WILLIAM L. PRICE
Arts and Crafts to Modern Design

William L. Price, c. 1914
(Photograph by Phillips Studio; Price and McLanahan Archives, George E. Thomas Collection)

William L. Price

Arts and Crafts to Modern Design

George E. Thomas

with an introduction by Robert Venturi

Princeton Architectural Press   New York

Published by
Princeton Architectural Press
37 East 7th Street
New York, New York 10003
212.995.9620

For a free catalog of books, call 1.800.722.6657
Visit our web site at www.papress.com

Editing and design: Clare Jacobson
Cover design: Sara E. Stemen
Text editing: Andrew Rubenfeld

Special thanks to: Ann Alter, Eugenia Bell, Jan
Cigliano, Jane Garvie, Caroline Green, Beth Harrison,
Mia Ihara, Leslie Ann Kent, Mark Lamster, Sara
Moss, Anne Nitschke, Lottchen Shivers, and Jennifer
Thompson of Princeton Architectural Press
—Kevin C. Lippert, publisher

Library of Congress Cataloging-in-Publication Data
Thomas, George E.
    William L. Price : arts and crafts to modern design/
George E. Thomas with an introduction by Robert
Venturi.
      p. cm.
    Includes bibliographical references and index.
    ISBN 1-56898-220-8
    1. Price, William L., 1861–1916. 2. Architects—
United States—Biography. 3. Architecture, Modern—
19th century—United States. 4. Architecture,
Modern—20th century—United States. I. Title.
    NA737.P685 T48 2000
    720'.92—dc21

                        99-050093

Table of Contents

Dormer, Magdalen College, 1896 (Architectural Archives, Philip N. Price Collection, University of Pennsylvania)

Acknowledgments

In the summer of 1971 I visited Atlantic City for the first time. Two years before I had acquired the Price and McLanahan archives at Freeman's Auction Company in Philadelphia. I went more as a lark than with any serious expectations, but knowing of William Price's work at the Traymore and Blenheim hotels from the materials that I had purchased, I decided to visit them. The exteriors of those great hotels looming above the ticky-tack of the small shops and billboards along the boardwalk—sculptural and shimmering in the summer light, bedecked with seahorses and seashells, enlivened by colored tile panels and crowned by domes—were a revelation. Twentieth-century architecture was not necessarily aesthetically impoverished. It was possible to design using modern materials in a way that delighted the eye and ravished the senses. I went inside and was overwhelmed by the scale of the spaces, the delicacy of the detail, and the amusing bits of ornament that caught my eye. More than half a century after they were built, these buildings remained fresh, strong, and interesting. Struck by my interest, one of the hotel clerks stopped me and told me to see everything that I could see as quickly as possible because the Traymore was to be demolished the following year. I went from ecstasy to grief in a moment.

Over the next year I led a campaign to save the Traymore, and ran again and again into the obstacle that no one had ever heard of its architect (it was usually attributed to McKim, Mead & White or to Thomas Edison). In our celebrity culture it is assumed that if the architect is unknown, his work must be of little value. Ada Louise Huxtable ignored my pleas to use the voice of *The New York Times* in the attempt to save a national treasure; after all, she asked, "Who is William Price anyway?" A few Philadelphia architects rose to advocate saving the Traymore. John Harbeson, Paul Cret's great student and the head of the successor firm of Harbeson, Hough, Livingston and Larson, wrote with passion about the power of the building which he remembered as a statement of the new possibilities of architecture in 1914—a few years after his graduation from the University of Pennsylvania. Henry Magaziner was interested in its construction systems and saw the merits of Price's architecture—he had graduated from the university when the Traymore was being rediscovered in the late 1920s. Robert Venturi pointed to its publication in *Masterpieces of American Architecture* and proclaimed the hotel a masterpiece of our own time. Although we were unsuccessful in the campaign to save the building, I have been caught up by Will Price ever since.

In the meantime I had advanced from the Atlantic City hotels to Price's Arts and Crafts community of Rose Valley. There was something of a Brigadoonish quality to that experience, for there I met Lucy Stephens, daughter-in-law of Alice and Charles Stephens, and through her, Will's daughter Margaret whose pug-nosed face and glasses still carried the look of her mother Emma Price from nearly a century before. Margaret's cousin Eleanor Price Mather was organizing a book on Rose Valley with Peter Ham and other members of the still active Rose Valley community, and I was asked to write an essay on Will Price's architecture. The rest of the country had forgotten Will Price but Rose Valley remembered and lay in wait to snare those looking for an architecture beyond the bounds of modernism. I was moved by their world and their desire to communicate an experience that remained as fresh in their memories as if it had been but yesterday that Will Price had been with them. More recently I have been sustained in my interest by Eleanor Price Mather's daughter Morris Potter who has preserved family records which were of inestimable value to my research. Similar praise goes to Will's grandson Philip Price who has carried on the family trade of acting, a bug which he inherited from his father, William Webb Price. Philip has cared for his side of the family history and has recently donated some of the material to Haverford College's Quaker Collection and the related architectural material to the Architectural Archives of the University of Pennsylvania. To the family my thanks are due.

In 1972 and 1973 I had the opportunity to work with James O'Gorman and Evan Turner of the Philadelphia Museum of Art on the exhibit that presented Frank Furness through the medium of Cervin Robinson's brilliant photographs and our research. Jim was never-endingly supportive, resulting in my asking him to be my advisor for a dissertation on Will Price, which he graciously agreed to do even though he was in the process of moving north to Massachusetts. I struggled for some time trying to fit Price into the usual categories of modernism and realized in the end that the history of modern architecture had somehow managed to miss almost everything in the culture that was clearly shaping the modern world. This was sobering and a bit terrifying for a graduate student but it eventually led to my conclusion that American modern was different from European modern in that Americans simply did what had to be done without much regard for theory whereas European modernism was essentially a phenomenon of an elite group that had no interest in the rising mass culture. I sent off my first chapter expecting the worst and received a postcard from Jim that said, "About time someone said this. Boil out the B. S. O'G" I've been boiling out the B. S. ever since.

While I was struggling with the question of how history could leave out a Will Price while presenting an architecture that had scarcely been built as the dominant architecture of the century, I met Robert Venturi at a talk that I gave on Will Price. Bob's family had been friends with the Mott family who owned the Traymore, and he had memories of being shown a rendering of the proposed additions to the hotel at the Mott lodge in the Poconos. Bob had attended the Upper School of Episcopal Academy which was located in another Price building, the house for John Gilmore. He had a strong affection for that richly evocative house as well as for the Traymore and the Blenheim which he attempted to save in 1978 by designing a modern frame for the front block of the building. *Complexity and Contradiction in Architecture* had been published in 1966 and Bob was completing, with Denise Scott Brown and Steve Izenour, *Learning from Las Vegas.* With their books as my shield, I felt able to attack the limitations of Euromodernism. They freed me to place Will Price in a larger and more inclusive American modernism, one that has diverged from the intellectualism of European modernism, incorporating larger popular themes which have since displaced much of the older high culture out of which the International Style now seems to have come. I have continued to learn from Bob and Denise and Steve ever since.

As I was completing my dissertation, I had the good fortune to encounter another Penn historian, Ted Hershberg, who was leading an interdisciplinary team looking at the industrializing city of Philadelphia in the middle of the nineteenth century. Their work prepared me to look beyond my discipline and has nurtured a generation of scholars whose research has transformed my understanding of Philadelphia. Philadelphia had become the city described by E. Digby Baltzell in *Philadelphia Gentlemen,* but a close reading of the facts about housing and wages as well as industrial process and design makes it clear that in the nineteenth century Philadelphia was the leading center of applied science and industrial innovation in the nation and probably the world. Ted's seminal study, *Philadelphia: Work, Space, Family and Group Experience in the Nineteenth Century* (1981), opened my eyes to the people who commissioned and inhabited the buildings that I studied and helped me place those buildings in the larger world of work and regional culture. Phil Scranton's escapades in industrial history have further opened my eyes and have in turn helped me understand how Frank Furness could achieve his remarkable buildings because he was working for a progressive clientele of engineers and industrialists, the men who ran the city after the Civil War. That in turn led to my better understanding of the world of Will Price when I returned to him after a twenty-year gap.

I would be remiss if I did not thank those who have made this project possible. As usual, I have done without the luxury of grants, fellowships, or any of the usual perks of scholarship but there is a certain simplicity in not having to deal with grants officers who understand old history and think that Philadelphia, the city in which the nation found its most vital ideals, is provincial. C'est la vie! My research assistants, students in Penn's Urban Studies and Historic Preservation programs, have joined me in looking at Will

Price and wondering about the histories that leave out the actual for the theoretical. I have thanked various students for research on individual projects in the catalogue entries, but I would be remiss in not thanking them as a group for keeping me engaged in a search that is the essence of the historical process. Domenic Vitiello, a former student at Penn and now at Massachusetts Institute of Technology, undertook the thankless but important task of checking facts. Needless to say, any errors are my own, and there are far fewer thanks to his careful work. The folks at Princeton Architectural Press deserve all praise and affection. They have taken Will Price on faith—and on the success of the earlier publication on Frank Furness. It is my hope that this project will reward their efforts and support. My dear wife Emily Cooperman has born the brunt of the pressures from my writing while she has been completing her own dissertation. I especially thank her for her patience when we were both trying to talk about our work at the same time.

George E. Thomas
Philadelphia
March 1999

Introduction

Robert Venturi

Ours is an era rife with historical revision, but here is a work involving historical discovery, exemplified in the architecture and career of Philadelphian William L. Price and enunciated within a broad context—technical, economic, social, aesthetic, and critical.

Although I grew up in a Philadelphia Quaker community as the son of parents who were interested in architecture, I learned of Price only in my mid-forties via George Thomas, who was completing his doctoral dissertation on Price at that time. But as a child and youth I heard the esteemed Quaker philosopher Jesse Holmes (Price's brother-in-law) speak at our monthly meeting house on several occasions; over the years my parents took me to performances at the Hedgerow Repertory Theater in Rose Valley (a community that Price founded), where I remember seeing the chief actor, William Webb Price (Will Price's son); I attended the Episcopal Academy, where I spent five years in the upper school housed in the John O. Gilmore mansion (designed by Price); with my parents I occasionally visited Arden, the Henry George Single Tax community (which Price co-founded); and I shopped for clothes in the boys' department of Jacob Reed's Store (which Price designed). I admired furniture from (Price's) Traymore Hotel—where my parents had spent their honeymoon. I saw it in the Pocono Mountains lodge of Joseph W. Mott (he had been an owner of the hotel and a client of Price). In the 1940s at the family lodge, Mrs. Mott showed me a beautiful rendering for an extension of that hotel. But, as I remember it, during all those experiences, the distinguished Philadelphia architect William Price—granted he had died several decades earlier—was never mentioned.

Here is a story that is perhaps generally American and particularly Philadelphian in terms of Price's faltering reputation but also in terms of his work and his career. These are characterized by Thomas as essentially pragmatic and particularly Quaker/Philadelphian as they evolved over time and responded to both everyday circumstances and ideal concepts. As described by Thomas, Price's work engaged parallel evolutions and multiple juxtapositions as it embraced a range of styles and types including—again pragmatically, not opportunistically—Philadelphian, Furnessian, industrial-Gothic vocabularies and

Project to restore and enlarge a William L. Price hotel in Atlantic City, Venturi and Rauch, 1977; project manager, Steven Izenour (Venturi and Rauch, courtesy Venturi, Scott Brown and Associates)

Ruskinian ideals; historical revivalist styles suited to capitalist, suburban, residential splendor; social- and socialist-oriented planning; and English-inspired Arts and Crafts architecture—for residential, communal, industrial, retail, and commercial-resort projects.

So here is an architecture or here are architectures that engage the immediate and the everyday, the practical and the realistic, and that balance the extravagant and the modest and then embrace ideals that are responsive as well as poetic. Here is an artist who is not theory driven—who is not a slave to consistency or a promoter of ideology. Here is an architect who valued richness over purity and acknowledged a variety of taste cultures and might thereby have anticipated a subsequent period of multiculturalism.

And then there is Price's precarious reputation, which succumbed in general to a cycle of taste where there is a reaction against the art of the immediate past (J. S. Bach had to be resuscitated by Felix Mendelssohn). It also succumbed in particular, as eloquently described by Thomas, to a kind of abstract-industrial-expressionist formalism in architecture and a kind or purist-elitist urban planing—where to a significant extent inclusive American pragmatism succumbed within the exclusive boundaries of a European ideology. And, of course, proper histories ignore commercial design, the arena of much of the most effective American design of the twentieth century—and thereby ignored Price's iconic seashore hotels as well as 1920s skyscrapers, classic Las Vegas buildings, and roadside vernacular.

And finally there is Price's lost reputation within the local context of Philadelphia, where a local prophet who is not mediocre enough can tend to fail rather than fare. Thomas amusingly questions why it is that various arguably contemporary equivalents of William Price—like Charles Rennie Mackintosh, Antoní Gaudí, Otto Wagner, H. P. Berlage, Peter Behrens, Louis Sullivan, and Frank Lloyd Wright, who were not Philadelphians—were not historically forgotten.

So here are eloquently acknowledged varieties of evolutions and complexities of juxtapositions that reveal a vital art within an immediate context—the art of William L. Price that was valid and vital for his time and is poignantly relevant for our time.

a kind of
purist-elitist
urban planning

William L. Price at his drafting board, c. 1913
(Price and McLanahan Archives, George E. Thomas Collection)

William L. Price:
On the Brink of the Twentieth Century

History is more or less bunk. —*Henry Ford*

America has always been the land of lone prophets without much but posthumous honor in their own country, which has been too busily engaged in exploiting its vast resources to take much interest in the spiritual consequences of its art, and Wright, Sullivan and Price were among the first to grasp the architectural possibilities of the new life and the new means of construction. Their names were known in Europe, while they still remained comparatively obscure among their fellow countrymen. —*George Howe*[1]

◄ *William L. Price and the Historiography of the Twentieth Century*

In 1930, with the drawings for his masterpiece skyscraper for the Philadelphia Savings Fund Society on his drafting board, George Howe described the struggle of the modern artist to be understood in the United States and offered his own explanation of the newly evolving architecture of the twentieth century which so confounded his peers and the broader public.[2] In his view, this brave new world of radio communications, movies, automobiles, and scientific method deserved an architecture that reflected the present and the future instead of depending on forms of the past. Placing his own recent work within a continuum that included other American architects such as "Wright, Sullivan and Price," Howe proclaimed the goal of expressing the quickening rhythms of modern life and the large scale afforded by new construction systems. Howe argued that, rather than beginning in Europe or in the seemingly more hospitable setting of academic Boston or avant-

---

1. George Howe, "What is This Modern Architecture Trying to Express?" *American Architect*, 137 (May 1930), 24.

2. Howe, 22–25.

garde of New York, the origins of the new architecture could be found in the industrial American heartland, designed by architects from Chicago and Philadelphia.

As the twentieth century ends, Louis Sullivan and Frank Lloyd Wright continue to be central figures in the history of American and world architecture. However, despite Howe's praise it is probably not clear, even to those who are literate in the history of twentieth-century American architecture, which Price it was that Howe included in his list. That it was fellow Philadelphian William Lightfoot Price to whom George Howe referred and not New York's Bruce Price or some other Price is clear both from Will Price's achievements and from the literature of the period. A year before the appearance of Howe's essay, Paul Cret remembered William Price as being "among those who shaped the present tendencies of American architecture," citing the Traymore and Blenheim hotels in Atlantic City and the Chicago Freight Terminal. These buildings continued to be published as American landmarks of modernism more than a decade after Price's death in 1916.[3] Price's impact on American design before the Depression was of such consequence that had a broader and less theory-driven history been the goal of post-World War II writers, he would have continued to merit a central place in the pantheon of American architects.

It was Will Price in his designs for the Traymore Hotel who established the sinewy and structurally expressive forms that became the model for both the tapering skyscrapers and muscular mid-rise buildings that became standards of eastern cities. (*fig. 1*) The style that is misnamed Art Deco (as if it originated in 1920s France) could as readily have been known as the Price Style or the "Vertical Style," the name used by Price's office. Price's design vocabulary for low-rise buildings, articulated by projecting piers crowned by caps that penetrate the parapet and denote the underlying structural frame as in the Chicago Freight Terminal, became the commercial vernacular of the day. At the modest scale of the suburban house, Price's office originated one important type of mid-Atlantic regional domestic architecture using colorful tile ornaments on gable-roofed volumes of stuccoed hollow tile whose shapes reflect the functions of the interior.

In the first generation of the new century, Will Price's career spanned the eastern half of the continent, from Quebec to Florida, with projects as far south as Puerto Rico, and from Atlantic City in the east to Chicago in the midwest. Price's corporate clients included the Pennsylvania Railroad as well as self-made industrialists of the modern world who commissioned hotels, railroad stations, retail stores, and private residences. To explore his ideas about community making in an age of suburbanization, Price designed several successful utopian communities including Arden, Delaware, a community founded

---

3. Paul Cret to the editor of the *Evening Bulletin* (17 July 1929); copy of letter in Walter Ferris Price Papers, Rose Valley, Pennsylvania.

on the principles of Henry George's Single Tax on real estate, and Rose Valley, Pennsylvania, an American link to the Arts and Crafts movement in Great Britain and where he made his home. It is a remarkable list of works, but one that lies outside the self-imposed aesthetic limits of modernism. Inclusive of a broader public where modernism was exclusive, commercially flamboyant where modernism was ascetic, earth-toned by means of local creek sands in stucco where doctrinaire modernism demanded harsh white or gray, and pragmatic and accommodating to individual clients where European modernism all too often was theoretical and reflected the goals of the architect, Price's architecture suggests ways in which contemporary design might have engaged the interests of a broader public (although this was rarely a goal of those who defined modernism). Had modern design evolved along the lines suggested by Will Price's work, lines that complemented the contemporary ideals of Sullivan and Wright in the midwest, post-World War II American architecture might have remained a part of the larger popular culture instead of being relegated to Tom Wolfe's "Cultureburg." Urban renewal might have been more urbane and less alienating and the edifying choice of many modern architects and historians to live in historic houses rather than modern designs might have seemed less ironic.

History without History

The twentieth century has been a century of forgetting as much as of discovery. Like the fate of ancient Roman emperors whose successors smashed their sculpted busts, chiseled their names off walls, erased their deeds from the written record, and rewrote history to corroborate the victor's view of the present at the expense of the past, the history of the architecture of the twentieth century has been similarly mutilated, and for similar goals. To the victors go the spoils. A history of the automobile based only on the experimental models of a few European manufacturers instead of on the cars marketed to the general public would have been no more accurate. In such a history the ancestry of the Citroën Deux Chevaux might be traced to Buckminster Fuller's Dymaxion car, but Henry Ford, General Motors, and Walter Chrysler, as well as the more recent Asian manufacturers, would be left out as too commercial, too popular. Modern history reflects changes in the purpose of its writers. From its original state as a chronological narrative incorporating the broad array of built objects, whose purpose was teaching architects how to design in historical styles, the goals of architectural historians were transformed. For most of this century historians have taken as their objective the ratification of the larger story of modernism—even at the expense of seminal events and individuals that played an important part in the evolution of modern design. No longer a narrative chronology, history became an analytical tool in the service of theory in which intention magnified the potential for distortion.[4] As Norman Cantor concludes, this new type of history is part of the larger fabric of an "antihistoricist" modernism that did not believe that truth lay in telling an evolutionary story. Modernism cared little for history; it was in fact hostile to it. Truth finding became analytical rather than historical. As T. S. Eliot, a prime theoretician of modernism, wrote in 1923, the "narrative method" had been replaced by the "mythic method." The historical approach in Eliot's view, was superseded by the very different program of concentrating on direct, inner, symbolic meaning, which was both completely external to history and irrelevant to considerations of temporality.... In the early 1930s, Eliot wrote: "All time is unredeemable / *What might have been and what has been point toward the same end*, / Which is always the present."[5]

The application of this subjunctive principle—"what might have been"—can be said to have shaped the history of modern architecture in the twentieth century. The 1932 exhibition at the Museum of Modern Art that announced the new theoretical framework for architecture also set the standard for history as cultural polemic. In the seminal catalogue essay that defined the style, Henry-Russell Hitchcock and Philip Johnson recast all that went before to fit their new canon. More brilliant was the public relations coup of the title chosen for the exhibit which gave its name, the International Style, to the new European architecture. Drawing on the methods of the scorned commercial culture, the authors manipulated public opinion by implying the widespread dissemination of the new design mode rather than acknowledging its true status in the 1930s—as a minuscule portion of contemporary building activity advocated by a handful of critics and clients.[6] Hitchcock and Johnson's text described a morphology of unornamented, asymmetrical buildings whose principal characteristic was the appearance of transparent volume rather than lithic mass and weight. Stressing the new architecture's contrast with scorned conventional design, the authors aimed their message at "a narrow, highly selective, learned and professional audience—the cultural vanguard."[7] For better or for worse, these characteristics and that audience have shaped architecture as well as architectural history and criticism ever since.

The founding of the Museum of Modern Art in 1929 and the International Style exhibit in 1932 marked the coalescing of a New York avant-garde whose orientation was eastward across the Atlantic. Henceforth, modernism would find its theories and fashion in the elite and effete settings of European studios and galleries instead of in the innova-

---

4. Norman Cantor, *The American Century: Varieties of Culture in Modern Times* (New York: HarperCollins, 1997), 43–66.

5. Cantor, 44. Emphasis my own.

6. This is not a new argument. It was the central thesis of my doctoral dissertation, *William L. Price: Builder of Men and of Buildings* (University of Pennsylvania, 1975) and it reappeared in Peter Blake's *Form Follows Fiasco, Why Modern Architecture Hasn't Worked* (Boston: Little,

Brown, 1977). Tom Wolfe's brilliant assaults on the cathedral of modernism, especially *The Painted Word* (New York: Bantam Books, 1976) and *From Bauhaus to Our House* (New York: Farrar, Straus & Giroux, 1981), capture the general hostility of the public toward European modernism as represented in both painting and architecture.

7. Cantor, 46.

tion rooted in American industry and democratic mass culture. In this context, Frank Lloyd Wright and his fellow midwesterners were incorporated into the historical texts only insofar as their work was relevant to European modernism. Will Price and the easterners who also helped break the hold of historical forms and shaped the new possibilities of contemporary design were left out altogether. Hitchcock and Johnson's *International Style* essay became the framework for future histories that left out more than they included. Every segment of American design was affected. East coast skyscrapers such as the Chrysler Building by William Van Alen were ignored by the new historians and denigrated for serving the commercial culture of capitalism. The California bungalows by Greene and Greene and Myron Hunt were discarded as too rustic in their use of natural materials and at the same time too sentimental. The richly ornamented federal buildings and museums by Beaux Arts designers such as Paul Cret as well as the sculpture-encrusted churches and public buildings of difficult-to-categorize architects such as Bertram Goodhue were pointedly ignored. Rather than address the expectations and interests of the broad public, the new architecture and the theory on which it was based were aimed at a rarified circle of the cognoscenti. After a century of rising public interest in design that culminated in Ayn Rand's still popular novel, *The Fountainhead*, the elite culture regained control of architecture by making it so refined, so intellectual that it was almost better as drawing or at most as a temporary exhibition pavilion than as actual buildings out in the weather and used by real people.

In the new historical construct American architects could practically be ignored. Frank Lloyd Wright was represented in Hitchcock and Johnson's text as little more than an artifact from the distant past, unworthy of illustration or significant discussion, dismissed for being too individualistic and not sufficiently responsive to the new "collective" culture. George Howe's PSFS skyscraper, now an acknowledged landmark of modern design, was criticized for the very qualities that made the building transcend European modernism: its connection to place, its representation of structure using a variety of materials, its articulation of multiple purposes. (*fig. 2*) Few other American architects were deemed worthy of study. In Hitchcock and Johnson's list of modern practitioners in the United States, four were Europeans: Oscar Stonorov, Ludwig Mies van der Rohe, William Lescaze, and Richard Neutra; the works of American-trained designers were represented by a gas station architect and Raymond Hood's severest skyscrapers. Every other architect, in an incredible turn of events, went from being the heroes of Howe's tale to being purged from the books.

With Europe-oriented historians and critics establishing the theoretical framework, American architecture was principally portrayed as a catalyst to European modernism via the publication of Frank Lloyd Wright's work in the 1910 Wasmuth edition. Ignored too were the successive tidal waves of American influences that rolled back across the Atlantic beginning with the 1876 Centennial Exhibition in Philadelphia. (*fig. 3*)

1. Price and McLanahan, Traymore Hotel, from southeast, c. 1940
(Price and McLanahan Archives, George E. Thomas Collection)

2. Howe and Lescaze, Philadelphia Savings Fund
Society (1931–33), looking southwest, 1976
(photograph by George E. Thomas)

3. Main Exhibition Hall, in Joseph M. Wilson, *The
Masterpieces of the Centennial Exhibition*, Vol. 3, *History,
Mechanics, Science* (Philadelphia: Gebbie & Barrie, 1876)

Buffalo Bill's Wild West Show inflamed European curiosity and became the basis for Puccini's opera, *The Girl of the Golden West*. Philadelphia's innovative factories became the focus of a torrent of articles about American industrial design and shop practice and led a worldwide transformation of work.[8] The movies became the new art form of the century and American influences spread abroad in the rhythms of jazz and blues. Fritz Lang's *Metropolis*, an homage to a country that Lang had only seen from New York harbor, and Adolf Loos' visit to Chicago for the World's Columbian Exposition hint at the excitement of Europeans in their first look at the United States. The arrival of the doughboys to save Europe and win the "war to end all wars" was but the cresting of a wave that had been building for almost half a century. From Antonín Dvořák's 1893 "New World Symphony," composed with a copy of Longfellow's poems on his music stand, to Igor Stravinsky's efforts at jazz before he had ever heard the music, European art forms were transformed by the anti-academic freedom of American art forms in music, urban design, and architecture. The continuing European interest in things American was further evidenced in an exhibit sponsored by the American Institute of Architects which toured Great Britain, the Netherlands, Belgium, and France in 1921 and 1922. All of these pieces of the story were left out of the histories of design in the twentieth century. Instead of telling the story of modern design as a product of the expanding industrial revolution and the mass culture of modern democracies, the Eurocentric history written in the 1930s proclaimed the failure of American nerve in the buildings of the White City of the Chicago Columbian Exposition as if the simultaneous closing of the frontier had reversed the tide of manifest destiny.[9] The notable exceptions to this story were the unnamed designers of grain elevators and the misunderstood genius, Louis Sullivan, who transmitted his artistry to Frank Lloyd Wright. After Wright the new historians claimed that the development of modern architecture shifted to northern Europe where it reached its apotheosis in the theory-driven architecture of Walter Gropius, Mies van der Rohe, and Le Corbusier. In this preferred account a suitably rigorous modern architecture had arisen not in suburbs of American midwestern cities or eastern industrial cities and coastal resorts but from pure reason, thus making it the worthy successor to centuries of European philosophy and theory.

As the twentieth century ends it is apparent that the more esoteric architecture becomes, the farther removed it is from the evolving culture. As a consequence of the realpolitik of the critics, the profession was reduced to a sideshow of the politics of the age. With the collapse of the Soviet Union, it is probably safe to rehabilitate individualism

---

8. Michael J. Lewis, "Modernism Without Program," in *American Architectural Masterpieces* (New York: Princeton Architectural Press, 1992), xvii–xxi.

9. George Edgell, *The American Architecture of Today* (New York: Charles Scribner's Sons, 1929) offers the cultivated American perspective just before the new theories changed design. Edgell was the Dean of the Faculty of Architecture at Harvard University and produced the book from his lectures for the Henry La Barre Jayne Foundation in Philadelphia.

and to consign collectivism to the ash heap. In the first years of this century Frederick Winslow Taylor advised industrialists and engineers to stop depending on precedent and to examine realistically the possibilities that new materials and new methods could bring to manufacturing. It is good advice for historians too.

> When starting an experiment in any field question everything, question the very founda-
> tions upon which the art rests, question the simplest, the most self-evident, the most uni-
> versally accepted facts; prove everything.[10]

Routes to the Past

Despite the best efforts of historians no erasure from history can be complete in the twentieth century if there is a will to search because there remain so many routes to the past. American architectural journals published a broad range of buildings that spanned contemporary design. Photographs illustrating the articles and, better still, advertisements as well as surviving early twentieth-century buildings of cities and suburbs present a radically different environment than that found in the histories. Indeed, no one who has looked at American cities—particularly the soaring skyscrapers of downtown New York or Chicago or the exuberant commercial architecture of resort cities such as Atlantic City, Miami, and more recently Las Vegas—can miss the gulf between what was built and the selections of doctrinaire historians. That the histories written to justify and support the values of the International Style ignored most of the built environment is evident at both ends of the spectrum. The heroic skyscrapers that became the symbol of American urbanism before the Depression were dismissed as "reactionary" or "middle-brow" by most academic historians.[11] The small-scale buildings that form the typical American streetscape, from shopping centers and gas stations to convenience stores and suburban houses, have simply been ignored, unworthy of the attention of serious historians. Only now, with the rise of interest in the broader culture, are these chief symbols of modern life being studied.

Fortunately, a few architects saw past the blinders imposed by critics and historians to the vigor of the commercial architecture of this century and reincorporated it into the canon of design. The 1966 publication of Robert Venturi's *Complexity and Contradiction in Architecture* began the rehabilitation of the architecture that had been purged from the histories. This book was followed in 1972 with the publication of *Learning from Las Vegas* by Robert Venturi, Denise Scott Brown, and Steven Izenour which established a purpose and a method by which the despised and rejected popular architecture of the twentieth

---

10. Robert Kanigel, *The One Best Way: Frederick Winslow Taylor and the Enigma of Efficiency* (New York: Viking Press, 1997). The quote is taken from John Dos Passos, "The American Plan," *The Big Money, U. S. A.* (New York: Houghton Mifflin, 1933; reprinted New York: Library of America, 1996 [p. 785]).

11. Typical is William J. R. Curtis, *Modern Architecture Since 1900* (New York: Prentice Hall, 1982, 2nd edition 1987), 217–227.

century could reinvigorate the ever colder and less engaging abstractions that modernist architecture had become. One of the consequences of both of these landmark texts (though perhaps an unintended one) has been the incorporation of early twentieth-century motifs into late twentieth-century design, the most famous being Philip Johnson's flip use of a broken pediment from the rejected Colonial Revival to differentiate the AT&T building from the other boxy modern skyscrapers in New York. Similarly Helmut Jahn referred to the form of the Chrysler Building in the twin blue skyscrapers that now tower over Philadelphia. More recently a Michael Graves design for a hotel at Walt Disney World has its roots in the now demolished seashore hotels of William Lightfoot Price in Atlantic City. These references to a lost past make it all the more appropriate at the end of the twentieth century for historians and practitioners to grapple with the ignored architecture that serves as the springboard to the present.

As the twentieth century ends, the career of William Lightfoot Price offers an opportunity to reassess early twentieth-century design independent of the distorting lens of European modernism and free of the cult of personality that has grown around Frank Lloyd Wright. Like Wright's Prairie Style buildings of the midwest, Price's architecture evolved out of the ferment of American society after the Civil War; like Wright's mentor, Louis Sullivan, Price was directly exposed to the ideas and office practice of Frank Furness, who could be said to have inoculated American architecture with the values of two of the great molders of our culture—Ralph Waldo Emerson and Walt Whitman.[12] And like Sullivan and Wright, Price found pleasure in the public spotlight, writing and lecturing to national audiences, arguing for his beliefs even as he refined his ideas. Despite the demolition of the vast majority of his important buildings, he remains accessible through his writings and through images of his buildings that his office carefully photographed and preserved.

Progressive Industrialists and Modern Design

As the following chapters establish, the link between Price's modern architecture and the industrial culture of Philadelphia and the midwest is not a coincidence. By the middle of the nineteenth century, in Europe and the United States, a chasm had opened between those who sought forms for the present from history and those coming out of industry and engineering who found their models in the progressive culture of experiment and innovation. Even in the 1850s, as modern iron and steel were being incorporated into bridges and railroad structures, English critic John Ruskin could state with absolute conviction that iron would never be an important building material—because it is not

---

12. See George E. Thomas, "The Flowering of an American Architecture," in Thomas and others, *Frank* *Furness: The Complete Works* (New York: Princeton Architectural Press, 1991), 26–33.

mentioned in the Bible. As the nineteenth century ended the academic culture of western civilization remained attuned to history as a navigational tool, as exemplified by G. W. F. Hegel's philosophical conclusion that ranked the social values of Christianity and the Prussian state as the highest achievements of evolutionary history. Henry Hobson Richardson's dependence on the forms of the Romanesque churches of the Spanish Pilgrimage Road for Trinity Church in Boston, and the turn toward classicism in the national practices of McKim, Mead & White and later Daniel Burnham were all part of the same trend.

Those choices missed the future. In other communities, including American industrial centers, architects and artists took their cues from mechanical engineers and industrial designers who deviated from historical models. Clients from this exceptional subculture served as the first sponsors of the evolving proto-modern architecture in cities such as Philadelphia, Pittsburgh, Indianapolis, and Chicago—the cities of the practices of Frank Furness, Will Price, Louis Sullivan, and Frank Lloyd Wright. Similar engineering-based subcultures made Glasgow, Prague, Barcelona and other industrial cities in Europe centers of architectural innovation as well.[13] Like fellow Philadelphian Frank Furness before him, Will Price was freed to design and build in ways that were fundamentally modern by this progressive clientele and by the peculiar circumstances of Philadelphia. Although no longer dominated by its Quaker minority, the city's leading families continued to send their children into trades and crafts that in turn led to careers in industry and manufacturing. Although they were outside of the mainstream of the evolving trans-Atlantic culture that was taking shape in New York and Boston, Philadelphians were comfortable setting their own course. Residents of Philadelphia continued to believe in their cultural independence, both as the birthplace of the nation and as a place where real value was created through manufacturing, and thus they could stand the scorn of outside critics who misunderstood the goals of Philadelphia designers. The generation of industrialists and manufacturers who became Price's clients had studied the new curricula at American colleges, finding their meat in the sciences of the modern world. These new men accepted and, one suspects, stimulated and challenged Price and his contemporaries to design an architecture that responded to the new, in the process offering an alternative

———

13. Philadelphia is no longer thought of as being linked to these industrial cities, but many of the innovations cited by Siegfried Giedion in *Mechanization Takes Command: A Contribution to Anonymous History* (New York: Oxford University Press, 1969) and listed as generically American innovations, were in fact Philadelphia innovations. These include Oliver Evans' first fully mechanized mill, innovations in standardization and scientific management, automation studies in the 1930s, and the invention of the computer in 1946. The British judges at the Centennial Exhibition made the same error in concluding that innovative machines were American in attitude, but missed the fact that most came from specifically Philadelphia shops, notably those of William Sellers and the Baldwin Locomotive Works.

to the financier's classicism of McKim's generation and the academic modernism that succeeded as the fashion of the next generation of elites.

Price's method was not a ruthless assault on all aspects of convention that characterized both International Style modernism and much of modern art. It would be Price's contribution to create an inclusive contemporary architecture, one that gave pleasure even to those who lacked the classical learning required by the historical revival styles of the old elites or the new sophistication of the avant-garde. Bold forms conveying structure and expressing function root Price's architecture in the Furness method. By broadening surfaces and simplifying detail, Price designed at the larger scale of twentieth-century mass culture. Because his clients demanded identifiability to serve their marketing goals, Price shaped highly individualized forms that readily became the commercial icons of their era. In an age of heroes, his name was well known. Like his now better known contemporary, Frank Lloyd Wright, whose wealthy clients commissioned expensive domestic masterpieces, Price's houses were as original in the use of modern materials, in open planning, and in the creation of new systems of ornament that captured their moment of creation. However, because of Price's deeply held beliefs about the relationship between American culture and democracy, much of his domestic work was modest, reflecting the economic circumstances of his clientele. These inexpensive houses spread the message of modernism into middle-class design in the mid-Atlantic region, becoming part of the contemporary vernacular before World War II.

Price faced and resolved issues that have shaped the twentieth century. For a generation after Price's premature death in 1916, American critics remembered his work. In the 1920s photographs and drawings of Price's great seashore hotels were exhibited in Britain and on the continent, receiving high praise for their innovative form and their expression of the emerging middle class. As the 1920s ended George Edgell, the Dean of the Faculty of Harvard's School of Architecture, included both the Traymore Hotel and the Chicago Freight Terminal in *The American Architecture of Today*.[14] In 1930, fourteen years after Price's death, a distinguished jury of American architects ranked Price's Traymore Hotel among the masterpieces of American design in the first third of the century. Later in the 1930s Charles Whitaker, a disciple of Louis Sullivan, saw in Price's midwestern landmark, the vast Pennsylvania Railroad Freight Terminal in Chicago, a logical continuation of the ideas of Sullivan. Unlike his master, Frank Furness, whose obituaries recalled his Civil War heroism and ignored his architecture, Price's achievements outlasted his life, forming the foundation of popular architecture for a generation. It would take the International Style exhibit of 1932 to erase the historical record that included the work of William L. Price.

———

14. Edgell, 290–291, 340–341.

4. Atlantic City, New Jersey, oceanfront, c. 1906 (Library of Congress Prints and Photographs Division, Detroit Publishing Company Photograph Collection, LC-D4-34770)

5. Price and McLanahan, Lincoln Apartments, Miami, c. 1919
(Price and McLanahan Archives, George E. Thomas Collection)

Working in the first consumer culture that was spawned by Philadelphia's great surge in industrial productivity in the late nineteenth century, Price's career forms a direct bridge to the design issues of post-World War II America and, at the end of our century, to the global society that shares the ever-expanding media-based communication systems of television, cinema, and cyberspace in a way that cuts across cultural and historical boundaries. Based on the foundations laid by Price and his contemporaries, it would be possible for architects to design independent of history for an ever-growing consumer society. Appropriately, Price's most innovative designs found their setting in New Jersey's Atlantic City In its present state, as a second-rate "Las Vegas-by-the-Sea," it is easy to forget Atlantic City's early twentieth-century role as a marketplace for American modern design. (*fig. 4*) Before World War II, Atlantic City was the "World's Playground," bringing the rich and famous to its boardwalk and hotels, and making it one of the disseminating centers of modern culture. That exposure spread the forms of Price's Traymore and Blenheim hotels across the nation and around the globe on postcards and saltwater candy box covers, making those buildings icons of the modern world. During the decade after World War I, Price's office continued to work in other resorts, most notably Miami which had become the successor to Atlantic City as a center of popular culture. By 1929 the forms which Price had pioneered a generation earlier were the signature motifs of the jazz age. (*fig. 5*) It would take the great economic Depression of the 1930s to end the wave of national confidence that began with Theodore Roosevelt's presidency. Then the American movement toward an original, contemporary, populist, and accessible architecture disappeared under the weight of opinion of academic aesthetes who championed European modernism while deriding the achievements of their countrymen. The journals of the day bear witness to the continuing echoes of Price's work. His career and its implications for a broadly defined American culture remain to be rediscovered as the twentieth century ends.

◖ *New Year's Eve 1900 in Philadelphia*

The past is behind us; the future lies before. We cannot tell either what tests and trials it may bring, or with what success it may be crowned. Let us then face it with courage, with confidence and with hope, and profiting by the lessons of the experiences though which we have passed, let us endeavor, all of us in our separate ways, to improve upon what has thus far been accomplished. And so The Inquirer wishes to its readers, one and all, a happy and prosperous New Year.[15]

Because it was Philadelphia that shaped the life and career of William Price, a brief excursion into the Quaker City of Price's formative years explains much about the goals and

---

15. *The Philadelphia Inquirer*, "Retrospect of a Year" (1 January 1901), 8.

above 6. John McArthur, Jr., Philadelphia City Hall (1873–1900), looking southeast, 1976 (photograph by George E. Thomas)

left 7. Fred Morgan, "The Old Century Hands Over the Keys," *The Philadelphia Inquirer* (31 December 1900)

means that are reflected in his career. Our encounter with William Price's city begins on the last New Year's Eve of the old century. In Philadelphia, December 31st, 1900, was a secular and patriotic celebration of the triumphs of the past century mingled with anticipation and hopes for the twentieth century. At eight o'clock in the evening the facades of City Hall flickered with the illumination of giant electric spotlights. In the huge courtyard 30-foot-high spruce trees brought for the occasion glowed with red, white, and blue electric lights while the 500-foot-high tower was outlined with fire. At 9:30 in the evening, the First, Second, and Third Regiments and the Third Battalion of the Sixth Regiment of the National Guard began a brisk march from the marshaling point at Broad and Spring Garden streets to a reviewing stand at City Hall and then continued on south to Washington Avenue. At 10 o'clock the doors of City Hall were thrown open to the public who for the first time witnessed the completed building that had preoccupied the city for nearly a third of a century. Finally, as December 31st, 1900, turned into January 1, 1901, the first moments of the twentieth century glowed with a display of fireworks that lighted the midnight sky and glinted off the shining, aluminum-plated tower of the new City Hall.[16]

The marble-sheathed, columned, and sculpted City Hall that opened to the public on that epochal evening was a Second Empire dinosaur whose design had been initiated before the Civil War for another site on Independence Square. There its vast bulk would have wrapped around the chief icon of the American Revolution, the Pennsylvania State House, known familiarly as "Independence Hall." Though the rest of the nation might sneer at the already outdated style of the new City Hall, the building bespoke the remarkable achievements of the Philadelphia during the previous century. (*fig. 6*) The vastness of the building, the innovations of its construction—from its fireproof (and nearly demolition-proof) building systems to its aluminum-plated dome some 500 feet above the street—and the rich sculptural program that told the tale of the region's settlement as well as its flora and fauna, were emblems of the extraordinary wealth and structural originality that were by-products of the world's most industrialized city.

Because of the accelerating pace of change in industry, the flood tide toward modern life was more obvious in Philadelphia than in Boston and New York with the result that the arrival of the new century was reported far more extensively in Philadelphia than in other eastern cities. As the old century ended *The Philadelphia Inquirer* barraged its readers with stories relating to the new century, filling its pages on Saturday, December 31st, 1900, and Sunday, January 1st, 1901. (*fig. 7*) The central theme of those articles was

16. *The Philadelphia Inquirer*, "Everything in Readiness for Advent of Century" (29 December 1900), 1. It is noteworthy that the twentieth century was particularly celebrated in industrial cities. *The New York Times* barely noted the event; the largest reference to the new century in that paper was an advertisement by the Philadelphia-based Wanamaker's Store. Otherwise, its chief mention was a small article about President William McKinley's views on future relations with Britain.

the transforming power of technology that had remade the Quaker City into the "greatest manufacturing city in the world."[17] One article touted the changes of the previous century, illustrating the post-Revolutionary city with 1799–1800 views by William Birch which were then contrasted with modern photographs of the each location. Like a turn-of-the-century *Contrasts*, but with the twist, that where Augustus Pugin had championed the middle ages as more spiritual and therefore to be preferred, the Philadelphia press celebrated the progress of the new age, depicting the lessening of physical effort and rising economic opportunity through the miracle of modern machines. Technologies that represented the height of progress a century earlier—stagecoaches and sailing vessels, scythes and flails, goose quills and messengers on horseback—were contrasted with innovations that had transformed modern life—railroads and steamships, typewriters and the telegraph, mechanized reapers and tractors. In Britain, half a century before, Pugin might nostalgically prefer the old world of the church and the cloister; by contrast Philadelphia newspapers at the end of a century of industrialization foresaw the industrial future as a way of empowering everyman in an age of prosperity.

Another, even greater testament to the wealth of the city than the new public buildings, could be seen from the observation platform at the feet of the statue of William Penn that crowned the tower of City Hall. From that vantage, as far as the eye could see, were some fifty square miles of row houses and factories, most of which had been built in the previous generation. (*fig. 8*) These buildings attested to both the dissemination of the wealth of the city to its industrial workforce and the means by which the wealth had been achieved. Unlike most of the world's industrial cities where workers were stuffed into barbell tenements and triple-deckers or worse, by 1900 the typical Philadelphia worker lived in his own two-story, three-bedroom row house with indoor plumbing and central heat that was furnished with the newest furniture, carpets, and fixtures purchased at the fourteen department stores that made Market Street the equivalent of Minneapolis' present-day Mall of the Americas. At the World's Columbian Exposition in Chicago in 1893, a typical Philadelphia row house was built in the Midway, attracting such hordes of visitors that the floorboards were worn through and had to be replaced. There could have been no better gauge of the wealth of the average worker of the Quaker City than the houses that gave Philadelphia its proud nickname the City of Homes.[18]

These houses describe the spread of industry-generated wealth into all classes of Philadelphians. Indeed, it is fair to conclude that by the 1890s the modern consumer cul-

---

17. Arthur Shadwell, "Industrial Efficiency: A Comparative Study of Industrial Life in England, Germany and America." The Englishman's report was cited in John MacFarlane, *Manufacturing in Philadelphia: 1683–1912* (Philadelphia: The Commercial Museum, 1912), 11.

18. John N. Gallagher, "Real Estate Holdings and Valuations," in Frank H. Taylor, ed., *The City of Philadelphia as it Appears in 1893* (Philadelphia: George S. Harris & Sons, 1893), 82–84, shows the plans and elevations of the house built at the Chicago fair.

ture had been born in the Quaker City and as a consequence, many of the issues of the mass culture of the twentieth century would first be explored in that city. At the end of the nineteenth century Philadelphia was one of the wealthiest cities in the world on a per capita basis. This wealth was made possible because Philadelphia industrialists in the second half of the nineteenth century had directed the transformation of manufacturing toward modern production practices and then had spread the fruits of that productivity in higher wages. Before the Civil War, in plants such as the Baldwin Locomotive Works, high piecework rates made it possible for individual workers to attain a high level of pay based on personal initiative and skill.[19] After the Civil War Philadelphia industrialists separated production from its craft roots in workshops through the process of industrial standardization—a movement led by William Sellers and fostered by the Franklin Institute of which he was president. The standardization movement ended the isolation of individual workshops by linking them to the goals of their clients, particularly the Pennsylvania Railroad which made standardization its corporate policy. As the home of the Pennsylvania Railroad and the Franklin Institute, Philadelphia businesses shaped national standards, learned of changes earlier than their competitors, and triumphed in head-to-head competition. A third innovation occurred at the end of the century when Frederick Winslow Taylor's idea of scientific management radically reshaped every aspect of work practices, producing remarkable increases in productivity.[20] Like the modern technology that supported the old-fashioned facade of City Hall, these achievements signaled the potency of Victorian progressivism that made possible the triumphant turn-of-the-century city awash in industrial wealth.

    The effects of this new wealth spread across the city in two distinct stages. In the 1880s rising wages and workweeks of nearly 60 hours provided for the construction of hundreds of thousands of two-story row houses that were built across the city. For the first time the bulk of the population had reached a level of economic stability to rent or purchase decent houses as well as the means to make them comfortable. In the 1890s actual wages rose only slightly but the struggle for the eight-hour workday saw a reduction in hours worked to around 50 per week, providing the second great luxury of our age, free time. Paralleling the rising wages were changes in the self-image of Philadelphia workers. By 1900 most Philadelphia workers in factories no longer identified themselves with the crafts on which their lives depended. Freed by higher wages and low-cost public transit, they lived in row house neighborhoods separated from their factories, thus reflecting their personal aspirations rather than the mere efficiency of proximity to work. White

---

19. John K. Brown, *The Baldwin Locomotive Works, 1831–1915, A Study in American Industrial Practice* (Baltimore: Johns Hopkins University Press, 1995), 146–150. Brown demonstrates the early increases in productivity, but doesn't take his story outside the plant to the emerging post-Victorian city.

20. The Taylor saga is told in Kanigel, 151–337.

painted porch fronts with pressed metal ornament in a remarkable array of ever-changing styles linked even these tiny houses to the consumer culture. Henceforth, Philadelphia workers saw themselves first as consumers, looking to their wages to provide a private house, then personal comforts, eventually an automobile and a family vacation at the New Jersey seashore or the Pocono mountains. The progress of science and its application to manufacturing, residence, and other aspects of everyday life transformed late-nineteenth-century Philadelphia and made the city a laboratory for the changes that would transform the rest of the nation and ultimately the globe in the next century.

Everywhere across Philadelphia there were other indications of the spread of wealth to the citizens of the industrial city. Philadelphia could claim that it produced more professional baseball players and had higher attendance at sporting events than other cities.[21] The city was dotted with recreational sites, that included high-stakes sculling races along the Delaware and the Schuylkill rivers (commemorated in paintings by Thomas Eakins) and one of the first modern football stadiums with the construction of the University of Pennsylvania's Franklin Field, the site in 1895 of the first Penn Relays and Penn's national champion football team the following year. Like Boston and Chicago, and exceeded only by New York's three teams, the city supported two professional baseball teams, the American League Athletics as well as the National League Phillies. For those disposed to more intellectual pursuits there were numerous clubs and organizations for music, theater, and light entertainment. On Christmas day 1895, Professor Woodville Latham demonstrated the first flexible film motion picture in B. F. Keith's Bijou Theater at 8th and Race streets, three days before a similar exhibition of the Lumière Cinematograph in Paris.[22] Turn-of-the century Philadelphians were the first generation to be molded by the media explosion of newspapers, magazines, and advertising. Philadelphia shaped many of these industries. When Harvard University sought an advertising business to profile in its Harvard Studies in Business History, it chose Philadelphia's N. W. Ayer & Son because its lineage included the nation's first advertising agency and because its prominence in the 1930s mirrored Philadelphia's continuing status as the center of the consumer culture. At the time of William Price's death in 1916 Philadelphia was also a center of movie production, with many films being produced in Sigmund Lubin's Indiana Avenue studio.[23] The cinema became the oracle of its generation, bringing the world to an ever-widening public. That same public read newspapers, learning of both triumphs and tragedies of the age—from the assassination of President McKinley which began the century to the sinking of the *Titanic*.

---

21. Horace S. Fogel, "Sports of All Sorts," in Taylor, 125. "If Philadelphia is not the base ball centre of the world, it is at least the home of base ball players. The Quaker City has furnished more good talent for America's National Game, than all the other leading cities combined."

22. Irv Glazer, *Philadelphia Theaters A–Z, A Comprehensive Descriptive Record of 813 Theaters Constructed Since 1724* (Westport, Conn.: Greenwood Press, 1986), 68.

23. Glazer, 22–23.

The wealth of the city could be seen beyond its limits in opulent suburban houses, a representation of wealth that is common to most cities, but also in the ring of amusement parks that gave pleasure to the working classes of the city, first Willow Grove Park, then Woodside Park, and finally Chestnut Hill plus other parks along the Delaware River.[24] Simultaneously New Jersey seashore resorts accommodated the new classes of vacationers, providing amusement parks and other facilities on the boardwalks which became standards of each of the new popular resorts. The amusement parks offered new types of experiences, often adapted from a mechanical contrivance that was based on what one already knew of life—rather than learned from history and reading. Freak shows and the Midway with its carnivals and shops became integral parts of the modern experience of permanent amusement parks near cities and at resorts while traveling circuses reached smaller population centers. Ever more elaborate rides (many of which were built by the Philadelphia Toboggan Company) used technological innovations to provide experiences of height and speed such as the Ferris Wheel and the roller coaster. By 1900 the amusement park visitor could even drive an automobile—although on fixed tracks—and in an eerie anticipation of Disneyland and Busch Gardens, turn-of-the century American amusement parks afforded a glimpse of many places of the globe without the bother of travel. These resorts reflected a rising disposable income and in turn heralded later phases of consumer culture that remain familiar aspects of modern life.

Thus, the tolling of the bells marking the new year and the new century celebrated an emerging mass culture that was represented across the vast metropolis in forms that were both national and peculiarly local. At Independence Hall the tower bell was struck twenty times for the twentieth century and 125 times for the years of liberty since the Declaration of Independence. As always Philadelphians were keenly aware of their special links to the founding of the nation. In the row districts south of City Hall final preparations were under way for another unique Philadelphia celebration, the New Year's Day Mummers Parade. This parade represented the private achievement of thousands of ethnic workingmen, who fashioned special costumes, learned musical routines, and marched in a variety of clubs and bands the length of Broad Street to City Hall. This was yet another intimation of the new popular culture made possible by surplus income and spare time. Though some anti-traditionalists had proposed that the parade march from north to south, it was determined that for the first day of the new century, the route would take its usual course from Reed Street in South Philadelphia to Girard Avenue.[25] This route took

24. Amusement parks have come into vogue for study, although the Philadelphia contribution is not singled out. See Margaret J. King, "The New American Muse: Notes on the Amusement/Theme Park," *Journal of Popular Culture*, 15, no. 1 (Summer 1981), 56–62. Judith

Adams, *The American Amusement Park Industry: A History of Technology and Thrills* (Boston: Twayne Publishers, 1991); David Nasaw, *Going Out: The Rise and Fall of Public Amusement* (New York: BasicBooks, 1993).

25. *The Philadelphia Inquirer*, "Everything in Readiness

workers past their own houses, arranged in neat rows like ranks of soldiers, past the immense factories where they earned their wages, through the new business district of the city with John Wanamaker's department store, around City Hall, and finally north on Broad Street toward the homes of the financial titans who controlled the factories, trolley lines and amusement parks. Despite the economic gulf between the paraders and the barons, they all increasingly shared a common culture that encompassed the worker with his family, the newly rich plutocrat, and even the patricians of the city. In the same decade that Thorstein Veblen had posited the development of a leisure class, working-class Philadelphians could be said, in however diminished a way, to share in the lifestyle of the elite in row house neighborhoods and seashore resorts. In Philadelphia the twentieth century arrived with a full head of steam.

Philadelphia and the Arts in 1901

For most of this century, and much of the last quarter of the last, it has been customary to overlook Philadelphia as a generating center of artistic ideas. Although in the 1830s Philadelphia had proclaimed itself to be the "Athens of America," Charles Dickens' 1842 characterization of the plainness of the city became both the national and international image, one that endures to the present. By the end of the nineteenth century, it was generally presumed that some Quaker gene was at work that eliminated aesthetics as a line of investigation by the region's citizens. Presumably it was this Quaker gene that simultaneously explained the hard realism of Thomas Eakins' paintings and also accounted for his commercial failure. The reputed difficulties that Eakins faced among philistine Philadelphians merely proved the case that twentieth-century historians have made about Philadelphia. In the last generation of the nineteenth century the national architectural press was also critical of Philadelphia, blaming Frank Furness for the aberrant designs of the city's commercial district and its institutions. Elsewhere in the United States architects headed toward history and Beaux Arts classicism, and away from the cultural independence advocated earlier in the century by Ralph Waldo Emerson and Walt Whitman. To be sure some critics, such as Bostonian Ralph Adams Cram, saw merit in Furness' "revolt," as an attempt to be "something besides cheap copyists," trying instead "to be live Americans, not dead archaeologists, [who] sought for vitality, originality, personal and ethnic expression." Still most critics found it necessary to criticize a lack of taste that made Furness' city the target of many diatribes in both the New York- and Boston-based architectural press.[26] Even local critics got into the act, as in the case of W. N. Lockington,

---

for Advent of Century" (29 December 1900), 1.

26. For a summary of the criticism of the Furness years,

see Michael J. Lewis, "Furness and the Arc of Fame," in Thomas and others, 121–136.

a British-born architect who remarked that Philadelphia architecture was "the most conservatively unarchitectural of the large American cities," and praised only a few buildings which he described as "specks of light in a dark red ocean."[27]

Machines and Aesthetic Expression

Despite these typical criticisms aimed at Philadelphia, it is apparent that as the twentieth century began Philadelphia was a center of innovation in design with substantial achievements recently attained in architecture, painting, and illustration. The case for the city's contribution in the visual arts is made in the Philadelphia Museum of Art's Bicentennial Exhibition catalogue, *Philadelphia: Three Centuries of American Art*, which lists a remarkable group of artists active in the city before 1903. These included the group of young artists later known as the Ashcan School, for their honest and direct depiction of the world, among them John Sloan, Robert Henri, and William Glackens (who had studied at the Pennsylvania Academy of the Fine Arts). Less noticed because they did not leave for New York City were those young artists and poets who continued to find their subjects in the progressive machine culture of the city such as Colin Campbell Cooper and Charles Sheeler.[28]

In the more fundamental but less studied field of industrial design the Philadelphia contribution was even more important because much of the industrial heartland of the nation looked to this city for innovation. In a city based on industry the impact of the tenets of industrial design on architecture surely warrants attention. Ironically, despite its obviousness, or perhaps because of it, this link has been ignored—apparently because the twentieth century has redefined Philadelphia's image from one of industry, its nineteenth-century characterization, to one of heritage and class consciousness, in actuality a by-product of the classism of the early twentieth century and more recently of E. Digby Baltzell's *Philadelphia Gentlemen*. A brief review of the literature of industrial design of the second half of the nineteenth century proves Philadelphia's importance as one of the nation's principal centers of machine making and industrial design. By the middle of the nineteenth century it was evident that a distinctly different approach to machine design was practiced in Philadelphia, one remarkable enough to be noted by those writing about industrial design. This took at least two forms. Philip Scranton, a historian of manufacturing, has demonstrated that New England machine makers comprehended the difference between their region and Philadelphia as one of values. Lucian Sharpe of the firm of Brown and Sharpe, manufacturers of measuring devices in Providence, Rhode Island,

27. W. N. Lockington, "Philadelphia's Architecture," *Builder and Decorator*, 5, no. 2 (October 1887), 17.
28. Darrell Sewell, ed. *Philadelphia: Three Centuries of American Art* (Philadelphia: Philadelphia Museum of Art, 1976). Cooper was ignored but Sheeler was included (501–502).

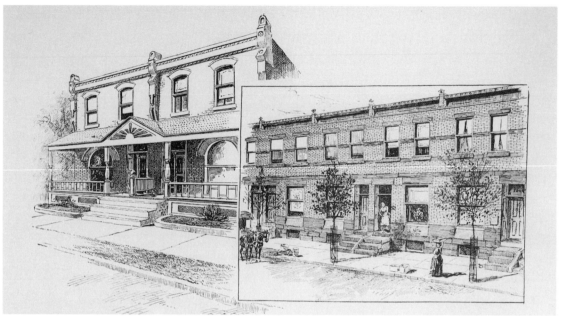

8. "Typical Philadelphia Homes," *Harper's Weekly* (1891), from Frank H. Taylor,
The City of Philadelphia as it Appears in the Year 1893 (Philadelphia, 1893)

9. Planing Machine, William Sellers & Company, in Joseph M. Wilson, *The Masterpieces of the Centennial Exhibition*,
Vol. 3, *History, Mechanics, Science* (Philadelphia: Gebbie & Barrie, 1876)

put it: "Our New England tool makers are all the time trying how cheap they can make tools [but] in Philadelphia the tool makers try how well they can make tools."[29]

Philadelphians agreed with this perception but also saw it as a question of design and not merely quality. Among the earliest to report on regional machine design was Edward Freedley who differentiated the machines made in the region from those of the rest of the country.

> The machine work executed in the leading establishments of Philadelphia, we may remark in conclusion, is distinguished by certain characteristics, which enable a competent judge to pronounce with confidence upon the source of its construction, or in other words to detect a Philadelphia-made machine by the "earmarks." Excellence of material, solidity, an admirable fitting of the joints, *a just proportion and arrangement of the parts, and a certain thoroughness and genuineness*, are qualities that pervade the machine work executed in Philadelphia, and distinguish it from all other American-made machinery.[30]

A generation later, at the Centennial Exhibition, a British judge found similar characteristics in the machine tools designed by William Sellers. The judge explained the award of the grand prize to Sellers, describing the machines from his shop as

> a collection of tools for working metal . . . remarkable [for] originality, without parallel in the past history of international exhibits. Besides it is thoroughly national in its characteristics. Every piece is worthy of an award, each one being of the highest standard in its particular class. The national characteristics included the nice fitting and precision, the *beautiful outlines that are imparted to each structure by the correct proportions that have been worked out in the determining of strength and form and the disposal of material to take full share of the duty.*

The British judge continued, praising the "scientific skill displayed in the application of mechanical force, for the daring in fearlessly breaking through the trammels of the past—without departing from true principles" and concluded saying "It is impossible to realize the full measure of such refined, mechanical, scientific and *artistic* merit by the foregoing remarks."[31] A century later William Sellers would be remembered as the man who introduced modern design principles in machines, who accepted their metallic character by painting them machine gray instead of red and green, who eliminated superfluous columns and other architectural details, and who stated the fundamental principle of

---

29. Philip Scranton, *Endless Novelty: Specialty Production and American Industrialization* (Princeton: Princeton University Press, 1997), 1, quoting "The Brown and Sharpe Manufacturing Co.," *Industry*, 2 (1889–90), 38.
30. Edward Freedley, *Philadelphia and its Manufactures: A Hand-book Exhibiting the Development, Variety and Statistics of the Manufacturing Industry of Philadelphia in*
1857 (Philadelphia: Edward Young, 1858), 328. Emphasis my own.
31. Francis A. Walker, ed., *United States Centennial Commission, International Exhibition, 1876. Reports and Awards, Groups XXI–XXVII*, Vol. 7 (Washington, D. C.: Government Printing Office, 1880), 14–18. Emphasis my own.

functional design that "A Machine looks right when it is right."[32] (*fig. 9*) This equation of form and function became a part of the Philadelphia culture that was absorbed by Louis Sullivan during his stay in Frank Furness' office in 1873—and it was presumably taught to Francis Price and William L. Price during their years in the Furness shop at the end of the same decade.

The British judge found similar characteristics in other Philadelphia-made machines including the steam engines displayed by the Baldwin Locomotive Works. Interchangeability of parts, ingenious adaptations of devices such as the water scoop, and safety devices such as the Westinghouse air brake all impressed the judge. Again the tendency toward functional design was noted and again it was linked to aesthetic purpose:

> The painting and general finish of the engine is planned with a view to quiet and harmonious effect, and is based upon the *principle that the purpose for which a locomotive is used does not admit of any merely ornamental devices: but that its beauty, so far as it may have any, should depend upon good proportions and through adaptation of the various parts to their uses.*[33]

The Centennial Exhibition exposed to American and foreign visitors alike Philadelphia architects' and painters' expressions of the modern world. Indeed the fair placed Philadelphia at the center of the global stage, as evidenced by historians of technology such as John Kouwenhoven whose *Made in America: The Arts in Modern Civilization* reports European fascination with American design, and Siegfried Giedion, who cites case after case of Philadelphia-based innovation in *Mechanization Takes Command*.[34] They describe as uniquely American the leadership in making and using labor-saving machinery and designing an aesthetic that responded to the new means of production, but both historians miss the essential concentration of these characteristics in the industries of the Philadelphia region. Philadelphia has been overlooked because the legend of the twentieth century places innovation in the United States in the midwest, especially in Chicago which was supposedly free from the "cultivated" European-oriented culture that stiffled American creativity. Philadelphia has also been viewed through the prism of the intervening Sesquicentennial Exposition which altered the city's reputation from one of innovation, the world view after 1876, to one of conservative stupor, the view after 1926. Much of this was deserved. Unlike the 1876 fair which introduced to the world Philadelphia

---

32. W. H. Mayall, *Machines and Perception in Industrial Design* (London: Studio Vista, 1968), 15. Mayall quotes Joseph Roe about Sellers: "Almost from the first, Sellers cut loose from the accepted designs of the day. He was among the first to realize that red paint, beads and mouldings, and architectural embellishments were false in machine design. He introduced the 'machine-gray' paint which has become universal, made the form of the machine follow the functions to be performed and freed it from all pockets and beadings."

33. Francis A. Walker, ed., *United States Centennial Commission, International Exhibition, 1876. Reports and Awards, Groups XV–XX*, Vol. 6 (Washington, D.C.: Government Printing Office, 1880), 236. Emphasis my own.

34. John Kouwenhoven, *Made in America: The Arts in Modern Civilization* (Garden City, N. Y.: Doubleday, 1948).

innovation in machine design and industrial standardization, the 1926 fair had as its centerpiece a recreation of eighteenth-century High Street and a three-story-high electric Liberty Bell. Henceforth, the nation would see the city as mired in the past and the earlier innovators from Philadelphia would be lost to view.

⊰ Philadelphia: The Poetry of the Present

The national interpretation of the Quaker City missed the reality that Philadelphia had long been freed from the past and from European forms by the rise of the city's industrialists as a force in shaping local institutions. By the 1860s the boards of the city's principal organizations including the University of Pennsylvania and the Academy of the Fine Arts were headed by industrialists who applied their own standards to the future of those institutions. In this circumstance Frank Furness, Joseph Wilson, and other architectural innovators received the bulk of their architectural commissions from such institutions, and in this period Philadelphia produced some of the nation's most imaginative architecture. (fig. 10) In a similar vein Elizabeth Johns has observed that after the Civil War Thomas Eakins and his students were preoccupied with scenes of contemporary life, although not in the sentimentalized mode of genre; painting was regarded as a form of documentation concentrating on the specifics of observation, and as such anticipated filmmaking and photography in the twentieth century.[35] Boxers sitting in their corners between rounds, rail hunters on their skiffs and eel spearers in the marshes, scullers resting after a race, swimmers at local creeks, and surgeons at work all afforded appropriate subjects for the artist's attention. In many of these images Eakins incorporated the new information of Eadweard Muybridge's photographs of animal locomotion, many of which had been taken at the University of Pennsylvania with the advice and support of Fairman Rogers, a civil engineer and former professor of civil engineering at the university. Rogers himself became the subject of Eakins' *The Fairman Rogers Four-in-Hand* (1879–80) in which the painter demonstrated his newfound understanding of the specifics of the gait of the horse as well as the effect of the relative speed of different-sized wheels of the coach. The present failure to cross interdisciplinary boundaries even in related fields of art and architectural history, let alone in the history of science and technology and the new social history of the 1970s, has resulted in often missing connections that would have been found between Frank Furness who designed the Pennsylvania Academy of the Fine Arts where Thomas Eakins taught and on whose board Fairman Rogers served. Also lost has been the larger interplay among the arts, the engineering disciplines, and the progressive industrial culture. That culture in turn provided numerous subjects for the artist as well as clients, inspiration, and technology for the architect as the side of the Pennsylvania Academy itself attests.[36]

———

35. Elizabeth Johns, *Thomas Eakins: The Heroism of Modern Life* (Princeton: Princeton University Press, 1983).

As the nineteenth century ended, and with Eakins as an example, a generation of Philadelphian artists, many of them working in the dozen local newspapers, depicted the modern world with increasingly unflinching honesty. Among these were John Sloan, William Glackens, and Robert Henri all of whom worked in Philadelphia as the new century began. Several of these young men occupied studios in the vaguely bohemian zone near the main press offices just west of Independence Hall, in properties that were losing tenants because of the shift of the business community west to the neighborhood of the new City Hall. Although most would soon leave for New York City during the first years of the new century, their presence in Philadelphia enlivened a city whose residents also included the great generation of illustrators, the link between high art and popular culture—Howard Pyle, then teaching at Drexel, N. C. Wyeth and other Pyle pupils, and lithographer Joseph Pennell. They reflected Philadelphia's continuing significant share of the nation's publishing industry, with the many magazines of Edward Bok's Curtis Publishing Company, as well as Lippincott and other presses active in the city. More than a few of these artists would find subjects in the great steel train sheds, the locomotives, and the belching smoke and steam of Philadelphia industry.

At the turn of the century the avant-garde in Philadelphia included Ezra Pound and William Carlos Williams who were studying literature and medicine at the University of Pennsylvania at the same time that Thornton Oakley and Morton Livingston Schamberg were studying in the university's fine arts program. Surely it was not a coincidence that Williams would continue to draw on machine images as a metaphor for efficiency in his poetry.[37] At the Pennsylvania Academy of the Fine Arts were Charles Sheeler and Charles Demuth who found new artistic subjects that expressed the new age, recording the height of the City Hall tower, the speed of the elevated lines, the power of engines. Thus it might have been anticipated that 1901 would be a fine moment for an architect to be alert to the possibilities of the new age. Reflecting the future of the city,

―――――――

36. As an example of this failure see Thomas Hughes, *American Genesis: A History of the American Genius for Invention* (New York: Penguin Books, 1989). Though working and writing in Frank Furness' and William Price's city, but apparently unaware of their work, Hughes wrote that "Europeans looked to Henry Ford and the United States for modern technology, but not for modern high culture—architecture, art and literature. European, not American, architects first sought ways to use in their buildings both modern production technology and an aesthetic vocabulary to express modern technological values, such as efficiency, precision, control, and system" (309). A careful examination of Frank Furness' Pennsylvania Academy of the Fine Arts finds all of these features in that building which influenced early modern European architects.

37. Williams described the process of making poems in machine terms: "A poem is a small (or large) machine made of words...there can be no part, as in any other machine that is redundant." William Carlos Williams, "Author's Introduction," *The Wedge* (1944), reprinted in William Carlos Williams, *The Collected Works of William Carlos Williams*, Vol. 2, 1939–62, ed. Christopher MacGowen (New York: New Directions Publishing Company, 1988), 54.

over the next generation most Philadelphia architects would turn from the industrial culture to the national trans-Atlantic culture centered in New York and Boston.

For an architectural parallel to Eakins' paintings in Philadelphia it is necessary to
look to the generation that reached maturity in the 1860s, represented by the work of
Frank Furness and the lesser known but equally important engineering-based design of
the Wilson Brothers. Through the nineteenth century Philadelphia's principal clients
were engineers who, since the centennial decade, had commissioned an original architecture that reflected the progressive values of industrial practice. Dismissed by critics in
other cities for designs that were viewed as unthinking expressions of a Quaker culture
that had no love for the arts, Furness and the Wilson Brothers were engaged in establishing methods of practice that would shape architecture in the twentieth century. These
Philadelphia architects were freed by the values of their clients, the industrialists of the
city who, since the 1850s had designed machines not based on precedent but on the belief
that form was derived from function.[38] With the example of Frank Furness and the
Wilson Brothers, Price explored the potential of steel and reinforced concrete to design
buildings of the scale that the twentieth century demanded.

Philadelphia's architects and engineers link the city to the half century of global
change that made the period between the Civil War and 1903 "the greatest period of technological change in terms of things that affected huge numbers of peoples lives in basic
ways."[39] As the twentieth century ends, the echoes of nineteenth century expansion, population growth and technological revolution continue to reverberate in our own era.
Although each recent period chauvinistically believes itself to be the locus of transformation of the modern world, there is good evidence to suggest that the second half of the
nineteenth century more profoundly affected the course of day-to-day life than any other
similar period of time. In transportation alone the changes were astonishing: reliable

---

38. See John Wolfe Barry, *Minutes of Proceedings of the
Institution of Civil Engineers*, 128 (1897), a London-
based publication which in 1896 reviewed Edward
Clapp Shankland's *Steel Construction in Chicago*. It outlined the developments of tall skeletal office building
construction. Also included were comments at the end
by engineers to whom Shankland had sent the paper
including William Le Baron Jenney, known to all as one
of the prime movers in the history of tall buildings (and
the former head of the American Society of Civil
Engineers) and one Joseph M. Wilson (of Philadelphia)
who commented that he had anticipated most of the
ideas being credited to Chicago in the ordinary course
of his work. And he had done it earlier and often better
(54–55). Set in the context of the problem of building

40. Albert Kelsey, photo essay of "The Dormitory
System of the University of Pennsylvania," *The
Architectural Annual, 1901* (Philadelphia: The
Architectural Annual, 1901), 179.
the underlying geology. It is in this same context that
Joseph Wilson saw the issue—as one of logical engi-
neering questions logically posed—and not of the par-
ticular search for innovation. In short this is an
American rational process toward a solution rather
than a European programmatic solution to fit a theory.
39. Robert C. Post (president of the Society for the
History of Technology), quoted by Steve Lohr, "The
Future Came Faster in the Old Days," *The New York
Times* (5 October 1997), sec. 4, p. 1.

left 10. Furness, Evans and Company, University of Pennsylvania Library (1888), looking east, 1991 (photograph by George E. Thomas)

below 11. Louis I. Kahn, Alfred Newton Richards Medical Research Laboratories, University of Pennsylvania (1956–61), looking north, 1976 (photograph by George E. Thomas)

steel-hulled steamships replaced wooden sailing ships; steam-powered locomotives succeeded animal-drawn wagons; electric trolleys supplanted the horse car; and, as the new century dawned, gas-powered automobiles offered the potential for independent travel. Only a few years later Robert Goddard's experiments with rockets would begin the push toward the limits of the universe. Similar progress occurred in public health, communications, home appliances, in short, in every aspect of life. The legacy of that era is the orientation of our culture toward the promise of the future instead of toward the past; the role of change has become the sole constant of modern life. After the Civil War Philadelphia was a laboratory of the future where, in the phrase of Albert Kelsey, "the poetry of the present" found expression in architectural forms.[40] In the first decade of this century William Price, alone of his generation, advocated the values of the city's heritage of innovation. Shaping the facades of large buildings along lines suggested by the nature of their materials and their purpose rather than according to principles handed down from history, Price evoked the character of the modern age in forms that became the basis of modern American style before 1930. The integrity of Price's approach was understood by Paul Cret and George Howe, who in turn advocated his work to their students. Certainly there is a recollection of Price's expressive construction in the Traymore Hotel in Louis Kahn's columns projecting through the parapets in the Alfred Newton Richards Laboratories at the University of Pennsylvania. (*fig. 11*) Through these Philadelphians, and especially through Robert Venturi and Denise Scott Brown who have rebuilt the bridges between design and popular culture, William Price's architecture will continue to resonate in American design.

---

40. Albert Kelsey, photo essay of "The Dormitory System of the University of Pennsylvania," *The* *Architectural Annual, 1901* (Philadelphia: The Architectural Annual, 1901), 179.

William L. Price, c. 1888 (Photograph by Walter Price, c. 1888;
Architectural Archives, Philip N. Price Collection, University of Pennsylvania)

Nationality, Ethnic Continuity, and Christian Civilization

The development of artistic architecture in America began after the Philadelphia Centennial. Good architecture of a certain class we had before that time, it is true; but that exhibition pointed the way to culture that speedily penetrated all forms of art and industry. The general movement toward higher artistic ideals inaugurated by the Centennial soon found expression in architecture. —*Barr Ferree*[1]

Centennial Roots

As the nineteenth century entered its last quarter, William L. Price apprenticed as a carpenter, finished the decade of the 1870s studying architecture with Frank Furness, and, in 1881 at the age of twenty, entered independent practice with his brother, Frank Price, in Philadelphia, the nation's second largest city. Unlike in New York City, which had become the center of the nation's finance and overseas trade, and in Boston, which remained an important national center of culture and commerce, architecture in Philadelphia was increasingly outside the national mainstream as evidenced by its lurid depiction in the northeast-dominated architectural press. Characterized as a dark industrial workplace whose architects produced bizarre variations on the already outmoded Victorian brick fashion, Philadelphia's downtown banks and suburban residences contrasted with the rest of the nation which had turned toward the light stone and brick of the Beaux Arts or the half-timber and pointed arches of the Gothic Revival.

New York- and Boston-based critics, writing for ever more cosmopolitan architectural journals advanced various theories for Philadelphia's failure to adopt the new historical styles that were sweeping the nation. These ranged from a curious lack of interest in things aesthetic, presumed to be caused by an anti-aesthetic bias of the resident Quakers,

---

1. Barr Ferree, "Artistic Domestic Architecture in America," *The New England Magazine*, 12, no. 4 (June 1895), 451.

left 1. Frank Furness, Provident Bank (1876–78), prior to demolition, 1957 (Architectural Archives, Frank Furness Collection, University of Pennsylvania)

below 2. James M. Price and Edward Markham at Blackwood, New Jersey, 1899 (Architectural Archives, Philip N. Price Collection, University of Pennsylvania)

to the ongoing influence of Frank Furness who was considered to be the Typhoid Mary of bad taste. William L. Price could be considered a test case for both theories. He was a Quaker who at various times used his Quaker roots as an excuse for his own aesthetic independence. In a 1907 lecture he explained his own work by stating: "Sometimes it is necessary to have these refractory and unpleasant people around to do the kicking for us. My own ancestors were kicked out of England as Quakers because they were so obnoxious and upsetting to things as they were."[2] Throughout his career Price worked in the Quaker City, absorbing its values and reflecting its standards. Will and his older brother Frank also were directly exposed to the ideas of Furness, learning the principles of the architectural profession in his office during the years that the Provident Life and Trust Company was under construction and Furness was arriving at the method that represented function through form. (*fig. 1*)

After leaving Furness' office Will and his brothers, first Francis (1855–1919, usually called Frank) and later Walter (1857–1951), joined the young architect's rebellion against the independent design of the Centennial generation. Like their peers across the nation who reached maturity in the 1880s, the Price brothers worked in the historical styles which represented the sophisticated trans-Atlantic culture developing along the mid-Atlantic and New England coast. It would have been a surprise if they had not taken this direction. In the first years of the twentieth century, fellow Philadelphians Walter Cope, John Stewardson, Frank Miles Day, Wilson Eyre, Jr., and Horace Trumbauer received the praise of lengthy articles by Ralph Adams Cram that touted their historicizing designs in contrast to the rogue architecture that had prevailed before in the Quaker City. Cram's capsule history of Philadelphia architecture was typical of the architectural press after 1880:

> Blessed with an early architecture of the very best type developed on this continent, it [Philadelphia architecture] sank first to a condition of stolid stupidity almost unparalleled, then produced at a bound a group of abundant vitality, but the very worst taste ever recorded in art, and then amazed everyone by flashing on the world a small circle of architects whose dominant quality was exquisite and almost impeccable taste.[3]

That Bostonian Cram found Philadelphia a topic of interest at the end of the century demonstrated that once independent Philadelphia had capitulated to the national taste and its architects were again worthy of being published in the national magazines.

Only a generation ago the question of stylistic choice seemed irrelevant in the theoretical framework of twentieth-century architecture. Two decades of postmodernism

———

2. William L. Price, "Modern Architecture," *The Artsman*, 4, no. 2 (January 1907), 228.

3. Ralph Adams Cram, "The Work of Messrs. Frank Miles Day & Brother," *Architectural Record*, 15, no. 5 (May 1904), 397.

have reinstated style as a theoretical question—although more as billboard signage of pop culture than the total integration of structure and purpose intended by the International Style moderns. At the end of the nineteenth century the question of style would have been basic to any architectural project and was essential to the self-definition of the architect as well. Architects selected styles for projects depending on context, purpose, and the preference of the client, and most architects were associated with a particular stylistic camp according to their personal interests and beliefs. After 1890 Beaux Arts classicism was the usual choice of the formalists such as McKim, Mead & White and Carrère and Hastings, while the moralists including Cram, Eyre, and Cope and Stewardson preferred the Gothic style. Either method could be supported within the framework of Hegelian historical determinism. Completely eclipsed as the century ended were the pragmatic functionalists such as Frank Furness. While fragments of nineteenth-century architectural theory were incorporated into the International Style, particularly the allied concepts of structural and constructive honesty that grew out of the Gothic Revival and the writings of John Ruskin and William Morris, other contemporary concepts such as Hegel's idea that racial memory and ethnicity were at the base of culture and by extension of architectural design withered in the lunacy of twentieth-century totalitarianism.[4] Still, it was only a century ago that Cram characterized the work of the young Philadelphians in Hegelian terms: "The Philadelphia group has stood and is standing for nationality, for ethnic continuity, and for the impulses of Christian Civilization."[5] Repugnant as such ideas may be at the end of the twentieth century, still they are part of the intellectual framework that informed choices made by architects at the end of the last century.

For Will Price and his brother Frank, both of whom had been trained in Furness' office where the moral framework of meaning and expression of function were the standard, it could have been expected that even though they departed from Furness' functional expressionism, they would come down on the side of the moralists, working in variations of the Gothic style rather than in the Beaux Arts. This choice, however, lay a few years in the future when Furness' vigorous work was fading and when the new historical choices were spotlighted by the 1893 World's Columbian Exposition in Chicago and by the rise of new architectural periodicals in the center of trans-Atlantic culture in New York City.

———

4. For the histories that shaped post-World War II design see Siegfried Giedion, *Space, Time and Architecture* (Cambridge, Mass.: Harvard University Press, 1941); Nikolas Pevsner, *An Outline of European Architecture* (Hammondsworth, England: Pelican Books, 1943); and Henry-Russell Hitchcock, *Architecture: Nineteenth and Twentieth Centuries* (Baltimore, Md.:, Penguin Books, 1958).

5. Ralph Adams Cram, "The Work of Cope and Stewardson," *Architectural Record*, 16, no. 5 (November 1904), 413. In the same article Cram characterized, "Day for taste, Eyre for personality, Cope and Stewardson for poetry" (411).

⅜ Family Roots and Values

The Philadelphia into which William Lightfoot Price was born on the 11th month, 9th day (November 9th), 1861, to use the Quaker style, was very different from the city in which he produced his mature work some forty years later. In the decade of his birth, the Civil War had drawn the cream of the city's youth into specialized military regiments, but Quakers, while advocating the abolition of slavery, rejected violence as a solution to human problems, forcing a choice between religious duty and military service. Those who remained members of the Society of Friends were further marginalized, continuing their drift from the mainstream of the community that had begun a century earlier during the years preceding the American Revolution. By the 1870s, although Philadelphia continued to be the principal center of their religion, Quakers were so reduced in number and so removed from positions of social and cultural leadership that it would have been astonishing had so small a sect shaped the aesthetic character of the city.

Instead, the designs that outsiders presumed to be based on Quaker values were actually the consequences of a culture controlled by progressive engineers and industrialists, men who were attuned to progress and not to precedent. Theirs was a workshop culture that valued experience over book learning and sought innovation as a product of their own work.[6] According to Lindy Biggs these industrialists had learned how to shape a factory building to become a part of the work process, in effect making it the master machine of the plant.[7] In Philadelphia most of the important post-Civil War architects, including Frank Furness, Joseph Wilson, Collins and Autenrieth, and Addison Hutton designed industrial buildings as an ordinary part of their practice. All would have been familiar with the new design strategies that were shaping industrial architecture. In its focus on industry and progress Philadelphia was like Glasgow, Prague, Barcelona, Chicago, and other industrial cities which were also regional centers of culture. As the nineteenth century ended there was a striking coincidence between the progressive communities whose leaders were engineers and manufacturers and the centers of work of such early masters of the modern movement as Charles Rennie Mackintosh, Antoní Gaudí, Otto Wagner, H. P. Berlage, Peter Behrens, and the Americans, Frank Furness, Louis Sullivan, and Frank Lloyd Wright.

The history of the Price family conformed in its broad outlines to the Quaker experience in the Philadelphia region beginning with the seventeenth-century migration across the Atlantic. William Lightfoot Price's life was a product of nature, by way of the physical and emotional characteristics of his family, and nurture in the manner in which

6. Monte A. Calvert, *The Mechanical Engineer in America, 1830–1910: Professional Cultures in Conflict* (Baltimore: Johns Hopkins University Press, 1967).

7. Lindy Biggs, *The Rational Factory: Architecture, Technology and Work in America's Age of Mass Production* (Baltimore: Johns Hopkins University Press, 1996), 47–53.

his parents' values were repeated in his own activities. Hence the Price family history warrants comment in order to understand the gathering forces that transformed a young Quaker, living on the edge of Philadelphia, into a designer of remarkable originality whose experiments in community planning and architecture for the expanding middle classes shaped twentieth-century America.

Philip ap Rhys was the first of his family to make the voyage to the new world, arriving in 1682 with the first wave of Welsh Quakers who had purchased from William Penn the so-called "Welsh Tract," the land which now comprises the western Philadelphia townships of Merion, Haverford, and Radnor.[8] By 1693 Philip ap Rhys owned 1000 acres in Haverford, a considerable property that represented significant wealth. During the next century the family grew in number and remained committed to the Quaker faith. As the eighteenth century ended the family was located near West Chester, where Philip and Rachel Price were progressive farmers in East Bradford Township. In 1795 Philip was asked to join the committee to found the Westtown School, a boarding school for Quaker children which he and his wife later served as superintendent and matron.[9] Although Westtown remained affiliated with the more urban Orthodox meetings, its rural location continued to connect young Quakers with their agricultural roots.

Will's father, James Martin Price, the grandson of Philip and Rachel Price, was born in 1825, a week after the death of his father Isaac. That event forced James' mother, Susanna, to move in with her parents-in-law where she applied her advanced education to teaching in the family's new venture, the Price School in West Chester.[10] The education of women had been a strong point of the Quaker community and it would continue in the Price family with many of its women graduates of Swarthmore College, including Will's wife Emma and their daughter Margaret. With farming and education as the family's principal trades, James Martin Price oscillated between the two poles of the family experi-

---

8. Welsh genealogy is complicated by the father's given name becoming the surname, thus changing for each successive generation. In the new world the Price family, like most of their contemporaries, shifted to a single patronymic, a conflation of ap Rhys which became Price. Certain given names regularly reappear in the family, most of all Philip and Eli. Thomas Allen Glenn, *Merion in the Welsh Tract* (Norristown, Penn.: Herald Press, 1896), 73.

9. The early history of the Westtown School is treated in two publications: Watson W. Dewees, *A Brief History of Westtown Boarding School with a General Catalogue of Officers, Students, Etc.*, 4th edition (Philadelphia: Sherman and Company, 1888) and Watson and Sarah B. Dewees, *Centennial History of the Westtown Boarding*

School, 1799–1899 (Philadelphia: Sherman and Company, 1899).

10. In 1831 Susanna remarried John Parvin Smith, brother-in-law of Sally Lightfoot, bringing the Lightfoot family into the enlarging circle of the Price family. As James Martin Price remembered it half a century later, the Price, Lightfoot, Parvin and Smith families formed a tight circle around the home of Philip M. Price at 12th and Spring Garden streets. Will's future wife, Emma Webb, grew up a few blocks away at 10th and Spring Garden where her father William ran a drugstore. Archibald McElroy, *McElroy's Philadelphia Directory for the Year 1853* (1853), James Gopsill's *Philadelphia City Directory for 1880* (1880).

ence. In 1835, after studying at Anthony Bohlmer's school for boys in West Chester, where he learned drawing and drafting, he entered the Westtown School where he later taught from 1848 until 1853. In the intervening years he served as an assistant teacher at the Haverford School (now Haverford College) and then attended the University of Pennsylvania, graduating second in his class with a Bachelor of Arts degree in 1847 and receiving his Master of Arts degree in 1850.[11] James' wide-ranging interests resulted in his being sent by the city of Philadelphia as a commissioner to the 1851 International Exhibition in London that is now remembered for the Crystal Palace of Joseph Paxton.[12] Literature and theater were other interests. While teaching at Westtown he was drawn into the circle of the bard of Chester County, Bayard Smith, and at the end of his life, he became the friend of celebrity writer Edwin Markham who had meteorically soared to fame on the strength of his poem "The Man with the Hoe," based on John Everett Millais' painting of the same subject. (*fig. 2*) The work had gained popularity as an image of the indomitable human spirit of the working classes—at a moment when industrialization and scientific management were transforming work, and socialism and Henry George's idea of the Single Tax were vying with capitalism for the future of the society. In 1901 these family interests in literature, the arts, politics, and ideas would coalesce in Will Price's communities at Rose Valley and Arden.

Sketching was another of James' interests reported in the family genealogical study and history written by his daughter Susanna Martin Price in 1929. Describing James as "tall and slender, much given to long walking trips with gun and knapsack, " she recalled that he "recorded many of these, illustrating them with his pencil." The surviving sketchbooks attest to the high level of competence gained at Bohlmer's school, including linear perspective which he used to record architectural, engineering, and natural subjects. Although Will Price may have grown up in a religious sect that conscientiously avoided sacred images, his father's enthusiastic illustration of his diaries anticipated his sons' artistic interests. When as a teenager Will and his cousins and nieces organized a group of youths who took as their name the Seekers After Knowledge, usually abbreviated "S. A. K.," Will illustrated the journals of their travels with vivid pen-and-pencil sketches until photographer Henry Troth joined their group and began recording the expeditions with a camera.[13]

---

11. W. J. Maxwell, comp., *University of Pennsylvania General Alumni Catalogue, 1917* (Philadelphia: General Alumni Society, 1917), 48.

12. James Price described the journey in a journal entitled "James M. Price: His Summer Jaunt Through Britain in 1851," Walter F. Price Papers, Rose Valley.

13. Will Price's sketches for the S. A. K. journals were in the possession of his daughter, Margaret L. Price in the early 1970s; a photo log of one of the later S. A. K. trips, entitled "So the S. A. K. Journeyed to Scalp Level, July 3rd to 17th, 1886," has been deposited by Will's grandson, Philip Nevin Price, in the Architectural Archives at the University of Pennsylvania.

3. House in Wallingford, Pennsylvania, birthplace of William L. Price (photograph by Walter Price, c. 1897; Architectural Archives, Philip N. Price Collection, University of Pennsylvania)

4. William L. Price, Westtown School at the time the Price boys attended it. Pencil perspective from Watson W. Dewees, *A Brief History of Westtown Boarding School with a General Catalogue of Officers, Students, Etc.* (Philadelphia, 1899)

In 1853, while teaching at the Westtown School, James married Sarah D. Lightfoot at the North Meeting at 6th and Noble streets in Philadelphia, near the Lightfoot home. The Lightfoots also had been farmers, mostly in the western counties around Philadelphia, but by midcentury, Sarah's brother Francis had moved into the booming city where he learned surveying from his uncle, Philip H. Price, the official surveyor of the Spring Garden District. Francis soon formed a real estate business with another cousin, Charles Walton, who was active in the streetcar suburb of West Philadelphia.[14] Later, James' sons found many of their early jobs among the circle of builders and real estate speculators who reshaped Philadelphia during the great boom period following the Civil War.

The years just before the Civil War were a time of economic difficulty for James Price who several times was forced to change jobs, usually at inopportune moments. In 1861 the family fortunes took a turn for the better when an aunt died, leaving James as the beneficiary of her estate. This inheritance made it possible for James and his small family to move to Wallingford where the family developed a moderately successful nursery business. There in a modest stone-and-frame farmhouse near Providence Road south of Media were born William Lightfoot, Charles, Caroline, and Anna, of whom only William and Anna lived to maturity. (*fig. 3*) This rural setting shaped Will's ideas of a family utopia which he would recreate forty years later when he acquired the nearby industrial village of Rose Valley for his experiment in community living. Presumably the farmhouse in Wallingford was the setting for Will's account of his first efforts at drawing which he recalled while living at Rose Valley:

> When I was five years old I stood beside the table where my older sisters and brothers were drawing from pictures in the *Farm Journal*, the only illustrated paper we had. Crude chickens, square pigs, straight-backed cows, and while listlessly watching their attempts, I was suddenly moved by a sense of power. I knew that I could draw, and scorning the easily erased pencil, my chubby untaught fingers seized pen and ink and drew a fair large bull.[15]

Although James held on to the Wallingford property into the 1870s, the family moved back to Philadelphia in 1867 as the post-Civil War recession deepened. James was forced to return to teaching and then became an agent of the newly formed Provident Life and Trust Company. Two years earlier, in 1865, as the nation's orgy of death was ending,

---

14. Susanna Martin Price, "The Story of the Price–Lightfoot Family culled from Innumerable Old Family Letters"(typescript, 1929; Architectural Archives, Philip N. Price Collection, University of Pennsylvania). Also in the same book is James M. Price, "The Ancestry of Sarah L. Price" (typescript), which reports that Francis followed the family business of surveying. Francis and his uncle laid out the Woodland Cemetery and Francis was the surveyor of the 24th Ward, the present university area. Francis Lightfoot Price was named for his uncle (3).

15. William L. Price, "Clouds and Swallows," *The Conservator*, 31, no. 8 (October 1908), 118.

members of the Society of Friends had organized the Provident Life and Trust Company, modeling it on an English mutual insurance organization, with the goal of securing "to Friends and 'others of like careful habit' the lower cost of insurance attaching to their superior longevity."[16] Unlike other insurance companies of the era which were little more than pyramid schemes for their operators, the Provident Company under the leadership of Samuel Shipley was carefully and soundly managed and steadily prospered. Ironically James Price found success in the direct sales of insurance rather than education or farming. For the first time in twenty years of marriage the Price family was secure. When James wrote to Will during a sketching trip to England in 1896, his fervent anti-William Jennings Bryan tone makes it clear that he had become a fiscal conservative with much to protect. Perhaps the economic turbulence of his early years shaped Will Price's future interest in schemes that linked economic and social utopias.

By the early 1870s the family had moved to West Philadelphia on the developing edge of a rapidly growing Victorian suburb. This location had the advantages of a short-ened commute to the Provident offices and proximity to the Lightfoot and Walton cousins.[17] Family closeness was a constant, as Eli Kirk Price, one of Philip and Rachel's ten children, recalled:

> The ten children of Philip and Rachel Price who grew up, by marriage made them twenty; all worthy, social and affectionate; all happiest when the children's children were gathered under the paternal roof. These were social occasions of hospitable entertainment.... A family union so cemented no one could think of marring and it never has been broken.[18]

Advanced Education

In 1875 the Price family moved to Lansdowne, then called Darby Station. Nearing his fourteenth year Will followed his older brothers and sisters to the Westtown School, beginning what was considered his advanced education. (*fig. 4*) Never committed to the values of classical education because of its pagan associations—the Quaker use of num-bers rather than the Roman names for the months was rooted in the same literal rejection of pagan content of any sort—Quakers readily sought to liberalize education. Around the Civil War the Westtown School joined the progressive movement eliminating require-ments in Latin and Greek and substituting new courses in mathematics, botany, and chemistry, thereby anticipating the curriculum revolution that would soon reshape the nation's colleges.[19] Unlike his older brother Walter who had followed his father's interests

16. William S. Ashbrook, *Fifty Years: The Provident Life and Trust Company of Philadelphia: 1865–1915* (Philadelphia: Holmes Press, 1915), 15. James M. Price is in a photograph of the early agents, facing page 60.

17. James Gopsill, *Gopsill's Philadelphia City Directory for 1873* (1873).

18. Susanna Martin Price, 4–5.

19. Watson and Sarah Dewees, *Centennial History of*

toward the classical education and eventually received a bachelor's degree from Haverford College and a master's degree from Harvard College, Will was drawn to Westtown's new scientific curriculum, studying physics and chemistry, both subjects of interest to the nearby industrial city.

If during school breaks in the winter of 1875 and the summer of 1876 Will had returned to his old North 39th Street neighborhood, he would have found it being transformed. Instead of a quiet suburb on the edge of the city, the rail yards just to the north had become the staging grounds for the West Fairmount Park site selected for the celebration of America's Centennial. On the edge of the park was constructed a vast temporary city of hotels, stores, and restaurants as well as the immense main exhibition buildings which would form the focus of the greatest mass event to date in the nation's history, drawing a quarter of the country's population. Certainly the family attended the Centennial Exhibition. There they would have seen evidence of the industrial might of the Quaker City, heard the steady beat of the giant Corliss engine as it powered the machines of the main exhibit hall, and reveled in the prospects of the modern world. Given the interest of two of James' sons in architecture, the family certainly visited the Fine Arts Annex where architectural and engineering materials were grouped together. The rows of perspective drawings and photographs presented a profession in flux, exemplified by two generations of architects, the older carpenter/pattern book designers such as Henry Hudson Holly, Isaac Hobbs, and John McArthur, Jr., and the young professionals notably Richard Morris Hunt and his students George B. Post, William Ware, Henry Van Brunt, and Charles Gambrill, not to mention such new stars as Gambrill's partner, Henry Hobson Richardson.[20] McArthur's stiff engraving-like drawings for Philadelphia's Second Empire City Hall contrasted with Richardson's painterly renderings of Boston's Trinity Church in Spanish Pilgrimage Road Romanesque and the rough-textured ink perspective of the William Watts Sherman House in Newport in the newly fashionable Old English Style.[21]

———

Westtown Boarding School, 184–185.

20. *Official Catalog of the International Exhibition of 1876* (Philadelphia: John Nagle, 1876), Department IV, 32–36. Among the architects winning awards were Gambrill and Richardson who were commended for "great fertility of invention," Carl Pfeiffer, Ware and Van Brunt, Sturgis and Brigham, Richard Upjohn, and John McArthur, Jr., whose public buildings of Philadelphia were cited for being "a colossal work intrepidly treated and richly deserving of recognition and award." Others receiving awards included "Viollet Leduc, Paris, France, William Burgess [sic]," and "the

Architect of Japanese Commission," commended for "the rich ornamental carving, altogether offering a capital and most improving study to the careless and slipshod joiners of the Western world." Francis A. Walker, ed., *United States Centennial Commission. International Exhibition, 1876. Reports and Awards, Groups XXI–XXVII,* Vol. 7 (Washington, D. C.: Government Printing Office, 1880), 663–667.

21. As Philadelphia's leading architect, Frank Furness did not display his drawings, relying instead on dozens of new commissions scattered around the city to present his ideas to the public. He did, however, exhibit

With the collective goal of dazzling Centennial visitors, Philadelphians rebuilt the center of their city in the decade after the Civil War. In the old downtown, near Independence Hall, Chestnut Street was lined with bristling attention-grabbing bank facades, including the new buildings for the Union Trust and the astonishing Guarantee Trust and Safe Deposit Company, both by Frank Furness. Nearby Walnut Street was lined with slightly more staid buildings for the insurance industry. To the west, at the intersection of Broad and Market streets was the promise of a new downtown in the granite base and marble lower walls of McArthur's mammoth City Hall was under construction on Penn Square. To the north and south were the spiky silhouettes of new civic buildings, notably James Windrim's Masonic Temple and Addison Hutton's Arch Street Methodist Church, and at Cherry Street the foundry-like massing of the Pennsylvania Academy of the Fine Arts by Frank Furness and George Hewitt.

In West Philadelphia a new train station by the Wilson Brothers greeted Centennial travelers at 32nd and Market streets, and Furness' newly opened Centennial Bank was conveniently located across Market Street for the safekeeping of tourists' valuables. Finally, the beveled front of Furness' bank led the eye along the diagonal of Woodland Avenue to the new buildings of the University of Pennsylvania. Philadelphia was in the eye of the nation, and for a moment received the praise of the architectural press. Furness' bold architecture in particular attracted the praise of a writer for the *American Architect and Building News* who reported that his designs were "full of life.... It is altogether the most interesting thing, to a student of architecture, to be seen in Philadelphia."[22]

In 1876, with the world suddenly at his doorstep and surrounded by the new architecture that was transforming the city, Will Price ended his Westtown education and turned toward his new objective, becoming an architect. Among elite Philadelphians, whether Episcopalians, Unitarians, or Quakers, it remained the custom for youths to be taught a trade before taking on professional education. Wherever possible, the core interest was supported, so that a future engineer might enter a machine shop and learn the trade of machinist. In the case of a future architect, as his daughter Margaret recalled, Will, like his older brother Frank, learned carpentry which, it was presumed, would provide steady employment if architecture did not work out, and would be of use to an architect.[23] Perhaps the brothers worked on the Centennial buildings during the final fitting

---

dogs in the agriculture section. See Pennsylvania Board of Centennial Managers, *Pennsylvania and the Centennial Exposition Comprising the Preliminary and Final Reports of the Pennsylvania Board of Centennial Managers*, Vol. 2 (Philadelphia: Gillen and Nagle, 1878), 103.

22. "Correspondence: Building in Philadelphia," *American Architect and Building News*, 1 (14 October 1876), 336.

23. Interview with Margaret Lightfoot Price (8 November 1970). Robert Kanigel, *The One Best Way: Frederick Winslow Taylor and the Enigma of Efficiency* (New York: Viking Press, 1997) quotes a Wilmington newspaper account of shop education for elite children in the same decade (108).

out prior to the opening of the fair in the spring of 1876. In any event, during his six-teenth and seventeenth years, Will worked in the building trades, learning the basic rules of thumb about building from a craft perspective.

Family tradition records that while Will worked as a carpenter he was also taking night courses at the Pennsylvania Museum School of Industrial Art. The Museum School had developed as offshoots of the Centennial Exposition and were intended to fulfill a role similar to that of the South Kensington Museum in London, providing guidance to designers and mechanics, thereby improving the competitive position of Philadelphia businesses. A committee of Philadelphians, Frank Furness among them, commissioned British industrial designer Christopher Dresser to give a series of lectures that persuaded the state to support the idea of the school.[24] The faculty of the new institution included architect Charles M. Burns, a Civil War veteran and one of the first graduates of the University of Pennsylvania's engineering program. Now remembered for his ecclesiastical work, Burns served as instructor in the artistic division; decorative artist George Herzog, who designed the period rooms in James Windrim's Masonic Temple, was instructor in historic ornament.[25] Ironically, despite Furness' initial support, the Museum School marked the beginning of the region's shift away from functional design toward historical sources. The school fell short of another of the objectives of its founders who had hoped to attract craftsmen as well as artists. The early catalogues list a few bricklay-ers, carpenters, and wood carvers among the attendees, but most of its pupils listed them-selves as students and clerks who saw in architecture a step toward the needed credentials of the new age.[26] Will was probably one of the carpenters listed as attending in 1879 when the family was once again in West Philadelphia.[27]

---

24. Architecture students are not listed by field of study in the early annual reports, but a few future architects can be found among the early prize winners including Edgar Seeler, the first to be listed as a prize winner in the 1886 report, and such later members of the Price office as John J. Bissegger and Carl DeMoll, both of whom were prize winners in 1888. Frank Price is listed as a prize winner in sculpture in 1889. In 1991 Linh Tran undertook research for my Urban Studies 272 class on the Price family at the School of Industrial Art and reports that Will was listed as "architectural draftsman" in the 1898–99 "Partial List of Former Students with Their Present Occupations." University of the Arts Archives. Other family members who attended the school were brothers Frank (1888–90) and Walter (1890–93) as well as sisters Mary and Susanna who attended in the same years. Pennsylvania Museum

School of Industrial Art, *School Circular, 1878–1900*, University of the Arts Archives.
25. *First and Second Report of the Board of Trustees of the Pennsylvania Museum and School of Industrial Arts, 1876–77* (Philadelphia, 1878), 8.
26. Copies of the *Report of the Board of Trustees of the Pennsylvania Museum and School of Industrial Arts* are on file in the Greenberg Library of the University of the Arts, the descendent of the Museum School. The 1879 *Report* (Philadelphia, 1880) noted the move of the school to the Franklin Institute (13). The following year it moved to 1709 Chestnut Street (1880 *Report* [Philadelphia, 1881], 5).
27. *Gopsill's Philadelphia City Directory for 1879* (1879). The directory reported that James M. Price was in insurance at 409 Chestnut Street (the address of Furness' Provident Life and Trust Company), and

◆ First Steps: The Young Architect

Even though Massachusetts Institute of Technology established architectural courses in 1865 and the University of Pennsylvania followed a year later, Will took the more conventional route of the period by studying in an architect's office. On 15 November 1878 Addison Hutton noted in his daybook that "James Price arranges for his son William to come about New Year's on trial."[28] Will remained in Hutton's firm for most of the next year, receiving a salary of $10 a week, double the salary of a laborer (and the same rate that Sullivan had received from Furness in 1873). Hutton had designed the first purpose-built offices of the Provident Life and Trust Company and was one of the competitors for the company's second building on Chestnut Street.[29] His reputation as a careful builder brought numerous commissions for the repair of failing structures, including the tower of Lehigh College's Packer Hall and the towers of the University of Pennsylvania's College Hall. After the Civil War Hutton depended on a continuous stream of young Scottish-born architects to keep his firm up to date in contemporary British fashion, suggesting that his own design sensibilities, formed in the years before the Civil War in the office of Samuel Sloan, were not able to adapt to the quickly changing fashions of the day.

Simultaneous with Will's entrance into the Hutton office, Francis Lightfoot Price entered the office of Frank Furness who had won the competition for the Provident Company's new building on Chestnut Street. This was the moment when Furness was arriving at his mature approach representing function through form so there could have been no greater contrast between his office and that of Hutton. Will joined the Furness office shortly thereafter.[30] During 1878 and 1879, the initials "F. L. P." and later "F. L. Price" in a logbook of payouts by the Provident Company for its new building prove that Frank Price was supervising the construction for the Furness office. That Furness had been hired by the Provident tells much about the broader perspective of Samuel Shipley and his partners. Heretofore Quakers had tended to hire Quakers, so, for example, Addison Hutton was the preferred architect of the Quaker colleges of the region, later being supplanted by younger Quakers such as Walter Cope and John Stewardson at the

---

living at 3322 Spring Garden Street. Frank was working at 309 South 3rd Street, the address of the Furness office.

28. Addison Hutton, Daybook for 1878 (15 November 1878), Quakeriana Collection, Magill Library, Haverford College.

29. Addison Hutton is treated in Elizabeth Biddle Yarnall, *Addison Hutton: Quaker Architect, 1834–1916* (Philadelphia: Art Alliance Press, 1974). See also Sandra Tatman and Roger Moss, *Biographical*

Dictionary of Philadelphia Architects: 1700–1930 (Boston: G. K. Hall & Company, 1984), 401–407.

30. The evidence for Will's work in the Furness office is in his obituary which lists the Furness office for his training. "William L. Price, Architect, Dead: Picturesque Figure in Art Life and Designer of Wide Reputation," *Philadelphia Real Estate Record and Builder's Guide,* 31, no. 42 (18 October 1916), 686. Frank Price's alcoholism was blamed by his family on his training outside of the faith in the Furness office.

end of the century. The decision on the part of the Provident leadership to hire Frank Furness, the son of the city's leading Unitarian minister, would not have been easily made; but by the late 1870s his strongly dissonant crescendos had transformed the staid image of banking on Chestnut Street. If the Provident were to compete successfully with other institutions, it would be well to have an eye-catching building which was Furness' forte. As James Price moved in the larger world of the Provident Life and Trust Company, he must have felt that it would be similarly advantageous for his oldest sons to learn architecture in the office that his business had hired.

Although we have no direct account from Frank or Will Price about the training that they received in the Furness office, it can be gauged from the well-known description of Louis Sullivan and the less well-known but more contemporary account by Allen Evans, Furness' later partner, as well as another by Albert Kelsey.[31] Each emphasized Furness' original ideas about architectural practice, ideas that were strongly attractive to young men who for one reason or another had not taken the academic route to training. In the case of Furness' method, Sullivan tells us that Furness "made buildings out of his head"—instead of out of books, as his partner George Hewitt was said to do. This interested Sullivan and placed Furness in the forefront of the shift away from architecture based on history to one based on function. Furness wrote about his method to Allen Evans' aunt (a friend of Furness' wife), who had inquired into the advisability of her nephew leaving the office of Samuel Sloan and joining that of Furness. Furness wrote in reply that "Mr. Sloan's way of working is so different from the way that Mr. Hewitt and myself [work] that I fear Mr. Evans would have to unlearn all that he has been through with Mr. S."[32]

Based on searching for means grounded in the constituent issues of the problem rather than in historical precedent, the Furness method would have been particularly appropriate in Philadelphia where industrial designers such as William Sellers and William Henszey, both later Furness clients, were transforming machine design and had established strategies that related function to form. Albert Kelsey, who later developed a close relationship with former Furness pupil Louis Sullivan, recalled a list of Furness' most innovative designs, many of them from before his time in the office in the 1890s, suggesting that neophytes were taken to see earlier examples of the office work perhaps as a means of demonstrating the office method. Both Price brothers would have encountered the evolving Furness method at the moment when it was being sharpened into a design tool.

---

31. George E. Thomas and others, *Frank Furness: The Complete Works* (New York: Princeton Architectural Press, 1991), 40–41.

32. Thomas and others, 41.

❧ *Philadelphia Architects: Generational Boundaries*

In 1878, while Will was working for Hutton, that office was located at 215 South 5th Street only a few blocks from Furness' office at 209 South 3rd Street. Most of the city's architects were within a block or two of each other, typically on the upper floors of the commercial buildings that vied for elbow room in the dense downtown. In the Victorian city there was a clear pecking order that found the more established firms within a block or two of City Hall then located in Independence Hall, the sole exception being the firm of John McArthur whose offices were at the new City Hall at Broad and Market streets, the construction of which would occupy his firm for the remainder of his career. Willis Hale's office was at 518 Walnut Street; the Wilson Brothers were at 410 Walnut; the Hewitts were located at 410 Chestnut. Younger architects tended to be pushed toward the west in the direction that the city would later move. In the mid-1880s Robert G. Kennedy, who had been in Addison Hutton's office, opened his own office at 725 Walnut Street in the row of houses built at the end of the eighteenth century by Thomas Carstairs, while Wilson Eyre, Jr., and Frank Miles Day operated offices in buildings of their own design in the 900 block of Walnut Street.[33]

The split between the older and younger architects represented by location was also apparent in professional affiliation. Most of the older architects were members of the American Institute of Architects, joining when the Philadelphia chapter was formed in 1869. Preoccupied with differentiating themselves from builders and demonstrating the worth that their efforts brought to building, architects in the Institute spent much of their time on the legal issues of profession-building: ownership and control of drawings, fees, competition, and so forth. For the younger architects those battles had been resolved and in their place were substituted the camaraderie and goals of another organization, the T-Square Club which was established in 1883 with Frank Price as treasurer, and Will Price, Wilson Eyre, Jr., and Robert G. Kennedy as founding members. It soon found a home amid the artistic organizations centered in the bohemian district of modest workers' houses in the north–south alleys paralleling the new commercial district on Broad Street.

Unlike the narrow professional goals of the AIA, the T-Square Club's purpose was "to promote the study and practice of architecture and the kindred arts, to further the appreciation of architecture by the public, and to afford its members opportunities for friendly competition in design."[34] Ironically, even as its members were advancing the

---

33. A contract between financier Edward Stotesbury and architect Robert G. Kennedy for the construction of a summer house in the suburb of Abington, dated 8 June 1881, suggests that after working in the Furness office, Will and his cousin Edward Paxon worked briefly for Kennedy. The contract was signed by

Stotesbury and Samuel W. Moore, presumably the Bouvier Street carpenter listed in *Gopsill's Philadelphia City Directory for 1880* (1880), and was witnessed by two men, Price and Paxon.

34. The divide in Philadelphia is described in "The Directory of the Architectural Annual" which summa-

cause of collegiality and design which could be appreciated in New York and Boston, its secondary goal of preserving "the historic and artistic monuments of Philadelphia" would shortly place it at odds with the emphasis on the present that had guided the leaders of previous generation. Led by Eyre, Day, and Cope and Stewardson, Philadelphia's future would be in the past, with the notable exceptions of the architects who passed through the Furness office—Will Price, Albert Kelsey, and George Howe. That change lay in the future, however, and in its first decade the focus of the club was on the issues that preoccupied the architects of the industrial city—construction, representation of function, and the role of new materials in design.

In 1900 the gulf between the two organizations seemed almost insurmountable with the T-Square Club on the rise and the AIA in decline. As the new century began the AIA had held but one meeting in the previous year and its membership had fallen to 30 while the T-Square Club's membership rolls had expanded to 156, with "eight regular monthly meetings being held, the annual meeting falling on the first Wednesday in May." The split told another story about the nature of architectural practice in Philadelphia as well. Most of the important commercial commissions of the city continued to go to the members of the Institute. In the 1890s the Wilson Brothers were the architects of the Philadelphia and Reading Railroad's new downtown terminal; Frank Furness won the commission for the vast enlargement of the Broad Street Station of the Pennsylvania Railroad; his former partner, George Hewitt, won the competition for the new stock exchange and in the early twentieth century his firm designed the downtown's chief hotel, the Bellevue-Stratford. The older architects designed most of the significant churches and public buildings of the region while the younger architects were limited to domestic commissions in the rapidly growing suburbs. This generational distinction between the masculine zone of business and the feminine zone of the suburb anticipated a similar pattern that arose in Philadelphia in the late twentieth century when another generation of older architectural firms, which had risen to prominence after World War II, received the principal urban commissions, while the younger firms, draping themselves in the trappings of the artist again found themselves limited to the smaller, more personal commissions and projects.

This generational split was acceptable to Barr Ferree who viewed it as a logical outcome of the scope of modern practice, where "the master of the country house is supposed to be likewise the master of the high commercial building." In Ferree's view there were good reasons for this split.

———

rizes the condition of the leading architectural societies and schools across the nation. *The Architectural Annual, 1900* (Philadelphia: The Architectural Annual, 1900), 262–285. For the Philadelphia chapter of the American Institute of Architects, see p. 274; for the T-Square Club, see p. 283.

> Modern American architecture is more complicated and diffuse than the architecture of any contemporary nation or of any past epoch. Our buildings are more varied, our conditions more complex, our needs more numerous, our materials more diverse, and our artistic qualities less acutely developed than any other people or in any other time. With all these complexities we have the additional disadvantage of having no style of our own, but of being free to choose where we will or where temporary fashion may dictate.[35]

In an age of specialization, as in other forms of work, architecture split along the cultural divide of contemporary life.

❧ F. L. and W. L. Price 1882–1893

Frank and Will Price formed their architectural practice in 1881 when the economy of Philadelphia was rapidly expanding, as the panic of 1873, which had caused Furness to lay off Louis Sullivan, finally ended. Locally productivity was rising as a consequence of William Sellers' efforts at industrial standardization and Frederick Winslow Taylor's experiments in scientific management. Over the next generation Philadelphia would lead the nation in units of new housing in vast row blocks near factory districts and in rapidly expanding railroad suburbs which housed the rising managerial and professional classes. In 1880 Francis L. Price was listed as an architect at 731 Walnut Street; the following year Will had joined the firm of F. L. and W. L. Price, Architects. The new office was in the midst of the bohemian zone of the city, sprinkled with art studios including those of Cecilia Beaux and later John Sloan, and small architectural offices including those of their T-Square Club compatriots. It remained there until the formation of Price and McLanahan in 1903.

Although no projects by the new firm were listed in the professional press until 1886, family letters describe the typical pattern of a young firm working for family and acquaintances.[36] No connection was more important than Frank's link to carpenter and builder Herman Wendell. In his late teens Frank had worked as a carpenter in Wendell's shop, continuing there for several years until he joined the Furness office as an architectural trainee. In 1883 James Price's letter to his son Walter, then studying classics at Harvard University, reported on the progress of the architectural business.

> The Boys' business has taken a forward move. Through Herman W[endell], they have secured & are drawing plans for 10 houses—moderate size pairs to be at once erected for *Drexel and Childs* on their 700 acre tract near Wayne sta. Penna RR. And this has been

---

35. Ferree, 452–453.

36. A letter from Walter F. Price, then studying at Haverford College, to Frank, 20 June 1880 ends, "I am very anxious about that court house plan and sincerely hope that thy 'Political' friends will be of service to thee. I hope I may be of assistance to thee when I come home in making drawing tables and helping fix things up in thy new quarters." Walter F. Price Papers.

followed after submission of their final plans, by the direction to prepare plans for 10 larger houses to be erected in spring. Moreover, South, Disston's bro.-in-law tells Frank that they are going ahead with Court House at Tacony, expect to build in spring. Did I tell thee that Will took 2 (excellent) 8x10 photographs of Herman's own house as a lever toward their first job at Drexel and Childs?[37]

Apparently the courthouse project that interested Walter three years before was still being considered, and the brothers had designed Wendell's house. Two years later Frank wrote to Walter, on the letterhead of "Frank L. Price, Architect, 731 Walnut Street": "We have quite a large job at Wayne for Drexel and Childs—twelve houses cost $50,000.00. Of course we don't get a commission on the lot, but still it is a very good thing."[38] (*fig. 5*) With the backing of Drexel and Company, the nation's most powerful bank, and the encouragement of the Pennsylvania Railroad, which offered low-priced commuter fares to the city as an inducement to purchase suburban houses along the railroad, Wendell and Smith constructed several hundred houses in Wayne, most of which were from designs by the Price brothers. As could be expected of young architects who had worked with an acknowledged master, the early houses could easily be taken as the work of a draftsman from the Furness firm. A wealth of inherited details characterize the houses: the deeply undercut brackets that carry overhanging upper stories; broad, oversized windows; and the clear description of interior function through fenestration shapes and sizes which Furness transmitted to his most apt pupils. Rather than becoming caricatures of the master, many of these early designs show an exuberance and force of massing that would anticipate the brothers' future work.

The decade during which the brothers worked for Wendell and Smith was an important one in the creation of the new market for middle-class housing. As evidenced by the popularity of upper middle-class houses based on Andrew Jackson Downing's pre-Civil War publication *The Architecture of Country Houses*, suburban houses had been the exclusive realm of the upper classes who could afford the twin costs of time and transit. Although Downing also included designs for small workers' cottages, the reality of the economics of the day meant that most workers remained in the cities near their work so that there was little call for modest suburban housing. Had workers been able to afford the costs of travel, they would still have been unable to afford their own houses because of the near impossibility of raising the money to purchase a house. In the post-Civil War years

37. James M. Price to Walter F. Price, 11 November 1883. "South" is either Thomas South, inspector of the Disston Saw Works, or Anna B. South, who is listed as a superintendent at the saw works (*Gopsill's Philadelphia City Directory for 1880* [1587]). Wendell continued his office at 14 South 32nd Street but was living at Powdermill Lane in Frankford (*Gopsill's Philadelphia City Directory for 1880* [1763]).

38. Francis L. Price to Walter F. Price, 28 November 1885. Walter F. Price Papers.

above 5. F. L. and W. L. Price, Tower House, Wayne, Pennsylvania, from Wendell and Smith, *Overbrook, Pelham, Wayne and St. Davids: Suburban Houses Built by Messr's Wendell and Smith* (Philadelphia, 1896)

left 6. William L. Price, armor hanging, third-floor great hall of Kelty, c. 1903 (Price and McLanahan Archives, George E. Thomas Collection)

across the nation, houses were typically purchased entirely for cash or with a mortgage that was paid off in a year or two. After the Civil War Philadelphia pioneered new types of financial institutions: the building society and the cooperative savings fund and loan association. They made it possible for the middle classes and soon even the working classes to purchase houses. By 1890 it was commonly understood that "Any industrious and frugal workingman living in Philadelphia may become a home owner if he desires, although to an outsider, who understands few, if any, of our many advantages, this statement will seem far fetched."[39] Five years later it was proudly reported that there were in Philadelphia alone 200,000 homes "occupied by single families...against a total of 130,000 in New York where the number of resident owners is estimated at only 13,000."[40] As the century ended the majority of new houses in Philadelphia were owner occupied, anticipating by half a century the home ownership rates of the nation following World War II and giving Philadelphia its proud name of the City of Homes.

Drexel and Company transformed the market for suburban home ownership by acquiring developable land and providing capital at moderate prices to builders to construct suburban houses for the rapidly growing industrial and managerial workforce. Middle-class suburbanization in turn transformed the shape and form of the city. Until the 1880s the location of housing had largely been determined by proximity to work, creating a dense urban center served by horsecar lines around which were industrial clusters of mills and housing. Increasing salaries, declining transit costs, rail and trolley lines that reached out to cheaper land, and the new financial institutions together initiated the great wave of suburbanization which continues to the present. By the 1890s, for better or for worse, the outlines of the modern city could be seen stretching north, west, and south fifteen to twenty miles from the center along the high-speed rail commuter lines.

Because of their pioneering role in creating the new middle-class railroad suburb, the Drexel firm developed many of the tools of modern real estate retailing. Competition with other developers for market share led to the widespread use of advertising as an important sales tool. In the case of the Wayne Tract, brochures and flyers were published and sales agents worked in a handsome real estate office, also designed by the Price brothers, whose half-timber detail and stone base quickly announced the design mode of the houses to those arriving by train at Wayne Station. At the outset the house designs were

---

39. John N. Gallagher, "Real Estate Holdings and Valuations," in Frank H. Taylor, ed., *The City of Philadelphia as it Appears in 1893* (Philadelphia: George S. Harris & Sons, 1893), 82.

40. The comparison with other cities appears in Franklin M. Harris, "Building Interests," in Frank H. Taylor, ed., *Souvenir of 12th Annual Convention of the*

Association of Master Plumbers, 1895 (Philadelphia: George S. Harris & Sons, 1895), 64. This is a later edition of Taylor's *The City of Philadelphia as it Appears in 1893*. For a summary of the building societies and their activities see Addison B. Burk, "Building Societies," in Taylor (1893), 85–87.

merely designated "A" through "F" but they were soon given names that reflected salient features. The house with a conical roof became the "Tower House"; the house with a strongly massed end carried on carved beams became the "Bruin Lodge"; and a cottage with crisp vertical wall gables was the "Flemish House." "Spacious secluded porch," "massive stone-work," "handsome effects in colored glass," "unique mantel," "stairway of oak, furniture finish," and "the very best of everything in this house" were promotional phrases in advertisements for these compactly planned houses. Equally purposeful were the perspective sketches of the interiors provided by the architects. These emphasized the flowing contemporary spaces, the fireplaces, and the stair landings, all picturesque features that would appeal to prospective owners. In one tiny sketch a wall hanging of shields and pikes suggests that Will was already collecting the un-Quakerly array of weapons that were the focus of his particular mania. (*fig. 6*) The Price office records that survive from 1893 through 1902 continue to mention individual Wayne commissions well into the 1890s.

It becomes easier to track the young firm in 1886 when the city began requiring building permits which were soon published in a building-trades weekly, the *Philadelphia Real Estate Record and Builders' Guide.* Its reporters gleaned information from architectural offices on new building projects that would be of interest to contractors and suppliers. In this publication most of the new firm's individual works can be identified. Its pages regularly mentioned the activities of Wendell and Smith who continued to hire the brothers as the principal architects for two huge Drexel development projects, Overbrook on the western edge of Philadelphia beginning in 1893, and the following year at Pelham, a suburb in Philadelphia's Mount Airy section. Both Drexel and Company and Wendell and Smith also retained the brothers for houses in Baltimore's Roland Park as well as in Essex Fells in the northern New Jersey suburbs of New York City, giving the brothers' practice an unusual level of economic stability but with the downside that much of the work may have been repetitive and perhaps less interesting.

While the brothers' business was getting established, the first published notice of Will Price as an artist occurred in the 1883 Annual Exhibition of the Pennsylvania Academy of the Fine Arts when a "Sketch for a Porte Cochere" was exhibited. From then on Will regularly submitted watercolors to the Academy's juried exhibits until 1894 when the T-Square Club began holding its own exhibitions at the Academy, thus providing a setting for the display of professional projects. These paintings ranged from perspectives of commissions (including the Kenilworth Inn in 1890) to local landscapes with titles such as "Afternoon Paradise" and "Summer Sketch." A number of Price's watercolors have survived including a view of the interior of a barn, dated "6-12-94," which may be the above-mentioned "Summer Sketch." Most of Will's other surviving watercolors date from his trip to England and the continent which occurred in July and August 1896. By that date brother Walter had already made four trips across the Atlantic (1889, 1890,

1892, and 1894), bringing back a treasure trove of sketches, watercolors, and photographs. Such trips were customary among architects of the period who used them to learn the forms and details of picturesque Europe that could be utilized in their practices.[41] The timing of the trips offer an insight into the seasons of the architectural year. With most construction beginning in early spring, architects were busiest from late fall, when financial planning was completed and projects were commissioned, to early summer, when projects were well under way and the important issues had been determined. Late summer was the time when architects could travel, enabling Will and Walter to continue the patterns established by the S. A. K. in the previous decade.

Will's and Walter's sketches were derived from the topographic watercolor tradition of Thomas Girtin and J. M. W. Turner of the previous century, but with an eye sharply focussed on architectural detail. Typically the views were skillfully composed, often juxtaposing a homely domestic structure with a famous landmark in the distance. Washes were handled with economy and skill, capturing the evanescent hues of place and time. By his early thirties Will was an accomplished artist, able to represent three-dimensional form, color, and texture on the two dimensions of paper. Whatever he could imagine he would be able to depict convincingly for his clients. This was the foundation skill of master architects of the end of the nineteenth century, and Will Price was a virtuoso. Throughout his career the presentation drawings that sold clients on projects were the works of his pencil and his brush.

❧ Personal Life

As was the custom of the day Will and Frank lived at home while they were setting up their business, and continued to reside there until their marriages.[42] In 1888 Will became the first of James' children to marry; Frank followed two years later. Rather than marrying within the Orthodox Quaker community, Will fell in love with bespectacled and lively Emma Webb, a graduate of Swarthmore College and the daughter of a pharmacist, William Webb, whose business was around the corner from the Price and Lightfoot homes in the Spring Garden neighborhood. The Webbs were also Quakers, but, as evidenced by Emma's attendance at Swarthmore College, were members of the Hicksite branch that had split from the Orthodox group in 1827 with so much animosity that the

---

41. Records of the trip and the itinerary are in the Walter F. Price Papers. Another trip that included many young architects, among them Elmer Grey, is the topic of "Letters and Notes Made During the Summer of 1892 in England, Italy and France, 56 Day Bicycle Trip with Joseph Pennell."

42. This custom was not confined to the middle classes.

Peter A. B. Widener recounts that his father and mother lived in the North Broad Street mansion of his grandfather for some time after their marriages and it was expected that children would live on the parental estate afterwards. *Without Drums* (New York: G. P. Putnam, 1940), 13–16.

7. Seekers After Knowledge at Scalp Level, 1886. Will is third from right, bottom row (Photograph attributed to Henry Troth; Architectural Archives, Philip N. Price Collection, University of Pennsylvania)

8. Wedding party of Will and Emma Price, 1888
(Architectural Archives, Philip N. Price Collection, University of Pennsylvania)

split remained active and hostile three generations later. The courtship of Will and Emma was conducted over several years, usually among the extended group of friends who banded together as the previously mentioned the Seekers After Knowledge. In the fall, winter, and spring the members met at each other's homes, presenting researched reports for group discussion, an idea that continues in Philadelphia in such arcane groups as The Informal Club. A record survives of the spring meetings of 1885 or 1886 indicating that discussion centered around the presidential administrations of Grant, Hayes, Garfield, and Arthur.[43] During the summer, picnics and hikes were popular activities, including extensive trips to faraway places such as Kezar Falls, Maine, and Scalp Level near Johnstown, Pennsylvania. Photographs, perhaps the earliest known by the later well-known photographer and Price cousin, Henry Troth, document the Maine and Pennsylvania trips, providing images of Will Price and Emma Webb as well as Emma's father William and his wife who accompanied the young people as chaperones and participated in the skits, costume dramas, and other activities. (*fig. 7*)

A letter from Will, written from Lansdowne, 5 May 1886, at the end of a period of extended illness, affords a peek into Victorian courtship, but also raises the first concerns about Will's health.

My dear Emma,

I have to go back to the large paper thee sees, it is about half past six & I am still in bed so I cant go & get any other.

Well dearest I am getting stronger quite rapidly now, yesterday I went down stairs three or four times to dinner & supped & in the evening walked around on the board-walk for quite a while. In the evening I read to the family for quite a long time & it did not hurt my eyes either. Little one, will thee marry me if I get bald? I find that my hair is coming out somewhat, but Aunt Sallie says it will come in at the same time so don't be scared.

* * *

These stars indicate that I have just had breakfast, they also indicate that I had too much & feel rather stuffy. When is thee coming out again dearest? and what train will thee come in?

Does thee know darling that by the time I get about for good, it will be only about six weeks untill you go away? It doesn't seem very long does it? & then thee will be away for two months. I suppose you will decide where the S. A. K. will go this week, and then thee will know whether you will be home for a few days before going to Easthampton, or

---

43. April 24th meeting on "Hayes 1876–80" included: "Foreign and Domestic Affairs"—Lizzie Webb; "Financial and Political Affairs"—W. L. Price; "The Temperance Movement"—Cassie Carr; "Leading Men and Issues of Our Time"—F. Saunders. In the previous week Emma Webb had researched "The Fifteenth Amendment" as part of the "Grant Administration." Other members included Walter F. Price, Henry Troth, Louella Troth, James Verree, Lilla Hollowell, Mary Willets, and Jesse Hoopes.

not. I do hope you will! It would break the time up somewhat & then if [I] could manage to go there for a few days it would break the time of separation considerably. I don't take any stock in being away from thee, it isn't soothing in any sense of the word, but as thee said, there won't be many more times; only I shall want thee to have just as good times as thee can in the summers after we are married, & I hope I can get off to go with thee a good deal, otherwise I don't know how I could stand it. Well dearest, I hope thee can get out again this week. I am afraid I will not be as patient as I have been now that I am much stronger. Thee knows how it is when you are getting well from a long sickness, so thee better come as often as thee can & prevent me from doing anything desperate.

Lovingly, Will

The S. A. K. trip for that summer was the excursion to Scalp Level, and a thin but animated Will can be seen with his circle in photographs.

Two years later, on 18 October 1888, Will and Emma were married and set up their home near Will's parents' home on North 18th Street in the streetcar neighborhood of North Philadelphia. The wedding party was largely made up of members of the S. A. K.: Will's brother Walter and sister Anna, Emma's sister Rebecca, wife of Jesse Holmes, future brother-in-law Nathan Kite, and Edward Paxon who, like Will, had continued from building into architecture and would remain a fixture in Price's firms for thirty years. (*fig. 8*) A year and a half after the wedding, presumably having given Will enough time to repent or perhaps to lead his new wife toward the Orthodox Quaker faith, Will was "read out of meeting" with the following proclamation:

> At a monthly meeting of Friends of Philadelphia held 2 mo 27th 1890, William L. Price, who had by birth a right of membership in the Religious Society of Friends, having accomplished his marriage contrary to the rules of our discipline, with a woman not in membership with Friends, and in a meeting appointed by and under the care of those who separated from Friends in 1827, and having also attended the meetings of that body, we have been concerned to treat with him on these accounts. But as he has not appeared to condemn these violations of our order to the satisfaction of this meeting, it has become our duty to testify that he has thus separated himself from us, and is no longer a member of the Religious Society of Friends.
>
> It is nonetheless our sincere desire that by obedience to the manifestations of the light of Christ in his heart he may see the importance of our testimonies in these respects and become prepared to be restored to membership among us.

Will and Emma remained devout members of the Hicksite branch of the Quakers for the remainder of their lives, and turned their family allegiance from Haverford College, where his older brother Walter had attended and later taught, to Swarthmore College, from which Emma had graduated in 1883 and where their son William Webb Price and daughter Margaret Lightfoot Price, and grandson Philip Nevin Price would later study.

Success: The Kenilworth Inn

In the summer of 1890 the Price brothers reached a new professional plateau when they won a commission for an immense resort hotel at Asheville in the mountains of western North Carolina. Less than a generation after the Civil War, northeastern railroads provided access North Carolina's Great Smoky Mountains which then became a center of tourism especially in the fall, winter, and spring. A cluster of fashionable hotels were built, several by Philadelphia architects, that made the sleepy town of Asheville a national resort renowned for its health-giving air among the pines.[44] A publicist for the Pennsylvania Railroad recounted the joys of "the bright valley of the French Broad."

> It is a land of bright skies, incomparable climate, and picturesque scenery whose praises have been sung by poets, and whose beauties of stream, valley, and mountain have furnished subject and inspiration to the sketcher's hand. The centre of this region, poetically called the "Land of the Sky," is Asheville.

With only the merest touch of hyperbole, the publicist concluded, "There is, perhaps, no more beautiful valley on the continent than this, and certainly none that would attract health-seeker, lounger, invalid, or dreamer."[45] At the end of the nineteenth century health was a major concern in American cities and Asheville was believed to offer a congenial climate of dry air with the smallest range between maximum and minimum temperatures in the United States.

Health considerations aside, the real catalyst for Asheville's growth was the construction a few miles out of town of Biltmore, the baronial mansion of George Vanderbilt being built by Richard Morris Hunt, with the landscape designed by Frederick Law Olmsted. Though Vanderbilt had done his best to conceal the vast extent of his operations, hoping to present a fait accompli to the nation, by 1890 the word had gotten out that a remarkable house was rising in the mountains near Asheville. To capitalize on the notoriety that such a vast project would bring to the area, Vanderbilt assembled a group of investors to build a great hotel on a nearby property.

---

44. In 1854 Asheville was described as "a flourishing post-village, capital of Buncombe county, North Carolina, is situated on the Buncombe turnpike, 1½ miles E. from the French Broad river, and 255 miles W. from Raleigh. It is on the route of the Western turnpike which is now in process of construction. It contains a bank, an academy, 2 newspaper offices and several churches. Population about 1000. The site of Asheville is ascertained to be 2200 feet above the level of the sea." Thomas Baldwin and J. Thomas, *New and Complete Gazetteer of the United States* (Philadelphia: Lippincott, Grambo & Company), 55. A contemporary description of the resort by W. C. Browning, an owner of the Kenilworth Inn, was published in *The Lyceum*, 2 (June 1892), 18–22.

45. Pennsylvania Railroad, *Summer Excursion Routes, 1887* (Philadelphia: Pennsylvania Railroad, Passenger Department, 1887), 18. Eight hotels with a total capacity of 1500 were already open, the largest of which was the Battery Park Hotel by Philadelphia architects Hazelhurst and Huckel.

For generations American urban hotels reflected the influence of Boston's Tremont House built by Isaiah Rogers in the 1820s.[46] Public rooms on the first floor made the hotel the parlor for a city; guest rooms above provided a basic level of comfort. What stylistic grace notes appeared on these urban hotels were masculine and crisp. In the case of the Tremont House, pilasters across the facade, a small Doric front portico, and a choragic monument on the roof as a belvedere linked the hotel to contemporary architectural fashion. Over the next half century resort hotels adapted the conventions of urban hotels to leisure settings along the Atlantic seaboard in Cape May, Atlantic City, and Newport, and at inland resorts where horse racing, gambling, and other recreations drew glittering crowds of monied people which in turn became part of the attraction.

Young architects are rarely totally prepared for their first major commissions. Lacking the documents that are available for the later years of the practice, we can only imagine the impact on what was probably at most a three- or four-man office whose two principals were 34 and 29 years of age respectively. Coming from Philadelphia where there were few examples of large nonindustrial buildings and where size was usually resolved by cobbling together many small elements, the scale of modern building was a problem that had not been effectively answered by the Furness practice and was thus unfamiliar to the Price brothers.[47] Heretofore they had designed nothing that was larger than suburban middle-class houses or perhaps a local courthouse, if the Tacony project was ever realized. With a budget of $150,000 the cost of the hotel was approximately thirty times greater than the individual Wayne tract houses, but like them it required a level of detail that conveyed domesticity and pleasures shared by vacationers. The published account in the *American Architect and Building News* was complimentary, describing a building of considerable size that dominated its setting by the theatrical device of a towering roof which was the focus of the main facade. The central block alone was some 200 feet wide to which were to be attached splayed lower wings of similar size but fewer stories, only one of which was built in the original phase. This composition placed all of the public and guest rooms facing the lawns and the views of "beautiful and rugged scenery." Rough stone walls at the base linked the building to the rock of the hillside, while the textures of shingled wall surfaces and the high roofs alluded to the mountainous landscape

---

46. Its influence was spread by William H. Eliot, *A Description of the Tremont House with Architectural Illustrations* (Boston: Gray and Bowen, 1830).

47. A letter in the Biltmore files from manager William J. Wallace to Charles McNamee, 19 April 1892, recounts difficulties with financing and conflicts over fees. The architects, following the conventions of the day, claimed a total commission of $5000 including the various fixtures, the furniture, the heating system and the elevator as well as for the unbuilt but designed wing. This was apparently not the custom in North Carolina, resulting in a threat of a lawsuit from the owners and architects. Biltmore Company Archives, Transfer Box 12. I am indebted to Harry Keiner, Archivist of the Biltmore Estate, for much new information on the project.

that formed the setting. Perhaps the high roof emulated Hunt's Biltmore then being constructed only a few miles away. (*fig. 9*)

The Kenilworth Inn was the first commission to indicate the future directions of the Price office, both in its function as a large resort hotel and in the effort to create a trademark image conveying the pleasures of a modern resort. Its name was a harbinger of the future as well. Previously Philadelphia hotels had taken their names from national institutions and icons—the Congress, the White House, the George Washington, the Mount Vernon. As the national culture was reoriented across the Atlantic by speedy and safe steamships and the transatlantic cable, European names conveyed sophistication and elegance. In increasingly Anglophile Philadelphia most hotels would take English names as in the case of the Kenilworth, and the later masterpieces of Price's career, the Marlborough, the Blenheim, and finally the Traymore. The Kenilworth shared one other feature with Price's later hotels and large-scale buildings. It no longer exists. In 1909 it was destroyed by fire.[48]

⚓ *The Operations of a Small Architectural Practice*

From surviving contracts, partnership agreements, and fee schedules it is possible to piece together a fair amount about the operations of larger architectural practices in post-Civil War America, but little has surfaced on how small offices survived. In the case of the Price office, a ledger offers a remarkable window into the operation of the firm. The ledger begins on "1 month" [January], 1893, with its columns labeled "Dr." [Draw] and "Cr." [Credit], and states the cash on hand from the previous year as $28.40. Weekly payments to the principals are recorded with Frank and Will typically drawing similar amounts that ranged, depending on fees received, from $5 per week to $15 per week toward an anticipated yearly salary of $2000 apiece. Draftsmen included brother Walter who had stopped teaching and now received the same $5 minimum, but without the irregular higher payments of $15 to $20 per week. Other draftsmen listed included Oscar Wenderoth, John J. Bissegger, Frank Martin, Carl DeMoll, and Edward S. Paxon. Most were hired as work required, but a few including Martin, Paxon, and Bissegger were fixtures in the office until its breakup in 1902, and then left for the new office of Price and McLanahan.

---

48. *The Philadelphia Inquirer* (15 April 1909), 1. The front-page article reported the probable death of the owner who had jumped from a window. The present hotel of the same name is the work of a midwestern architect, D. J. Dreher. See *Chicago Architectural Exhibition, 35th Annual Exhibition* (Chicago, 1922), 225. The Kenilworth was not a financial success, apparently because there was no summer market and "The Southerners are all poor and will pay very little for board. The money comes in when the wealthy northern people come here in the winter. It would, therefore, seem to be for the Kenilworth Inn but one short season each year." Memorandum of Charles McNamee to George Vanderbilt (3 November 1899), Letter Book, p. 60. Biltmore Company Archives, Transfer Box 45.

9. Richard Morris Hunt, Biltmore (1888–95), Asheville, North Carolina, from north terrace, 1902 (Library of Congress Prints and Photographs Division, Detroit Publishing Company Photograph Collection, LC-D4-14327)

10. Frank Furness, Clement A. Griscom residence (c. 1881), Ardmore, Pennsylvania, from Wells and Hope, *Philadelphia Suburban Houses* (Philadelphia, c. 1886)

Young draftsmen of the city circulated between practices of like interests and the young men of the Price brothers' office were no exception. In 1896, for example, Oscar Wenderoth and Carl DeMoll (Will's future brother-in-law) were in Frank Miles Day's office at 925 Chestnut Street, while John Bissegger was temporarily working in Edgar Seeler's office at 328 Chestnut Street. There was an entrepreneurial component to the office as well. Some payments were designated as commissions, suggesting that when draftsmen brought work into the office they received a portion of the fees. Thus, in January 1893 one line for Edward S. Paxon reported $15 commission while the next line was for his regular pay. At the bottom of each page were totals for draws and credits reflecting the far greater value of the dollar then and the lower expectations of a workforce which was only beginning to realize the higher wages of Taylor's management revolution. The first month in 1893 reported draws of $366 and a balance of $377—which less the balance brought forward at the end of 1892 shows that income was slightly less than outgo. The second page of the ledger is more alarming for outgo exceeded income by nearly $100, caused by payment of six months' rent with the only fees those for the Chestnut Street mansion of Monroe Smith (Herman Wendell's partner) and a small fee for a house for the Roland Park Company in Baltimore. This carried the office forward through February and March.

A quick perusal of the ledger illustrates the costs of doing business as the century ended. Rent to James Dingee (perhaps a father of the draftsman of the same name in the Furness office) amounted to $27.50 a month. As blueprints became the normal means of communicating architectural information, regular payments began to appear for Williams, Brown and Earle and for the Philadelphia Heliograph Company ranging from $10 to $12 a month. In 1895 a new engraving-like hand script replaced the handwriting of Walter Price, indicating that he had moved from office manager to a member of the architectural staff, and that a secretary had been hired in his stead at a lower salary. Here and there are occasional expenses for "Type-Writing" marking the shift to the new technology. In 1899 the office was wired for a telephone with payments of $15 per month, or nearly the salary of a draftsman.

In this era before the income tax, office accounts and personal accounts were regularly mixed. For example, on 25 February 1893, a payment of $25 was reported to a bookseller, R. M. Lindsey, with the side note "on act. of Violet-le-Duc [sic]." This represented part of the price of the illustrated multivolume set of Eugène Viollet-le-Duc's *Dictionnaire Raisonné du Mobilier Française de l'Époque Carlovingienne à la Rénaissance.*[49] In May another $47 went toward payment for the set. When weekly salaries for a draftsman were $5, the purchase of a set of books at several months' salary might have seemed extravagant, but

---

49. Paris: Librairie Centrale d'Architecture, 1858–75.

in the 1890s the Price brothers, like most of their contemporaries, depended on historical models for details, making books such as the *Dictionnaire* as important as drafting tables and pencils in the capital costs of a practice.

For the rest of the decade of the ledger, Will's book purchases included a wide array of publications that indicated the broadening perspective of the young architect. The *Boston Sketch Club* was acquired in the summer of 1893 and Ticknor and Company's *American Architecture* a few months later. This was followed by books of photogravure plates including Smith and Packard's multivolume *European Architecture*, whose acquisition just before Will's trip to Europe in June 1896 may have been intended to guide his travels. Periodical subscriptions also provide an overview of contemporary practice and included at various times *The Architectural Record*, *Architectural Review*, and *Brickbuilder*, particularly when they included projects by the firm. In 1893 the office paid for two years of *Arte Italiano*. The shelves of the small office would have groaned under the weight of those tomes but each was crucial in providing sources for designs that would have given customers comfort knowing that they were getting architects in touch with the larger artistic world and not the personal idiosyncrasies of the outmoded Victorians such as Frank Furness and Willis Hale. Whenever a major commission was received, back bills would be paid and a few new treasures would join the library. In 1894, with the Alan Wood fees providing a sense of well-being, Will spent the extraordinary sum of $1000—two years' salary for a senior draftsman—for a collection of "foreign photos" taken by fellow architect Frank E. Mead. The initial payment alone was $100.

The pattern of fees for architectural commissions is also revealing. The credit side of the ledger quickly draws attention to the income which was typically received in amounts of one or two hundred dollars. A new client usually would pay up to half of the estimated commission on account with additional payments reflecting the completion of the drawings and, where contracted, supervision of work. Interspersed with the minor fees, however, were great chunks of cash that represented the enlarging scale of the brothers' practice as the boom of the 1880s continued into the next decade. With their victory in the competition for Alan Wood's palatial dwelling in West Conshohocken first came $1000 and then another $3500, a portion of which represented the subcontracting of interior decoration. A final payment of $2497.69 attests to the palatial cost of the mansion. Monroe Smith hired the brothers to do an immense house on Chestnut Street in West Philadelphia and sent a first payment of $500 followed by additional payments. These payments encouraged the brothers to take on staff, purchase books, and expand the capital of the office. Each of these large projects carried the office for a considerable period of time, but the hiring of additional staff as well as the payment of larger salaries representing overtime quickly ate into these sums. The regular payments from Wendell and Smith for their development houses evened out the boom-and-bust cycle, but still there were dry spells, especially during the downturn in the mid-1890s when the principals were not paid at all for periods of time.

In August 1893 an entry in Walter's hand reports "W. L. Price successor to F. L. and W. L. Price" and, at the end of the ledger, there is an accounting of the regular payments that were made to Frank to buy out his share of the business. Henceforth, when Frank found a project, he would receive a commission like the draftsmen. Frank remained on the payroll until the dissolution of the firm in 1902 and then was listed on and off in city directories as working for Walter. At the time of the sale, there was increased evidence of Frank's illness that probably forced him to sell his portion of the practice to Will. Immense payments to doctors scattered through the accounts may represent the cost of caring for Frank—and the resulting stresses may have resulted in additional medical expenses that are listed for Will.

The following spring after Frank was bought out, an entry listed new capital of $2000 representing Walter F. Price's purchase of an interest in the business. That purchase was made possible by a loan to Walter from Mrs. Webb, Will's mother-in-law. The loan from Mrs. Webb is evidence of another aspect of small business in the late nineteenth century. Today's easy credit was not available to most individuals and businesses, forcing small practices to depend on family and friends for the short-term bridge loans that made it possible to survive the slow periods. The Price ledger is dotted with such loans. Price's boyhood friends in the S. A. K. such as James Verree and Edwin Forsyth provided small loans as did Will's father, his mother-in-law, and later aunts and uncles on the Lightfoot side of the family. In the parochial world of Quaker society families and friends lent to each other and supported the businesses that in turn were largely composed of cousins and nephews.

The ledger offers one final insight into the architectural practice. When the total fees of each year were measured against the expenses of staff, book purchases, office costs, and so on, the principals of the firm were always a little behind their estimated salaries, carrying a debt forward to the next year. In years of economic depression, such as characterized 1896 and 1909, staff members were laid off, the principals went without salaries, and loans were taken from family and friends to carry on. Even for a relatively successful practice as that of Will Price, architecture remained a marginal business, capable of carrying firms when times were good but draining the spirit when times were bad. Little has changed in the succeeding century for too many beleaguered architects.

Prodigy Houses

The immense fees received from Alan Wood mark another aspect of the changing architectural profession and its role as an indicator of the regional economy. In *The Architecture of Country Houses* (1850), Andrew Jackson Downing had asserted that the republican villa rather than the palace or the castle epitomized American democracy. During the decade after the Civil War, the national cultural bias against vast expenditure on personal luxury faded, and conspicuous expenditure became the rule—as evidenced by Richard Morris

Hunt's huge Vanderbilt mansions in Manhattan, Newport, and North Carolina, and by the turn of direction toward palatial houses designed by elite firms such as McKim, Mead & White and Peabody and Stearns. Representing the new money generated by finance and even wartime profiteering, these great mansions became the prime subjects of the architectural journals of the day.

In Philadelphia in the 1870s and 1880s, where industrialists continued to invest more in their plants than in their homes, even fabulously wealthy entrepreneurs such as Clement Griscom, head of the Red Star Steamship Lines, and Alexander J. Cassatt, president of the Pennsylvania Railroad, commissioned Frank Furness to design relatively modest dwellings. (*fig. 10*) Another of the differences that distinguished the industrial culture from the new trans-Atlantic culture centered to the north, was that this plainness resulted in few Philadelphia-area houses being published in the national press until Philadelphians joined the national course toward conspicuous consumption in the 1890s. Unlike finance, industry required continuous re-investment and thus did not generate the kind of surplus cash that permitted conspicuous consumption as it had in New York City. It would take first the economic expansion that arose out of William Sellers' development of industrial standardization and then the vast increase in profit that resulted from the scientific management practices of Frederick Winslow Taylor to produce a sense of well-being that enabled the children of the old industrialists to change from building the modest homes of the past to the mansions of the Gilded Age. Because these clients came from a different generation than their parents, their architects came from a new generation as well. The conspicuous expenditure of wealth was something new in Philadelphia. The earliest of the post-Civil War parvenu mansions in the Quaker City was the palatial brownstone that Willis G. Hale designed in 1887 for the Widener family at the crossroads of North Philadelphia, where Girard Avenue, the main route to Fairmount Park crossed North Broad Street, the center of the nouveau riche of the city.[50] Hale shifted from copying Frank Furness' innovative brick designs to trying his hand at the historicism that Richard Morris Hunt had used to represent the ambitions of the Vanderbilts a decade earlier. From this point on Philadelphians of the new generation would look toward history and fashion as represented by New York.

By the 1890s Philadelphia architects—whether serving the old elites such as Cope and Stewardson or Wilson Eyre, Jr., or the nouveau riche, such as Horace Trumbauer—designed houses of display of such size that they might be called "prodigy houses," the term used for the great houses of display built during the reign of Queen Elizabeth at the end of the sixteenth century.[51] Although display remained something of an anomaly in

---

50. George E. Thomas, "Peter A. B. Widener Mansion," *Philadelphia: Three Centuries of American Art*, ed. Darrell Sewell (Philadelphia: Philadelphia Museum of Art, 1976), 421–422.

Philadelphia, especially for Quakers, the Price office came to be identified with these vast houses, beginning with Alan Wood's mansion and with great mansions for John Gilmore (1899) and William Scott (1903). These houses exemplified the changes that had occurred in domestic architecture after the Civil War. Before the war Andrew Jackson Downing had argued that because American society did not tolerate aristocratic institutions as such, architecture should find the appropriate scale and character that represented the American republic. Downing understood, however, that this modest scale need not restrict design to a few types reflecting social standing as in Britain and France. Indeed, it was preferable that architecture represent the individual. Downing suggested that a banker might choose a simple, rational, rectangular building—the preferred characteristics of a banker—whereas an eagle might more aptly find an aerie. A generation later in 1879, Martha Lamb, writing in *The Homes of America*, proclaimed that "the salient features of domestic architecture are to a considerable degree the outward manifestation of the individual man. A man's dwelling in the most complete mold may be regarded as a type of his whole private life."[52] As Downing predicted and Lamb confirmed, individualism had become the norm of the Victorian house, sometimes rising to excess, but as in the case of Calvert Vaux's design for Frederic Church's Olana, or Edward Tuckerman Potter's Hartford home for Mark Twain, the goal was portraiture, though with an increasingly expensive frame.

As the last decade of the nineteenth century ended, houses had become emblems of status in a society that more and more judged worth by the ability to consume conspicuously. A new consumer culture had evolved. At its low end it permitted Philadelphia workers to own their own row houses and to spend time at the seashore in the summer; at its high end the new scale of industry and finance enabled clients to build houses that could only be called palatial. With the nation reading in newspapers and magazines of the excesses of New York society in their Fifth Avenue mansions, Newport "cottages," and north Jersey shore houses, even previously plain Philadelphia joined the consumer culture whose upper end Thorstein Veblen had described in *The Theory of the Leisure Class* (1899).[53] According to Veblen an individual denoted his worthiness not only in terms of

---

51. For an analysis of the social split represented by architectural patronage in Philadelphia, see George E. Thomas, "Architectural Patronage and Social Stratification in Philadelphia, between 1840 and 1920," *The Divided Metropolis: Social and Spatial Dimensions of Philadelphia, 1800–1975*, ed. William W. Cutler III and Howard Gillette, Jr. (Westport, Conn.: Greenwood Press, 1980), 85–123.

52. Martha Lamb, *The Homes of America* (New York: D. Appleton Company, 1879), 10. Later, on page 148, she describes "Cottages...as variously adorned as the idiosyncrasies of human character." Architecture thus became an analog to phrenology.

53. New York: McMillan, 1899; reprinted New York: Penguin Books, 1994 (115).

his financial standing but also by his ability to consume. The apparent costliness of home, clothing, and other material possessions expressed the value of objects to bring honor to their purchaser. Out of this arose what Veblen called "the pecuniary canons of taste," meaning if it looks expensive, it is good.[54] Simplicity lost out to elaboration and complexity. More was more.

Architects did not miss the message. One California architect, W. J. Cuthbertson, analyzed the topic of "Commercialism in Architecture" and applied it to domestic design. Beginning with the question of a "National Style," he suggested that because of the facilitation of communication, "Nationalism in architecture is no more and the architecture of the world is now cosmopolitan. Now commercialism, or more correctly speaking 'Mamonism' is the preponderating feature of the later part of this century." He continued:

> The private individual must not allow another to eclipse him in the ornateness and costliness of his house as he will lose the respect and trust of the community to which may be credited the striving after novelty and strong effects, a species of advertising which is another aspect of the predominating spirit of the time.[55]

❧ The Alan Wood House

In 1893 Alan Wood sponsored a competition for a new house on the bluffs above the Schuylkill River overlooking his steel plant. Two years earlier, while the Price brothers were putting the finishing touches on the Kenilworth Inn, they saw Biltmore, Hunt's recreation of a Loire valley chateau for George Vanderbilt. This experience transformed their design method, and henceforth they would design with an eye toward historical sources. The mansion that the Price brothers designed for Alan Wood was their first opportunity to work in correct historical style.

Woodmont, as the mansion was called, was an immediate triumph, imitated by other architects, and never eclipsed in the Philadelphia area in terms of ornateness and costliness. Especially astonishing was the five-story-high great hall rising to the peak of the immense tile-clad roof. In an age seeking "novelty and strong effects" this was a novel and strong effect indeed, although the thought of heating it in this day of higher energy costs is daunting. As a design the house occupies a transitional position in the Price brothers' career, for despite attention to French Gothic detail, in plan the building was still very much a compact Victorian design. Like Furness' houses of the previous decade, Woodmont's central hall was surrounded by a ring of smaller rooms that served the specific functions of dining and retiring, cooking and serving. As a project reflecting the youthful exuberance of the architects, it is remarkable but it missed the formality of Beaux

---

54. Veblen, 115–116.

55. W. J. Cuthbertson, "Commercialism in

Architecture," *California Architect and Building News*, 13, no. 9 (September 1892), 49.

Arts planning that Hunt had introduced into Biltmore, and it also missed the careful integration of plan and detail that characterizes the works of those architects who had trained in schools rather than in offices. Nonetheless, it remains one of the premier landmarks of its day, having attracted the flattery of imitation by such architects as Horace Trumbauer, whose Grey Towers for the William Welsh Harrison family followed two years later.

The "cosmopolitan" styling of Woodmont had another consequence for it could have been built in Newport, or Long Island, or any of the new suburbs of Boston or Pittsburgh. As Cuthbertson noted, a national cosmopolitan character had arisen so that by the end of the century the origins of domestic designs published in architectural journals were no longer apparent without reading the caption information about architect and locale. History had triumphed—in McKim's libraries and triumphal arches in New York City, in Cope and Stewardson's Gothic scheme for Washington University in St. Louis, in Longfellow, Alden & Harlow's Richardsonian designs in Pittsburgh. Unlike the risks of originality there was comfort in the past—even though within the walls of the new houses and office buildings coursed gases, fluids, and electricity needed for sanitation, heating, and lighting. By the century's end, electricity had brought the magic of instant and efficient lighting and, for a few families, connections with the wider world via the telephone. As a result of these changes the irony of the "historical" house now seems almost overwhelming—not unlike John Constable's nostalgic images of rural England painted as the industrial revolution was changing his world.

Philadelphia had found its own distinct character during the industrial revolution in the early nineteenth century. In the post-Civil War years its most engaged and important citizens, whether engineers, architects, doctors, or artists, were comfortable in the modern world. As the century ended, Will Price had joined the national style and rejected much of what he had learned in Frank Furness' office. Until the construction of the Blenheim Hotel in 1905, his published projects and his principal work took the form of monumental mansions for the newly wealthy. He would design large Gothic stone mansions in a region defined by the routes of the Pennsylvania Railroad—as far west as Indianapolis, Indiana, where he designed the house for the canned pork and beans manufacturer Frank Van Camp. (*fig. 11*) Other Price mansions appeared along the route of the Main Line of the railroad in Lancaster and Pittsburgh. As Philadelphia captains of industry built their new homes in the suburbs, away from their mills and factories, and traded in their offices at the plant for downtown offices, sent their children to Harvard, Princeton, Yale, Bryn Mawr, Smith, and Vassar, and vacationed at the national resorts, Will Price and his contemporaries served their desire for national acclaim with mansions that looked to Europe and the past.

11. Price and McLanahan, Frank Van Camp residence, Indianapolis, Indiana, 1905
(Price and McLanahan Archives, George E. Thomas Collection)

12. William L. Price, "House Number 6, A $2,200 House for a Small Square Lot," from William L. Price,
Model Houses for Little Money (Philadelphia: Curtis Publishing Company, 1898)

⊲ *Midlife Search*

On the above evidence, the Will Price of the 1890s would seem to have held little promise to be a significant national influence in the new century. Unlike his near contemporaries Walter Cope, John Stewardson, Frank Miles Day, and Wilson Eyre, Jr., Price's rural Quaker background did not give him the connection to elite Philadelphians who were the usual sources of important commissions. Instead Price worked for developers, industrialists, and financiers rather than for the gentry whose connections gave Cope and Stewardson their national collegiate practice, or who hired Eyre for city and country houses, or who hired Day for churches and institutions.

Even as the 1890s marked Price's drift toward national architectural trends, there were hints in the second half of that decade which anticipated the future. In July 1896 the *Philadelphia Real Estate Record and Builder's Guide* reported that "A large amusement park is to be erected in this city by a stock company which has engaged Mr. Price and he is presently obtaining a few pointers from European architects."[56] This was Will's first trip overseas, finally giving him the chance to see the historic buildings on which his practice depended. For Will it was an overwhelming experience, confirming all that he had learned at Biltmore, and offering a remarkable insight into himself that he recalled in 1908:

> Always I could draw: and soon my fingers were never wholly satisfied with my horses; ever there was something the horses lacked.... Till one day of rolling clouds and vibrant sky, looking forth and down, my fingers grabbing some cold stony railing of a high balcony, shared with gay-clad elders quite unlike my duncolored Quaker family, I was conscious of grey towers behind me and of unheard of stony stairways lately climbed, and on my right, down, far down, ran a winding street, swelling here below into a tiny square, stone paved and flanked with gabled, beam-crossed fronts of houses gay with paint and carving, and just below the level of my eye, roofs, strange red roofs of crockery, strange windows, filled with laughing faces and waving hands, and great split banners, swaying in the summer air.... No fairy story, for I knew none. No frozen picture from a picture book. My picture books were the Penny Magazine and a natural history with no color and little drawing in their plates. And there I was on this traceried balcony, no longer the shy country Quaker lad, but self-contained and sure—sure as I was when I drew pictures of strange uncouth grotesque forms....
>
> It wasn't till years afterwards that I recognized those strange heads my childish fingers had drawn as gargoyles, as of stone not of scaly flesh, for I knew nothing of such things then—for many years had no knowledge of Gothic architecture: and then later, later as an architect, I revisited France, the cross-timbered carved front of old houses looked somehow incomplete until a vision of my rolling clouds brought them back gay in paint and gold, many-colored, new.[57]

---

56. *Philadelphia Real Estate Record and Builder's Guide,* 11, no. 31 (29 July 1896), 615.

57. Price, "Clouds and Swallows," 118–119.

On this trip Will went out of his way to meet members of the William Morris circle including C. R. Ashbee and others involved in the Guild of Handicraft. Price was strongly drawn to Morris' ideas of a humane society and for years afterward read aloud and with great gusto from Morris' writings after Sunday dinner. The Morris ideal as exemplified by Ashbee would be put into action in Rose Valley.

Will's family grew along with his architectural practice. Margaret Lightfoot Price, the first of four children was born in 1890 and was followed by William Webb Price in 1891 and Ruth Kirk in 1893. With three children the North Philadelphia row house was too small. In 1894, when Will began designing houses for Wendell and Smith's upscale community at Overbrook, an opportunity to own a larger house presented itself—if it could serve as the model house of the new community, accessible to potential buyers. The first house in Overbrook at 6334 Sherwood Road was for the Price family. Early sketches dating from June of that year show that Will first conceived of his house as linked to adjacent houses in order to present a relatively monumental composition which would have occupied much of the street frontage of the block. It was eventually constructed as free standing like the larger houses that Price was designing elsewhere. Richly detailed on the exterior and with leaded glass lighting the stair landings, this house attested to Will's success. Within were fourteenth-century French cabinets in the library, modern leaded glass windows of Price's own design, and a floridly carved verge board on the front gable which distinguished the house from those that surrounded it. Another feature, a great third floor room that could serve as an assembly hall or small theater, suggests that Will's love of theater had survived the transition from the Seekers After Knowledge to married life. Despite the Gothic exterior, the house was lighted by electricity with copper pipes serving as conduit, and wiring insulated from the pipe by a resin. With heat provided by a central steam plant serving the Overbrook community, the house was complete and luxurious in every way and a far cry from the small houses that Price was simultaneously designing for Edward Bok's *Ladies' Home Journal*. (*fig. 12*)

Despite its comforts there were drawbacks to the new house at 6334 Sherwood Road which must have caused Will to begin thinking about the nature of the modern suburb. Here for the first time in his life Will was separated from the other members of his family, surrounded instead by members of the new managerial and corporate elite who shared common economic resources but little else. With his father and brothers Walter and Frank living on South 4th Street, in the vicinity of the Provident Life and Trust Company and the brothers' architectural office, and with his fellow Seekers After Knowledge scattered around the city, Will was more isolated than ever before. Two years later his father bought the house immediately to the rear on Drexel Road and Will and his parents were reunited. With his brother Walter still living at home, the extended family was as close as a short walk across the backyard. The family unity was shattered three years later in 1899 with the sudden death of James Price. Will used his portion of the inheritance to begin construction of a much larger house—called Kelty—which stood across City Line Avenue in Lower Merion. (*fig. 13*) Like in the Sherwood Road house, family rooms were in the front with an angled rear service wing, and like the earlier house, it was Gothic in detail with an even larger third floor assembly hall and theater, this time with an articulated stage. (*fig. 14*) Here Will was just across the side yard from one of his important clients, banker and social activist John Gilmore.[58]

As his economic position rose with the success of his practice, Will returned to his search for knowledge that would engage him for the last two decades of his life. His new interests were strengthened by a widening circle of acquaintances each representing future directions. In the mid-1890s Will began a series of plans for "Houses of Moderate Cost" for Edward Bok, publisher of *The Ladies' Home Journal*. Although Bok himself was a shameless self-promoter, the magazine was a national publication that spread Price's name beyond the limits of the city. It also provided the opportunity to explore modest houses, something that would distinguish Price's career from most of his contemporaries'. In 1898 Price received a commission to design Bok's house in Merion. Also at this time Price encountered Horace Traubel, principally remembered as the chronicler of Walt Whitman but in the 1890s a founder of the Contemporary Club and the Philadelphia branch of the Society for Ethical Culture as well as the editor of a widely read political monthly, *The Conservator*.

It was Traubel who linked Will to much of the intellectual ferment in the Quaker City, especially the political and economic ideas of fellow Philadelphian Henry George whose call for a Single Tax on land resonated across the industrializing nation in the last generation of the nineteenth century. In the mid-1890s as Frederick Jackson Turner reported the closing of the American frontier and with the nation mired in a deep economic recession which slowed manufacturing and threw farmers off their land, Price joined the first generation of blue-denim-clad idealists who marched through Delaware, attempting to persuade its citizens to make it the nation's first Single Tax state. In 1896 Will even went so far as to run for city council on the Single Tax slate but was soundly defeated. The Single Tax idea would gather in artist Frank Stephens, businessman Joseph Fels, and banker and neighbor John Gilmore too.

The last years of the 1890s would add another to Price's forming circle—Martin Hawley McLanahan, who had trained as an architect at Washington College but was principally a real estate investor and speculator. In the summer of 1899 McLanahan hired Price to design a house on the western Main Line at St. Davids Station. Although overlaid

---

58. It was in Gilmore's Price-designed mansion that a Señor López called for Philippine independence. Will's daughter Margaret recalled the horror of learning that the nice man on whose lap she had sat when he was a guest at the Price home had been hanged when he returned to Manila (interview, 7 November 1970).

13. William L. Price, William L. Price residence (Kelty), Lower Merion, Pennsylvania, c. 1902
(Price and McLanahan Archives, George E. Thomas Collection)

14. William L. Price, Kelty, third-floor great room, c. 1902
(Price and McLanahan Archives, George E. Thomas Collection)

by historicizing detail, the McLanahan House was one of Price's most original early designs. Free-flowing space linked all of the public rooms of the first floor while the details of the public spaces reflected the curvilinear art nouveau that in Price's words "had a good substantial kick," and indicated his growing interest in breaking out of the historical design mode. The gesso relief of the fireplace and the murals of the end wall of the living room were to date Will's closest approximation of the English Arts and Crafts style, here reflecting his growing interest in the movement's forms and philosophies. It is likely that McLanahan found his way to Will because of the firm's success in Wayne, including a newly constructed house for Alan Reed which was similar in scale to the future McLanahan home. But it is also possible that they shared interests in the Arts and Crafts movement, the Single Tax movement, and any of the other organizations that preoccupied Will at the end of the century and in which McLanahan participated in the twentieth century.[59] In addition to sharing many of Will's interests, McLanahan had access to almost unlimited capital through his marriage to a daughter of Charles Schoen, the inventor of the steel box car and the steel tire for locomotive wheels.

As the 1890s ended Will was ensconced in his own palatial residence and working for a circle of industrialists and activists. A flurry of new commissions again linked the Price firm to the larger world. In 1898 a Quaker hotel operator and grandson of the founder of the Lehigh Coal and Navigation Company, Daniel White, hired Price to design a sun room addition that would mask the Victorian facade of the Traymore Hotel on Atlantic City's beachfront. Two years later Daniel's brother Josiah hired the firm to design a new hotel across Park Place from the Traymore, which would be named the Marlborough. An American heiress had just married the Duke of Marlborough and steamships were making the Atlantic crossing in just a few days with little hazard. Old world doings and events were part of the daily grist for the American press and Philadelphia had joined the rest of the nation in following European events.

With his link to Whitman's scribe Horace Traubel as well as to the activist circle of Philadelphia artists, Will Price was reconnected to the American vision transmitted by Ralph Waldo Emerson and Walt Whitman to Frank Furness, and on to Furness' best students. In 1901, with his fortieth birthday looming, Will helped found a Single Tax colony in Arden, Delaware, and shortly after made the purchase of the land that would become the Rose Valley experiment. In the fall Will moved back to the countryside of his youth. The twentieth century was dawning.

———

59. Price had already worked in 1897 for the Charles Scott Spring Company, the business where Charles Schoen had learned the steel business, and had also designed a house for Charles Scott. See checklist for 1897 and 1900.

William L. Price as the Mikado, c. 1907
(Photograph by Ellis Photography; Architectural Archives, Philip N. Price Collection, University of Pennsylvania)

Brave New Worlds:
Price's Utopian Visions

Nearly all of our people live either in houses built to sell, without individuality or other relation to the inhabitants than selection of the least unfit by them; or they live in houses designed by architects who did not and could not know them and their life, and who in the most part were more interested in their art than in the object of their art.

—*William L. Price*[1]

❧ *Community in the Age of Roosevelt*

In April 1900 the young governor of New York, Theodore Roosevelt, addressed the Hamilton Club of Chicago in a widely publicized speech entitled "The Strenuous Life," which gave public expression to his personal values.[2] Himself a child of the Gilded Age, Roosevelt attacked materialism and the commercial spirit, denounced "ignoble ease" and praised "the doctrine of the strenuous life, the life of toil and effort, of labor and strife." After Chicago Roosevelt's westward trip took him through Kansas where William White, editor of the *Emporia Gazette*, prophetically proclaimed "He is the coming American of the twentieth century."[3] In 1900 the Republican Convention met in Philadelphia and nominated William McKinley of Ohio to a second term as president of the United States with Roosevelt as his running mate. Their term of office began in March 1901.

Before 1901 had ended, Americans would experience powerful premonitions of the future. On 6 September 1901, at the Pan-American Exposition in Buffalo, New York,

---

1. William L. Price, incomplete typescript, "A Plea for Democracy in the Domestic Architecture of America" (c. 1909), 1. Price and McLanahan Archives, George E. Thomas Collection.

2. Nathan Miller, *Theodore Roosevelt: A Life* (New York: William Morrow, 1992), 330.

3. Miller, 331.

1. Rose Valley before renovations, 1901
(Photograph by Henry Troth; Price and McLanahan Archives, George E. Thomas Collection)

2. Arden Green, Arden, Delaware, 1999 (Photograph by George E. Thomas)

an assassin's bullet mortally wounded President McKinley. Eight days later McKinley was dead and the reins of the nation were turned over to the 42-year-old vice president. During his nearly eight years in office, Roosevelt's dynamic personality shifted the presidency toward the activism that has characterized the modern era. Already famed for his years in the west and as a Rough Rider during the Spanish-American War, Roosevelt engaged the nation by his capacity to take risks in pursuit of noble goals. Exemplifying the "strenuous life" in word and deed, Roosevelt and his family were agents of the shift toward the youth culture that remains a hallmark of our society to the present and under Roosevelt the office of the president became the focus of the nation's energies.

Around the time that Roosevelt became president, just before Price's own fortieth birthday on 9 November 1901, Will Price moved his family from their large house in Overbrook to a recently finished apartment in a row of renovated workers' houses in Rose Valley, an abandoned mill village west of Philadelphia. (*fig. 1*) The row of houses had been adapted from Will's design to serve as the Guest House for the Arts and Crafts village modeled on structures described in William Morris' utopian novella, *News from Nowhere*. Roofed in red tile in accord with Morris' imagined villages of twenty-first-century postindustrial England, ornamented with Mercer tile panels on a sandy yellow field of new stucco, and fronted with new porches that proclaimed the desire to spend time amid the beauties of nature, the Guest House denoted the principal themes that would characterize Price's Rose Valley architecture. With few exceptions Rose Valley houses were set in gardens, designed to incorporate elements of the regional vernacular, constructed of local materials, and related to other buildings of the village in a way that visually represented a community of shared values and interests. Tile ornament set into stucco walls became the hallmark of what Price called "Rose Valley architecture," defining whenever these elements were used the architect's and client's shared commitment to the modern world. Will Price had joined the revolution of the twentieth century.

Antecedents to Innovation

Although it seems likely that Arden and Rose Valley were consequences of the conjunction of Price's fortieth birthday and the new century, there were numerous antecedents in his family history and in Will's enlarging circle that hinted at his coming radical changes in lifestyle and eventually in his architectural practice. The widening circle included the aforementioned Frank Stephens, and Horace Traubel as well as several of Price's architectural clients, among them John Gilmore and Martin Hawley McLanahan whose access to capital made it possible to put Price's theories into action. There was another antecedent to Rose Valley: Will's first trip across the Atlantic in the summer of 1896. From purchases of decorative materials for houses under construction and later as a result of his acquaintance with C. R. Ashbee, Will encountered members of the English Arts and Crafts community. Price's mentor Frank Furness had steadfastly avoided going to Europe on the grounds that the charms of its architecture might be too seductive. For Will, already seduced by history since his encounter with Hunt's Biltmore, the direct experience of the charms of the English countryside reinforced his interest in the delights of preindustrial cottages and their village settings. Most important was Price's discovery on that trip of the local color and regional character that even now remains an essence of the English countryside. It was this quality that Price realized was lacking in the restless competition between houses in the suburbs that he had designed in the previous decade. Perhaps in those English villages Will saw the essential similarity to many of the villages of his childhood. Indeed, it was this very character that Thomas Nolan, professor of architecture at the University of Pennsylvania's School of Architecture, saw in the farm villages of the Pennsylvania countryside.

> The suburbs of Philadelphia, and much of the country in the adjoining counties, have often been compared in their general character and appearance to the English counties in the southwest, especially Devonshire and parts of Somerset....
>
> Some of the immediate suburbs make one think of quiet old English towns. There is scarcely a trace of the American "newness" about them; and there are lanes that wind about and lead over and beyond, lined with vine-covered walls and shaded by some fine old trees....
>
> There is something, too, about the very atmosphere of these places that at least suggests some phases of English rural home life, and it is admittedly more distinctly obvious here than in the suburbs and neighboring country of New York or Boston or any of the larger American cities.[4]

Unlike modern suburbs, in which each house was as different as possible from its neighbor in style, material, and shape, older English villages were still characterized by a vernacular simplicity of form and unity of material that joined the entire array of buildings, from cottages and shops to the village church and the principal estate buildings. Henceforth, whenever Will had the choice, he would seek to recreate local character in design through the use of local materials and forms.

Will's belief that communities should embody and sustain the values of their shared society grew out of the same trip. In 1888 C. R. Ashbee had established the School and Guild of Handicraft in East London which moved to Essex House in 1890, but closed two years later. Four years later Ashbee made a lecture tour of the United States, including a visit to Philadelphia and six weekly lectures at Reading, Pennsylvania on "The Historical Conception of English Character and Citizenship."[5] Price may well have looked

---

4. Thomas Nolan, "Recent Suburban Architecture in Philadelphia and Vicinity," *Architectural Record*, 19, no. 3 (March 1906), 167–193.

5. Alan Crawford, *C. R. Ashbee: Architect, Designer & Romantic Socialist* (New Haven, Conn.: Yale University Press, 1985), 66–67.

for Ashbee in London and he would probably have also seen Quaker industrialist George Cadbury's planned village at Bourneville, which had begun construction in 1895, a year before the trip.[6] When Price returned from England, imbued with Morris' and Ashbee's approaches to craft production, he began to write about the negative implications of the second phase of the industrial revolution which was playing itself out in the Philadelphia of William Sellers and Frederick Winslow Taylor. For Price and his fellow visionaries the solution to these large social problems began with political action such as the Single Tax, first in Delaware and later in Philadelphia. Responding to the economic crisis of 1873 which was a harbinger of the economic stresses of the remainder of the century, Philadelphia native Henry George, then a California newspaper writer, editorialized about his theory of the heretofore unexamined and unsuspected links between prosperity and poverty. Six years later in 1879, George published *Progress and Poverty* which over the next generation sold more than two million copies, an astonishing number in a nation of 100 million people. George warned that progress could be one of the causes of poverty rather than a solution to it, especially if its benefits were not spread to the workers who were the actual cause of increases in productivity.

> So long as all the increased wealth which modern progress brings goes but to build up great fortunes, to increase luxury and make sharper the contrast between the House of Have and the House of Want, progress is not real and cannot be permanent. The reaction must come. The tower leans from its foundations, and every new story but hastens the final catastrophe.[7]

As George pointed out, famine and low wages were as common in areas where there were too few workers as where there were too many. Progress, George hypothesized, was not created by wealth alone; rather, it was created by the greater productivity of the worker and the appropriate use of capital. Working from this model George argued that greater employment would lead to a differentiation of skills which in turn would lead to increases in productivity. If workers were paid a living wage, they would consume more, thereby increasing demand. Thus, the "laborer in performing the labor really creates the fund from which his wages are drawn.... as the efficiency of labor manifestly increases with the number of laborers, the more laborers, other things being equal, the higher should wages be." In Philadelphia George's thesis would ring true, because Taylorism had produced both specialization and productivity which in turn led to rising wages. These wages fueled the great surge of row house construction that announced the birth of the con-

---

6. For the Arts and Crafts perspective on Bourneville see Mabel Tuke Priestman, "Inexpensive English Houses That Might Be Adapted to American Uses," *Artistic Houses* (Chicago: A. C. McClurg, 1910), 94–105.

7. Henry George, *Progress and Poverty, An Inquiry into the Cause of Industrial Depressions and of Increase of Want With Increase of Wealth ... The Remedy*, Centennial Edition (New York: Robert Schalkenbach Foundation, 1979), 10.

sumer economy which appeared first in and around industrialized Philadelphia, and later came the characterize the nation after World War I.

George's central focus was on the issue of land ownership because in a nation that was still largely agrarian, he theorized that land rents, land speculation, and commercial monopolies were the chief causes of economic depressions. To resolve the problem, he identified one sovereign solution which he italicized for emphasis: *"We must make land common property."*[8] This George proposed to do by a Single Tax on land, raising taxes to a confiscatory level that would force the sale of land to those who had an economic use for it, or alternately returning land to public ownership. It was this tax that became the rallying cry of George's adherents. Rejecting social Darwinism with its implications of imperialism and racism, George called instead for a society based on the Judeo-Christian values of "equality, freedom and justice for all men," as exemplified in the potential of American democracy.

> Civilization is co-operation. Union and liberty are its factors…the law of human progress…proves that the making of land common property…would give an enormous impetus to civilization, while the refusal to do so must entail retrogression. A civilization like ours must either advance or go back. It cannot stand still.[9]

Henry George's theories quickly entered the national political sphere, forming the basis for much modern economic and political theory. In 1886 he ran against Republican candidate Theodore Roosevelt for mayor of New York City, both losing to the Democratic machine. Twelve years later George was again in the race for mayor of New York when he suddenly died. As the nineteenth century drew to a close, George's ideas still had the force of a new discovery and drew social idealists, Will Price among them, to its banner. In the mid-1890s members of the Philadelphia Single Tax Society hoped to validate George's ideas by persuading Delawareans to adopt the revolutionary system of taxation only on land. It was probably in that organization that Will met many of the colleagues of his later years, notably Horace Traubel and Frank Stephens. Their efforts in Delaware were soundly defeated but their fervor continued even after George's death.[10] George's ideas of shared social responsibility and Roosevelt's program for the strenuous life were blended in Will Price's deeds as the twentieth century dawned.

In the spring of 1900, acting on Will Price's idea of testing the Single Tax theory by founding a village based on its principles, Will, Frank Stephens, and Stephens' future

---

8. George, 328.

9. George, 524. This discussion of Henry George and his ideas is derived from Edward Rose, *Henry George* (New York: Twayne Publishers, 1968) which provides a modern treatment of George's theories and career.

10. Henry Seidel Canby, *Age of Confidence: Life in the*

Nineties (New York: Farrar and Rinehart, 1934). Canby recalled the "blue-coated army of propagandists, speaking at street corners, dropping handbills at our doors, arguing even with the peach farmer on his lonely plantation" (115).

wife Eleanor Getty sought a retreat in the countryside where low-priced land would permit experiments in new forms of community and in the production of artistic objects.[11] Philadelphia's economic boom had drained the countryside of its youth, making it possible to buy at reasonable prices small farms whose land had been exhausted. Will was drawn to these experiments and these communities would preoccupy him for the rest of his life. At his death he was simultaneously living in the Arts and Crafts community of Rose Valley, serving on the board of trustees of Arden, and serving on the board for a proposed Single Tax community to be put into effect in the principality of Andorra, which had been purchased by Fiske Warren, another of Will's regular associates for utopian schemes.[12]

Arden and the Single Tax: Politics Represented in Community Form

On the 12th of June, 1900, Frank Stephens purchased a 162-acre farm just across the Pennsylvania state line in Delaware with the intention of forming a community based on George's principles.[13] Stephens was a graduate of the Pennsylvania Academy of the Fine Arts, a former pupil and brother-in-law of Thomas Eakins, and a partner with fellow Academy student Colin Campbell Cooper, Jr., in the decorative arts business of Stephens, Cooper and Company.[14] In establishing Arden, Frank Stephens was one of many who sought an alternate to the industrial society as the nineteenth century ended. Many of these American experiments occurred in the northeast near those industrial centers which were being transformed by modern work methods. Five years before Arden's founding Elbert Hubbard established Roycroft at East Aurora, New York, for the production of furniture; Ralph Radcliffe Whitehead's Byrdcliffe Colony at Woodstock, New York, followed in 1901; the New Clairveau community near Montague, Massachusetts, was another center. The locations of these communities in the region of the "Burnt Over District" along the Erie Canal as well as a second cluster of communities in California, plus the groups associated with William Price near Philadelphia were not coincidental. Each of these areas had historically attracted residents who sought salvation of one sort or another. As the new century began the same regions were overlaid with Arts and Crafts societies that sponsored exhibitions of the products of their members, and frequently fostered communal activities.[15] Clearly Arden anticipated many of the themes of

---

11. For a recent overview of Arden's history see Mark Taylor, "Arts and Crafts and the Single Tax: The Utopian Experiment at Arden, Delaware," *Style 1900*, 10, no. 3 (Summer/Fall 1997), 46–51.

12. "Single Tax Experiment in Andorra," *The New York Times* (16 April 1916), sec. 6, p. 5.

13. Frank Stephens, Autobiography, manuscript, in the Stephens Papers, Arden Archives.

14. Stephens had turned in Eakins for pulling the loincloth off a male nude in the company of female students, resulting in Eakins being fired from the Academy.

15. A summary of many of these organizations is included at the end of Janet Kardon, ed., *The Ideal Home 1900–1920: The History of Twentieth-Century Craft in American* (New York: Harry N. Abrams, 1993), 236–276.

the twentieth century, not the least being the search for means to express individuality and establish self-worth in a supportive and creative community.

In October 1901 Stephens formed a board for Arden which included his friend Will Price and Frank Martin (a long-time member of the Price firm) and "deeded it to humanity forever." Arden, as their experimental community was called, based on Shakespeare's idyllic setting in *As You Like It*, would be the first of many efforts to wedge the door of social equality open a bit further.[16] For Arden Will developed a community plan which deserves to be better known. The plan gave to Arden, a tiny community scaled to the economics of the working classes, the type of sophisticated planning common to only a few elite communities such as Llewellyn Park in New Jersey. Unlike the wonderful gorge that formed the common space of Llewellyn Park, the Delaware property lacked great scenic distinction. Its chief asset was a small stream, Naaman's Creek, on the east side, with farm buildings from its earlier use to the south. By incorporating the stream valley as a natural preserve into the eastern edge of the community and by preserving the woodlands on the west (dubbed Sherwood Forest, doubtless a reflection of the success of the recent publication of Wilmington native Howard Pyle's *Adventures of Robin Hood*), Price framed the community with wooded buffers separating the village from the highways surrounding it. Building sites were outlined by a road system that divided the community into two zones, the "Woodlands" on the east and "Sherwood" on the west. These zones were centered around shared common spaces that provided areas for recreation, theater, and a community Gild Hall in an abandoned barn. Houses would be tightly clustered around these spaces, like a New England village with a central common, affirming the democratic sharing of resources that was the basis of Henry George's idea.

Plots for houses were valued according to size as well as proximity to community resources and protected landscape borders, with the intention that the land rents rather than sales would carry the shared expenses of the community. But because of Henry George's insistence that labor should not be taxed, no increases would be incurred due to the construction of a house or other improvements. For the first decade there was a provisional character to most of the cottages which were little more than wood tents providing shelter during summer months when it was pleasant to escape the city. Permanent building activity began with the construction of a guest house and a studio building tellingly named the Red House, in homage to the house at Bexleyheath, Kent, where William Morris had opened his studio and had begun his manufacturing. Located on the village green these simple and rustic buildings established the architectural character of the community. (*fig. 2*)

———

16. Arden is the subject of a master's essay by Eliza Harvey Edwards, "Arden: The Architecture and Planning of a Delaware Utopia" (University of Pennsylvania, Program in Historic Preservation, 1993).

In 1909 Joseph Fels gave the community funds to redesign the barn to better serve as the Gild Hall and to undertake designs for several cottages which, according to the terms of the gift, were to be "subject to Will Price's order, several thousand dollars to build at once four or five cottages from that master craftsman's designs; with one stipulation that they should be permanent and artistic in character with stone foundations and cellars, hollow brick and concrete walls, and above all, literally the red-tiled roofs so beautiful in the scenery of Britain and the Netherlands."[17] These houses drew on the architectural vocabulary which Will had previously established at Rose Valley. Most notable of these was Frank Stephens' own cottage on the green with "Tomorrow is a New Day" carved into the beam above the main entrance. It was a worthy motto for a community that included Upton Sinclair, Scott Nearing, and "Mother" Ella Reeve Bloor.

❧ *Rose Valley*

Over the summer of 1901 as Price and Stephens planned their community, Will may have held discussions with his own family on whether or not they would join such a rough-and-tumble village. Despite being connected to Philadelphia by the Baltimore and Ohio Railroad, Arden did not have the resources to be much more than a summer colony and it must have been apparent that it would be more concept than reality for many years. Distressed by his own isolation in the suburbs of the Main Line, Will knew that Arden would be even more removed from the people and ideas that interested him. To involve his own family in such an experiment he would have to build another community, one closer to the city and in an area that could provide schools and other necessities.

In April and May 1901 Will Price purchased nearly 80 acres of land including the water-powered mill buildings and workers' houses in the valley of Vernon Run, a tiny tributary of Ridley Creek.[18] Eleven weeks later on 17 July 1901 Price along with Martin Hawley McLanahan, John Gilmore, Edward Bok, and Howard Stratton (director of the Philadelphia Museum School) incorporated the Rose Valley Association whose purpose

---

17. *Arden Club Talk* (March–April 1909), cited in Edwards, 58.

18. Delaware County Deeds, Book F #10, p. 1102; Book M #10, p. 223. An extensive bibliography has developed on Rose Valley, beginning with Eleanor Price Mather, "This Was Rose Valley: A Study in Planned Community," *Friends Intelligencer* (16 January 1954), 32–34; "Rose Valley Renaissance," *Friends Intelligencer* (20 March 1954), 156–158; Peter Ham and others, *A History of Rose Valley* (Rose Valley, Pa.: by the Borough, 1973); William Ayers and others, *Rose Valley: A Poor*

Sort of Heaven, A Good Sort of Earth (Chadds Ford, Pa.: Brandywine Museum of Art, 1983); George E. Thomas, "Rose Valley Community," in *Philadelphia: Three Centuries of American Art*, ed. Darrell Sewell (Philadelphia: Philadelphia Museum of Art, 1976), 465–467; George E. Thomas, "William Price's Arts and Crafts Community at Rose Valley, Pennsylvania," *The Ideal Home 1900–1920: The History of Twentieth Century American Craft*, ed. Janet Kardon (New York: Harry N. Abrams, 1993), 125–135.

3. Rose Valley shops with Will Price in rear, c. 1903 (Price and McLanahan Archives, George E. Thomas Collection)

4. Rose Valley Guild Hall, stage set for *The Mikado*, designed by Will Price, c. 1907 (Price and McLanahan Archives, George E. Thomas Collection)

was "the manufacture of structures, articles, materials and products involving artistic handicrafts." Suggesting that he was of two minds about making the dramatic jump to a new community, Will was simultaneously completing his new house Kelty on property acquired from John Gilmore. Designed during the winter of 1900 and largely constructed over the following summer, the lifestyle and carrying costs of the new house might have kept Price thrall to the medieval past. Fortunately Will and his family lived during the summer and winter of 1901 in Rose Valley and henceforth would cast their lot with the future there.

By October 1901, a month before his fortieth birthday, Price and McLanahan had adapted one of the mill buildings to serve as a furniture shop for the production of the superb Gothic revival pieces of the sort that Price had provided his clients during the previous few years. (*fig. 3*) This, it was hoped, would be the first of several "banded shops" on the William Morris model which would encourage other artists to join the community. To ensure quality and to manifest guild values, the seal of the community, a wild rose surrounded by a belt, emblematic of the banded shop, would be awarded to work that met exacting standards for craftsmanship and honesty in manufacture as determined by the community board. Here Price intended to challenge the modern production methods which increasingly fragmented Philadelphia manufacturing into specialties that in his view devalued both work and product.

By the end of the nineteenth century, in the city where such brilliant eighteenth-century craftsmen as William Savery and Thomas Affleck had made Philadelphia furniture synonymous with the highest quality in the nation, and where, after the Civil War, Daniel Pabst had produced remarkable custom furniture and paneling for Frank Furness, it had become nearly impossible to find cabinetmakers skilled in all the aspects of their craft. In only one generation of labor specialization, Philadelphia workshops had been so transformed that Price could scarcely find even a two- or three-man workforce for his shops. In 1904, in a talk about the value of manual training courses in public schools, Will recalled his difficulty in finding workers for Rose Valley.

> A couple of years ago, some of us tried to start some little shops at Rose Valley. I went to one of the oldest and best cabinet makers in the city of Philadelphia and asked him if he could get me two or three good, all-round cabinet makers. He said, "Well, I think I could get you two." That is, only two in a city of over a million people. I said: "I want young men." "Oh!" he exclaimed, "these men are so old they will probably die before you get them out there." He added: "You cannot find a young cabinet maker because there is no use for him. I can get you a good dowel sticker, or a good man on the lathe or mortise machine, but there is no such thing as a cabinet maker in the cabinet making shop." That is of course not absolutely true; but nearly all of the good men are foreigners—very few of them are Americans. That is the situation in one of the most simple, direct and important of the crafts left to us.[19]

Not only was it hard to find craftsmen who were absorbed in their work but, as Price observed further in the talk, there were significant social consequences to be considered. A nation of "button pushers" could not long remain a republic, and while industries based on such systems might make goods profitably, Price warned that "it does not make character; and you cannot get character as a by-product of such labor."[20] In the suburbs of Philadelphia where William Sellers' standardization had become the watchword of the regional economy and where Frederick Winslow Taylor had transformed work from traditional craft to modern industrial production, Price took on the moral issue of the effect of production methods on character using Rose Valley as practical laboratory experiment and philosophical allegory.

◄ Rose Valley Planning

With land purchased and the shops under way, Will and his fellow adventurers settled into the existing buildings of the old mill village to begin to shape their community. In the Price family living room in the Guest House, on 12 December 1901, was held the first meeting of the "folk mote," the government of the new Rose Valley community.[21] The system of government was a reflection of the idealists who created it. During the early years of the community the meetings were attended by the entire spectrum of the community, from the woodworkers in the shop and the artists of the Guild Hall to the Prices and later the McLanahans and Schoens. The list of attendees of the first meeting, held at the home of "freeman W. L. Price" is of note, both for the characterizations of the residents, and for their relationship to each other: "Dr. Caroline Smith, First Chairman; Susanna M. Price [Will's sister], teacher; Josephine DeMoll, mother of children; Carl de Moll, her son, craftsman; Mary his wife, skilled in growing flowers [another of Will's sisters]; Clara Merrick, skilled in household economy and lover of children [of the bridal party of Will and Emma and housekeeper for the Price family]; Elizabeth Warrington, "Chaperone of us all" [and aunt of Will Walton]; Will Walton [with Elizabeth, cousins in the Lightfoot line, working in Will's office], who sings and draws houses with his hands to the satisfaction of freeman Price; Frances Day, artist, children's portraits; Mrs. Day; Walter F. Price, architect of renown and sketcher of promise; Mrs. E. W. Price, wife of W. L. raiser of children; Anna Margaret Kite [another of Will's sisters and wife of Nathan], lover of

---

19. William L. Price, "The Attitude of Manual Training to the Arts and Crafts," *Proceedings of the Eastern Manual Training Association* (Philadelphia: Eastern Manual Training Association, 1905), 16.

20. Price, "The Attitude of Manual Training," 16–17.

21. Minutes of Folk Mote, 12 December 1901, "Chronicles of the Folk: being the true and full tale of the doings and sayings of the Dwellers in Rose Valley in folk-mote assembled. With a short tale of the first folk mote and a tale of the chaos that went before. This book having been made in the year of our Lord MDCC-CCII and in the year of the Association 1." Manuscripts in Rose Valley Borough Offices, Rose Valley, Pa.

children, kindergarten; and Nathan Kite, tiller of the soil."[22] At the first meeting Carl DeMoll, Francis Day, Nathan Kite, and Will Price were asked to chart the course of the community, while Walter Price was given the task of making a map of the waterways and drainage pipes and Francis Day was authorized to purchase a "town lamp" to be tended by the members of the community.

Another meeting took place four days later at which Will presided, "he being skilled at government and the father of the town." At that meeting the question was raised as to who should take part and, most particularly, at what age children would become voting members. "Some held that children were too young to vote and their minds too small to grasp the full import of what was going on; others that children were not so dumb as they looked, and they had rights and ought to be allowed to express them." On further consideration, it was decided that children who had reached the age of five could vote. A generation before universal suffrage the Rose Valley residents concluded that all community members, men, women, and children alike should be able to participate in decision making. At the same meeting it was determined to present a lecture series, Will Price to talk on William Morris, Walter Price to talk on medieval guilds, and William Evans to talk on the local birds.[23] Community improvements, festivals, and entertainments were later topics and took the form of medieval pageants and Gilbert and Sullivan musicals which were performed in the Guild Hall. (*fig. 4*)

Unlike Arden, Rose Valley contained both association land and private land. Homes could be constructed on privately owned land across Rose Valley Road from the association property, but initially the residents made use of existing buildings on association land for homes. These included the mill workers' row houses which were adapted to make the community Guest House and the mill foremen's houses which were turned over to the shop workers—in itself a symbolically significant promotion from the uniformity of the row to the twin houses of management. Other existing houses, including a late-eighteenth-century country Georgian house (once occupied by Bishop William White who gave Rose Valley its name) and the small Victorian frame house at the gate lane, were renovated as modern living quarters. Two larger existing Victorian houses became the homes of Will Price and his brother Walter who also provided a home for their recently

---

22. Only Francis, Mrs. Day, and Clara Merrick were not in some way part of the extended Price family. Later community residents included John Maene, a Belgium-born sculptor; Eleanor and Yarnall Abbott, fellow graduates of the Pennsylvania Academy with Alice Barber Stephens; F. Morgan Townsend; and Pennsylvania Museum School graduate and architect in Will's offices, John Bissegger.

23. Minutes for 16 December 1901. The Chronicles continue, describing the various activities of clearing land, planting gardens under the supervision of Mary DeMoll, floods along the creek that inundated even the new shop as well as a lecture by Elizabeth Packard of England on "Socialism and the Brotherhood of Man" (3 February 1902). The first Shakespeare entertainment occurred in the spring (5 May 1902).

5. Rose Valley, new bridge over Vernon Run, toward Guest House and workers' houses, c. 1905
(Photograph attributed to M. Hawley McLanahan; Price and McLanahan Archives, George E. Thomas Collection)

6. William L. Price, "Attractive Dining-Room with Casement Windows,"
from William L. Price, *Model Houses for Little Money* (Philadelphia: Curtis Publishing Company, 1898)

widowed mother Sarah Price. These buildings were technically outside the limits of the association. When Will and Emma moved from the Guest House to their larger house in the spring of 1902 they requested permission to continue to be considered as citizens of Rose Valley.[24] Once the row of workers' houses was renovated into the Guest House and following the model of a Quaker community, a committee of overseers was established including Emma Price, Caroline Smith, and Anna Kite. A year later, in the fall of 1903, Martin Hawley McLanahan became a member of the association along with Henry and Mary Hetzel and Henry and Emma Troth. Two years later Charles and Alice Barber Stephens and Charles and Elsie Schoen were added to the list of citizens.

Because the founding of Rose Valley corresponded to Will's new public persona as a writer/lecturer, we know much about his thinking during the planning of Rose Valley. If the shops resulted from his dissatisfaction with Taylorism, Rose Valley, like Arden, resulted from his quest for a communal way of life. This goal was the theme of his essay in the first issue of *The Artsman*, which began publication in 1903 at the beginning of the third year of Rose Valley.

> Here are slowly gathering together people who do things—writers, musicians, craftsmen, art workers, and those who think the simple life with some human touch worth more than the strain and show and haphazard of your ordinary communities. Here the tiniest cottage may be built side by side with a more spacious neighbor. And why not? Certainly our fitness to associate together upon simple human conditions should not be gauged by our incomes.[25]

That Will was thinking along the Single Tax ideals of Arden is also clear, for he emphasized his own lack of interest in profiting from any development that might occur: "There is no land speculation at Rose Valley, vaunting the beauties of nature in the market place. There whatever increase of value comes by reason of the growth of the community goes into the general pocket."[26] A plan of the community published in *The Artsman* in 1907 shows the evolution of the community. Unlike the open farmland of Arden, which gave the designers freer rein, Rose Valley's plan was based on an existing network of roads and clusters of buildings. The focus of the community was at the intersection of what is now Rose Valley Road and the lane to the mill. (*fig. 5*) Formerly this had been the center of the old industrial village with houses near mill buildings, all located near their sources of waterpower. At that intersection was the row of houses that became the Guest House, and across the street were the original cluster of mill foremen's houses that were occupied by several of the shop workers. The nearby Bishop White house was occupied by John Maene, Price's longtime wood carver and an instructor at Drexel Institute, and whose

24. Chronicles, 5 May 1902.
25. William L. Price, "Is Rose Valley Worth While?"
The Artsman, 1, no. 1 (October 1903), 10–11.
26. Price, "Is Rose Valley Worth While?" 11.

family have remained residents of the village to the present. Beyond, to the north toward Media, were Victorian houses that were part of the railroad suburb, including the house that Will's family soon occupied. A new lane was carved out around Will Price's house to provide access to tiny cottages that were the homes of several of the artists who had joined the community, including photographer and childhood friend Henry Troth and Henry Hetzel, a teacher of manual training in Philadelphia. By this act of planning which juxtaposed the tiny cottages of his friends near his large house, Price proved that real estate values were less important than community. In Rose Valley ideals would rule over economics.

Three large tracts on the opposite side of Rose Valley Road were occupied by Hawley McLanahan, his father-in-law, Charles Schoen, and later another of Schoen's sons-in-law, Martin R. Jackson. Opposite the Price home on the main road to Media was the home of Alice and Charles Stephens which Will had created by adding to an existing barn which then became studios for the two artists. Interwoven in a tapestry that encompassed the village were homes of industrialists, artists, wood carvers from the mill, and draftsmen from Will's office as well as Walter Price and other family members. Shared interests and not economics determined community. Although only portions of the land were held in common as in Arden, still every resident shared access on common walks throughout the property. Public space was reserved along Ridley Creek and in the pond on Vernon Run which became the summer recreational center and the ancestor of the present swim club.

Architecture as an Expression of Life

The opportunity to design the domestic architecture of Rose Valley came at an important time for Will Price. Heretofore his clients had either been large corporations who used Price's designs to sell houses in suburban developments or wealthy individuals whose personal taste reflected the wave of historicism that crested in the 1890s. Having worked in the Furness office, Will would have remembered the representative realism of the Henszey and Griscom houses that were completed while he was a draftsman but, like his T-Square Club peers, he too had ridden the wave of taste that favored history over direct expression of purpose. Two houses at the end of the 1890s marked a correction in course, first, the art nouveau-influenced McLanahan house with its flowing interior spaces, curved ceilings, and Pre-Raphaelite painted ornament, and second, the rougher, more masculine design of the Walter house in nearby Wallingford. There, in a house nestled in its own hollow, far removed from the main highways, Will designed a straightforward piece of construction essentially devoid of historicizing ornament. Although the stonework now reads as of its period and the diamond cut into the plane of the front bay is clearly a motif of turn-of-the-century shingle style, the house was resolutely vernacular in inspiration and avoided the historical details that tended to overwhelm the large houses of the period.

In many regions of the country, by the middle of the 1890s, simplicity was becoming a common antidote to Victorian complexity, characterizing artistic house design to the extent that Barr Ferree observed that "the most noticeable element of strength in the most artistic of recent domestic work is unadorned surface." Ferree linked this change to the "value of mass in modern building…made clear by Richardson," so that "building speaks for itself as a building, and not for its value as a medium for the display of architectural variety."[27] Thus Will was a part of his generation, mirroring evolving popular taste when he attacked the complex overlay of pattern and hard glossy finishes of the Victorian age and advocated simple materials and natural finishes that in turn were naturally allied with the English Arts and Crafts movement. The natural beauty of materials became a theme in Price's columns in *The Ladies' Home Journal* and continued into the next decade. In one article he wrote:

> Woodwork…should be simple in the extreme—usually mere, flat, thin bands, designed to show the grain…and never cover[ed] with coat after coat of varnish or paint to hide its beauty…. There is nothing more beautiful than an open-grained or large figured wood like chestnut, cypress, or even hemlock, without filler or paint, merely sandpapered to smooth a surface and waxed to bring out a grain.[28]

While Rose Valley was beginning, Will was asked to give a lecture to the Ontario Association of Architects in Toronto, a group which would invite him back several times over the next few years. The 1902 talk was published by the association and from there found its way in the autumn of 1903 into *American Architect* which had long been the voice of the American profession. There Will enunciated several themes that would preoccupy him for the rest of his career. First and foremost was the relationship between client and architect. Architects might strive for artistry but to Price, as a professional, his task was to serve the client and not simply his own interests.

> Having secured our client, the first question for us is, what next? Shall we build around that client our shell or his fitting shell? Now when we stop to think of it, how often are we trying to build the best possible monument to ourselves and not the best possible house or building for that man?[29]

It was a question that has preoccupied the profession for more than a century. Is the architect hired to do what he likes and is known for, or is he hired to portray the values and interests of the owner? For Will the answer was absolute:

---

27. Barr Ferree, "Artistic Domestic Architecture in America," *The New England Magazine*, 12, no. 4 (June 1895), 460–461.
28. William L. Price, *Model Houses for Little Money* (Philadelphia: Curtis Publishing Company, 1895), 90–91.
29. William L. Price, "A Philadelphia Architect's Views on Architecture," *American Architect*, 82, no. 1452 (23 October 1903), 27.

> what we are going to have to do if we are going to have real architecture is to make our
> product more than beautiful, more than fitting to the situation, primarily fitting the man
> that is to live in it, or the purpose for which it is to be used.

There were risks with this approach that Price accepted.

> That means a pretty savage thing sometimes; it means if we are going to build a house for
> a vulgar man, that we must build a vulgar house. It would not be architecture if we did
> not. It must be better than that man; it must be what that man might be, it must represent
> that, but unless it has in it some element of that thing which makes him the vulgar man, in
> my judgement, it is not architecture at all.

While Will grappled with this question he was also beginning to understand his obliga-
tions to his own time. In the 1890s designs for *The Ladies' Home Journal* he had discovered the merits of simplification, albeit expressed through the vehicle of historical
revivals which took the form of finding the right English cottages or the appropriate vernacular farm building as model. (*fig. 6*) Simplification would become a hallmark of modernism in its rejection of the superfluous and the handcrafted. It also was a sign of the
reform movement which chose aesthetic reduction enriched by craft elements over the
machine-made surface complication that characterized the products of the industrial revolution. Because it was so readily made ornament had become an element of all classes of
consumer objects, although as Ruskin and later Veblen pointed out, there was more honor
in the expense of costly hand-labor than in cheap machine-made decoration. Still,
Victorians were certain that more was more. Post-Victorians such as Price saw the potential merit in less—although not necessarily to the ultimate reduction of Mies' dictum that
less could truly be more. But certainly as a means of arriving at a new style appropriate to
the new age, the paring away of extraneous elements could be a method. When young
Philadelphia architects had adopted the historical styles that brought them into line with
their east coast peers, Victorian surface complication was merely supplanted by an alternate historically derived overlay of Gothic half-timber and stone carving, Renaissance
compound arches framing windows and doors, and classical columns and ornamental
detail. The palette of Philadelphia architects lightened too, although not to the extent
that limestone and marble came to predominate for house facades as in certain streets in
New York City. Philadelphians remained too aware of the redness of their colonial city to
abandon totally the color scheme of their forefathers, even though tan and orange-brown
brick as well as tan stucco became popular for a time.

In the case of Rose Valley it is likely that the aesthetic simplification that characterized the early buildings was a response to economics and time. During the first year,
with the goals of quickly and economically renovating the Guest House and the other
small houses of the village, Will turned to the simple local palette of fieldstone and stucco
of the barns and farmhouses. Perhaps he had attended Elmer Grey's lecture on the merits
of the vernacular at the T-Square Club. Undoubtedly he would have been aware of Wilson

Eyre, Jr.'s turn toward simplification in Philadelphia suburban houses. On the cottages and Guest House Will avoided the fictive overlay of half-timber which had typified the stuccoed surfaces of the Overbrook houses for the Drexel Company, or of his own recent house, Kelty.

Beyond the relation of the building to the client was the larger issue of the relation of architecture to society. In the 1902 lecture Price hypothesized that "we have come to a time when neither the civic nor the religious is the ideal around which we build our civilization, but the individual, the domestic."[30] This idea can be traced to Andrew Jackson Downing's *The Architecture of Country Houses* (1850) and before that to Ralph Waldo Emerson, both of whom understood the relationship between the core values of American society and the buildings that served the people. To Downing republican social values formed the underpinnings of domestic architecture. Paralleling this notion was the concept that a house could express the individuality of its owner, an idea that had long been accepted for royalty but had not been applied to the middle classes. Houses built along these lines contrasted with houses in the English countryside which served as markers of the permanence of social strata in their plan and size, suggesting that life courses were unchanging save for a fortunate few. Americans expected social change and by the middle of the nineteenth century had come to expect the imprint of personality and interests on architecture as well. To Price, working in Philadelphia for middle-class clients, cost became a primary consideration that shaped design: "We do not often have palaces to build; we are not working for Gould or J. Pierpont Morgan, but for each other, the average community which we find around us."[31] Though Will was perfectly happy to accept commissions from men of fabulous wealth, including Alan Wood, John Gilmore, Charles Schoen, and Frank Wheeler, most of his Rose Valley clients were from the "average community."

For the 1902 lecture Price returned to the principle of unity that characterized English villages he had seen and drawn in 1896. This could be achieved Will suggested, by using local field stone together with stucco, "the roughest sort of dashed work or pebble dash" which would make for handsome houses that would fit into their setting. Its greatest value was architectural, "It gives us mass, it does not chop the surface up."[32] Despite having mass and simplification as a goal, Price acknowledged that it was all to easy too slip into historical overlays.

> Of course we use a great deal of timberwork down with us, and I am sorry to say we very
> seldom use it honestly; most of our timberwork being stuck on the outside of the house
> and not part of the structure. That, of course, is inexcusable, there is no possible excuse

30. Price, "A Philadelphia Architect's Views on Architecture," 27.

31. Price, "A Philadelphia Architect's Views on Architecture," 27.

32. Price, "A Philadelphia Architect's Views on Architecture," 27–28.

for it, so far as I can see—I do it myself, but I am ashamed of it and I am trying to stop.[33]

Finally, in his wide-ranging talk, Price addressed the great topic that concerned Rose Valley and its artisans, the role of the machine in manufacturing and the resulting aesthetic value of its products.

> This machinery question is a vital one, and one we cannot ignore—as to where we can drawn the line on the machine, I was trying to make a distinction, and I think I can make one. I think you will agree that the place where we can draw the line is this—just so long as a machine is a tool with which a man works, it is a benefit, no matter how highly it may become developed; but the moment it ceases to be a tool, and becomes a mere automatic machine, into which material is fed, and out of which a product comes without any volition of the man who is working it, then that machine becomes an immoral affair, and the product of it becomes absolutely worthless as far as the art world is concerned. That seems to me to be the place to draw the line.[34]

This was Morris' position and one that was shared by most of the Arts and Crafts movement. So long as the machine enabled the worker to be effective and enhanced the process, it could be an artist's tool; when it was part of a system of production simply to make multiple versions of someone else's idea, it no longer has merit.

The problem, in an age of cheap, mass-produced ornament, was whether the architect could guide his client toward simplification.

> Now can we get the people we build for, and the people we build with, to go with us and return—if it be a return—towards a more simple method of construction? I think we can. I think that there is one way we can do it if no other, but it would be a drastic method. That would be to cut off all the ornament, make the thing absolutely simple and plain, with only the essential features in it. I think we can go a step farther, and instead of cluttering up the inside or the outside of our houses with numberless mouldings and brackets...without any special meaning except that our ancestors or forefathers did it in marble or some other material, for I am afraid that is the reason we put most of those things in, we can eliminate most of these things and substitute for them extreme honest simplicity in construction, and a little bit of good carving, for we still have the carvers left to us, and some of the carvers and decorators are really artists and artisans. That seems to me a most practical line of elimination. Cut the quantity of it down to the quick, if need be, to get the quality a little where we want it. We can do that, and the people will go with us,

---

33. Price, "A Philadelphia Architect's Views on Architecture," 28.
34. C. R. Ashbee, Memoir, I (December 1900), 241–242, Victoria and Albert Museum, London. In Chicago Ashbee reported on meeting Frank Lloyd Wright and quoted his view of the machine. "My God," he said, "is Machines and the art of the future will be the expression of the individual artist through the thousand powers of the machine."

for they are just as sick of the uninteresting wall-papers and truck that their houses are cluttered up with as we are. I have had no difficulty in getting people to allow me to simplify their houses for them. The tendency of ornament comes from the architect rather than from the client almost every time. Of course there are exceptions and people want a lot of gaudy ornamentation and display; and I think in these cases we had better give in to them. I think that is possibly the best way to cure them. It is a little rough on us, but I think we had better suffer it if we can make architecture possible in the doing of it.[35]

Will expanded these ideas a few years later in article entitled "Choosing Simple Materials for the House." He began:

The advantages of the use of common and rough local materials seem to be to be three-fold. First, they are cheap; second, they are easily obtainable; and third, they are beautiful. Burroughs says somewhere that a house should be built of materials picked up at hand and in a large degree he seems to me to be right. Not only for sentimental and practical reasons but because it tends to produce types—tends towards a pleasing homogeneity in local style that is altogether good.[36]

Recalling his experience of English villages, Will raised the banner of regionalism.

We have boxed the compass architecturally, raking over the world's scrap heap of styles and the supply man's scrap heap of materials and, as a consequence, urban and rural districts alike are for the most part marred not only by a total lack of local significance in architecture, but by any lack of homogeneity in style, material or color.[37]

As to style, where he had his own choice as architect he argued that the true purpose of ornament was "the expression of ideals" rather than the art of some far-off people. Seeing the political meaning behind the unthinking adoption of English forms, Price rejected their cost and their character with the ultimate goal of building for the American present.

We are building cut stone English gardens which stand for generations of landlordism and servitude. We are building marble Italian gardens which stand for the exclusions of the palace. And later on we will build American gardens which will stand for democracy and homeliness....

Build your house and your garden (for your house is not a home without a garden, or your garden a garden without a house), to fit the needs of yourself and your friends.... Build it simply, for we are at heart a simple people, joying in the doing rather than the having. Build it of the materials next at hand, and you will wake up some day to

---

35. Price, "A Philadelphia Architect's Views on Architecture," 28.

36. William L. Price, "Choosing Simple Materials for the House," *Country Houses and Gardens of Moderate Cost*, ed. Charles Osbourne (Philadelphia: House and Gardens, 1907), 33. The same article appeared under a slightly different title, "The Value and Use of Simple Materials in House Building," *House and Garden*, 8, no. 3 (October 1905).

37. Price, "Choosing Simple Materials for the House," 33.

7. Workers designing fireplace in Rose Valley Guest House, c. 1902
(Photograph attributed to M. Hawley McLanahan; Price and McLanahan Archives, George E. Thomas Collection)

8. Alice Barber Stephens' barn before it was adapted into her house, c. 1903
(Price and McLanahan Archives, George E. Thomas Collection)

find that we have an American architecture, as typical and expressive as the world has known.[38]

Such architecture took time for nature to smooth and soften its materials, and for those in haste Will scornfully chided, "If you have not time to wait, build in a suburb." But by using local materials, "simple backing-stone walls, your rough plaster, and your weather-stained wood," the effect would not be of poverty and meanness, but one which would bear proof of its native character.

There was another advantage to simple materials. They gave the workers who built the house the opportunity to involve themselves with the process, to add their own lives to the building. Having worked in the Furness office, where a specification could be as simple as "For the beam ends, give me your best detail," Price remembered the era before the taste for historical style made every detail dependent on precedent and when craftsmen knew the character of their materials because of generations of contact. (*fig. 7*) This tradition had been lost, and Price hoped that it could be reborn.

> But don't think when you have taken time and thought as to plan, that the work is done. You will have to give the mason, the joiner, and the plasterer a chance, and by giving him a chance, I don't mean signing a contract with him. If he cannot add some touch of individuality to his work, you have planned in vain. You must coax his interests into your walls. You must make him a mason, not merely a fulfiller of specifications. You cannot specify the unknown individuality that must be built stone by stone into your wall. You say that you cannot find such skillful and artistic masons? Have you tried? But we have made him very shy, and with our exact specifications, our deadly detail and superior knowledge, we have well-nigh crushed him out.... This feast of simplicity to which I ask you is no unattainable mecca of the rich. It does not lie in palace land, but is here, holding out its hands to rich and poor alike, in every countryside, when we shall have sense enough to hear its call.[39]

For the ultimate test of worth, Will proposed that one "Accept Morris's comprehensive summing up: 'Have nothing in your house that you do not know to be useful, and believe to be beautiful.'"[40] Finally Price drew on eastern design, another culture that had found beauty in simplicity.

> The Japanese have taught us, among some other things, the beauty of the grain of even the commonest woods. The Japanese not only know the beauty of simple backgrounds for their priceless treasures, but they also know that the value of this beauty is enormously enhanced by the fact that the treasures they show have no competitors. How we "civilized" people envy them and how little we emulate their methods![41]

---

38. Price, "Choosing Simple Materials for the House," 37.
39. Price, "Choosing Simple Materials for the House," 39.
40. Price, "Choosing Simple Materials for the House," 39.
41. Price, "Choosing Simple Materials for the House," 41.

Despite the overarching theme of simplicity derived from the vernacular, Will added one other important idea that turned toward the ideals that would shape the later architecture of Rose Valley. He wrote: "Architecture to be fit, must fit need and purpose and environment—fit the living purpose, not the dead precedent."[42] He had opened with a similar idea in the 1902 talk, "There is only one thing worse than ignoring precedent, and that is following it."[43] This was Price's dilemma: his training and culture were aimed at the past, but revival for its own sake went against the goals of the new society in which he lived.

Rose Valley Architecture

In the summer of 1904 *The Artsman* reported that the Guest House had been the home of the well-known illustrator Alice Barber Stephens and her husband, Charles Stephens, the cousin of Frank, and himself a well-known illustrator of Native-American themes. *The Artsman* added:

> Mr. and Mrs. Alice Barber Stephens have finally determined to settle in the Valley. They have got control of the land on the right of the road leading down from Moylan to the shops. The old barn remaining on the property will be remodeled for a studio. A residential extension will be added with Will Price to design the new building.[44]

Next June *The Artsman* reported that Charles and Alice Barber Stephens had "taken full possession of their house, which under Price's inspiration has become a significant factor in the landscape."[45] (*fig. 8*) In the house that was added to the barn, Price demonstrated his first, still-hesitant steps away from history toward the vernacular. A second story was added to the barn which, because it faced north and south, provided northern light for each studio. A house was joined to the barn by a projecting octagonal stairwell which separated the home from the artists' work spaces. The open spatial flow of the McLanahan house in St. Davids was again tried here using an entrance vestibule joined to the living room by an open screen and flowing into the dining room through large pocket doors that made it possible to use all but the kitchen as a single open space. Combining adaptive reuse with sensitive addition the Stephens house stepped away from the culture of conspicuous consumption.

Will's text on the house conveys an approach based no longer on history and fashion but on simple facts represented by the needs of the owners and the possibilities of a south-facing site. It was as if, riding back to Moylan on the 5:38 with Frank Furness, he had finally understood Furness' methods of twenty years before.

---

42. Price, "Choosing Simply Materials for the House," 33.

43. Price, "A Philadelphia Architect's Views on Architecture," 27.

44. [Horace Traubel], "From the Artsman Himself,"

The Artsman, 1, no. 10 (July 1904), 393–394.

45. [Horace Traubel], "From the Artsman Himself," *The Artsman*, 2, no. 11 (August 1905), 367.

This house grew, as all houses should grow, out of the needs of the owners and the opportunity offered by the site.

In this particular case the site included an old stone barn, and as part of the demand was for two studios, the whole house may be said to have grown out of these facts. The barn doors fortunately opened north, and changed to windows, gave the desired studio light; the pleasant outlook as fortunately lay to the south and included an old spring house that had crept in between the trunks of giant sycamores and nestled in the hollow so that its roof was nearly level to the ground.

The old barn standing near the road was converted into first and second floor studios, the old timber roof being rebuilt for the upper studio, and large windows and fireplaces being built into the old walls.

The house rambles off from the fireplace end of the studios and is connected to them by an octagon stair hall. It is built in part of field stone so like that in the old barn that it is almost impossible to tell old work from new. The upper part is of a warm grey plaster, and the roof is of red tile. All the detail is as simple and direct as possible, and the interior is finished in cypress stained to soft browns and greys and guilty of no finish other than wax or oil.

The dining room is paneled to the spring of a flat elliptic ceiling which is covered with Japanese gold paper, as are the walls of the living room.

The other rooms are finished with a simple cypress trim, with the walls in plain tones of water color or flowered papers to match the old-time furnishing.

It is what it was intended to be—the home and workshop of busy artists, and the grounds and garden growing up around are of the simple and direct character that might be expected to result from the old environment and the new life growing up within.[46]

This factual character of the plan carried over to the exterior. By subdividing the house into volumes that represented the interior spaces, the scale was reduced to one appropriate to the valley; the studios were in the barn, the stair set off the living room, and a bend in the axis differentiated the dining room from the kitchen beyond. In this distinction of spaces through volume and fenestration, Will returned to the lessons of the Furness houses of the previous generation by describing the separate facts of the house. The plan also followed the ideas that Furness had initiated, away from the cubic mass of a four-square plan that conserved heat, toward a linear plan that gave each room at least two exposures.[47] The walls of the house followed the lines of the stonework of the barn, but

---

46. William L. Price, "Mrs. Alice Barber Stephens' Studio, Rose Valley, Moylan, Pa.," typescript, Price and McLanahan Papers.

47. While Will was in the Furness office, the Shipley house was constructed which marked the new linear direction. See George E. Thomas and others, *Frank Furness: The Complete Works* (New York: Princeton Architectural Press, 1991), 235–236.

above the first story shifted to stucco over hollow tile, below a red tile roof. Different window shapes reflected the various uses of the rooms and were the principal exterior ornament. Apart from a Mercer tile thunderbird set into the end of the barn toward the road, the new house was entirely without extraneous carving and trim. On the barn a hint of Gothic detail in a studio window and some half-timber in the added floor of the barn survived the rigorous simplification of Price's design. The result was a house that related to the regional vernacular while meeting modern needs.[48]

Despite his own expressed preferences Will continued to receive commissions for vast houses in the Gothic manner, although how much suffering they caused him while curing the clients of their desire for gaudy ornament cannot be told. In Rose Valley Will could persuade his friends to build in a manner that was without ostentation and thus was removed from the directions of the "pecuniary canons of taste," as Thorstein Veblen had termed the goals of the culture of conspicuous consumption. During the next few years four additional significant commissions came to Price and McLanahan in Rose Valley: McLanahan's own home, the large estates of McLanahan's father-in-law Charles Schoen and another Schoen son-in-law Martin R. Jackson, and over the decade, a continuous series of alterations to the stone Victorian home of the Price family. With the backing of his father-in-law McLanahan acquired most of the western side of Rose Valley which included several houses. One was a modest frame farmhouse at the top of the ridge that separates Rose Valley along Vernon Run from the larger valley of Ridley Creek. This would become Hawley McLanahan's house. On the opposite side of the valley was the Civil War-era farmhouse that had been the home of Antrim Osborne, the owner of the mills of Rose Valley's initial industrial phase. It became the home of Charles Schoen.

For the McLanahan's dwelling Will wrapped the old frame farmhouse with a hollow tile exterior which was then stuccoed in the gray plaster that he preferred and ornamented with panels of Mercer tile. The new front was composed of large bays on either side of the central door which was spanned by a massive segmental arch that joins the front plane of the bays. This gave the facade a broad, sculptural treatment that recalled the contemporary work of C. F. A. Voysey and, to a lesser extent, C. R. Ashbee. Anticipating the future directions of the Price and McLanahan hotels and railroad stations, the McLanahan house marked the beginning of using Rose Valley houses as a test laboratory for form and detail. Within, massive stone fireplaces enlivened an otherwise simple interior.

---

48. The Stephens house was among the most published of Price and McLanahan's domestic commissions. See Mabel Tuke Priestman, "Alice Barber Stephens' Unique Suburban Home," *Suburban Life*, 6, no. 1 (January 1908), 11–13. This was republished with different illustrations in Priestman, *Artistic Homes* (Chicago: A. C. McClurg & Company, 1910), 32–41. See also Charles DeKay, "A Studio House in Rose Valley," *Arts and Decoration* (March 1911), 198.

Will's house was a different story. It had been built in the 1890s as a conventional square-plan Victorian of the local gray stone below a slate roof with little to recommend it as design. Given the amount of work that was flooding through the office and the additional time required to help keep Arden and Rose Valley on track, the fact that Will found time to adapt what was otherwise an acceptable house is telling. By carrying interior walls on concrete beams, Will opened the closed cells of the Victorian house. Over the next few years he added handsome concrete and tile fireplaces. In the dining room, which as always was the center of his home, he lopped the corners of the room with built-in cabinets and fireplaces to create an elongated octagonal space. This he spanned with a geometric beam system and lighted with a segmental-headed window. In this one room in his own house he could be in a space of his own design.

A Rose Valley Visitor: C. R. Ashbee

In 1908 C. R. Ashbee made his second tour of the United States, visiting the many American communities that were exploring the Arts and Crafts. He had been to the United States before in 1900 centering his visit on the east coast. In the fall of the year Ashbee reached the Philadelphia area where he toured the Drexel Institute (now Drexel University) and Swarthmore College before going to Bryn Mawr College which he found attractive for its intensity, but a bit surprising in its "Anglo Mania."[49] At the end of the first trip Ashbee traveled as far west as Chicago where he encountered Hull House's Jane Addams, "The embodiment of moral power." There he saw the new Rockefeller-funded University of Chicago which he dismissed as "a miserable affair when looked at...as the expression of a great idea in building." He concluded: "No wonder the younger architects, like Lloyd Wright, kick at Tradition."[50]

On his second journey to the United States Ashbee was interested in American changes to the Arts and Crafts idea. He remarked on the democratic energy and commitment in producing art objects which could be afforded by a larger population rather than the precious hand-crafted objects of the English Arts and Crafts movement which remained rooted in Ruskin's classism. After all one of the consequences of Ruskin's demand for honesty in materials and workmanship was either the perpetuation of low wages to keep such crafts affordable or the exclusion of the growing middle classes from the arts because they could not afford them. Although Rose Valley's furniture had been so

---

49. C. R. Ashbee, Memoir, I, 207–210. Ashbee quoted M. Carey Thomas, Bryn Mawr College's dean, as referring to Swarthmore as a "Matrimonial Agency," and reported that at Bryn Mawr "marriage is discouraged, and indeed the life is made so comfortable, interesting and luxurious, that I can understand girls staying on permanently as many do, under the autocratic rule of Miss Thomas" (210).
50. Memoir, I, 232.

9. William P. Jervis' pottery workshop with molds and finished pots, c. 1903 (Price and McLanahan Archives, George E. Thomas Collection)

10. Villa in Italian style, from Andrew Jackson Downing, *The Architecture of Country Houses* (New York: D. Appleton, 1850)

11. Price and McLanahan, office and cottage for Fiske Warren, Harvard, Massachusetts, c. 1913, from *American Architect*, 105, no. 2000 (22 April 1914)

expensive that only the wealthiest could afford it, William P. Jervis' Rose Valley pottery had taken the opposite tack, relying on molded clay forms to save the time at the wheel, making it possible instead to lavish effort on the glazes. (*fig. 9*) In a similar vein the Rose Valley shops had accommodated machine tools which, so long as they were directed by the craftsman rather than driving the schedule of production, were viewed as an asset.

In the fall of 1908 Ashbee reached Rose Valley.[51] Despite the closing of the shops a year before, Ashbee professed himself delighted with what had attempted there. Months earlier in an entry in his memoir, Ashbee had situated Will Price prominently on a page that reviewed the first decade of the century, along with Joseph Fels and the Single Tax movement.

> In that first decade of the century, the fantastic absurdities of American life were as much in evidence as the realities. Senator Clarke of Montana, "The Copper King," was building his crazy house on Vth Avenue in as many styles, ancient and modern as his architect could collect; old Professor Sumner at Yale was generalizing charmingly about "Mores; "Rose Valley Price," the Quaker architect was momentarily bitten and fighting with Joseph Fels for the Single Tax.[52]

Ashbee's November entries were devoted to Will and Rose Valley.

> "Rose Valley Price," the architect, is really fine; there is something prophetic about him. He is perpetually rising up and cursing the system. I forget which of the minor prophets had a sense of humor, but he has. You see it in the quaint twitch of his ugly Socratic little nose, and he flashes illuminating anecdotes and witticisms at you.
>
> He has, like most of us who have studied the arts and crafts and feel the humanity underlying the movement, the conviction that if the movement is to find itself, it must speak in a voice of its own and not in the language of back numbers, the beaux arts, the "old Colonial." His own beautiful handling of Reid's [sic] Store in Walnut Street [sic] is a good expression of the man—and he has no patience with the work of McKim and White and others who stand for traditional culture. He reminds me often of Lloyd Wright. It is a fine trait that impatience of the past, but only when it has genius or taste as a starting point.[53]

The two men must have walked around center city Philadelphia and seen Frank Furness' and McKim, Mead & White's Girard Bank because Ashbee recalled:

> He pulled me up sharp the other day near the new marble banking house of the Girard Trust, or whatever it is called, pointed a jeering finger at the big dome—asked derisively why bankers when they dropped into architecture had to "do it in classical temples," and then added, "that bloody dome is so tight that if it were pumped up another couple of feet it would go pop."[54]

---

51. For a more complete account of Ashbee's American tour see Crawford, 151, 213–214.

52. Memoir, III, 8.

53. Memoir, III, 41.

54. Memoir, III, 41.

A trip to Rose Valley followed which opened political topics.

> There's room for the scholars as well as the socialists and its good to hob a nob with both.
> Price has an entirely healthy and original view of life. He took us out to Rose Valley to
> spend Saturday to Monday there, and we enjoyed it. It was a wild and simple and refined
> life they were leading—a sensible and human Bohemia. He read us long extracts from Mr.
> Dooley over the supper table, took us to one house after another of his neighbors and
> friends, till we were bewildered with new faces.
>
>   Price and Dr. Holmes, his brother-in-law and I plunged intermittently into
> socialism, aesthetics and single tax. "Things'll come through all right," he would cry, "if
> we could only quit this fool life we're all of us leading." I think he has gotten a little farther
> than most.[55]

Over the weekend they visited Swarthmore College which Ashbee had not seen since
1900. Ashbee noted: "Price took us to Swarthmore. It was disappointing." The new
Carnegie Library built on the campus was not to Ashbee's liking, and, worse, it was not
by his friend.

> It is admissible for a mere aesthete like myself to lie, when his whole philosophy of life is
> challenged over a tea cup, but I hate to see it in a Quaker. Why can't they let architecture
> alone, stick to their own tradition of simplicity and resources instead of—well! Price and I
> withdrew into a corner of the library to talk it out together, the skimped stone quoins of
> the building etc.
>
>   "Quakerism is played out," said Price, "it won't look the facts of life in the face
> any more. It's full of sham and humbug and pretense." "That's a bit hard," I said, "but they
> ought to have let you build their library for them—as thee's a friend." He laughed and we
> both longed for old John Woolman again to upset the tea cups and dance on the ice
> creams.[56]

❧ *Rose Valley: Transition from Workshop to Artist Community*

The industrial phase of Rose Valley lasted only a few years. Between 1904 and 1905 a pottery shop run by William P. Jervis operated in a small addition to the Guild Hall which
also housed a bookbindery and studios for artists such as Howard Stratton, Alice Barber
Stephens, and Francis Day. Labor discontent, in large measure caused by the continuously
rising wages of Philadelphia, made it impossible for the shops to pay at the same level.
The closing of the shops in 1906 changed the tenor of the community from one that had
something of the paternalism of Elbert Hubbard's East Aurora or Gustav Stickley's
Craftsman Farms to one that more nearly represented the social and political goals which

---

55. Memoir, III, 42.   56. Memoir, III, 44.

had interested Price for a decade. Price was able to reduce his own time commitment as others in the community took increasingly leading roles. But a dark cloud loomed, for the lack of manufacturing meant that the original loans for Rose Valley were not being paid. By 1911, when it was clear that the loans could not be met, Hawley McLanahan and Charles Schoen proposed the first of a series of bail-outs by purchasing all of the land of the community with the exception of the Guild Hall and an acre and a half of land around it which would be rented at market value, a fee which was further reduced when it was announced that the Schoens and McLanahans would pay two-thirds of the rent. In August of that year the sale was completed.[57]

Ever the real estate operator McLanahan proposed to subdivide the large hillside framed by Rose Valley Road and Possum Hollow Road into a "garden suburb" of houses the sale of whose lots would pay off the original debt of the community. There was the chance that such a change would introduce the liabilities of railroad suburbs into the community, but, by hiring Will as the architect and by establishing limits on the sales of lots to prohibit speculation, they hoped to avoid larger problems which had prompted the formation of the community in the first place. For Will the houses presented a remarkable opportunity. For the first time he could design essentially without a client, with full design freedom. Coming at a time when he was finally breaking free from historicism in his designs for hotels and apartment houses in the midwest and along the shore, it was a significant opportunity. The houses were intended to attract the type of people who had originally founded the valley, and thus were of modest scale and design. By using contemporary industrial materials, particularly hollow tile for walls and partitions, costs could be held in check. The first group of five houses consisted of two pairs of mirror image houses plus a house of more elaborate plan. The pair closest to the road took the form of a T plan with a broad gable across the wing of the T, while the rear pair, overlooking Vernon Run valley, were based on a linear one-room-deep plan, recalling Downing's mid-nineteenth-century designs for Italianate villas in their massing. (*fig. 10*) The middle house was more complex, taking the form of a W in plan, since been enhanced by additions at the ends of the wings. Despite differences in plan and size, each of these houses shared Rose Valley's common vocabulary of materials and forms. Local stone formed the foundation and was woven into upper walls to the zone of the base of the porch. Walls were stuccoed with the tan sand from the creek and ornamented with geometric panels of Mercer tile, some of which were designed in Rose Valley fashion by the workers themselves. In their economy they continued the line of investigation that Price had begun almost a generation before

57. The history of the collapse of the community is told by Eleanor Price Mather, "The Arts and Crafts Community" and "The Early Folk," *A History of Rose Valley*, ed. Peter Ham and others, 9–44. See also Chronicles, especially the meetings for December 1912 and March 1913.

for *The Ladies' Home Journal*, but where the earlier houses had been conventional and based on historical forms and details, these were strikingly original, shorn of historic detail, simplified in form, and clearly modern in intent. That Price's intentions were toward a modern architecture suited to his time and place is clear from the text published with details of the houses.

> No idea of false construction is to be gathered from any of the details. Under a present day impulse, new structural conditions as exemplified in concrete and hollow tile have been accepted. These demand a specific surface treatment and naturally point the way to the accomplishment of a plastic art whereby perhaps an indigenous expression, typically American is to become established.[58]

As Price neared his fiftieth birthday he had found his artistic direction, one that resulted in modest modern houses for American artisans and young professionals. At the same time he was making a similar definitive shift in his designs for large buildings. The path for domestic architecture which had begun as a response to regional character and vernacular design had finally reached the fundamental principles of reflecting one's own time in "a plastic art" with an "indigenous expression, typically American."

In the final issues of *The Artsman* in early 1907, Will published the text of a lecture on the subject of modern architecture. He continued the theme in an article in Gustav Stickley's *The Craftsman*, which had become the organ for a beguiling mixture of political exhortation, design theory, and household design and decor. Will Price's article, "Is American Art Captive to the Dead Past?" fit the tone of the magazine as well.[59]

Will began by asking "How long... will the Renascence hold us in its grasp?" It was a question that could have been asked by William Morris or more recently by Frank Lloyd Wright. Morris' lecture in 1889 to the Arts and Crafts Society on "Gothic Architecture" found wide circulation and was published four years later. It forms the basis for much of Will's interpretation of history, and one suspects of Wright's as well. Will had been a confirmed Gothicist in his early work and still believed in its inherent virtues as advanced by Morris and English historians who saw in the Gothic a "frank expression of materials and the wants and customs of their own day."[60] As late as 1910 Wright's views were similar: "A revival of the Gothic Spirit is needed in the art and architecture of modern life."[61] In his essay Price advocated the "rock-ribbed Gothic of Whitman" rather than

---

58. Price and McLanahan, "Group of Houses at Moylan, Rose Valley, Pa.," *The Brickbuilder*, 20, no. 9 (September 1911), 185.

59. William L. Price, "Is American Art Captive to the Dead Past?" *The Craftsman*, 15, no. 1 (February 1909), 515–519.

60. William Morris, "Gothic Architecture," lecture given to the Arts and Crafts Society, 1889; published by Kelmscott Press, 1893; republished in G. D. H. Cole, ed., *William Morris: Selected Writings* (London: Nonesuch Press, 1948), 475–493.

61. Frank Lloyd Wright, *Ausgefürhte Bauten und*

"all of the curled darlings and simpering niceties of a borrowed culture." Quoting Oscar Wilde that "The educated man's idea of art is always the art that has been; the artist's idea of art is the art that is to be," Will demanded that artists leave their "dead cloisters" and "come out in the free air." He concluded:

> If our American life is half-way worth the boast we make for it, why is it not good enough for our inspiration?
>
> Carlyle says, "Originality does not consist in being different but in being sincere." And there is not only the very soul of individuality in art, but also of style in art. For if we were sincere, our work would vary from type as we individually vary, but also as we are much alike in the same environment, so our sincere work would have much in common, and that is the thing we call Style. Not a fixed form, but the expanding expression of a common impulse. So if we were sincere as we are like our fathers, so would our work follow theirs, not as imitation but as like expression, and as we are different and beyond our fathers, so would our work be different and beyond their work.
>
> Not the feeble, book-learned Colonial of our day, for we are no longer colonists, but the full-blooded expression of a giant Democracy; the strong, rude conqueror, not the feeble dependent of an outworn social creed. And some there are groping for this real Renascence, not a resurrection mind you, but the re-birth of art. Here and there a free man lifts his head. Here and there a potter lifts his clay out of the common style....
>
> Look at your achievements. Look at the architectural triumphs of even ten years ago, and ask yourselves if they will live, if they have anything to say, any new thoughts to thunder down the hollow vault of time. We are a people in the forming, and so have all peoples been when they really lived, and we must build for the moment and go on, and if you don't care to build for the scrap heap, don't build, for it will all go there. But if you build truly, some stones shall stand, some detail will cling to the robes of art and become part of the great new whole. Better to lay two bricks together in the new way that tells a tale, than to build a temple for the money changers with no thought in it less than two thousand years dead.[62]

In this article the constituent elements of Price's theories can be deduced: certainly from nineteenth-century England, John Ruskin, Thomas Carlyle, and William Morris and more recently George Bernard Shaw and Oscar Wilde. From the United States Price knew Walt Whitman and Ralph Waldo Emerson, sources which he wold have discovered in Furness' office as well as the writers of the American Arts and Crafts movement who were published in *The Artsman*. They form a rich array of sources indeed but the style of

Entwurfe (Berlin: Wasmuth, 1910); reprinted in Bruce Brooks Pfeiffer, *Frank Lloyd Wright: Collected Writings*, Vol. 1, 1894–1930 (New York: Rizzoli, 1992), 110.

62. Price, "Is American Art Captive to the Dead Past?" 518.

the first pair of houses of the Rose Valley Improvement Company, with their planar walls, corner towers with overhanging roofs, and asymmetrical form, suggest another source, one that became apparent in another piece that Will wrote for *The Craftsman,* "The House of the Democrat." That source was Andrew Jackson Downing.

"The House of the Democrat" was published in *The Craftsman* in 1910, and republished in Gustav Stickley's *More Craftsman Homes* in 1912. There Price returned to the antihistoricist theme of the 1909 article which in turn had become Stickley's own thesis in the introduction to the book, "A Word About Craftsman Architecture." Stickley stated the goals of Craftsman design as "a style of building suited to the lives of the people...the result not of elaboration, but of elimination...[that] is the secret of beauty in architecture." Stickley concluded that "There can be no doubt in my mind that a native type of architecture is growing up in America."[63] This was the theme of Price's article which followed Stickley's introduction. "The House of the Democrat" brought together Price's principal ideas—the rejection of historical forms that spoke of "slavery or serfdom—and advocated an architecture that represented the values of American democracy. Paraphrasing Downing's thesis of a half-century before about the appropriateness of the villa as a representation of the values of the republic, Price called for homes in the country in forms that would rely on the beauty of nature for their ornament.

> When at last we shall build the house of the democrat, its doors shall be wide and unbarred, for why should men steal who are free to make? It shall be set in a place of greenery, for the world is a large place and its loveliness mostly a wilderness; it shall be far enough away from its next for privacy and not too far for neighborliness; it shall have a little space knit within a garden wall; flowers shall creep up to its warmth, and flow, guided but unrebuked over wall and low-drooped eaves. It shall neither be built in poverty and haste, nor abandoned in prosperity; it shall grow as the family grows; it shall have rooms enough for the privacy of each and the fellowship of all....
>
> The rooms of his house shall be ample and low, wide-windowed, deep-seated, spacious, cool by reason of shadows in summer, warm by the ruddy glow of firesides in winter, open to the wistful summer airs, tight closed against the wintry blasts, a house, a home, a shrine; a little democracy, unjealous of the greater world....[64]

More than fifty years earlier Downing had sketched the same themes in remarkably similar phrases.

> In this most cultivated country life, every thing lends its aid to awaken the finer sentiments of our nature. The occupations of the country are full of health for both soul and

---

63. Gustav Stickley, "A Word About Craftsman Architecture," *More Craftsman Homes* (New York, 1912; reprinted New York: Dover Publications, 1982), 7–9.

64. William L. Price, "The House of the Democrat," in Stickley, 7–9.

body.... The heart has there, always within its reach, something on which to bestow its affections. Happy is he who lives this life of a cultivated mind in the country....

The man of sentiment or feeling will seek for that house in whose aspect there is something to love. It must nestle in, or grow out of the soil. It must not look all new and sunny but show secluded shadowy corners. There must be nooks about it where one would love to linger, windows, where one can enjoy the quite landscape leisurely; cozy rooms where all domestic fireside joys are invited to dwell. It must, in short, have something in its aspect on which the heart can fasten upon.... [65]

Linking ideas of "sentiment" and "feeling" with the call for a house to "nestle in, or grow out of the soil," Downing established the goals of the American home which are derived from the ancestor of our homes, the English cottage. In Rose Valley, from the Guest House of 1901 to the Improvement Company houses of 1910, Will was successful in persuading his clients and friends to build according to regional character with inspiration from the present. When other architects began to design everything in a house even to the hostess' dress, Will persuaded his friends and relatives that it was better to build a shared garden and to join in communal activities. The few highly individualistic houses of the community, culminating with Howell Lewis Shay's immense Gothic mansion of 1923, missed the essential point of Rose Valley. In the shared vocabulary of cottages and mansions, Guild Hall and gates, there was a representation of community. This need is still longed for today as evidenced by such end-of-the-century manifestations as Celebration and Seaside, Florida. How much richer these recent communities might be if they manifested the communal engagement of a folk-mote that chose activities through consensus; if they were designed and built by the members of the community who were urged to leave their imprint on their houses and gardens; and if they worked toward the idea that a community was about shared interests and not equal bank accounts.

Utopian Epilogue
In 1930 Upton Sinclair wrote a brief autobiography that recounted his experiences to that point, and included an extensive account of his year and a half as a resident of Arden after he had gained fame as the author of *The Jungle*.[66] He described his tiny cottage built with the funds from that best-selling book and constructed for him by Frank Stephens, a house which ended up costing more than twice its estimate. He remembered with fondness Scott

65. Andrew Jackson Downing, *The Architecture of Country Houses* (New York: D. Appleton, 1850), 258–263.
66. Upton Sinclair, *American Outpost* (New York: Holt, Rinehart & Winston, 1930). After the success of *The Jungle*, Sinclair had helped found a utopian community at Helicon Hall near Fort Lee, New Jersey. It burned in an accidental fire. He then moved to Fairhope, Alabama, another Single Tax community, and then lived at Arden from 1910 to 1912 (230–243).

Nearing, the University of Pennsylvania professor who had dabbled in socialism and then went far beyond in his political questing. And he offered a recollection of Will Price:

> There was Will Price, Philadelphia architect, genial and burly—what a glorious Friar
> Tuck he made—or was it the Sheriff of Nottingham? He sits now in the single taxers'
> heaven, engaged in spirited debate with William Morris over the former's theory of a rail-
> road-right-of-way owned by the public, with anybody allowed to run trains over it! He
> had the misfortune to fall in love with my secretary, and she was in love with some one
> else; a mixup which will happen even in Utopia.[67]

Presumably Will was affected by an Ardensque *Midsummer Night's Dream* or perhaps a momentary response to turning 50.

Rose Valley and Arden were not Price's only experiments. In 1911 Fiske Warren, a fellow Single Taxer and the heir to a New England paper fortune, retained Will to design a house and office in Harvard, Massachusetts. (*fig. 11*) In this New England setting Will looked to the local architectural forms, producing a design that was derived from the vernacular of the New England farmhouse. In vernacular fashion, the front of the house was south facing front and was connected via a long rear wing and breezeway to the garage. Constructed of hollow tile and concrete, like the late houses of Rose Valley, it was in accord with Will's goals of expressing an indigenous American design based on local character. Will was involved in other small communities that Warren supported, serving with Frank Stephens as trustees of Halidon, Maine. Five years later, in the spring of 1916, with World War I occupying center stage, Warren decided that the Single Tax had not been tried on a sufficient scale to test it properly. He began the process of buying a portion of the principality of Andorra in the Pyrenees to attempt a Single Tax country. Among his first acts was to establish a board similar to that which led Arden, and once again Will Price was called upon to serve.[68] Letters from Warren to Price report on initial visits. Perhaps there was to be a community built along Price's plans, but Price's death and the broadening effects of World War I ended the idea.[69]

Rose Valley and Arden anticipated many of the themes about residence, personal expression, and independence that would appear in the United States in the twentieth century. Both communities were removed from urban centers, anticipating the flood of the middle classes to the suburbs and the country that, for better or for worse, has character-

---

67. Sinclair, 232.

68. "Single Tax Experiment in Andorra," *The New York Times* (16 April 1916), sec. 6, p. 5.

69. Although Price's impact on Andorra appears to have been negligible, it is worth noting that the country's economy continues to show the effects of the twentieth-century vision. It remains an oasis of duty-free shopping, which is the basis of the economy. Present guidebooks describe it as "consumerism gone mad." Mark Ellingham and John Fisher, *Spain: The Rough Guide*, 7th ed. (London: Rough Guides, 1997), 661.

ized American planning. More concentrated that Wright's Broadacre City because they were scaled for walking, Rose Valley and Arden have remained effective communities. Both Rose Valley and Arden have continued to attract residents with shared interests anticipating the idealism that enriched the 1960s in the United States. In addition Rose Valley and Arden were nostalgic in recreating the preindustrial village, a quality that resonates in modern suburbs and seashore resorts which now seem escapist, even absurd as the twentieth century ends.

As the twentieth century began, Price sought to build Morris' dream of a humane society in Rose Valley and Arden, communities whose buildings were reflections of the shared goals of their residents. Even though Rose Valley's period of industrial reform and production was brief, it has proven to be a durable model for a community. The theatrical and artistic activities that began as offshoots of Will Price's Seekers After Knowledge, then moved to the upper rooms of his houses in Overbrook and Merion, became the Rose Valley Chorus which continues to the present. (*fig. 12*) The Guild Hall where the community performed Gilbert and Sullivan as well as early plays by W. B. Yeats became the home of Jasper Deeter's repertory theater company and remains as the Hedgerow Theater. During the depths of the Depression, Rose Valley residents formed their own school, built it with their own hands, and staffed it.[70] Rose Valley retains its idiosyncratic variety of houses whose families share common interests if not equal incomes. Descendants of the original residents still live in Rose Valley. Perhaps one day the borough will establish a museum that celebrates this most remarkable American achievement, a shared community that welcomed a modern architecture shaped out of the indigenous materials of its region. Arden has been even more successful, remaining true to its core belief in the Single Tax, and to the social ideas of Henry George, Frank Stephens, and Will Price. Every month community dinners in the Guild Hall draw the diverse community together. Arden was so successful that it has replicated itself as Ardentown in 1922 and Ardencroft in 1950.

The Rose Valley community wrote its own obituary for Will in a November 1916 letter to Emma Price.

> The Rose Valley folk wish to express to Emma Price and her family their sincere appreciation of the value and rare character of her husband, William L. Price, and the unique connection which he had to our community, which had grown about him, following his intense desire to gather around him earnest craftsmen and those sympathetic with the honest handiwork controlled by art and skillfulness.

———

70. Grace Rotzel, *The School in Rose Valley: A Parent Venture in Education* (Baltimore: Johns Hopkins University Press, 1971).

above 12. William L. Price, Rose Valley drum, executed by John Bissegger (Price and McLanahan Archives, George E. Thomas Collection)

right 13. Playbill for "The Artsman," May 1917 (Architectural Archives, Philip N. Price Collection, University of Pennsylvania)

The early history of Rose Valley shows the high standards attained by some of these artists. The spirit of Will Price's ideal never has been lost, though it has grown, as we know, into a rare place for individual homes, rather than a working center.

We wish now to acknowledge our recognition of the fact that through his lifetime, he has sustained the spirit, and we believe has spread the heart of these ideas as far as his creative genius touched or his companionship reached.[71]

The following spring, in May 1917, the community produced for the first time Will's play "The Artsman," which he had written in 1902 in the first bloom of excitement of the making of his community. Performed at the Rose Valley Guild Hall on May 5th and 12th, it sold out and was performed again in June and July. (*fig. 13*)

Horace Traubel remembered Will Price's achievement at Rose Valley and Arden in an essay in *The Conservator* for October 1916:

One of Price's dreams was Arden. The other was Rose Valley. Neither came true in substance. But both of them always came true in his idealism. He always felt sure nothing right could finally lose and nothing wrong could finally win. Other men fought the fights of the flesh, which are the fights of destruction. But he fought the fights of the spirit, which are the fights of salvation. He was against the war that demanded the surrender of the body. He was against the peace which demanded the surrender of the soul. Price was in short uncompromisingly modern in structure. He was all windows and doors. He was a house without walls. He didn't have any earth to stand on. And he didn't have a roof over his head. He appreciated the medieval arts. But he hated art as a tradition. He was willing to listen to the past. But he rejected all inheritance. All time was the morning to him.[72]

71. The letter was signed by Alice Barber Stephens, Cornelia Needles Wright, and Margaret Scott Oliver. It is recorded in the Chronicles, November 1916.

72. Horace Traubel, "An Architect of Buildings and People," *The Conservator*, 27, no. 8 (October 1916), 102–103.

Will Price inspecting Traymore Hotel, spring 1915
(Architectural Archives, Philip N. Price Collection, University of Pennsylvania)

Architecture as the Utterance of the Living

The other force to which I have referred may be called architectural, for it has for its aim the introduction into our architecture the true living spirit of the art and the age, without which it can never be a live national art. I mean the introduction of modern ideas, modern forms, modern methods, adapted to the life, habits, modes of thought, resources and appliances of the day. —*Ernest Flagg*[1]

ᐊ *Progressivism and the Industrial Heartland*

As the nineteenth century ended Philadelphia's young architects in the T-Square Club allied themselves with others of similar interests across the nation to form the Architectural League of America and once again raised the question of whether the United States would produce a national style. Established architects in New York and Boston advocated a trans-Atlantic architecture based on Beaux Arts method and historical detail but many of the League members continued to find purpose in the Victorian goal of expressing the national culture. The location of the League's national conferences in St. Louis in 1898, Cleveland in 1899, Chicago in 1900, and Philadelphia in 1901 not by chance encompassed the industrial heartland, places where the progressive engineering-based culture still contested for leadership of the nation. It was from these cities that the League's membership was principally drawn and it would be there that the siren call of a modern architecture would continue to be heard by young American architects.

The League's goals can be gauged from *The Architectural Annual* which was published in Philadelphia and edited by Albert Kelsey, a graduate of the University of Pennsylvania's architecture program and a veteran of Frank Furness' office. Perhaps recalling

---

1. "A Letter by Ernest Flagg from the Symposium Published in the T-Square Catalogue, 1899," in Albert Kelsey, ed., *The Architectural Annual, 1900* (Philadelphia: The Architectural Annual, 1900), 31.

Furness' views, Kelsey took the editorial position that Beaux Arts and archeological methods were inimical to true modern design, resulting in an architecture that was "servile" and "decadent." In the text accompanying a photo-essay on the new dormitories at the University of Pennsylvania designed by Cope and Stewardson, Kelsey scoffed at the historicizing designs whose seventeenth-century details denoted the "romance of an alien past" when they might have reflected "the poetry of the present." Elsewhere Kelsey quoted Philips Brooks, the rector of Richardson's Trinity Church in Boston, and a former Philadelphian, who asked "What is there anywhere more poetic, anything that more appeals to the imagination than the brilliant advance of natural science?"[2] When the League looked for a champion it found Frank Furness' pupil from a quarter of a century before, Louis H. Sullivan, and in his work saw the expression of the idea that "America is the great modern nation in the external activities, and has already given its name to the wholesale nature of modern methods."[3]

As a champion of the innovative culture that spanned the post-Civil War period to the beginnings of the twentieth century, Louis Sullivan was chosen to address the Cleveland meeting of the League in 1899. Kelsey used Sullivan's text to counter a speech given the same year by Henry Van Brunt, president of the American Institute of Architects. Van Brunt had been a pupil with Frank Furness in Richard Morris Hunt's studio two generations earlier, but in the intervening years had chosen the safe side of design and theory. His address was vacuous and self-congratulatory, lauding the rise of university courses in architecture where design was learned from history, a gradually increasing membership in the Institute, and greater professional control of competitions. He concluded from this evidence that the profession had reached "an era of tranquil and promising development."[4]

---

2. [Albert Kelsey], "Expression in Architectural Forms," *The Architectural Annual, 1900* (Philadelphia: The Architectural Annual, 1900), 19.

3. Although Sullivan was dropping from view at the beginning of the twentieth century, his ideas and work continued to be published in *The Architectural Annual*. The 1901 issue opened with a photograph of Sullivan (10) and included him in a list of "talented and proficient architects as Messrs. Sullivan, Furnace [sic], Eyre, White, Wright, Codman, Stevens, and Spencer" (14). It also included some of the most important papers written on Sullivan during his prime, "Louis H. Sullivan, Thinker and Architect," by A. W. Barker (49–66) and "Louis H. Sullivan, Artist Among Architects, American Among Americans," by Charles Caffin (67–68). The previous issue of *The Architectural Annual* (1900) included

Sullivan's address to the Architectural League, "The Modern Phase of Architecture" (27). Another Philadelphia connection was the publication by the Philadelphia-based *Lippincott's Magazine* of Sullivan's "The Tall Building Aesthetically Considered" in 1896. Americans in the industrial corridor were paid the flattery of European imitation in industrial and architectural imitation. This is missed by Lindy Biggs and most other historians who see the connection via Gropius in the early twentieth century. Lindy Biggs, *The Rational Factory: Architecture, Technology, and Work in America's Age of Mass Production* (Baltimore: Johns Hopkins University Press, 1996), 164–165.

4. [Henry Van Brunt], "President Van Brunt's Address, 1899, *The Architectural Annual, 1900* (Philadelphia: The Architectural Annual, 1900), 30.

There could have been no greater contrast in the speech which Sullivan gave in the same year. Where Van Brunt looked backward, Sullivan raised the banner of the future recalling in his speech the cadences and images of the address given by Frank Furness' father, Reverend William Henry Furness, to the American Institute of Architects when it met in Philadelphia in 1873.

> Perceiving as I do, the momentous sway and drift of modern life, knowing, as I do, that the curtain has risen on a drama, the most intense and passionate in all history, I urge that you throw away as worthless the shopworn and empirical notion that the architect is an artist—whatever that funny word may mean—and accept my assurance that he is and imperatively shall be a poet and an interpreter of the national life of his time.

For Sullivan American architects must achieve an original architecture befitting their heritage:

> you will realize at once and forever that you, by birth, and through the beneficence of the form of government under which you live—that you are called upon, not to betray but to express the life of your own day and generation. You will realize in due time, as your lives develop and expand, and you become richer in experience, that the fraudulent and surreptitious use of historical documents, however cleverly plagiarized, however neatly repacked, however shrewdly intrigued will constitute and will be held a betrayal of trust.[5]

Positioning himself with the young architects of the League, Sullivan closed his address proclaiming, "Your youth is your most precious heritage from the past. I am with you."[6] There were few architects from the younger generation who would join Sullivan in the quest for an architecture of their time.

In the same year that Sullivan addressed the Architectural League, the T-Square Club of Philadelphia held a symposium on modern design and debated whether a national style was possible. Once again the national fashion for historical designs both Gothic and classical came under a blistering attack, this time by Beaux Arts-trained New Yorker Ernest Flagg.

> One of these forces [warring for control of design] may be called archaeological: it is founded upon the dry bones of the past, and in general stands for the unthinking, unreasoning imitation of foreign buildings and ancient styles which were out of date and abandoned by the people who produced them centuries ago, which have nothing to do with modern ideas, and the imitation of which for our use is inconsistent with the dictates of common sense. The Chicago Exhibition was a characteristic product of these methods. The love for this sort of thing, not the thing itself, be it understood, but the modern imitation of it, is fostered by a sickly sentimentalism and a love for the picturesque divorced

---

5. Louis H. Sullivan, "The Modern Phase of Architecture," 27.

6. Sullivan, 27.

from reason, which to satisfy its unhealthy longings would stamp out all virility and substitute imitation for invention in design.[7]

Although there is no proof that Will Price attended these meetings, still the debate certainly stimulated him as he neared his fortieth birthday. It is evident that Sullivan's and Flagg's views were only a trickle in a modest current that ran through the industrial heartland against the tide of history and academicism, both of which had the support of the Institute, the universities, and the national architectural press. Remarkably the national architectural press found nothing to say on the subject of the new century. Another article by Flagg pronounced the end of regional differences thanks to high-speed communication. It was his conclusion that France was in the lead in architecture and clothing fashion "because there is in the French mind a quality which fits it to lead in such matters, for the bondage of the other nations is entirely voluntary."[8] The contrast between Flagg's opposing directions in his articles of 1899 and 1900 was telling in that the articles were aimed at Philadelphia and New York City audiences respectively who had responded to the new century with the equally telling contrast—with delight and wonder in Philadelphia and with a corresponding yawn in New York.

Out of the industrial heartland came a continuing flood of innovation, the hallmarks of the twentieth century, with several crucial inventions occurring in 1903. In that year Henry Ford opened his automobile factory and the Wright brothers flew the first airplane. In Washington Theodore Roosevelt's administration established the principle of federal involvement in land policy and economics. As 1903 began, Will Price turned over his residential practice to his brother Walter and opened a new firm which was announced in *The Philadelphia Inquirer*:

> The architectural business heretofore conducted by William L. Price at 731 Walnut Street is now conducted by Mr. Price and M. Hawley McLanahan under the firm name of Price and McLanahan.[9]

❧ M. Hawley McLanahan: A New Partner

Trained as an architect at Washington College, Martin Hawley McLanahan (1865–1929), Price's new partner, was employed in the real estate firm of Whiteside and McLanahan which rode the crest of middle-class home ownership in the Philadelphia region. Despite his training, there is little evidence that before he joined Will Price, Hawley McLanahan

---

7. "A Letter by Ernest Flagg," 31.

8. Ernest Flagg, "American Architecture as Opposed to Architecture in America," *Architectural Record*, 10 (October 1900), 178–180. Flagg contrasted style (a "slow system of evolution") with the short-term cycles of fashion, arguing, "It is natural that as communication becomes more rapid between different sections, these local differences should disappear, and this is exactly what we find has happened." On this premise it was logical that fashion-conscious Europe would export its styles to the United States (179).

9. *The Philadelphia Inquirer* (9 January 1903), 12.

had ever practiced architecture; indeed, he had hired Will to design his country house at St. Davids Station. His marriage to Elsie Schoen, the daughter of industrialist Charles Schoen, gave McLanahan access to capital and linked him to the industrial culture that dominated Pennsylvania.

With McLanahan as a partner in the architectural practice as well as co-owner of the Rose Valley furniture shops and shortly after a resident of Rose Valley, the two men were linked during the workday, in the evenings, and on holidays. The first act of the new partnership was to rent offices at 1624 Walnut Street, located in a part of the expanding downtown that was growing up around the new City Hall. The space was decorated as befitted its dual role as architectural office and showroom for the Rose Valley shops. A massive oak mantle, carved and constructed by the shops, accented the front room which was also ornamented with pieces of furniture from the shops, Will's collection of medieval weapons, Turkish carpets, and bookcases holding the numerous volumes of the firm's architectural library. (*fig. 1*) It was, in short, the bohemian counterpart to an artist's studio and calculated to attract the right sort of client. Upstairs, in a room reserved for Horace Traubel, *The Artsman*, the literary voice of Rose Valley, was published.

The new partnership and the new location also signaled significant changes in the pattern of commissions. Before 1903 Price's office had primarily served clients with residential projects in the city and its suburbs, with a few side trips to Atlantic City. Beginning in 1903 McLanahan's connections resulted in projects that reached well beyond the city. The first of these were in the center of the state at Hollidaysburg where the McLanahan family had roots.[10] Less than two years after the new practice had begun the firm was designing stations for the Pennsylvania Railroad from Pittsburgh to Chicago and large private residences in principal cities along the route, including Lancaster, Pittsburgh, and Indianapolis. What had been a small, regional domestic architectural practice centered on the decorative and suburban became a national practice that asserted an interest in construction methods and the world of business.

———

10. Unlike the decade of 1893–1902 when we know a lot about Price's practice from the office ledger, no such documents have come down to us for the Price and McLanahan office. However, unlike the early years of the office, which occurred before the publication of the *Philadelphia Real Estate Record and Builder's Guide*, the second phase of practice is well documented by that weekly journal of architecture. In addition Price and McLanahan's photographic archives, acquired at auction in 1969, provide commission numbers, making it possible to determine where gaps occur, and in some instances include office correspondence which was used to wrap glass negatives. The records were apparently sorted in 1925 when McLanahan sold his portion of the business to Ralph Bencker. Most of what survives includes negatives taken by McLanahan as well as earlier office materials. A second cache of material was for a long time stored at the Chrysler Museum in Virginia. It has recently made its way to the Athenaeum in Philadelphia where it is presently being catalogued.

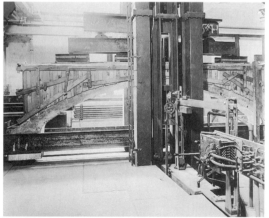

above 1. Price and McLanahan office, 1624 Walnut Street, c. 1906 (Price and McLanahan Archives, George E. Thomas Collection)

left 2. Lesley Testing Laboratory, Towne School of Engineering, c. 1910 (courtesy of University of Pennsylvania Archives)

◁ Reinforced Concrete: A New Material for a New Age

Before 1900 Philadelphians had played an important but understudied role in the evolution of the structural and aesthetic possibilities of iron and steel construction. Frank Furness had used iron trusses and cast-iron columns with expressive intent at the Pennsylvania Academy of the Fine Arts and his skylighted, glass-and-iron-roofed banks on Philadelphia's Bankers' Row showed Centennial visitors the role that new materials of the industrial age could play in expressing the architectural possibilities of the era. Equally significant were the structural innovations developed by the Wilson Brothers, who as the chief designers for the Pennsylvania Railroad were able to spread their professional insights the length of that vast rail system. The standardization movement, initiated in Philadelphia during the Civil War, had entered a new phase with the goal of establishing specifications and capacities for materials based on scientific testing. This movement was centered at the University of Pennsylvania's Towne School of Engineering where much of the testing took place under the eye of Edgar Marburg.[11] Marburg had begun his career in the Edgemore Iron Company of William Sellers and in 1898 was a co-founder of the American section of the International Association for Testing Materials, the forerunner of the American Society for Testing Materials. He took on the task of overseeing technical committees on the standard specifications for iron and steel and on concrete and reinforced concrete. When Robert Lesley, founder of the Association of American Portland Cement Manufacturers, gave funds to the Towne School to establish the Lesley Testing Laboratory, the new material could finally be systematically studied.[12] (fig. 2) During the early years of the twentieth century this basic research gave Philadelphia architects access to information about the material, making the region the nation's center for the use of architectural concrete. The concrete structures that were hallmarks of the work of Louis I. Kahn and the Philadelphia School of the 1950s and 1960s were rooted in the research at the Lesley Laboratory half a century earlier.

Under the influence of Hunt's Biltmore, Price rejected the Furness method of representing modern materials. In the 1890s Price used steel in large houses but his interest was history, and since steel was not used in historic buildings, it was not featured in his designs. Hence, when Will designed the mansion for Alan Wood, whose steel company was one of the giant industries of the region, steel was employed to carry the great spans

---

11. A recent corporate history of the American Society for Testing Materials ignores its links to the Towne School and Professor Marburg.

12. A synopsis of Lesley's career can be found in W. J. Maxwell, comp., *General Alumni Catalogue of the University of Pennsylvania, 1917* (Philadelphia: General Alumni Society, 1917), 68. Lesley graduated with the class of 1871, worked as an assistant editor of the *Philadelphia Ledger*, then became a manager of the Cumberland Cement Works in 1882, before organizing the Association of American Portland Cement Manufacturers in 1902. For ten years he was the vice president of the American Society for Testing Materials and was also a manager of the Franklin Institute.

of the first floor and frame the vast roof, but it was generally invisible behind the oak cladding of the great hall. Although this covert use of steel was in line with the decorous conventions of late nineteenth-century design it contrasted with the Victorian expressionism of Furness and his contemporaries who had celebrated steel's aesthetic and structural possibilities. After the Civil War and spurred by the progressive industrialists of the city, elite Philadelphians reveled in the aesthetics of new material. In the 1870s Charles Wheeler, another local steel industry titan, had dictated that in exchange for his donation toward the construction of Bryn Mawr's Church of the Redeemer, "iron [would] be used and treated as such."[13] Other Victorians such as James P. Sims shaped steel into the exposed flying buttresses of the Holy Trinity Chapel in Philadelphia while Frank Furness made the stairs, columns, and ceiling of the concourse of the Baltimore and Ohio Railroad Terminal from the new material. In a similar mode Furness carried the grand stair in the entrance hall and spanned the reading room of the University of Pennsylvania Library with massive exposed steel girders.

With the Association of American Portland Cement Manufacturers centered in Philadelphia, it was just a matter of time before the question of the appropriate expression of the material would be applied to concrete. It was immediately apparent that reinforced concrete construction had the potential to resolve the important architectural issues of fireproofing and soundproofing while producing structures of sufficient stiffness to resist wind loads and with sufficient strength to rise many stories. Mass concrete, as represented by Carrère and Hasting's late nineteenth-century hotels in St. Augustine, Florida, could be molded and faced to resemble quarried stone but steel-reinforced concrete could be both linear and planar, sculptural and geometric. With the guidance of the scientists at the Towne School of Engineering in the early years of the new century, the physical attributes and structural possibilities of concrete were better understood while its aesthetic nature remained to be determined.

Jacob Reed's Sons' Store

At the end of Price and McLanahan's first year in business, a previous residential client, Alan Reed, commissioned a new clothing retail building in the still shifting downtown. In addition to heading his own clothing manufacturing and retail business, Reed was a member of the board the American Cement Company.[14] Perhaps he saw an opportunity to advocate the new material in which he had an interest. In any event, when his new store was announced, it was reported that it was to be constructed of reinforced concrete and faced in brick. Just before Price received the commission for Reed's new store, he had given the

---

13. This document in the Church of the Redeemer's archives was pointed out by Maria Thompson.

14. Moses King, *King's Philadelphia and Notable Philadelphians* (New York: Moses King, 1901), 71.

lecture for the Ontario Association of Architects in which he stated his belief that the present had its own claims to expression. Jacob Reed's Sons' Store would be his first opportunity to work in the material for which he would be known for the rest of his life.

Just as mid-nineteenth-century architects had detailed cast iron to look like stone and wood, Will initially detailed concrete along the lines of masonry, forming an interior arcade of concrete columns with elaborate basket capitals and spanning openings as if with stone or steel. For the exterior he reverted to traditional masonry with stone columns carrying stone lintels which in turn carried brick walls. Although the skeleton within was reflected in the facade, there was no direct expression on the exterior of the new construction material. The broad mortar joints and rough brick of the upper walls may have alluded to earlier uses of concrete such as the great concrete domes of Byzantine design and the broad mortar joints of the early Christian churches in Ravenna. Ravennate too were the columns and basket capitals in limestone that were incorporated into the exterior. Similar forms were cast for the reinforced concrete columns and capitals of the interior colonnade which were ornamented with Mercer tile. In the sparkle of tile mosaics on the upper levels and in the broad mortar joints of the brickwork there are references to Wilson Eyre's University Museum of the previous decade. (*fig. 3*)

Fortunately Will's background in the Furness office saved him from designing a staid commercial front. The previous summer he would have been reminded of his teacher's method when he was commissioned to add a balcony to Furness' Penn National Bank (whose board included Alan Reed). For that post-Centennial building, designed while Will was in the office, Furness had used overscaled Palladian windows, a long-vanished element of eighteenth-century Philadelphia Georgian, to light the multistory banking room. (*fig. 4*) With the Palladian window restored to convention by the Colonial Revival, Price and McLanahan reverted to Furness' transformation of scale to call attention to the street front of the store by enlarging the window so that it became the entire lower story of the building. What should have been on a wall became the wall itself, an eye-catching reversal of the norm calculated to attract attention.

The shape of the Palladian window had a formal logic of its own for the purposes of the shop front. The great central arch framed a grand entrance while the rectangular openings on either side formed giant display cases for the suits and haberdashery of the men's store. The same forms then extended into the interior as a barrel vault running the length of the store. Carried on concrete columns and beams of a primitive slab-and-beam system spanning the width of the central hall and from the colonnade to the party walls, it denoted the hierarchy of the store display with suits and overcoats in the "nave" and the lower side "aisles" containing the cases for shirts, ties, and the other furnishings of men's dress. Price also evoked Furness' technological showmanship in the interior of the store. Lunettes, introduced into the barrel vault at the interval of the column bay, were lighted from the rear by electric lights which gave the effect of the showroom as free standing. A

above 3. Wilson Eyre, Jr., Walter Cope, John Stewardson and Frank Miles Day, University of Pennsylvania Free Museum of Art and Science (1896), looking south, 1976 (photograph by George E. Thomas)

left 4. Frank Furness, Penn National Bank, 1881 (Architectural Archives, Frank Furness Collection, University of Pennsylvania)

heretofore repressed side of Price's architectural persona, the delight in the possibilities of new materials, appeared whenever the opportunity for striking commercial design offered itself. Although illusionary electrically lighted arcades became a commonplace of commercial design, the potential for plastic, sculptural space of the main shop floor pointed the way to the future. The Jacob Reed's Sons' Store was important in another way too. Where most of the young architects of the T-Square Club had were largely restricted to domestic architecture, the commission for the Jacob Reed's Sons' Store returned Will Price to the commercial arena which continued to be dominated by the older architects. Henceforth, Price and McLanahan would compete with the older firms for the commercial work of the city, wresting the Pennsylvania Railroad commissions from Price's master, Furness and from Furness' contemporaries, the Wilson Brothers. It would be in commercial designs that Price would find the architectural mode that has since defined much of the twentieth century in America.

ᴥ Architect for the Western Division of the Pennsylvania Railroad

Equally as important as acquiring a new partner whose interests lay in the larger commercial sphere was Price's fortunate connection to the city's premier corporation, the Pennsylvania Railroad. Deeply rooted in the engineering culture of Philadelphia, the Pennsylvania Railroad had continued to hire Frank Furness for its urban and suburban stations long after his expressive and personal approach to design had lost favor nationally. Only in New York and, beginning in 1904 in its Western Division beyond Pittsburgh, did the railroad begin to take on the garb that characterized corporate architecture across the nation. In New York City, McKim, Mead & White snatched the downtown Pennsylvania Station from Furness although their brilliant use of steel in the shapes of Roman vaulting was a effective nod to the industrial culture of the nation's largest corporation. At the beginning of the twentieth century, the Western Division of the Pennsylvania Railroad was led by James Turner, Will's brother-in-law.[15]

In the spring of 1905 James Turner commissioned a house from Price and McLanahan in Pittsburgh's stylish east end. The previous fall Turner had commissioned Price and McLanahan to design the first of a series of new railroad stations that would stretch from Pittsburgh to Chicago. The first of these stations, in the growing suburb of

---

15. For James Turner see *Prominent Families: 1913, Pittsburgh, Suburban Districts and Adjacent Towns* (Pittsburgh: The Index Company, 1913), 244, which lists James Turner at 5220 Ellsworth Avenue. See also Charles Rook, ed., *Western Pennsylvanians* (Pittsburgh: Western Pennsylvania Biographical Association, 1923), 62–63. It describes Turner as a Baltimore Quaker who by 1920 was vice president of the Pennsylvania Railroad Company. In 1902 he was elevated to third vice president of the lines west of Pittsburgh, rising to second vice president in 1907. As director of midwestern railroads he was in a crucial position to provide work for Price and McLanahan.

Allegheny, was announced in March 1905 as "unlike any other station building around here. The estimated cost of the proposed buildings will not fall short of $250,000 and may go considerably beyond that."[16] On the site was an 1870s brick Victorian building, a vestige of the adaptation of the German *rundbogenstil* to industrial and railroad buildings. In contrast to the warehouselike volumes that had sufficed for railroad architecture of the earlier generation, Price's design was decked out in stepped gables, bands of limestone set in the brick, and at one corner a stylish clock tower. At first glance its historical detail makes it hard to tell if the building was designed by a New York or Boston historical revivalist but beneath the overlay of ornament there were connections to the international engineering culture. The facade reflects the forms and details of the Flemish Gothic Revival, apparent in two Amsterdam landmarks of the previous generation, P. J. H. Cuijper's Amstel Station and H. P. Berlage's Beurse. A nearly contemporary American example in another industrial town is the federal courthouse and post office in Paterson, New Jersey, which was based on the meat market at Haarlem, Netherlands.[17] As the Richardsonian Romanesque ran its course, the Flemish style became a popular alternative to the Beaux Arts.

Inside, the concourse of the Allegheny Station was a very different story from the civic and historical forms of its exterior. There the architects juxtaposed historic masonry details and modern construction in a way that was Berlage-like in its directness and force. Instead of using Grueby faience tile to clad the structure as they had in the waiting room, the architects simply spanned the concourse with a lattice of giant reinforced concrete beams infilled with operable steel industrial sash on the perimeter and closed in overhead with glass block set into a waffle slab to form skylight panels in the ceiling grid. Neither moldings nor cornices concealed its tough industrial power. As their understanding of the material grew, the architects began to find forms that differentiated concrete from steel, notably in the curving transition from the horizontal to the vertical plane of the column which denoted both the wind-bracing of the structure and the architect's idea that in reinforced concrete, column and beam were continuous. Price's use of reinforced concrete drew the attention of *The Railway and Engineering Review.* The space compares favorably to Otto Wagner's Postal Savings Bank in Vienna of the same years.[18] Direct, powerful, and industrial in character, the concourse of the Allegheny Station was an appropriate entrance into Pittsburgh and the fitting work of a pupil of Frank Furness.

---

16. *Pittsburgh Dispatch* (24 March 1905), 2.
17. According to James Van Trump the Paterson Post Office was designed by Wentworth and Vreeland of Paterson. James Van Trump, *Life and Architecture in*

Pittsburgh (Pittsburgh: Pittsburgh Landmarks & History Foundation, 1983), 226–227.
18. *The Railway and Engineering Review*, 47, no. 28 (21 September 1907), 820–823.

Over the next five years Price and McLanahan would design other stations in western Pennsylvania at Brownsville and Washington, in Ohio at Steubenville and Canton, and in Indiana at Converse, Hartford City, Ridgeville, Dunkirk, and Fort Wayne, culminating with the Chicago Freight Terminal and additions to the Indianapolis Terminal. These commissions brought Price into contact with industrialists along the route of the railroad. By the end of 1905 Price and McLanahan had prepared a book of their most important Philadelphia houses to show potential clients in the region the nature of their work. Soon a satellite office in Indianapolis was necessary to handle commissions for large residences including those of Indianapolis meatpacker Frank Van Camp and his assistant Thomas Jackson.

"The Utterance of the Living"

While the sphere of the office expanded to the west, Price and McLanahan were asked to consider how they would handle an annex to the Marlborough Hotel in Atlantic City. In that hotel of 1901 the slate shingled exterior recalled Asheville's Kenilworth Inn with a tall French roof above shingled upper walls in turn supported by a stone base. A high roof again carried the stylistic message but in typical Philadelphia representational fashion, window size denoted interior function: bay windows lighted the guest rooms; small windows lighted the bathrooms. Describing the new luxury of a private bathroom with each guest room, the facade itself formed part of the advertising for the hotel. Within, the interior was ornamented with two features that hint at Price's grasp of the potential for flamboyant commercial design of the future. In the lobby was a great eight-sided fireplace that functioned, not to warm the building, but to create a central focus, a gathering spot. Toward the rear of the building was the dining room which was the other great space of the hotel. A vast columned hall, it was illuminated at one end by an immense leaded glass dome lighted from above by electric lights that made it a glittering space day and night. The forest of columns and the many dozens of tables and hundreds of chairs were emblematic of the era's growing pleasure in the excitement of the crowd. Here, amid hundreds of fellow diners, highlighted by the sparkle of crystal and the buzz of conversation, a sensation of pleasure would rise, heralding the banquets and dinners of the emerging middle-class culture.

For the Marlborough annex Price was given a new challenge. Like other seashore towns during the previous generation Atlantic City had been devastated by a series of wind-whipped winter fires, so the goal of making a new fireproof hotel was both a marketing and a safety decision. If the building happened to look incombustible because of its radical form and material, so much the better. The client for the Marlborough Hotel and the Blenheim Hotel, as the annex was called, was Josiah White, grandson and namesake of the pioneer who had designed and built the Lehigh Canal, successfully bringing the anthracite coal to Philadelphia that powered the engines of the industrial revolution. In the 1890s hotelier Josiah White pioneered the idea of keeping hotels open year-round, making Atlantic City the nation's playground and giving it a reason to build at an urban density near the ocean. A risk taker with vision, White accepted the idea of building in concrete to avoid potential problems with the availability of steel and because he thought that the sound of carpenters nailing wood forms would be quieter than riveting steel and thus would be less disruptive to his guests in the nearby Marlborough.

The opportunity to design a second hotel for Josiah White came when Price was still working out the aesthetic possibilities of concrete. After Jacob Reed's Sons' Store which was essentially a trabeated column-and-beam system with a fictive concrete vault, Price had begun to understand the aesthetic potential of concrete in the Allegheny Station. Unlike riveted steel which was used to build rectilinear cages that had to be faced with fireproofing materials, concrete had the potential to be both sculptural and linear, simultaneously forming columns and floor slabs as well as the exterior surface material of the structure. This had important implications for a unified aesthetic expression, one which could make possible a significant step away from conventional construction toward modern design.

Not surprisingly for a Philadelphian whose culture believed in a relationship between form and expression, the question of how concrete should be used became the focus of Price's thinking and writing in the next decade. Price's transition from a system of concrete construction to the aesthetics of reinforced concrete can be seen in the Blenheim Hotel. In its bony armature and astonishing domes and towers emerged Price's intention of creating an architecture that would reflect the virtues and vices of the modern world. That Price made the leap in Philadelphia is all the more remarkable because of the gradual erosion of the progressive engineering culture. Taking its place was a new generation whose celebration of the past had increased the nation's awareness of its heritage but at the significant cost to the Philadelphia region which turned from the present to the past. As the century ended S. Weir Mitchell and other Philadelphia writers were recreating the flavor of the founding years of the nation in historical novels including *Hugh Wynne* and *The Red City* that contrasted with the realistic currents of the modern novel in their nostalgic sentiment. The former novel had a frontispiece by Howard Pyle captioned "In the presence of Washington."[19] For Philadelphians, a century after the city's role as the nation's capital had ended, time and space could be compressed in so simple a recollection. In the nearby countryside the rolling landscape of stone farmhouses and fields would have been but little changed from their appearance 125 years earlier, forming a constant reminder of the events that had taken place there.[20] The virile, graphic

---

19. Mitchell's *Hugh Wynne: Free Quaker* was serialized in *The Century* in 1896 and 1897 and published as a book in 1904; *The Red City* followed in *The Century* in 1907–8 and as a book in 1908.

images by Howard Pyle and his pupils, among them N. C. Wyeth, became the nation's image of its history while the work of Pyle's pupils who moved to other regions of the nation established the mythic character of the still vital but, with the closing of the frontier, passé west. But was America merely the historical ghosts who had founded the nation or was it the throbbing engine of the present? In the Philadelphia of Frank Furness, William Sellers, and Thomas Eakins the choice could be made between the two directions, but by the early twentieth-century most Philadelphians found the past more glamorous. Only the adventurous few persisted in following the course of the present.

It is not surprising that, living only a few miles from the Pyle circle, Price was stimulated by the same images and was drawn to the same type of costume dramas and displays which, from the days of the S. A. K., had remained a favorite amusement. Just as artists collected costumes and paraphernalia that gave verisimilitude to their images, architects had similar trophies; Price's were medieval armor, Moorish robes, and Turkish rugs, while his neighbors at Rose Valley, illustrators Charles and Alice Barber Stephens, had notable collections of American Indian and colonial garb. (*fig. 5*) At the University of Pennsylvania School of Architecture costumed pageantry formed a part of the teaching of the historical styles. These emblems of the past conflicted with the remembered values of the Furness office and with the strident celebration of the present advocated by Horace Traubel and his hero Walt Whitman.

With Rose Valley as his home and confronted by the goal of inventing an architecture that reflected his own era, Will Price based his approach on his own growing understanding that architecture could not succeed as art if it did not express contemporary life. In this view he was moving away from the Arts and Crafts movement based on the Gothic Revival of Morris toward the American Arts and Crafts movement's interest in progressive contemporary but not necessarily revolutionary design. The conflict that had become apparent to Will in 1903 over the dishonest use of half-timber in domestic architecture spread to other areas of his practice. Writing on furniture design for *The Artsman* in 1904, Will for the first time acknowledged the worth of the American present.

> But convention decrees that certain so-called established styles are correct, and we still
> make precedent our guide, accepting our taste without analysis second-hand. This leads
> us into errors more ludicrous than mere mistaken taste and less excusable than we know.
> It fills our streets with Italian and French renascences, and our countryside with Spanish
> and English houses, and our homes with wretched imitations of palace furniture, all of
> which may or may not be very beautiful, but certainly is not American and therefore is not
> art. For this is America, and art is the utterance of the living not the dead.

———

20. N. C. Wyeth was one of those who recalled the flow of history in Chester County. Betsy James Wyeth, ed., *The Wyeths by N. C. Wyeth: The Intimate Correspondence of N. C. Wyeth 1901–1945* (Boston: Gambit, 1971), 20, 47.

5. Rose Valley costume party, with Charles Stephens in Plains Indian garb and Will Price as Arab, c. 1908
(Price and McLanahan Archives, George E. Thomas Collection)

6. Price and McLanahan, Blenheim Hotel under construction, spring 1906
(Price and McLanahan Archives, George E. Thomas Collection)

> When America finds itself we will have national arts and not till then, We must
> put off the cloak of pretense, cease judging either ourselves or our work by dead stan-
> dards, and work in the material at hand to meet the daily needs of contemporary life.
>
> This is not a plea for wild vagaries in design.... But it is a plea for the self-asser-
> tion of that sincerity out of which all real art grows.[21]

In 1905, with the Rose Valley shops closed and the future of the community and its values
in doubt, Price asked, "Shall we copy the architecture and the chairs of our ancestors?"
And again he reached the conclusion that life was of the moment: "Most certainly not,
except in methods or details which remain perpetually modern."[22]

Having decided that it was only appropriate to design in ways that were both modern and American, Price was forced to rethink his design approach, taking his cues from
the system of construction and the purpose of the building rather than any historical
style. A 1906 paper delivered by Will to the Philadelphia meeting of the Association of
American Portland Cement Manufacturers, illustrated with construction photographs of
the Blenheim Hotel, records his thinking as that building neared completion. (*fig. 6*) He
began with a brief overview of the current situation: "We have, both here and abroad, a
comparatively large number of concrete buildings which are structurally good, but in
most cases are treated merely as a skeleton on which a building apparently of brick or
stone is hung—a makeshift and a sham, whether the actual work is done by structural
steel or a concrete frame developed therefrom." Working from the Philadelphia premise
that accurate description bordering on the literal was appropriate, Price described his
understanding of the nature of concrete construction and its effects on design.

> But reinforced concrete used even as a skeleton offers opportunities for design not offered
> by any other material. A steel frame building is no stiffer than its joints, and in buildings
> of greatly varying heights or loads, allowance must be made in design to take up undis-
> tributed settlement, or serious cracking will result, while in concrete, the building, if
> properly designed structurally, and properly built of proper materials is a monolith.[23]

It was this quality that Price had attempted to represent in the curved transition between
the columns and beams in the Allegheny Station, and which he again used in the window
openings of the Blenheim. Thus, according to Price's understanding of reinforced concrete, tall volumes could be juxtaposed against low portions without differential settlement, and it was even theoretically possible for a concrete structure to withstand a great

---

21. William L. Price, "Some Humors of False Construction, *The Artsman*, 1, no. 9 (June 1904), 321–328.

22. William L. Price, "Architecture and the Chair," *The
Artsman*, 2, no. 5 (February 1905), 163.

23. William T. [sic] Price, "The Possibilities of

Concrete Construction from the Standpoint of Utility
and Art," published by the American Portland Cement
Manufacturers Association as "Bulletin #2," republished in *American Architect and Building News*, 89, no.
1579 (March 24, 1906), 119–120.

storm that washed out much of the foundation. After warning manufacturers of the dangers of any falling off in the quality of their product which would make concrete less predictable, Price added:

> It all looks so easy, just the building of boxes and the casting of concrete and steel in moulds, and where the law or better, knowledge does not protect us, all sorts of liberties are going to be taken, owing to the desire to save materials and the large factor-of-safety usually allowed.[24]

Recounting his own experience in the Allegheny Station where reputable contractors had used dramatically different calculations for the strengths of materials, Price reiterated, "I can see grave dangers ahead, both from the effect of failures upon the public and the passage of too stringent laws."

Price then reflected on the opportunities represented by the new material beyond its obvious comparison with steel and masonry. As Price saw it after the construction of the Blenheim, the real interest lay in its "greater possibility as a plastic material." Instead of being built of individual blocks and pieces, concrete was formed from continuous volumes, laid up with a shovel and trowel and poured into molds. For Price these qualities then required ornament that could also be molded, or "run or fashioned" in the manner of plaster while colored tiles could be inset into the concrete and used as copings to protect overhangs. If these different characteristics were respected, it was clear that new forms would result.

> It is evident that this would and should make a wide departure from Classic forms and accepted styles—that it means, in fact, a new architecture, although it will not be necessary to abandon all precedent. We shall want walls, windows and doors in any case, and must learn to build them in their accepted forms. But in a material so plastic the forms of openings and mouldings may be expected to vary much from those necessary to an architecture dependent on arches and lintels.[25]

In addition to questions concerning the nature of the material, Philadelphia architects, used to designing in the row house modules of the preindustrial city, were now confronted by the problem of the scale introduced by modern construction methods. The rationalist Wilson Brothers had resolved modern scale by using the column grid as the basis for design, but architects such as Furness and Willis Hale approached the larger volumes of modern construction as surfaces for additional ornament to the point that the building's structural character nearly disappeared. In the case of the Blenheim, Price grasped the importance of simplification seeking "simple wall openings, few and simple mouldings and a total lack of cornices." His goal was "to use a solid wall, pierced by the simplest of

---

24. Price, "The Possibilities of Concrete Construction," 119.

25. Price, "The Possibilities of Concrete Construction," 120.

openings, in an effort to reduce to the minimum the chopped-up appearance of buildings that of necessity have many windows and small unbroken wall-spaces."[26] By using balconies to cast the horizontal shadows customarily produced in classical architecture by cornices, and by using multistory bays instead of pilasters Price was able to transcend the immense size of a 400-room hotel and in the process "preserve this feel of wall... [thereby] destroying any semblance of stone and giving it a plastic character that seems appropriate." Linking purpose and construction Price's conclusion could have been made by William Sellers half a century before: "It is along the line of simple and direct expression of the purpose and mode of construction of building that architecture grows when it is really growing, and cement in its manifold possibilities spreads before us a new field for the imaginative designer."[27]

Price focused his lecture on issues of construction safety and surface character. As a result other aspects of design in concrete were not discussed. The Blenheim Hotel was built using a complicated system of poured-in-place columns and slabs that were clearly intended to carry much of the aesthetic load. By pulling the columns forward to the plane of the facade and recessing the infilling block, Price established an underlying rhythm based on the columns that gave order to the immense volume of the building. This would become a recurring theme. In the case of the Blenheim the voids were infilled with hollow tile and the entire surface was coated in a smooth concrete skin to create a monolithic expression of the unity that Price believed was inherent in the material. An overlay of cast tile ornament modeled in the forms of seashells, crabs, seahorses, and seaweed linked the building to its place at the seashore. With forward-curving solaria reaching toward the boardwalk, a domed front tower containing the premier hotel rooms, and an L-shaped rear wing framing the shared court with the Marlborough, the Blenheim suggested the form of a lobster. It was immediately acknowledged as a masterpiece whose opening was aimed at the media moguls with telling effect.[28]

---

26. Price, "The Possibilities of Concrete Construction," 120.

27. Price, "The Possibilities of Concrete Construction," 120. An excellent summary of the knowledge about reinforced concrete just after the construction of the Blenheim is contained in W. L. Webb and W. H. Gibson, *Cyclopedia of Architecture, Carpentry and Building*, vol. 4 (Chicago: American School of Correspondence, 1909). It covers the available information on the material, summarizes systems of reinforcing as they were evolving, and provides excellent information on relative costs of steel and concrete as well as a revealing summary of labor costs for a garage in Philadelphia (305–307). Of note is the concentration of projects cited in the Philadelphia region, confirming the importance of the research at the University of Pennsylvania (344). The Blenheim is illustrated (293) with a caption that states "This Magnificent Structure, Built Throughout of Reinforced Concrete is Especially Noteworthy as the Most Elaborate Application which has Yet been Made of this New Material of Construction. It is Located near the Famous 'Boardwalk' Overlooking the Ocean."

28. One of the early visitors was N. C. Wyeth who attended the 4 May 1906, Periodical Publishers' Association of America dinner. See David Michaelis, *N. C. Wyeth* (New York: Alfred A. Knopf, 1998), 148, 464.

A year after its completion, in a lecture on the topic of modern architecture before the Ontario Association of Architects, Price recalled the opposition of his own staff and the doubts of the owner.

> When the Blenheim was about half finished, some man met the owner and said: "Look here how in the world did you ever have the nerve to start a building like that?" and he replied: "My architect said he had to have some damned fool to try his experiment on and I guess I am it." He asked me what style it was and I said, "I do not know unless it is Atlantic City, period of 1906." That is what it was trying to be. I think [it is a mistake] to change the construction and not change the design. In the Blenheim Hotel I tried to be honest to a certain extent in that very direction. We had in the Exchange, concrete construction, which is absolutely expressed in the resultant forms in the ceilings, and where we had [the need for] big beams there are still big beams, and where the spans were smaller they were smaller beams. The construction is honestly accepted, and it does not seem to be very shocking, either to the public, or to many of the architects who have seen it. They do not like to admit it, but they do like certain things about it: at least they tell me so. You can say what you please after I go. But it is a fact that in that building, I really was trying to accept the problem as I found it, against the judgement of my entire office, and I had to do the work in the face of considerable opposition. I fortunately, or unfortunately, as remains to be seen, had a client that I had built for before, and as he had made a good paying concern of the other hotel, he was amenable to reason, or amenable to unreason, as the case may be, and he let me do pretty nearly what I pleased.[29]

In 1905 when Price was persuading Josiah White of the merits of the new design, he already had reached the central idea that would guide him for the next decade: "Here we are in an condition which is certainly not Classic, not Renaissance, not Gothic in its habit of thought. It is a business age."[30] Because the values of business had overwhelmed the larger values of community and human relationships, Price contended that architects should be "preachers as well as mere interpreters of the public mind," with a special obligation to point out the horrors that Lincoln Steffens, Ida Tarbell, Upton Sinclair and other muckrakers were spreading across the pages of the national press. Price's Quaker background required personal responsibility and witness, leading Will to demand:

> If we have a factory to build, and that factory is to be a place where little children are ground to death, as they are in the silk mills in Pennsylvania, we ought to make the gates of that factory look like the gates of Hell, and we should paint over the door, 'Abandon

---

29. William L. Price, "Modern Architecture," *The Artsman* 4, no. 2 (January 1907), 227–238 and *The Artsman*, 4, no. 3 (April 1907), 239–278. Perhaps tellingly, this would be the last issue of *The Artsman*. The idea of the

architect as preacher goes back to William Henry Furness' address to the AIA in Philadelphia in 1873 when he charged the profession to be "street preachers."
30. Price, "Modern Architecture," 259–260.

> hope, all ye who enter here,' and be honest about it.... If we really expressed the sordidness that exists in our time in the architecture that surrounds life, it would not stand a minute, or at least for a very short time.

Seeing Atlantic City as a mixed blessing—a place of resort for the monied classes but also a place where workers were lured to spend beyond their means—Price placed the Blenheim in the same context, describing his goal as the truthful expression of "the use and purposes, the ambitions of these people, and I will try to make it hurt just a little."

> I built a hotel last year, and I know it hurts a little. I know there are architects that it hurts, and yet they cannot help but admit, many of them at least, that it is an expression of the purpose for which it was built and of the place where it was built: that it is an expression of the gay and sumptuous life, as it was meant to be, of the people that go to Atlantic City.

The Blenheim Hotel was an expression of its moment in time rather than a reference to other cultures and other places. Firmly rooted in the present, it became, with Daniel Burnham's Flatiron Building in New York City, an icon of the present. Price understood the revolutionary nature of his achievement.

> What I want to say will be, I hope, rather anarchistic—rather in the direction of taking a shot at certain ideals and ideas that seem to me to be false in our architectural work. In talking about modern architecture perhaps I ought to define a little what I mean. It is very differently looked at. The Beaux Arts man says that modern architecture consists in following out certain continuous historical precedents, as expressed in the Schools of Paris, and that the Beaux Arts people are in line with that succession architecturally; that though the work may be bad in every other way, still that is the path we should pursue. However, that is not the kind of modern architecture I want to talk about. I was told today that Mr. Cram...thinks that the Gothic architecture was nipped in the bud by an obtrusive and immoral Renascence, and that what we ought to do is go back and take up the Gothic where our predecessors left off, and arrive at something really splendid. I think he is partially right in his premise but entirely wrong in his conclusion. He is right when he says that the Gothic was interrupted before it reached its full flower.
>
> What I mean by modern architecture is architecture that accepts its own age and its own want and its own feelings as its standard, rather than any mere standard of excellence or beauty in design. That seems to me what constitutes the modern way of looking at things.[31]

Despite a busyness of surface and details that recall the Spanish late Gothic, the Blenheim Hotel was a seminal event in the evolution of the modern culture. Unlike the Allegheny Station, which was dependent on historical sources and requires some knowledge to understand fully, the Blenheim stood as a new creation, a gray-tan monolith that was a

---

31. Price, "Modern Architecture," 227–228.

left 7. William L. Price, "A Detail of the Erectheum," *Catalogue of the T-Square Club* (1905–6)

below 8. William L. Price, Chicago Union Station. Glass plate negative of lost pencil drawing on paper. (Price and McLanahan Archives, George E. Thomas Collection)

celebration of the present. In the manner of Frank Furness, the hotel's forms and fenestration represented the functions within while the building's character was expressive of the scale and energy of the modern age. Its astonishing front elevation, a dome flanked by front towers and chimneys, presented a roofless modern volume whose parapets capped vertical walls, doing away with the customary pause of eave line or cornice that usually began the termination of a structure. The resulting design was no longer an archeological assemblage of historical forms requiring prior knowledge for understanding and appreciation. The values of Philadelphia's industrial architecture, an architecture whose forms represented the specific functions within, had reached the great commercial establishments of the beachfront. No longer speaking in the dead languages of the past, the new architecture was intended to be accessible to the new middle classes who had never made a grand tour of Europe. (*fig. 7*) Signifying the values of the business age, this architecture's goal was not the creation of an harmonious urban totality, rather it was a commercial howl that was marketed through the originality of its design. The Blenheim set the stage for the flamboyant architecture of all future American playlands from Atlantic City to Disneyland and Las Vegas.

With the exception of Price and McLanahan's architecture, the first years of the twentieth century saw Philadelphians turning away from the culture of innovation toward one rooted in the past. The premier engineer-architect, Joseph Wilson, had retired at the end of the 1890s and died in 1902; Frank Furness, although continuing in his practice, had turned over most of the design work to younger associates, his bold touch evident only in a few railroad station commissions. Howard Pyle, not Thomas Eakins, was the vital force in teaching. Of the younger generation of Philadelphia architects, Walter Cope and John Stewardson were already dead. Wilson Eyre, Jr., had stopped seeking commercial commissions in the 1890s and by 1900 had largely restricted his practice to escapist suburban residences. Frank Miles Day had broadened his practice to colleges and universities, but most were designed in the historical styles of Europe. As the children of Philadelphia's engineering elite began attending Princeton, Yale, and Harvard and studying literature and architecture, the progressive culture of the city was replaced by one that celebrated its own history, not that of engineering and design, but colonial ancestry and the American revolution. Genes replaced genius in the pantheon of the city. By 1903 John Sloan and most of the other newspaper artists who had been drawn to the city by its raw industrial energy had decamped for New York which was strengthening its hold on the national media.

The leading institutions of the city were changing as well. The University of Pennsylvania was no longer headed by a scientist who was comfortable with the designs of Furness and the Wilson Brothers. Its new leader, Charles Harrison, a sugar manufacturer, had replaced Frank Furness as the campus architect with Cope and Stewardson and Frank Miles Day, thus giving the institution its romantic Gothic appearance. The university's School of Architecture was headed by Warren Laird, a graduate of the École des Beaux Arts, and the professor of design was French-born Paul Cret. The contrast between research being undertaken in medical and engineering laboratories and the campus architecture was obvious to Albert Kelsey who compared the "romance of the alien past" of Cope and Stewardson dormitories and laboratory facades with the Furness approach which he characterized as reflecting the "poetry of the present."

Although the culture of the city's elite was changing rapidly, two important clients resisted the shift toward history—the Pennsylvania Railroad and the Atlantic City hotel operators. As cultures they were far apart, for while the railroad continued as a bastion of engineering values of the late nineteenth century, the hotel operators sought originality to achieve commercial identity. Price managed to work with both groups, satisfying their goals while working out his own interests. Atlantic City had become a mixing bowl that drew vacationers and conventioneers from the entire eastern seaboard, earning it the nickname of "the nation's playground" and bringing Price and McLanahan to the attention of a national audience.[32] With the construction of and publicity for the Blenheim, Price and McLanahan found opportunities for work beyond the limits of the region. This reversed the historic condition of localized architectural practices, initiating instead the pattern of Philadelphia architects of the twentieth century. In this century, Price and McLanahan, Louis Kahn, Romaldo Giurgola, and Robert Venturi, while expressing the values of the industrial culture of the city, have received their most important commissions outside their native region. By the second half of the century's first decade Price's future lay along the western routes of the Pennsylvania Railroad and at the booming beach resorts of the Atlantic coast.

❧ Chicago Terminal

With the completion of the Blenheim Hotel, Will and Hawley visited Europe together. Some hint of the itinerary can be guessed from photographs in the office records dated 1906, and showing views of Spain, France, and Germany. Will's photograph of the Erectheum, published as the frontispiece to the 1907 exhibition catalogue of the T-Square Club, indicates that they traveled as far as Greece, probably reaching Constantinople. (*fig. 8*) For most American architects of the period, such a trip would have confirmed the directions of a career reflecting the values of the Beaux Arts or the Gothic Revival. But seeing the landmarks of the continent at age 45 produced a different effect on Will than it had a decade earlier. Although much of the trip, particularly the portion in Spain and Turkey, was conceived to provide information related to the new types of work the office

---

32. For a history of Atlantic City see Charles Funnell, *By the Beautiful Sea: The Rise and High Times of That*   *Great American Resort, Atlantic City* (New York: Alfred A. Knopf, 1978).

was pursuing, Will had already reached the conclusion that the best work was of its own period, not a revival grafted onto a later culture. Will had seen England and France in the 1890s, admired their landmarks and adapted them to his design. But in 1906 he was convinced of the merits of his own age, and when it was his choice, he would remain a designer of his own time.

Shortly after returning from Europe, Price and McLanahan received an opportunity that reiterated the merits of the present. In 1907 the Pennsylvania Railroad began a plan to relieve congestion in the downtown Chicago with a new terminal that was to be designed by Price and McLanahan. This unleashed other forces that led to the plan for Chicago prepared by Daniel Burnham. The story is largely restricted to the period after 1911.[33] But Price and McLanahan's elevation drawings for a "Chicago Terminal Station," dated 1908 and 1909, prove that even before the Burnham Plan was initiated, the Pennsylvania Railroad had begun exploring its options for a new building. The problem of scale now had to be solved in what was to be the largest building containing the largest room that the firm had ever imagined.

Side and front elevations dated 1908 show a building already largely developed along lines that are more "modern baroque" than Beaux Arts classicism. (*fig. 9*) Symmetrical in massing, the only exception being a clock tower on one side of the building, with details drawn from modern sources, it seems at first glance to be the most classical of any of the office's mature designs. With the simultaneous construction of McKim, Mead and White's Pennsylvania Station in New York City and Burnham's Union Station in Washington, the Pennsylvania Railroad expected their Philadelphia architects to produce along similar lines. However, instead of the multilayered and skylighted space designed for New York, Price's scheme was based on the great European terminals, most likely the vast hall of the Frankfurt railroad station which he had seen on his trip.[34]

Two photographs of the now lost pencil elevations of the station from the street sides show a longitudinal barrel vault intersected by a cross transept of nearly equal size which would have contained the main waiting rooms. An immense porte cochere projected from the central transept and a great portal centered under the curving volume of the roof was probably repeated at the far end of the building. Small-scale fenestration around the lower perimeter suggests that the corners of the building would have been infilled for use as offices for the railroad while the main hall would be a vast and airy

---

33. Carl Condit, *Chicago 1910–1929: Building, Planning and Urban Technology* (Chicago: University of Chicago Press, 1973), 59–88.

34. The similarity of design, down to the central mass of figures raised above the entrance arch, suggests that the scheme was developed by Walter T. Karcher who was in the office and had made a specialty of railroad stations at the University of Pennsylvania. See Daniel [sic] M. Karcher, "The Science of Cities," *Architectural Annual, 1900* (Philadelphia, 1900), 202–203.

left 9. William L. Price, Chicago Union Station, side elevation. Glass plate negative of watercolor. (Price and McLanahan Archives, George E. Thomas Collection)

below 10. Beach site, Overhanover, North Carolina, 1909 (Price and McLanahan Archives, George E. Thomas Collection)

room—not unlike the great arched concourse that Theodore Link had introduced into the American railroad station in St. Louis and which had become the characteristic feature of stations around the globe.[35] Unfortunately no plans or elevations of the track side of the station survive. Whether it was intended to sit entirely above the train traffic with tracks passing below as in New York's Pennsylvania Station or Philadelphia's later 30th Street Station, or whether it would have served as a stub-end station with all of the tracks terminating against the opposite wall, is unclear.

A watercolor of one end of the building was made the following year. It fills in additional details about the construction. The exterior would be the red brick that was the uniform of most Pennsylvania Railroad buildings, with limestone for the base, window surrounds, parapets, and carved ornamental bands and sculpted decorations. The sculptural motif of massed figures supporting a globe was another reference to the Frankfurt railroad terminal (and other contemporary European public buildings) and is like Frank Lloyd Wright's use of a similar motif for the facade of the Larkin Building of 1904. The puzzle is how the building would have been constructed. In the French and German examples the great halls were little more than extensions of the train shed into the station and thus were built of steel arches carrying secondary framing which in turn supported gabled roofs on the exterior, and from which a plaster ceiling following the curve of the arch was suspended. Logically, the Chicago Terminal would have followed the same construction system. Still there are questions. Price was known at the time for large-scale work in reinforced concrete, and much of the detail would seem to conform to the motifs that he had developed for that material, particularly the curving frames linking the jambs of windows to their lintels. More telling may be the rounded volumes and the secondary ribs of the roof which appear to support a small grid unit that could be glass block infilling the roof surfaces in the manner of the Allegheny Station of three years earlier. Even more telling may have been what appear to be massive masonry buttresses that provide a visual transition from the outer wall to the main hall. Were they merely decorative or, if the structure was of concrete, were they intended to have a role in buttressing a concrete arched span?

The details suggest that the architects proposed to build transverse concrete ribs joined by concrete girders, spanning the interior in one giant space. It would be easy to dismiss the idea as impossible were it not that, at the same time in Philadelphia, engineer George Webster was completing construction of the world's largest reinforced concrete arched span carrying the Walnut Lane Bridge across the Wissahickon Valley. Built using

---

35. Carroll Meeks, *The Railroad Station in History* (New Haven, Conn.: Yale University Press, 1956) and Nikolas Pevsner, *A History of Building Types* (Princeton: Princeton University Press, 1976) both cover the railroad station. Contemporary stations were surveyed by Karcher, "The Science of Cities," 197–212.

wood forms, and spanning some 233 feet with a height of 200 feet, it easily surpassed the scale of the Chicago Terminal. For the first time Price had envisioned volumes and forms worthy of the plasticity of the material.[36]

Overhanover: Dreams and Visions

With the Rose Valley shops closing at home and a national economic slump as well as losses in several architectural competitions including the Scranton and Wilkinsburg Stations for the northern division of the Pennsylvania Railroad and a campus plan for the Western University of Pennsylvania, 1907 and 1908 were difficult years for the office.[37] Hawley McLanahan took on the daunting task of finding projects across the eastern half of the nation. In the previous decade surplus income across much of American society had made resorts successful year round, so McLanahan went looking for opportunities for new resorts along the Atlantic coast. With the ocean as the primary focus and the railroads the national transportation system, McLanahan turned to the southeastern seashore which was slowly breaking out of the two generations of economic depression stemming from the Civil War. A generation after the Kenilworth Inn had proven a financial disaster because southerners could not afford modern hotel costs, the "New South" had returned as a center for sports and health-related activities.

1909 is an important year in the evolution of modern architecture in the United States. In the midwest Frank Lloyd Wright, after completing the Robie house, departed from the field. In the United States an economic boom began that would crest five years later with the global inflation generated by World War I. Price's firm expanded in these years, gaining the capacity to handle larger projects, and moved to larger offices, first to 1529 Walnut Street and then to 1418 Walnut Street, each move placing the office closer to the core of the business district. In 1909, with the Blenheim Hotel the hottest draw in Atlantic City, Price and McLanahan were discovered by the nation's developers and rode the roller-coaster of great expectations. The first of these projects was a design for an immense new resort on the coastal islands off North Carolina's mainland in the vicinity of Wilmington. It was there that the main north–south railroad, the Atlantic Coast Line, returned to the coast from its inland route from Washington and Richmond. During the

---

36. Condit indicates that various station projects were put on hold during the completion and acceptance of the Burnham Plan for Chicago (260–264), and then resulted in the construction of the Union Station after 1913 from Graham, Burnham and Company's plans (269–284).

37. David Hackett Fischer, *The Great Wave: Price Revolutions and the Rhythm of History* (New York: Oxford Uni-

versity Press, 1996) summarizes economic conditions in the early twentieth century, at the moment when the rising price curve of the modern era begins. He offers a remarkable synthesis of economic and cultural data that confirms the rise of the consumer culture. Despite rising population which usually triggers inflation and poverty for the working population, wages rose because of unions, the social safety net, and rises in productivity.

winter of 1908-9 McLanahan and a New York-based photographer made numerous visits to the North Carolina coast, returning with large format panoramic views of the sites which included barrier islands, the main inlet, cypress swamps, and loblolly pine forests. (*fig. 10*) Long tangles of Spanish moss and clusters of mistletoe contrasted with the scrub vegetation of the mid-Atlantic coast. With land secured the consortium organized by McLanahan relied on Will's renderings to raise money for actual construction.

Because McLanahan's developers had no interest in interacting with the local community except as a source for labor, they were not restricted to purchasing land near the existing villages and cities. To make up for the lack of an existing urban center, Overhanover was to be an all-encompassing vacation resort. An entire new town would be constructed on the mainland connected by an automobile causeway to the outer beaches. With Americans discovering the automobile, the mainland community was bounded by a nine-mile highway which could double as a racetrack. Following the earlier model of Arden, six golf courses were laid out in the residential zone to provide green space. Although most of the houses were to be built in a developer's grid framing the main road, many of the nearly 200 house lots were along waterways, reflecting a boating component made possible by the development of small gasoline and diesel engines. There was even a sanitarium at a secluded point on the far side of the resort reiterating the continuing link between health and the ocean.

Like so many earlier railroad resorts, grand hotels would be the initial draw, luring potential buyers of home sites. Three immense oceanfront hotels, each different in character, were to be constructed on the beach while another would be built on the mainland facing the inlet and serving as a year-round center. The promoters of Atlantic City had named streets for the states and capital cities of the nation; at Overhanover the hotels were named the Raleigh, for the state capital of North Carolina, the Wilmington, for the nearby county seat, and the Onslow and the Hanover, for the state's ocean counties. Flanking the causeway were two giant water towers whose sculpted planes transformed what were utilitarian structures into a monumental gateway.

Like most of the great projects of the next decade, Overhanover turned out to be a maddening will-o'-the-wisp, but Price's rendered perspectives afford insight into the evolution of the firm's approach to the design of large structures, designs which would became brick and concrete in the next decade. The surface effects were not unlike the sculptural passages of the Blenheim. And as with that hotel a concrete armature would be framed and infilled with hollow tile forming octagonal towers containing tanks to pressurize the community's water supply. At first glance the resulting towers recall those designed by the firm for the Schoen house in Rose Valley but with a significant change in scale and in architectural character. The raised frame that surrounded recessed central panels in each bay and represented the underlying structure, was spanned by a segmental arch which in turn framed a three-light window above a decorative panel of tile set in the surface of the tower. The elements of the base then curved inward in a sweeping taper, an effect that reappeared at the top of the tower. Forms that on the Blenheim Hotel had been abrupt and additive were smoothed and sculpted, creating smooth transitions from one plane to the next. The effect was as if the water tower had been sculpted from plaster, realizing Price's intention of representing the inherent plasticity of the material. Unfortunately the drawings do not reveal exactly how the shapes would have been made—by poured-in-place molds or as a concrete skin over conventional block masonry in the manner of Erich Mendelssohn's Einstein Tower of a decade later. The medium, however, was less important than the message: architecture could be sculpture seen in the round. At the moment when Wright was defining a strategy of breaking the volume into planes, Price was working toward the opposite goal, one which transformed the rectilinear grid of modern structure into iconic and sculptural forms. The evidence of the skyscrapers of the 1920s suggests that Price was on the track that would be fruitful until the rise of International modernism.

Despite Gothic remnants such as gargoyles poking out of the tower just below the springing point of the segmental arches, the effect of the water towers was startlingly original, anticipating by a decade the expressionist vein of design in concrete. Two of the hotels, the Raleigh and the Wilmington, were by contrast more conventional, having colonnaded centers with long wings interrupted by projecting gabled volumes with central chimneys recalling the Schoen house facade. The elevation for the third beachfront hotel, the Onslow, called for a raised central block of six stories flanked by eight-story towers with subtly curving lower wings on each side, each terminating in towers. Like the Blenheim the lower stories would contain public spaces, in this case with access from under the hotel to a grand stair to a row of permanent beach shelters along the oceanfront, apparently one per hotel room. The side wings were organized like the rear wing of the Blenheim with pairs of bays articulating the long wall and concrete brackets supporting an overhanging enclosed balcony forming a cornicelike closure to the wings. In the central block Price pushed beyond the additive character of the Blenheim toward the more sculptural character of the water towers by joining the balcony to the bays in an oversized reproduction of the curved transition between columns and beams that he had used on the expressed frame of the Blenheim. The sculpted planes of the upper levels of the water towers reappeared on the end towers of the blocks. Again Price described the plasticity inherent in concrete, conceiving three-dimensional forms that in the future would reappear in his designs for concrete.[38]

———

38. Overhanover was exhibited in the *18th Architectural Exhibition of the Philadelphia Chapter of the American* *Institute of Architects and the T-Square Club* (Philadelphia, 1912).

Despite the huge effort as reflected in the photographs, community plans, and renderings, Overhanover was never built but the lessons learned became the basis for the next decade of design, first in a successful seashore hotel project and soon after in a second round of railroad stations for the western division of the Pennsylvania Railroad. The Clarendon Hotel, as the new resort was called, was constructed at Sea Breeze, Florida, where the Atlantic Coast Railroad again touched the coast. Rendered perspectives show that it was to follow the composition of the Onslow with a central block framed by lower wings. (*fig. 11*) The central block would be the first phase with the wings to be built if the market merited additional construction. With the exception of the projecting porch, the building's lines were simpler than the sculpted volumes designed the previous year. Like the Blenheim and the Overhanover water towers, there was more than a hint of Spanish flavor in the details of the Clarendon with large panels of Mercer tile ornamenting the upper walls and buttresslike forms at the corners. Some of those shapes were vestiges from the Gothic houses of the previous decade. More progressive was the general simplification of surface demonstrating that Price was coming to terms with scale. What was appropriate at small scale seemed busy when it was large. Larger buildings required greater discipline.

The McLanahan search along the coast produced additional projects including a hotel design at Daytona for the Palmetto House, an immense golf-centered resort at an inland site at Aumond, Georgia, and a remarkable scheme for the Hotel San Cristobal in San Juan, Puerto Rico. None of these projects was built. It would take the shift of the nation to the automobile led by midwestern industrialists to re-energize the Florida coast with the focus on Miami. After World War I the midwesterners who had hired Price's office in Indianapolis took the firm to Miami where it led the design of that new recreational mecca. There, Price and McLanahan designed the aquarium, apartment houses, and the houses for Carl Fisher and Frank Wheeler, establishing a second front where the firm's nonhistorical architectural vocabulary could flourish.

Western Vistas

In 1910 the firm's interests once again were directed to the west. Three years earlier James McCrea had been elevated to head the Pennsylvania Railroad with James Turner as his assistant; for the first time, the railroad was led by men whose training and interests were with the division west of Pittsburgh.[39] During the McCrea era acquisitions by the Pennsylvania Railroad in Indiana and Ohio resulted in commissions for new stations beginning with Steubenville, Ohio. Only five years earlier Price's designs for the stations

39. George H. Burgess and Miles C. Kennedy, *Centennial History of the Pennsylvania Railroad* (Philadelphia: Pennsylvania Railroad Company, 1949), 517.

11. Price and McLanahan, Clarendon Hotel, Sea Breeze, Florida, 1910
(Price and McLanahan Archives, George E. Thomas Collection)

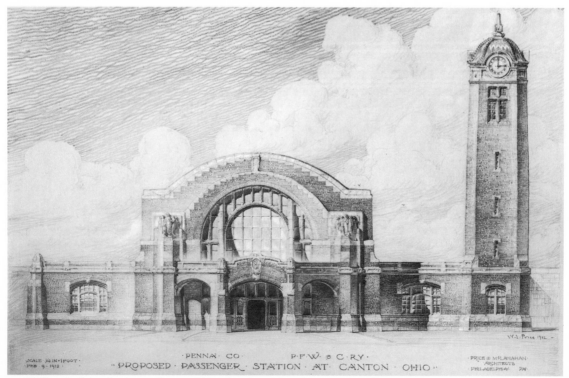

12. William L. Price, Station at Canton, Ohio, elevation. Glass plate negative of lost pencil on paper.
(Price and McLanahan Archives, George E. Thomas Collection)

in Allegheny and Washington, Pennsylvania, had been vertical in massing and historical in detail, essentially late Victorian buildings rooted in the past. Standing on the edge of the midwestern prairie, the new station at Steubenville reflected Price's continuing evolution.

Unlike the Allegheny Station which required an office level above the waiting room, the Steubenville Station was a conventional Pennsylvania Railroad structure that could have its principal spaces side by side at track level. Responding to the flatness of the west Price made the chief feature the great sweep of the horizontal line of the overhanging sheltering roofs linking the main station and the freight building. The composition was complemented by a muscular frankness in the structure. Unlike the load-bearing masonry walls of most suburban stations, Price and McLanahan designed a skeleton of reinforced concrete which was largely sheathed in sand-colored brick, with recessed paneled piers denoting the position of the columns. The observant viewer might have noted that the massive brackets projecting from the piers that flanked the entrance and the canopy which they supported were built of reinforced concrete. But the most direct expression of the material was the concrete parapet that projected through the roof, marking the entrance. Coped by tile blocks whose sinuous curves suggested the flow of the prairie and ornamented with decorative panels of Mercer tile, the Steubenville Station was Price's most successful small-scale modern design, and demonstrated the maturation of the office as Will neared his fiftieth birthday.

The features of the station design, especially the long horizontal roofs, raise the question about what Price knew of the midwestern architects of the Prairie School. As the century ended Philadelphia, more than most eastern cities, had remained closely linked to the industrial heartland. Since the Civil War the Pennsylvania Railroad had funneled the products of the nation's midsection from Chicago through Philadelphia and there was a constant line of travel between the two cities, represented by Louis Sullivan's decision in 1873 to make his way to Chicago from Philadelphia. The affiliation of the T-Square Club with the Architectural League was another aspect of that relationship. Hence, it was not coincidental that midwestern journals published Philadelphia designs when most east-coast publications had dropped the designers of the Quaker City. For example, the *Inland Architect* was the last non-Philadelphia publication to include a Furness design, while Philadelphia publications kept an eye on midwestern developments. It was Philadelphia's literary magazine, *Lippincott's*, that published Louis Sullivan's "The Tall Building Artistically Considered" and it was the Philadelphia-based *Architectural Annual* that celebrated Sullivan's career at the turn of the century. In the twentieth century *The Ladies' Home Journal* published seven of Robert Spencer's designs for farmhouses, introducing the nation at large to the directions of the Prairie School, while simultaneously serializing a tale of the encounter of eastern values with Chicago in "The Russells in Chicago, the Experiences of a Young Boston Couple Who Moved to the West."[40] Five years later *The*

Ladies' Home Journal selected a Frank Lloyd Wright house in the series on houses of moderate cost begun by Will Price a decade earlier.

As William Price was about to design the Steubenville Station, he would have certainly known of the new architecture of the midwest via *The Ladies' Home Journal*. And, as H. Allen Brooks demonstrates, many of the early works of the Prairie School were published in the *Architectural Record* beginning around 1905 and continuing throughout the decade. Will Price's office ledger for 1900 includes subscription payments to the *Architectural Record* and it is reasonable to assume that Price and McLanahan continued the subscription. Another source on modern design directly available to a Philadelphian was the T-Square Club annual exhibition and published catalogue. In 1899 it included many of the designers associated with the Arts and Crafts movement from Great Britain, among them C. F. A. Voysey, C. R. Ashbee, Aston Webb, and C. Harrison Townsend. In 1900 the exhibit committee selected several Elmer Grey cottages and the following year included his cottage designed for *The Ladies' Home Journal* series on houses of moderate cost. Grey had been the star of the 1900 Architectural League convention in Chicago with a paper on the subject of "Indigenous and Inventive Architecture," making it likely that his work was included in the T-Square Club exhibit in response to that talk.[41] And because he had toured Europe with Walter Price a the beginning of the decade, his drawings certainly would have been scrutinized by the Price brothers.

After the first year or two of the twentieth century the sea change that transformed Philadelphia from a center of innovation could be seen in the T-Square Club exhibits and in the merger of the T-Square Club and the American Institute of Architects. Selected projects of out-of-town architects were almost invariably pompous designs by a Beaux Arts classicist such as Cass Gilbert or picturesque Gothic churches by Ralph Adams Cram. With the arrival of color printing, the color frontispiece often told the tale. In 1903 the T-Square Club memorialized the later Walter Cope and published one of his watercolors of the Ghiralda; in 1904 it was given to Carrère and Hastings' Cleveland Trust Company. In the year of the triumphant display of Price and McLanahan's Blenheim Hotel, the frontispiece was a black and white photograph of the Erectheum—taken by W. L. Price. Clearly the rapprochement between the AIA and the T-Square Club undercut the latter's modernist direction. Only when Albert Kelsey or another committed modernist was on the selection committee would original projects by midwesterners, such as Louis Sullivan's design for Petty's Island in the Delaware River, be chosen for exhibition.[42]

---

40. Emily Wheaton, "The Russells in Chicago," *The Ladies' Home Journal* (1901–2).

41. H. Allen Brooks, *The Prairie School* (Toronto: University of Toronto Press, 1972) discusses Elmer Grey (40–41). The link to Grey in the T-Square Club exhibit committee for those years may have been William C. Hays who soon departed for the west.

42. The papers of the T-Square Club are in the Historical Society of Pennsylvania, and good runs of the journal exist in local libraries. Kelsey was on the

With the continuing links between Philadelphia and the midwest it should come as no surprise that Price incorporated standard devices of the period into the Steubenville Station design. The segmental-headed window with a curved mullion was a favorite motif of Voysey. The horizontal planes of the sheltering roofs and the flattening of forms were common in the midwest but, unlike Wright who in small-scale buildings used stucco over wood in lieu of concrete, the structural expression was Price's own. This linked him to Sullivan's generation and others trained by architects of the post-Civil War years who saw in the expression of construction and function the way to the future. Finally, the striking patterns of decorative tiles on the parapet and the tapering, tile-capped concrete shafts of the light standards out front were peculiarly Price's and reflected the aesthetic he was evolving at home, in Rose Valley's Improvement Company houses at the time.

National Vision and Western Opportunities

Between 1910 and 1914 most of the buildings actually constructed from Price and McLanahan designs were in the midwest. An equal number of unrealized projects along the Atlantic seaboard from Newport to Puerto Rico would hold out the hope of vast economic success. One unusual commission outside of these clusters was for a studio in Stamford, Connecticut, for Gutzon Borglum. Remembered now as the sculptor of Mount Rushmore, Borglum and his brother Solon had distinguished careers as figurative sculptors, exhibiting regularly at the T-Square Club and other local venues. Price and Borglum had begun collaborating around 1909 on the Newark Lincoln Monument, a work finally completed in 1913.[43] But it was probably through their shared interests in progressive politics that the two men first met. In a biography by Borglum's wife, the genesis of the studio was remembered as the work of "friend William Price of Rosedale [sic], near Philadelphia, who had helped him with the Newark Lincoln and other work." The studio was located overlooking a small creek and accessible by a footbridge; it was constructed of local stone laid up naturally, recalling the indigenous construction of the region. The exterior was barnlike, complete with a giant doorway—needed when modeling a horse and rider inside the studio. Within, a massive fireplace spanned by a Cyclopean lintel and supported on immense brackets hinted at the future work of Borglum.[44] During the proj-

---

committee that selected Sullivan's project in 1907.

43. Robert J. Casey and Mary Borglum, *Give the Man Room* (New York: Bobbs-Merrill, 1952), 108. This book establishes 1908 or 1909 as the date of the commission of the Newark Lincoln Monument, but it was not installed until 1913. Mary Borglum recalled, "The architect who drew up the plans for the setting was an old friend, William Price" (102). This suggests that the two men knew

each other for some time, beginning years before the studio project and probably accounting for the commission.

44. Indicating the totality of Price's fall from memory, a biography by Lincoln Borglum overlooked Price entirely, claiming that the studio was of his father's "own design." Lincoln Borglum and Gweneth Reed DenDooven, *Mount Rushmore: The Story Behind the Scenery* (Las Vegas: KC Publications, 1977), 22.

ect, Will's health problems surface again and henceforth appeared with ever more alarming regularity. In a letter to the carpenter of the roof trusses, dated 26 April 1911, it was reported that "The detail of gable over the main entrance, we cannot send you until it has Mr. Price's approval. Mr. Price has had trouble with his eyes and will not be in the office before to-morrow."[45]

The midwestern chain of commissions continued in summer of 1910 when Price and McLanahan had plans on the boards for a small railroad station at Converse, Indiana, and a larger station at Fort Wayne. Fort Wayne was an "important division and junction point on the main Chicago to New York line of the Pennsylvania system" which required both modern passenger facilities and extensive offices.[46] This station, now much altered by 1950s repairs, stands as one of two surviving monumental structures by the architect, the other being the addition to the Indianapolis Terminal. There can be no doubt as to the origin of the design; the barrel-vaulted hall flanked by curved, largely symbolic buttresses and intersected by lower abutting wings is certainly a miniaturization of the unexecuted Chicago project. Even the ornamental sculptures capping the piers that frame the central hall and terminate the buttresses were part of the earlier project. The cross vault of the Chicago station also survives in the design in the gabled roofs of the office wings on either side of the central hall. The crisp rectangular window and door openings and the light steel canopy suspended from the iron frame of the glazed diaphragms that infill the main facade were intended to indicate a frame of structural steel rather than concrete. Apart from material and scale there was another significant difference between the Fort Wayne Station and the Chicago Terminal. As a trackside terminal the Fort Wayne structure presented a difficult problem of transition from the ground level waiting room to the elevated track level. This the architects resolved by a concrete and glass waffle-slab roofed passage to a tunnel under the tracks from which rose stairs to the platforms.

The waiting room consisted of a single large space spanned by a barrel vault which contrasts with the gabled exterior profile of the roof. Skylighted bands, lighted by a clerestory under the gable, brought natural light into the space, recalling the French terminals that Price had seen a few years earlier. The color scheme of the both exterior and the interior was light and bright limestone and yellow-tan brick woven into a striking essay in tapestry brickwork. Its geometric character contrasts with the curvilinear coffers of the vault where "run in place" plaster profiles recall Price's interest in art nouveau a decade earlier. Despite the drama of the entrance from the track level and the effective massing of the building, the standard Pennsylvania Railroad passenger station benches overwhelm the modest waiting room and the result seems miniaturized.

———

45. J. Fletcher Street to Stacy Glauser & Sons, 26 April 1911, Price and McLanahan Papers.

46. Portion of a flyer for "NWEMCo," Price and McLanahan Papers.

The ghost of the Chicago Terminal reappeared the following year when the office was asked to design a new station at Canton, Ohio. (*fig. 12*) Apparently its size would have been comparable to the Fort Wayne station, but sensitive to obvious difficulties of scale, Price revised the design toward the massing of the Chicago Terminal, lowering the curve of the roof vault, simplifying the side wings to make them subservient to the central mass, and developing the facade into more plastic and massive elements. European stations were recalled in the massed sculpted figures capping the chunky piers flanking the entrance. The composition was given a picturesque touch by a tall campanile similar to the offset tower which would have been a part of the Chicago station.

Opportunities Along the Atlantic Coast

In 1912 alone McLanahan's search for large-scale projects resulted in at least six designs for resort buildings, hotels in Newport, Rhode Island, northern New Jersey, a second hotel in Asheville, an inland golf resort in Georgia, and a seashore hotel in Puerto Rico as well as a pier in Atlantic City. Of these the project that came closest to construction was the immense ocean pier stretching out from the beachfront of Atlantic City. Docks and piers have been a staple of seaside resorts introducing city dwellers to the world of seafarers and watermen. By the early nineteenth century wood and even iron piers were being constructed for recreation, and by the end of the century, modern techniques were applied to the problem of construction at the edge of the sea. Atlantic City was the setting for the most ambitious of these projects: the Steel Pier, designed by James H. Windrim in 1898, was extended and overlaid with new features at numerous times in the twentieth century.[47] At the turn of the century its proprietors could work a crowd into a frenzy of excitement by doing nothing more than hauling a net around the pier and dumping the resulting contents on the deck.

At the end of 1911 or the beginning of 1912 a group of New York and Atlantic City businessmen hired Price and McLanahan to design a mammoth reinforced concrete pier that would stretch more than 2500 feet into the ocean at a site near Tennessee Avenue, just to the north of the Traymore and the Marlborough–Blenheim hotels.[48] It was a remarkable vision, but one that gave a premonition of coming changes in what had been Philadelphia's sphere of influence. Before this New York capital had only rarely intruded into Philadelphia markets; its arrival marked an important step in the marketing of the "City by the Sea" as a national resort, and projects of this scale would be central to that

47. The Windrim project was reported in *The Philadelphia Inquirer* (9 December 1898), 12, and additions were reported in *The Philadelphia Inquirer* (17 November 1900), 15.

48. Numerous letters, mostly between J. Fletcher Street and the Hennebique Construction Company, survive as do glass plate negatives of the proposed elevations and perspectives of the pier in the Price and McLanahan Papers.

development. That Price and McLanahan of Philadelphia were selected as the architects is also telling, indicating that they were known for innovative design that could help in the marketing of the project. The Blenheim's striking facade continued to produce results.

The Exposition Pier would be the midway of the Chicago Fair recreated on a surface thrust into the Atlantic Ocean—and with luck and design it would seem even grander than its setting. A spectacular entrance pavilion would lead from the beach into a barrel vaulted hall which once again was a rethinking of the Chicago Terminal. At its rear, visible along the entire beachfront, would be a fifteen- or twenty-story observation tower derived from the railroad station clock tower, and beyond were a 3000-seat theater, a convention hall, shops, restaurants, and amusement buildings finally ending in a vast open deck ordered by colonnades that was to contain an outdoor bazaar. Three eight-by-ten-inch glass plate negatives were necessary to photograph the side elevation at a scale that would be visible. The principal buildings that were fully developed as designs drew on the forms that had been evolving in the office during the previous years, with vestiges of the Overhanover water towers, the great curved planes of the Chicago Terminal, and the celebratory volumes of the Blenheim, all recapitulated but with a breadth of surface and larger and more sculptural forms. Price had learned the value of reusing effective pieces from earlier projects. The pier had the added edge of an amusement park which may have been the cause of some truly original pieces, especially the orange-and-green tile domes growing out of flat roofs at the boardwalk.[49] These shapes would reappear a year later in the even more remarkable Puerto Rico hotel project. In the setting of Atlantic City, where the Blenheim dominated the boardwalk, if the shapes of the pier buildings seemed exaggerated, so much the better. Perhaps Will remembered Furness' bank designs along Chestnut Street, each demanding attention and competing with earlier buildings. Overlaying the big volumes were an array of festive towers, minarets, and pagodas which would give a dreamy silhouette—especially as they emerged from the gilded fog of the early summer morning.

Something of the division of labor between the architects and the engineers, the Hennebique Construction Company of New York, can be learned from the surviving fragments of correspondence between the two offices. It was the engineering firm that proposed using water jets to sink the wood pilings on which the structure was to be built and suggested a simpler system of concrete caps above the pilings which would be held in place by the weight of the slab. Engineers had begun to learn of the problems created by modern scale and in the case of a pier of several thousand feet, they suggested steel expansion plates regularly spaced the length of the structure. This practice would not

49. Reproductions survive of a lost Jules Guerin paint-   and colorful domes.
ing of the pier showing warm yellow tans for the walls

become common for another generation with significant consequences for the survival of early reinforced concrete structures of any size.[50] The Price office determined the column dimensions and their reinforcing for the incidental structures above the main slab, leaving only the large buildings such as the theaters for the engineers. Presumably the architect's calculations were based on standard formulas developed at the Towne School of Engineering, and were confirmed by the engineers. In May 1912 preliminary contracts were signed for clearing access to the site and by the fall test borings were made for footings in the vicinity of the great tower that marked the entry near the surf line. Construction would begin the following spring.

With the plans in hand the developers ran into a storm of a different sort, an economic downturn that affected the capital markets. In desperation they retained the brilliant architectural renderer of the day, Jules Guerin, to add jewel-like hues and flat tones to Price's perspective. By the spring of 1913 Will was involved, writing to James Turner to see if he knew anyone in Pittsburgh who might be interested in funding the scheme. With vast quantities of Pittsburgh money pouring into another seashore project down the coast in Cape May, no one in western Pennsylvania cared to throw more money into the Atlantic Ocean. There was not even money to pay Guerin for his rendering. Although the pier continued to be mentioned in office correspondence for two more years, it never became any more real than the Guerin perspective.

During the same years similar fates befell half a dozen related projects. Their numbers reflected the economic boom after the recession of 1909, and their failure to be constructed demonstrates their essentially speculative nature and the problem of similar projects competing for the same pool of capital. It would be nice to think that the office was being paid for its work, but it is likely that much was on speculation.[51] As exercises in design these projects show the effort of the office to merge its sympathy with the Spanish baroque as analogous to concrete with the debased forms of modern classicism which had become the basis for contemporary festival architecture beginning with the White City of the Chicago fair and continuing in early twentieth-century exhibitions such as the Pan-American Exposition in Buffalo and the Louisiana Purchase Exposition in St. Louis. Conflicting with these tendencies was Will's instinct to work resolutely toward contemporary construction and detail as a representation of modern life. It was not an easy conflict to resolve and it was made more difficult, one suspects, by the desire of owners to

50. In Philadelphia in the 1930s a triangular concrete-framed building designed by Magaziner and Eberhard for the University of Pennsylvania pushed itself off its foundations because of a lack of expansion joints.

51. McLanahan's role as the business manager of the firm is evident in letters requesting payments for over-due fees. One such letter of December 1913 to the directors of the Aumond project reports that payment was a year overdue; a letter to Philadelphia attorneys to collect carries the handwritten note that the fee had been received, less ten percent for the lawyer's fees.

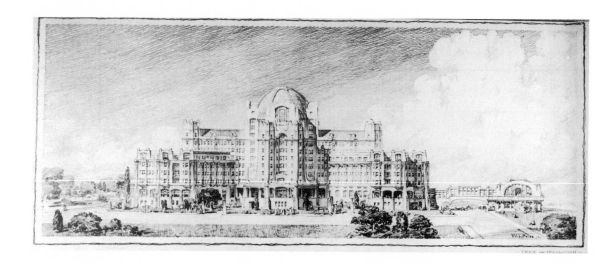

top 13. William L. Price, Essex and Sussex Hotel, Spring Lake, New Jersey, elevation. Glass plate negative of lost pencil drawing on paper. (Price and McLanahan Archives, George E. Thomas Collection)

center 14. William L. Price, E. W. Grove Park Hotel, elevation. Glass plate negative of lost pencil drawing on paper. (Price and McLanahan Archives, George E. Thomas Collection)

bottom 15. William L. Price, proposed apartment house for Frank W. Wheeler, Indianapolis, Indiana. Glass plate negative of lost pencil drawing on paper. (Price and McLanahan Archives, George E. Thomas Collection)

have projects that were conventional and acceptable and at the same time original and therefore notable. For an architect born in 1861, whose generation had largely stayed with history, Price's transformation was all the more remarkable.

The conflicts rooted in Price's training resulted in many projects beginning with a conventional historicizing approach but as they developed moving toward the contemporary forms that increasingly interested Price. Those that remained in the first stages are less interesting while those that continued to develop show more links to the mature work that engages the eye nearly a century later. This pattern can be seen in many of the hotel projects which typically featured a central block flanked by long wings and terminating with end towers in the manner of the Onslow Hotel. The conflicting aesthetic forces within the office are indicated by the overhanging roofs of the Spanish revivals and the incorporation of overscaled buttresses and volutes complementing the vertical accents of towers. Vestiges of historical detail were often juxtaposed against the broader surfaces ornamented with tile panels overlaying sculptural planes that seamlessly merge chimneys and walls, balconies and arches to create new and original forms. These tendencies can be seen in the facade of the proposed hotel for Newport of 1910 and the scheme of the following year for the additions to the Essex and Sussex Hotel and the Dunes Hotel, both of which were to be constructed in Spring Lake, New Jersey, a Victorian resort that had fallen behind Atlantic City and was seeking to keep its New York clientele. (*fig. 13*)

The dialogue between client and architect comes through in letters relating to a new hotel for Asheville, North Carolina. Despite earlier difficulties with the Kenilworth Inn, Asheville had continued to be a successful regional resort and, with the rise of the "New South," local developers saw the opportunity to add to its previous renown. In 1911 the office was asked to enter a limited competition for E. W. Grove's proposed hotel which was to bring the grand hotel of the Atlantic seaboard to the older railroad resort. Price's earlier Kenilworth Inn had been an artistic if not an economic success before its destruction by fire in 1909, making him a logical choice as one of the competitors. The owner of the project, E. W. Grove, was a St. Louis pharmaceutical manufacturer whose flagship product was Grove's Bromo-Quinine. On a visit to Asheville he found the dry air and moderate temperatures beneficial to his own health, with the result that he purchased a large property on Sunset Mountain where he proposed to sell residential lots. When this strategy did not succeed, he decided to build a hotel modeled on the Yellowstone Inn but of native stone instead of logs.

Office correspondence referring to a meeting in Philadelphia with Grove's representative, William Randolph, indicates that a design similar to the Kenilworth was the client's wish, with the main intent to represent the setting in the Asheville mountains. By February 1912 plans and a large perspective had been submitted which Will followed up with a letter describing the central ideas. (*fig. 14*) The hotel was to be built in stages with the central block functioning as a complete building and with the capacity to extend the dining room "almost to an unlimited extent...owing to the fan like shape...which gives a great expanse of window and view." As to the elevation, Price commented:

> We have indicated the use of the rough boulder and mountain stone with plaster walls on hollow tile above, the roof to be covered with dull green, glazed tiles such as you saw in our office. We have put a great deal of timberwork on projecting eaves and balconies suggested by the forest setting of the building which otherwise will be practically fire-proof.
>
> For a building of this size, we felt that a design in the character of the Chateaus of the Austrian Alps was more applicable than the chalet form. The chalet character could be readily expressed in the cottages, garage and mountain summit house; producing with the hotel a most harmonious effect.
>
> We have had great pleasure in working out this scheme and believe that some such plan as this if carried out in the manner which you talked to us would provide the most attractive and comfortable resort establishment in America.[52]

The letter hints at conflicts that were unresolved. The client had asked for a chalet which the architects felt was the wrong style for the scale for the project. Will had offered an olive branch by suggesting that the chalet style would be right for the small buildings. The client wanted the chalet and, not getting what he wanted from his east coast architects, eventually built the Grove Park Inn in a crudely rustic style that recalled the Adirondack lodges of the previous generation and the great western railroad hotels of the day but missed the sophisticated interplay of massing and angles of the facade which made Price's scheme richer. A conciliatory letter from Will followed expressing regret that he had not met the wishes of the client. He had failed to observe a principle that he had enunciated in the 1903 speech in Ontario—the architect's job is to give the client what he wants while elevating him. But unless the building is what the client wants, the project is doomed from the start. The architect of the present structure was Fred Loring Seely, Grove's son-in-law, "a former newspaperman in Atlanta...who proceeded to design without an architect, and to build without a contractor."[53] Built of reinforced concrete and faced with boulders, it was in effect based on the central themes of Price's design but lacks the high roofs and clustered towers which were the hallmarks of the Austrian style that gave Price and McLanahan's perspective such force.

Houses for Plutocrats

Four domestic projects marked the maturation of Price's ideas about regional character in modest buildings. In 1911 Will was commissioned to design a house and office for Fiske Warren in Harvard, Massachusetts, the site of one of the principal Shaker communities

---

52. William L. Price to William Randolph, E. W. Grove Park, Asheville, North Carolina, 28 February 1912,

Price and McLanahan Papers.
53. *The Grove Park Story* (privately published, c. 1970).

and the setting for Warren's attempt at a Single Tax village. Warren, heir to an immense New England paper fortune, had been a backer of Price's Arden community, and was a staunch advocate of the Single Tax and other utopian schemes. In 1911 he brought Will to his estate at Harvard, beginning a group of projects which would end with the purchase of a large portion of Andorra. Although the design of Tahanto, as the Warren office and cottage were called, is less satisfying than Price's next houses, the central idea was important. For Warren, Price designed a modern version of a New England farmhouse with a gable-roofed front block attached to a long rear wing that in a local farmhouse would have connected to a barn. There was an inherent logic to vernacular architectural forms, a logic that Will had felt in the local architecture of Rose Valley. This logic did not rise from fashion but rather from the facts of climate, solar orientation, availability of materials, and living patterns. Because sound domestic architecture needed to be rooted in its place, when Price designed for a different setting, he changed his vocabulary to address the place.

Two mid-Atlantic houses were based on the same conclusion. In 1911 Price and McLanahan received a commission for a house for George G. Greene, the son of the industrialist whose pharmaceuticals factory dominated Woodbury, New Jersey. Having returned from Pasadena, California, where he had encountered western contemporary design, the client sought the most progressive architect in the Philadelphia area and found that the only choice was Will Price. Will designed a gable-roofed house with steep slopes appropriate to the region's wet weather and bright stucco surfaces overlaid with Mercer tile ornament. In a slightly more conventional vein Price designed a house in Chestnut Hill on the edge of Philadelphia's Fairmount Park for Joseph Woolston. Again the gabled-roof forms reflect the shapes of the rolling Pennsylvania valleys and the region's weather, while the carefully calculated orientation offered a sunroom and porch as a screen against the heat of summer and the cold of winter. The exterior details, incorporating decorative tile into pebble-dashed stucco over hollow tile walls, reflected the vocabulary that Price had developed; again concrete lintels spanned windows in hollow tile walls. The vernacular logic of Rose Valley had spread to all of Price's domestic work.

While he was designing the Warren and Greene houses, Price received a group of commissions for a real estate development, a hotel, and a large house all for the Indianapolis industrialist and automobile promoter Frank Wheeler. The fact that the initial contacts were for large-scale public buildings suggests that the connection was made through McLanahan's search. A long, narrow perspective of the Wheeler Heights development dated 1912 shows a low hotel, clearly the Raleigh from the Overhanover project, nestled in trees on a crest of land above a man-made lake. A design for the downtown Indianapolis hotel was closely related to the large seashore hotels around 1911 and 1912. (fig. 15) Wheeler had big visions, but these projects never came to fruition. Wheeler along with his neighbors Carl Fisher and Joseph Allinson were pioneers in the auto parts business and together developed the Indianapolis Motor Speedway as the medium for their advertising. In June 1911 Wheeler retained Price and McLanahan to design a mansion on land adjacent to his associates that befitted his rising economic station. Fisher had already erected a large but plain house while Joseph Allinson was building a house from the designs of an Indianapolis architect, H. L. Bass. Wheeler selected Price and McLanahan for his house.

In early June 1911 the office sent a proposal to Wheeler. Shortly thereafter a representative of the office, probably Ralph Bencker, visited the site and took small views in all directions showing as far as the eye could see the boundless horizon of the prairie, interrupted here and there by a tree, and on the side toward the road by telephone poles. The photographs show a farm, complete with barn, farmhouse, and wash on the line. On one side, in the distance, can be seen Fisher's house, screened by trees. Bleak scarcely describes the emptiness. Wheeler had big ideas for his property. The waterways of the Chicago fair would be recreated on the midwestern prairie. A depression would be excavated—using animal power—to produce a formal lake filled by artesian wells. Off to one side of the lake was to be an irregularly shaped water park with islands and landings, a "shady pond" according to the site plan, with a teahouse serving as a landing for a custom-designed gondola. The near side of the lake would be framed by the mansion which would be linked by a pergola to a giant water tower containing Frank Wheeler's pool room and private office. It was an opportunity at the scale of the Wood mansion of three decades earlier but for a client who was attuned to the modern world and who desired a house that celebrated the present. At fifty Will was ready for the task.

The office put its best men on the project. Will handled the larger design issues and assigned Ralph Bencker, already running other midwestern projects, to serve essentially as clerk of the works, while J. Fletcher Street handled the landscape design and selection of plant materials. Siting was simple. In the foreground, near the road, was a tennis pavilion and courts with the house to the rear and slightly off center, balanced by the reflective surface of the lake and the vertical accent of the water tower to the side. A grove of trees sheltered the smaller "shady pond" and restricted the view along the edge of the property toward the Fisher house. Behind the house, staff quarters were constructed on axis with the lake and the entrance to the pond, while a guest house was to be constructed on a spit of land between the two watercourses, in the quiet rear of the property.

The house reflected the conclusions that Price had reached on the Warren building. A house should respond to the character of the site—in this instance the overwhelming horizontal of the prairie which might be interrupted by secondary vertical accents. The plan met the social circumstances of a midwestern American family. Reception occurred in a nearly central hall with a grand stair on axis with the vestibule which faced the main drive. A small receiving room to the right of the hall offered a space for private conversation but the room most used would be the drawing room at the corner of the house that opened out onto paved terraces. These would have served as outdoor extensions of the living spaces during nice weather. Together these three front rooms formed a suite around the stair, once again opening the interior into free-flowing space. Modern central heating and the decompartmentalized openness of modern life were reflected in the design. To the rear, where they would receive afternoon light, would be the dining and breakfast rooms, parallel to the rear service corridor linking them to the pantry and kitchen. Asymmetrical, with each space sized to its purpose, with windows shaped according to the character of the activities within and oriented according to views and terraces, the house was a logical expression of the lifestyle of a successful businessman. Despite the recurring vertical corner buttresses and chimneys rising through the gable ends, the effect is one of peaceful repose.

In keeping with the plan, the facades were modern and direct. A yellow-tan brick which must have resonated with the greens and clay tones of the landscape forms the walls of the house. Laid in Flemish bond, and accented by geometric bands of tile in greens, yellows, and blues—the colors of the sky and prairie—and roofed by broad planes of green Spanish tile, the exterior nestled into its landscape with remarkable grace. In a strongly welcoming gesture the entrance portico projects slightly and is capped by a parapet whose segmental curve recalled entrance of Price's railroad station at Steubenville. There is no doubt as to the location of the entrance, no concealment; it is direct, sincere, assertive. The palette of materials and shapes are shared by the other structures of the estate, beginning with the entrance gateposts whose tapered shafts capped by sculptural pier caps would become familiar in the ornament of the Traymore Hotel and the Chicago Freight Terminal. Crowning the complex was the powerful sculpture of the water tower whose upturned roof corners, particularly when juxtaposed against the teahouse by the water and the Japanese lanterns of the rock garden around the shady pool, betray the exotic sources of the design.

The Wheeler house was similar in scale to the Steubenville Station and like that building was constructed on an armature of reinforced concrete. Once again curved transitions between columns and beams denote the structural system in accord with the office's by then conventional manner. Where needed for structural logic, columns were free standing, as in the hall or incorporated into walls. The structure was given warmth by wainscoting but, unlike the houses of the previous generation which would have followed medieval models, here Price used plain surfaces of book-matched grains, joined by wooden butterfly clasps and crowned by simple moldings. By stopping the paneling below the transitional curve of the columns rather than cladding the entire height as well as the beams, the underlying concrete structure is revealed and the wood describes its role as purely decorative surface.

Although Price and McLanahan were proud of the results, office correspondence reveals strains in the relationship between architect and client. A letter between Will

Price and Frank Wheeler in the spring of 1913, as the project was winding down, gives a picture of the difficulties over fees. The sense of hurt is probably familiar too.

April 22, 1913
Mr. Frank. H. Wheeler,
Indianapolis, Ind.

My dear Mr. Wheeler:-
If I did not know you so well, I should regard your last two letters as insulting. I know that you no more believe that we are trying to "hook" you than that you are trying to get something for nothing from us.

  We have taken your word for the account from the beginning and have based our charges on our regular schedule as sent to you with letter of June 7, 1911 and accepted by you in your letter of June 9th, except that we have only charged you at the flat 6% rate for all work, even interior cabinet work, decorating, gardening, etc., on which our schedule calls for 10%; and that we have given you such supervision as no job I know of has had, our Mr. Bencker with your foreman having practically built the house which under our schedule and according to established practice would entitle us to 2¼% additional or 8¼%—see schedule "Separate Contracts".

  As to the gardening, we not only laid out the whole scheme of roads, walks, pools, etc., but a large part of the planting was not only planned by us but the actual planting lists made out by our Mr. Street in connection with your former gardener. You have repeatedly said to me personally that we were entitled to a commission on all such work from the front back to the vegetable garden, with which, we had nothing to do. You agreed with me that this road, grading and planting cost $5,000, we both stated it was a guess, but in the fact of your repeated statements about this work it does not go very well to have you now say we are trying to "hook" you. Perhaps it wasn't $5,000, we do not know. You have the accounts, we are quite willing that you should fix the amount, so our understanding is clear.

  As to the Tobey work, it was solely on your own statement of what was due us that we were acting when we made the account. You told me, the next to the last time that I was out, that you had given Tobey the hangings according to the original scheme as made up by Mr. Robertson and myself here and in Chicago, also that you had ordered some of the furniture according to the original designs, on which you said we were entitled to commission, but bought some on which we were not, with which I entirely agreed. We wrote to Robertson in accordance with this as follows: "Will you please send us a statement of the contracts on the Wheeler work which your firm has? Mr. Wheeler could not remember these accounts, his impression was that the decorations were $5,000 which corresponds with our recollection and the draperies he did not seem to about, my recollection was that they were about the same amount. I also understand from him that some of the furniture as originally designed, they are ordering. Kindly send us a statement of what this was and the price as Mr. Wheeler desires to make settlement of the contracts on which were entitled to commission. Of course, we are not entitled to commission on furniture he bought from you with which we had nothing to do. An immediate reply will greatly oblige." Our commission on this work is for selection and approval not for drawings.

As to the leaded glass, we designed this glass for the place, but I was not willing to have it made as ordered to do by you, unless you saw one sash of it for color, etc. this was the lower windows which was to be mainly plate glass so that the garden could be seen through it. The upper windows were nearly all of colored glass and these lower ones could also be for the same price. We believed as the designers of the house that we knew what should go there and still believe that the glass designed for this window, the dining room and the conservatory are right. The window sent out I told you, would not be the right size, it was only a sample so that we should be sure of the color being what you wanted.

As to the traveling expense account, it is according to our printed schedule sent you and according to general architectural practice; with this exception: we have made no charge for excess time as called for, our interest in your place was so great that we have given unusual service and have not even charged according to the regular rates and our printed schedule of charges.

Very truly yours,

Price and McLanahan,

By WLP[54]

After the letter the project was quickly back on track, with designs for a guest house and a servants' residence. At the end of May there was a letter on the final touch to the estate, the shipping of the gondola for the ponds. Ralph Bencker handled the correspondence because he had "a great deal of experience with boats."[55] After nearly a decade out of the national architectural press for domestic commissions, the Wheeler house received thorough study and applause in an article in the *International Studio* by Harry Blackman Sell entitled "Good Taste and the Mansion." Beginning with the premise that good taste and mansions are rarely found together, Sell was both surprised and delighted with what he found.

Fortunately to-day there are arising men who see their opportunities and who grasp them. Men who have the vision, the bravery, and the energy to disregard the worn forms of the past and to put into the sixth figure a studied understanding of the conditions of the problem, the personality of the client and the fundamental laws of good taste in building.

---

54. William L. Price to Frank H. Wheeler, 22 April 1913, Price and McLanahan Papers.

55. Ralph B. Bencker to Frank H. Wheeler, 23 May 1913, Price and McLanahan Papers.

Such a man is William L. Price, and such a commission was the home of Frank H.
Wheeler, built high on the crest of a prairie billow just outside the city of Indianapolis,
Indiana.

As one approaches the house from the high road, the feeling grows stronger and
still stronger that this is truly American architecture.[56]

Price had incorporated into his domestic designs Thomas Carlyle's principle (which he
had paraphrased in *The Artsman*) that "originality does not consist in being different but in
being sincere."[57]

❧ *The San Cristobal: Intimations of the Future*

Although the San Cristobal Hotel in San Juan, Puerto Rico, would turn out to be another
will-o'-the-wisp, it preoccupied the office first in 1910 and again in 1912. In order to create a tourist industry, Puerto Rico offered incentives which would give premier hotel sites
to developers free of local taxes if the operator guaranteed construction and operated the
hotel at a profit for ten years. The benefits for the entire island were outlined in the
prospectus:

Apart from these briefly outlined advantages, the erection of a GRAND HOTEL, becomes at
the same time an important aid to the working classes, who, by means of their labor will
erect it. The fabulous sum of $500,000 will be invested in the above enterprise, the benefit
of which will be shared by that country and its artisans who shall take part in the erection
of the same.[58]

The 1910 plan for the San Cristobal was Spanish baroque, reflecting the culture of the
island. The decorative patterns of the glazed tile roofs and the rich ornamental brocade
over the upper surfaces recall Spanish churches that Price had seen in his European venture of 1906. Like the Overhanover hotels and the project for the Grove Park Inn, the
building could be constructed in phases with the core facilities occupying the central
block. Many of these designs were slipping back toward historical forms, so the fact that
none of the them was constructed is no loss. Indeed, had one been built, it is possible that
the next phase of Price's career would never have arrived. Instead their principal role is to
make what came next, in 1912, all the more remarkable for its freshness of conception,
and all the more regretted because it was never constructed.

Two drawings of the final design survive, a perspective dated 1912, and a plan
dated 28 January 1913. Perhaps it was the simple cubic masses of modest Spanish-influ-

---

56. Harry Blackman Sell, "Good Taste and the
Mansion," *International Studio*, 57 (November 1915),
xi–xv.
57. Price, "Modern Architecture," 229.

58. "Copy of letter re Porto Rico Hotel," provides
details on land costs and incentives; the quote is from a
fragment of a letter filed with the Puerto Rico hotel
project, Price and McLanahan Papers.

enced houses that attracted Price's attention or the massive sculptural character of the great cliffs and fortress overlooking San Juan harbor. In any event Price abandoned the Overhanover scheme and designed with an abandon that would characterize his last projects. Instead of a dominant central mass Price reversed himself and designed a rectangular almost clifflike volume with an entrance pavilion in the center facing the main highway. It was joined to a wing, off to the side, that contained entrance doors on either side of a fireplace, with another wing that was more or less an extended octagon overlooking the cliffs and the ocean. Each volume represented the large functions of the hotel, the exchange or lobby with a patio under the entrance block, a ball room and connecting lobbies in the central wing, and the dining room and related banquet rooms in the octagon. This plan took Price back to his beginnings as a Victorian architect free to confront design as a consequence of facts.

The perspective is even more remarkable. Working from the plan instead of from precedent, Price was free to sculpt a plastic mass that was lacking in applied details and historical references. Instead, with the exception of the buttresses at the corners which repeat the forms of the fortifications of the harbor, Price designed in broad masses, interrupted by a few balconies for scale and shadow but principally described by fenestration and volume. The huge windows of the lower level lighted an interior porch surrounding the central "patio" which was cooled and soothed by an indoor fountain. Rising from this dramatic space was an interior court surrounded at the upper levels by the single loaded corridors providing access to guest rooms and covered by an immense roof pavilion ventilated by large windows. Unlike the roof-capped volumes of earlier hotel projects, this scheme was surmounted by a pavilion which lighted and ventilated the central court and by astonishing flying saucerlike domes similar to those of the Atlantic City pier entrance which was being designed at the same time.

Sleek, sculptural, rising to an array of forms depicting marvelous opportunities, the San Cristobal is eerily timeless. Unrivaled by any designs of its day, the San Cristobal affords a view into the future of a concrete architecture, one of plastic richness that could have set architectural imaginations flying free before European modernists attached machine rhetoric to design with such limiting consequences. Anticipating Tony Garnier's World War I sketches of a *Cité Industrielle*, the San Cristobal has the air of a dream. We can only wonder at what so dramatically reshaped Price's vision. One possibility seems likely. In the summer of 1912 mortality again loomed as it hadn't since his fortieth year. A letter to the owners of the Essex and Sussex Hotel apologized for failing to get drawings for a prospective redesign of the building sent off in time, noting "I had no thought of being away this summer. My doctor advised a two month's rest, from which I have just returned."[59]

---

59. William L. Price to Mrs. S. E. Urie, Spring Lake, N. J., 20 September 1912, Price and McLanahan Papers.

⋲ *Last Years: The Traymore Hotel*

As if hastening toward a finally visible goal Price's career speeded up as his health declined. 1913 was a relatively slow year. The office finished the Wheeler estate and completed minor parts of the railroad projects in the midwest. An addition to Jacob Reed's Sons' Store would have reminded Will of how far he had come in a decade. As 1914 began with few projects in the office, the situation was once again desperate. In the spring of that year Daniel White decided to enlarge his hotel, the Traymore, which stood across Park Place in Atlantic City from his cousin Josiah White's Marlborough–Blenheim Hotel. Whether simply good business or intrafamily competition, White's goal was to create a landmark that would make his hotel the signature building of the resort. The difficulties of getting the project going are well told by the attorney, L. Stauffer Oliver, whose account offers a remarkable insight into the risks involved in putting together such projects.

> About that time, the owner of the old frame Hotel Traymore at Illinois Avenue and the Boardwalk in Atlantic City, decided he wanted to build an outstanding new structure as a monument to his lifetime in the hotel business in that city. So he got together a group of three younger men; his manager, Joseph W. Mott, and the two architects, Price and McLanahan of Rose Valley, who had designed the modern eight-story structure he had previously had erected at the Boardwalk end of his frame hotel.... He made them an unusual proposition. If they would finance and build a beautiful modern hotel, he would take the company's preferred stock issue in full payment of his land, the new structure at the Boardwalk end and his very valuable good will. They were to receive all of the common stock for their services as promoters....
>
> In addition to the first mortgage and the bonds secured thereby, a bond and second mortgage, and new corporation's charter, by-laws, and minutes, there were many contracts to be negotiated and drafted. All went well until the construction company demanded a surety bond as a guarantee that the second mortgage money would be available when needed. Once news of that demand became known, virtually everyone wanted similar protection, and the intricate financing structure, which the three men had so painstakingly built, began to fall apart and they began to lose heart. After a prolonged struggle they became convinced that the situation was hopeless.
>
> Although taken merely to do the legal work of incorporating the hotel company, drafting the mortgages and accompanying bonds, the corporation minutes, and the many contracts for such items as the hotel building, the decoration thereof, the elevator system, the American and European plan kitchens, the furniture and the furnishings, I could not, after all the work I had done, sit by and see the enterprise collapse....
>
> Finally, I concluded to have a show-down. So I set ten a.m. on a Friday in mid-summer, 1914, as the time for settlement at the Guarantee Trust Company in Atlantic City. All the parties met at the time and place stated and we haggled and negotiated from

ten a.m. until ten thirty p.m. When we left at that late hour, the mortgage and all contracts had been signed and delivered.

On the morning of the following day, the newspapers were full of blazing headlines—World War I had broken out in Europe. Before ten a.m that day, the brokers who had underwritten the first mortgage called me on the phone and said, "Oliver, if you had been one day later, your damned hotel would never have been financed."[60]

The Traymore was financed and a project that had been discussed for two years went into construction. The project began with the assumption that the 1906 Boardwalk wing would be preserved as an integral part of the design. Fortunately, although its secondary details were less sculptural than Price's later works, the cruciform plan and the domical and barrel vaults of the roofs could be incorporated into the final project. The long site suggested a main facade facing Illinois Avenue; by adding progressively longer wings on the Park Place side, rear rooms could still get an ocean view or at least see the park and the silhouette of the Blenheim to the south. With a raised central block distinguished from the main slab by domed towers and a lower inland wing which more or less duplicated the mass of the original wing, the architects were able to develop an effective composition whose deviations from symmetry were masked by the scale of the building and the oblique angles of view along Illinois Avenue.

Using all of the techniques that he had mastered in the previous five years, Will gave order to the facade by pairs of bays joined at their tops by spanning arches visually supporting the crowning domes. Above the parapets immense curving volutes formed a transition to the domes while the masses of the building stepped in toward the center without the interruption of a roofline. The resulting towers created vertical accents that read like the skyscrapers of the next decade. The remarkable effect was the building as a whole. Despite the slablike form of the Illinois Avenue front, the upper levels of the facade were new and unique, a vast sculpted mass, a sand castle that honored Price's vision of the plasticity of concrete and the modern potential of the material. Clad in the sand-toned bricks that Price had used for a decade, and accented with brilliantly colored tile pier caps at the points where the columns protruded through the parapet, with gilded domes and barrel vaults, the Traymore was the first large-scale public building to exploit fully the plastic potential of concrete. The desire of the architects to build according to their plans was understandable.[61]

---

60. L. Stauffer Oliver, *The Bench Is a Hard Seat: An Autobiography* (Philadelphia: Dorrance and Company, 1965), 6–8. Oliver's fees went toward a Rose Valley house designed by Price and McLanahan. Price was not so lucky. At his death the capital contribution represented by his designs for the Traymore had yet to pay him a cent.

61. A full account of the construction of the Traymore is contained in George Thomas, "A House Built on Sand," *Via* 7, ed. Paula Behrens and Anthony Fisher (Philadelphia: Graduate School of Fine Arts, University of Pennsylvania, 1984), 8–21.

The contractors were able to get on site immediately after Labor Day, with the closing of the old hotel at the end of the season. A remarkable log of 300 film negatives records the construction process. When the site was cleared varying numbers of wood pilings were driven to the point of resistance and then capped by masses of concrete which served as footings for the columns of the building. In some instances, quicksand was hit, forcing changes in the location of footings. Because it was the goal to build the entire 600-room building in less than nine months, steel cores were added to the columns of the lower levels to carry the weight of the building while the concrete cured and gained in strength. Photographs taken week by week show the building rising through autumn storms and a spring blizzard, gradually being clad in its tan brick. One view shows as many as fifty masons building the perimeter wall while a snowstorm rages across the site. Attesting to its importance, Price made regular inspection visits during its construction.

With the construction well under way the office turned to the possibilities of the interior decor. Price thought of N. C. Wyeth who had become the hottest graphic artist of the day and asked him to Rose Valley to discuss doing the decorations. Wyeth's letter to his brother of his 18 January 1915 meeting with Price records the vision of the architect.

> Yesterday was a great day for me, and like all fine experiences I could wish that you had shared it with me.
>
> A week ago George Harding asked me to meet him on Sunday noon at the home of Chas. H. Stephens (better known perhaps as the husband of Alice Barber Stephens of magazine fame). "The meeting," he said, "is to discuss the possible decoration of a luxurious hotel now building in Atlantic City."
>
> I accepted the invitation of course, and so, in the downpour and almost summer's heat of yesterday's storm, slopped my way to Rose Valley—the home of Mrs. Stephens near Philadelphia.
>
> The event of the few hours in Stephens' home was as full of charm and stimulus as one could well assimilate, but which was overtopped by the visit we payed to William Price, architect.
>
> If ever a man emanated the electric force and energy of Roosevelt, Price is the man! Such enthusiasm, such virility, such exquisite taste and refinement perfectly mixed with a wholesome manliness I have seldom seen, except, as I say, in Roosevelt, and I imagine, in such men as Riis, Phillips Brooks, Rabbi Wise and all those where we feel that the force the animal, the *brute*, has *not* been dulled by finely directed....
>
> With all this fabulous mosaic of music, philosophy and Oriental art as a background, we went into Price's sanctum (in itself a temple and place of worship), and there he unfolded his scheme for the interior design, furnishing and wall decoration of the $2000 [sic, $2,000,000] hotel at Atlantic City.
>
> With his back to the window, and seated crosslegged on a broad divan, he built up for us a prodigious vision of the vast structure. His ringing, insistent keynote was

modernity, modernity! A beseeching appeal to us to face our modern spirit and customs unflinchingly, and to cease thinking that unless a building resembles the Parthenon, or a mural decoration resembles Angelo or Donatello, that it is "rotten." That we *must* recognize that our life today, from the frenzied, circus-ridden antics of Billy Sunday to the spendthrifts and money gluttons who patronize hotels of a resort, are *realities*, just as Nero and his extravagant retinue were realities, feasting their eyes on a gladiator's battle, or gloating over the sacrifice of Christians in the arena. That to paint, sculpt, or design classically is merely to be true to your era.

On this line he talked for an hour and drove and redrove home his arguments with pointed analogies.

To all this I am profoundly sympathetic. It is what I profoundly believe, and with the stimulus of an older, stronger man that I am behind me I shall be able to escape the shackles of tradition and evolve something modern.

And, now I have an opportunity. A gorgeous underground café; stark in its simplicity; a great black marble dancing space dropped below level, upon which are coral-colored tables and chairs: huge pillars, four of them supporting a glass ceiling which is in reality a lake filled with Japanese goldfish! From the dance floor one gazes at the sky through the water and the flashing goldfish. The great flat walls and pillars are to be painted in blues, emeralds and whites, interpreting the feel of the deep sea! Such a chance! Mermaids, flying fish, seaweed, spume and glittering bubbles, rising, rising, like champagne in a glass!

Last night, I couldn't sleep, but I evolved my scheme and unless something unheard of happens, the scheme will go through with a rush!

The huge banquet room is another matter: 65 x 80 feet, fountains, huge glass globes with goldfish magnified as big as shad! Illuminated jets of water running like gold and jewels, Chinese rugs of pumpkin yellow and jet black pillars![62]

Coming shortly after Wyeth had been cut adrift by the death of his mentor Howard Pyle, the encounter with Will offered N. C. a new guide. A humorous sketch of Will resulted, one that shows him seated surrounded by his collection of weapons, his foot against a stack of the pamphlets he had just authored on the importance of peace, with the ironic title, "The Prince of Peace," with the "n" of Prince crossed out to make the title "The Price of Peace."[63] (*see color plate 21*) In June, with the hotel scheduled to open in days, N. C. sent along another report.

We are arriving at quite remarkable results—Harding and I. The Hotel itself is attracting nationwide attention on account of its size, cost, completeness and numerous *features*, the

---

62. Betsy Wyeth, ed., *The Wyeths*, 482–484.
63. The watercolor is in the possession of Philip Price, grandson of Will. The pamphlet at Will's feet is "Peace Man or War Man," Will's testimony against World War I.

above 16. N. C. Wyeth in studio painting scenes from *Treasure Island* for children's playroom, Traymore Hotel (Architectural Archives, Philip N. Price Collection, University of Pennsylvania)

left 17. Price and McLanahan, plaster model for 40-story addition to Traymore Hotel, 1916 (Price and McLanahan Archives, George E. Thomas Collection)

> most talked about being the "submarine café." With the room only half done, *7000* people visited it on Sunday! And the manager had to sign away and publish in the local papers that admission to the café would be prohibited until completely done.
>
> We are spending every hour our energy will stand to finish by Friday, midnight. Saturday, a banquet for 400 hotel managers from the principal hotels east of Chicago will be given in this room. A remarkable advertisement![64]

Wyeth reported that it was his paintings for a *Treasure Island* publication that got him the work. He was soon painting the *Treasure Island* scenes in the children's playroom. (*fig. 16*)

With its central position where the Atlantic City beachfront bulged out, Price's Traymore Hotel became the classic background of every beach view of the resort. It was immediately celebrated in the national architectural press with an important article in *Architectural Record.*

> Atlantic City, despite its great fame as a seaside resort, presents from an artistic standpoint a most disappointing appearance. Its famous hotels are for the most part only frame structures, devoid of any attempt at architectural embellishment, within and without. But to this rule there are notable exceptions, and a great improvement in recent years is to be noted. Several of the larger hotels have been rebuilt or added to, and the newer buildings are in almost every case far superior to the older ones. The most important of these works, both as to size and architectural character, is the Traymore, recently completed from the plans of Price & McLanahan of Philadelphia.[65]

After noting that the same architects had designed the Marlborough–Blenheim Hotel which, it was observed, was "of grey stucco, with rather acid green terra cotta ornaments...too rococo in character," the Traymore was found to have a "greater sobriety," with a color scheme reported as "soft, pinkish brown, with touches of yellow and green, culminating in the yellow tile domes, 234 feet above the ocean."

> Its very unusual design has been the logical consequence of its location and importance and can fairly be considered a great triumph for its architects, who have provinced an edifice that is striking without undue ostentation or expense, and festive in character without descending into frivolity.

The City by the Sea had found its ultimate urban image, an architectural landmark whose fame was spread by millions of visitors, and in turn added to the fame of the resort as its forms became the characteristic devices of the 1920s.

---

64. Betsy Wyeth, ed., *The Wyeths*, 487. Shortly thereafter, N.C. was given the decoration of the children's play room in one of the domes on the top of the hotel which he peopled with his figures from *Treasure Island*. None of these murals survive, but an oil sketch of the mermaids and seafoam of the Submarine Grill remains in the possession of the Price family.

65. John J. Klaber, "America's Greatest Seaside Hotel—The Traymore, Atlantic City, N. J.," *Architectural Forum*, 27 (November 1917), 119–123.

Chicago Freight Terminal: A Jacket Big Enough for the City of Broad Shoulders

The commission for the Traymore Hotel occurred nearly simultaneously with two other major commissions, one an addition to the Indianapolis Union Terminal to elevate the trains above the streets of the downtown and to provide an immense concourse under the tracks; the other for a vast freight terminal for the Pennsylvania Railroad in Chicago. Both mark further stages in the evolution of Price's work.

The significance of the Chicago Freight Terminal is easy to gauge. Its monumentality marked Price's growing mastery of scale. Just as large buildings need relatively simple forms to be graspable by the eye, when they go beyond immensity to become gargantuan there is often a need for secondary articulation so that the building can be grasped. In the case of the Chicago Freight Terminal with a facade several city blocks long beside the Chicago River, the solution was to subdivide the building into large masses with a secondary rhythm established by the pier caps breaking though the parapet. On the Polk Street front a giant tower rose nearly 150 feet above the street. With clock faces on its four sides, it was the quintessential symbol of the railroad that established national time zones and prided itself on its clockwork precision. The tower was more than just advertising for it contained three stories of storerooms; above them were giant water tanks that pressurized the fire-suppression sprinklers. Its slightly tapering form, made stronger by the chamfers of the upper facades, added to the sense of height. Elongated volutes linked the base of the tower to the mass of the building and were repeated in buttresslike elements that formed a transition between the lowest masses of the Polk Street facade and the upper levels of the building. It is hard to imagine that these elements had a structural role but their purpose in making the Polk Street facade a powerful sculptural form is clear.

Here the volutes were symbolic in purpose, recalling the design almost eight years before of the Chicago Railroad Terminal. The Polk Street elevation was going to be Price and McLanahan's chance at immortality in Chicago, and they were going to take their best shot. Achieved before the New York City zoning law which mandated such setback forms so that light could reach the bottoms of its canyons, this spire and the centerpiece of the Traymore, heralded the tapering, stepped-back spires that became the skyline of American cities of the 1920s. Photographs of a plaster model used to develop the tower indicate one of the means by which the office arrived at the increasingly plastic vocabulary of its late buildings. Because so few architects ever work on such a scale, the lessons of the side elevation had less impact than the towered Polk Street facade, but its progeny can be seen in other freight terminals for the Pennsylvania Railroad and the equally immense Sears, Roebuck northeast distribution center in Philadelphia by the Chicago architectural firm of George C. Nimmons and Company. Charles Whitaker (who kept Sullivan's memory alive until his rediscovery by Hugh Morrison) asserted that the Chicago Freight Terminal "grew naturally out of the theories of Louis

Sullivan."[66] In 1973 Carl Condit gave it high praise:

> the excellence of their architecture is still apparent.... The huge steel-framed building contains more than 1,500,000 square feet on its five levels making it the most generously scaled structure of its kind. The rectangular volume of the station building encloses five transverse light courts under skylights with sawtooth profiles in section. The long silhouette of the whole mass is repeatedly interrupted by slightly projecting wings and the low upward-swelling curves near the end bays, but the feature that dominates the surrounding area is the octagonal clock tower rising 190 feet above the street level at the north end of the building. The visible manifestation and the emblem of the metropolitan rail system for much of its history, the tower in this case also provides space for two utilitarian functions.... The interior construction is distinguished chiefly by the massive concrete floor slabs common to railroad freight stations and warehouses, the maximum loading factor being 300 pounds per square foot.... The huge red-brick enclosure, punctuated by a few small windows, is marked by a bold massing that is a little restless...but it possesses a monumentality that adds powerful rhythmic accents to the long rectilinear vistas of its rail and river setting.[67]

"No Particular Type of Architecture"

The last important midwestern work of the firm was the track elevation in Indianapolis which had its beginning in 1915. Unlike the Traymore Hotel and the Chicago Freight Terminal, which transformed the external forms of American tall buildings, the Indianapolis structure has almost no external presence, being essentially a reinforced concrete deck carried on concrete piers whose principal facade is a narrow triangle at one street intersection, and a bridge above a street adjacent to the station. The soft greens and tans of the terra-cotta panels of the bridge hardly offer a clue to the riot of secondary cooled purples, greens, and orange-tans of the terra-cotta tiles of the interior. A local writer in the *Indianapolis Star*, unaccustomed to nonhistorical design, reported that it "was of no particular type of architecture."[68] The palette of 1920s Miami had arrived in the brilliant colors and bold modern forms of Price and McLanahan's work in Indianapolis. There was another direct connection to Miami. In 1918, with the end of World War I, Carl Fisher and Frank Wheeler would take the firm of Price and McLanahan with them to Miami where they would shape the architectural vocabulary of the next great American seashore resort. By then, however, Will Price was dead, and the office was running on forms which had evolved in the years before 1916.

---

66. Charles H. Whitaker, *Ramses to Rockefeller* (New York: Random House, 1934), 329.
67. Condit, 265–268.

68. Quoted by Wesley I. Shank, "Union Station, Indianapolis," Historic American Building Survey (1971).

Last Projects

In 1916 two more projects appeared to offer yet more excitement for the office. One was Fiske Warren's Single Tax scheme in Andorra, which because of the war came to nothing. In the fall of 1916 *The New York Times* published an account of a proposed addition to the Traymore by Price and McLanahan. The hotel had been so successful that its owners conceived of adding an immense 30- to 40-story tower at the inland end of the 1914 building. (*fig. 17*) After rising above the inland wing for ten stories, the domed tops of the main block would be repeated in a domed tower surrounded by slightly lower subsidiary domes. Taller than any of Atlantic City's hotels, it would have doubled the number of rooms to nearly 1500, making it one of the largest hotels in the world. N. C. Wyeth was to have a hand in the decorations, for in a letter of 16 October 1916, the day after Price's sudden death, he remarked, "We had planned much ahead."[69] Will's illnesses of the previous five years had been the prelude to a massive stroke; the fire that had glowed within and had left Will looking ever more frail in the previous few years, was extinguished.

Wyeth's account of the Quaker service attests to the impact that Will had on his associates.

> I have attended not more than five funerals in my life. All were impressive of course, and although in every case I came away with firmer resolves and more serious intents, I don't know that I ever experienced the sensation of positive exhilaration and constructive desire as I derived from the services last Tuesday.
>
> Price was a Quaker—naturally the services were Quaker, that rare spirit that one finds in its original genuineness only in a few communities, such as Rose Valley, Pa. This little home on Tuesday was the mecca for the best of them and a remarkable spirit prevailed.
>
> There were no flowers to speak of (not enough to be depressing). There was no official speaker.
>
> When the time set for the services had arrived there was perfect silence. This lasted say ten minutes. One could feel veneration and prayer vibrating through the rooms. Then out of the silence in another part of the house spoke a voice, gentle but very audible, in a cheerful conversational tone: it said something like this:
>
> "I knew Will Price from early manhood. The first meeting was in a railroad station and I was late for a train. I had two heavy satchels and Will Price grabbed one of them and said, 'Come On!' and ran, holding the ticket gate open until I got there. He has run ahead many and many a time since, with our heavy satchels, and has held the gate open for us to enter. Some of the satchels were too heavy or else he ran with too many—"
>
> And so it went on. Then he (Dr. Holmes of Swarthmore College) stopped and there was an eloquent five minutes' silence, and still another voice from a different part of

---

69. Betsy Wyeth, ed., *The Wyeths*, 538.

the house spoke in those same kindly, sincere tones, once in a while breaking, but regaining poise, would begin again.

This lasted an hour and then we all went away to our homes. There was silence with all the moving of people and of carriages, and so the event floated into my mind, became fixed there forever and I moved away undisturbed, but *fiercely illuminated, stimulated, resolved*, and happy—yes happy, that I had known, even for only two years, such a *man!*[70]

———

70. Betsy Wyeth, ed., *The Wyeths*, 539–540.

McLanahan and Bencker, proposed addition to Traymore Hotel, Atlantic City, 1925 (Chrysler Collection, Athenaeum of Philadelphia)

Epilogue

❧ The Office in the 1920s

Will's death at 54 ended a remarkable career that spanned the promise of Frank Furness' work to Price's own realization of a modern architecture at the scale of the modern world in the years before World War I. Unlike the European architecture that grew out of the cultural catastrophe of World War I, whose practitioners pared away the delight of ornament and the content of form to delineate their hostility toward a failed past, Price's architecture was a positive response to the stimulation and excitement of the early twentieth century. Whether in Philadelphia or Atlantic City or Chicago or the suburbs of Indianapolis, Price designed buildings that were both heroic and engaging, forming one of the poles of progressive design in the United States for the next few decades.

For nearly five years after Price's death the firm continued under the name of Price and McLanahan. In 1921 chief draftsman Ralph B. Bencker was elevated to partnership in the renamed firm of McLanahan and Bencker. With the end of World War I the firm resumed its national practice, working from Quebec to Florida. In the booming automobile resorts of south Florida, Price and McLanahan were the architects for Carl Fisher's first buildings in the swamps that became Miami Beach, designing the Yacht Club, the aquarium, the Flamingo Hotel, the Alton Beach Apartments, and the Lincoln Apartments as well as Fisher's house. Among their more remarkable surviving projects is Star Island, an artificial island made out of the muck of Biscayne Bay. Bounded by seawalls and protected from intruders by its own drawbridge and gatehouse, it was the first of south Florida's gated communities. The water tower in a shared central green recalled earlier examples of the office's signature sculpted structures.[1]

McLanahan and Bencker remained the principal progressive firm of the Philadelphia region through the 1920s, relying on the vocabulary of the Price era for high-rise towers

---

1. Significant material on Price and McLanahan's later work is held by the author as well as the Athenaeum of Philadelphia.

including the Rittenhouse Plaza and Garden Court Plaza apartment houses and the Guarantee Trust Company (the successor to the bank for which Furness designed one of his most memorable buildings). The small-scale modern design mode continued in suburban banks and the brilliantly toned Equitable Trust Company in Atlantic City as well as the Musical Arts Club on the 1900 block of Ranstead Street in Philadelphia. The firm's identity with modernism was affirmed when it was selected to design the Automat restaurants of the Horn and Hardart chain. For nearly forty years Bencker continued that commission, expressing the synthesis of the machine and consumer cultures in an important anticipation of modern fast food with strong corporate identity. In 1923 McLanahan and Bencker received the T-Square Club's gold medal for the firm's contributions to design with specific mention of the Traymore Hotel. Two years later they won the prestigious commission for the Pennsylvania Building for the Sesquicentennial Exposition, where they again displayed the firm's characteristic forms in a celebratory court of honor framing views of a towered facade. Bencker's written remarks on the building place it within the intellectual framework of the office, recalling Price's theories of more than a decade before.

> In its design no forms have been borrowed from European prototypes to make it 'Classic,' nor has it followed the "Colonial" precedent, thus relegating it to a single past expression of our national life. Its trend is modern, and its dominant note the 'vertical' motif which is gradually asserting itself as the typical American contribution to architectural expression.[2]

Among the last works to show the signature forms of the office was the corporate headquarters on Washington Square of N. W. Ayer, the nation's first great advertising agency.[3] Clad in limestone, ornamented at the top by four-story-high figures of Truth in Advertising, and accented with a remarkable program of modern carving, it continued the sculptural massing that had interested Will in the previous decade.[4] However, instead of reflecting an underlying skeleton of concrete, by the late 1920s under Bencker's direction, the structure was steel and its sculpted sheathing of limestone was a surface cladding rather than a description of the underlying structure. What had been essentially representational, an extension of Gothic principle denoting structure and function in Price's office, had become stylistic mannerism under Bencker. Like 1920s European modernism Bencker's architecture had become one of surface rather than reality.

---

2. Ralph B. Bencker, "The Pennsylvania State Building," *American Architect*, 130, no. 2508 (5 November 1926), 384.
3. For a history of N. W. Ayer see Ralph M. Hower, *The History of an Advertising Agency: N. W. Ayer & Son at Work* (Cambridge, Mass.: Harvard University Press, 1939). The building was described as "reflecting in a restrained manner the influence of the *art moderne* which was just beginning to spread in the United States. The decorative motifs throughout are modernistic and symbolize fundamentals of the advertising business."
4. Ralph B. Bencker, "N. W. Ayer & Co.," *Architectural Forum* (October 1929), 432–471.

↭ European Exposure

In 1921 and 1922 works by the firm of Price and McLanahan were included in a traveling exhibit of American architecture organized by the American Institute of Architects which toured the major cities of Britain and Europe, including Glasgow, Manchester, London, Brussels, and Paris.[5] The big projects by the New York firms drew the attention of most of the reviewers, but a reporter from the *Philadelphia Record* quoted one English reviewer who paid special note to the Traymore and its implications.

> Within the past twelve months, there have been many evidences of the growing recognition abroad of American Architecture, the latest being the fact that the Royal Golden Medal for architecture (a benefice founded by Queen Victoria in 1848 and awarded annually since) has been awarded for this year to Thomas Hastings of New York. The Evening Post of that city, commenting editorially with pardonable pride upon this achievement of a New York artist, remarks that "further testimony to what the Royal Institute has described as 'the pre-eminent merits of the architectural work now being done in the United States' was afforded by an exhibition of contemporary American architecture which took place in the London galleries of the Institute in 1921."
>
> It will be of further interest, especially to Philadelphians, to recall that during the exhibition in the London galleries the work of Philadelphians came in for a very large share of the praise of British observers. The work of Paul Cret, as exemplified in the Central Public Library of Indianapolis, was hailed by a writer in the London Mercury as "unmistakably impressive." But this writer reserved his highest praise for the Philadelphia firm of McLanahan & Bencker. He found one building, he says, "the most interesting of all those that were shown," the Traymore Hotel in Atlantic City. He says:
>
> I suppose that Atlantic City is an American Blackpool. Those who consider it in this way will be predisposed by their natural dislike of such places to include in that dislike the colossal hotel that seems to dominate the front. Yet let them imagine Atlantic City unpeopled and in ruin, then they will feel with me the mass and outline of the hotel has something of the boldness and mystery, the scale and grouping of a medieval cathedral. If they still dislike this building it will be because they have learned to regard the dogmas of professional practice as infallible, dogmas which have been formed by a study of the past which was once present, fresh and adventurous. We have been taught to hate windows,

---

5. Most of the projects exhibited were the works of the usually named architects, Carrère and Hastings, McKim, Mead & White, and so on, with Price and McLanahan's work representing modern tendencies. There are numerous brief references that make it possible to follow the tour throughout Europe, including the *Journal of the American Institute of Architects*, 10, no. 8 (August 1922), 301, and the *Journal of the Royal Institute of British Architects*, 29, no. 1 (12 November 1922), 22.

glazed in two sheets of plate glass placed under flat segmental arches—such windows as we see in the back walls of London flats. Yet the lines of this building, in spite of commonplaces like this enclose a grouped mass which masters the mind and compels a wonder not very different from admiration.[6]

Shaping the Present Tendencies

Ironically, even as the Traymore was receiving international admiration, Will Price was being forgotten while McLanahan and Bencker rode on the reputation of his work. In 1928 the dean of Harvard's School of Architecture, George Edgell, included Price's Traymore Hotel and the Chicago Freight Terminal in his landmark survey, *American Architecture of Today,* and showed a remarkable appreciation of these buildings as modern works of art. Edgell described the Chicago building as "prosaic" in purpose with "a fortress like dignity…severe, even forbidding…but no one would call it dull."[7] The Traymore was applauded for its solution of modern scale.

> Here the scale is tremendous. The building is broken into pavilions, in turn accented with verticals in the form of superimposed bays. This continues to the tenth story, where a balcony, flung wide on corbels, makes a powerful horizontal. Above that an attic, stepped in masses, and domes produce a skyline of rare picturesqueness and force. The Traymore is really the old picturesque seaside hotel, purged of its gambrel and filigree translated into the terms of stern modernism, with its picturesqueness preserved.[8]

But there was a drawback to the praise, for the Chicago Freight Terminal was identified as the work of McLanahan and Bencker, and Edgell hesitatingly referred to the Traymore's architects as "Price* and McLanahan," with the asterisk referring to a footnote that stated, "I believe the late William L. Price is responsible especially for the original design."[9] This loss of recognition distressed Paul Cret who wrote to the editor of *The Philadelphia Evening Bulletin* to correct the error:

> [Will Price] deserves to be remembered among those who shaped the present tendencies of American architecture. His friends would like to see that his name is not forgotten when mention is made of such works as the Traymore, the Marlborough–Blenheim, or the Pennsylvania Railroad Freight Terminal in Chicago.[10]

In 1930 George Howe placed Price in the American pantheon and in the same year, the Traymore Hotel was again published as exemplifying the best of modern American design in *Masterpieces of Architecture in the United States.* According to Paul Cret's preface it

---

6. "American Architecture," *The Philadelphia Record* (9 July 1922).

7. George Edgell, *The American Architecture of Today* (New York: Charles Scribner's Sons, 1928), 384.

8. Edgell, 340–342.

9. Edgell, 342.

10. Paul Cret, letter to the editor of the *Evening Bulletin* (17 July 1929).

was one of two dozen designs chosen as representing "the highest achievement of contemporary American architecture."[11] Selected by a jury that included Cret as well as American modernists Harvey Wiley Corbett, Raymond Hood, Milton Medary, and Harry Sternfeld, the Traymore was still considered a landmark of modern design nearly a generation after its construction; its tapered volumes, vertical facade elements, and signature domes and spires were regarded as a source for the skyscrapers of the 1920s.

After World War II the Blenheim Hotel made a cameo appearance in Peter Collins' *Concrete: The Vision of a New Architecture*, but because the purpose of his book was the ratification of the stripped industrial forms of European modernism, Price's other work was ignored.[12] The next major inclusion of Price's work would be in Carl Condit's *American Building Art* and there for its innovative structural use of concrete rather than as innovative design. The Museum of Modern Art exhibition, "The International Style," organized by Henry-Russell Hitchcock and Philip Johnson had intervened in 1932. Hitchcock and Johnson proclaimed the merits of collective architecture over that produced by individualists just as Aldous Huxley was writing *Brave New World* and George Orwell was writing *1984*. The Depression and World War II broke the links in the chain of memory, replacing the landmarks of the 1920s with the goal-oriented histories of the modern age. Architectural historians, freed by the new architectural curricula from teaching young architects how to design in historical styles, turned their attention to the social and geopolitical polemics of modernism.

With the goals of architectural theory set by European architects and writers and the history of American architecture shaped to prove connections to European modernism, Price disappeared from the histories of American architecture—as did Frank Furness and many of the men who had shaped the architecture that was actually built rather than the architecture that the theoreticians advocated. Caring principally about the link of European modernism to Frank Lloyd Wright, the history of American architecture was inverted toward the midwest in a sequence that went from Richardson to Sullivan to Wright to Europe. Blindered by expectations, the link between innovative architecture and the industrial and engineering-based culture of the American heartland was lost. There is no greater irony in the history of modern architecture than this shift, for even as historians such as Siegfried Giedion, Lewis Mumford, and Henry-Russell Hitchcock celebrated the achievements of engineers they ignored the centers of the engi-

11. Edward W. Hoak and Willis H. Church, *Masterpieces of Architecture in the United States* (New York: Charles Scribner's Sons, 1930), 2. With Cret involved, the architects listed were Price and McLanahan. The introductory text on the Traymore was written by Charles Harris Whitaker, Sullivan's disciple.

12. Peter Collins, *Concrete: The Vision of a New Architecture* (New York: Horizon, 1959), 87–88, praises the Blenheim as "the most strikingly rational attempt to exploit both the structural and aesthetic values of concrete."

neering culture where it might have been reasonable to expect to find architectural forms conveying the possibilities of the new technologies. Had they followed the nuggets back to the vein, they might have linked the achievements of Louis Sullivan to the ideas and values of Frank Furness and understood the progressive goals of Furness' architecture. Rather than dismissing Sullivan's Furness-inspired work, as an "incredible corruption of form inspired by the bold vagaries of Frank Furness," Hitchcock might have probed its underlying meaning and in the process found Furness' Philadelphia contemporaries the Wilson Brothers—as Carl Condit was able to do when he focused on building technology rather than on style.[13] For that matter, Hitchcock might have discovered that George Howe came out of the Furness shop as well—and following the same vein might have even found Will Price who had carried Furness' expressive vocabulary of shaped and sculpted volumes into the scale of the twentieth century.

Concentrating instead on the architecture of the generating centers of the architectural media, Boston, New York, and later Chicago, Hitchcock missed the story of the engineering progressives of the American heartland who had provided the basis for the great genealogies of modernism as it developed in America, and produced the work which engaged the interest of Europeans before World War I. The similar forms of H. P. Berlage and Price at the turn of the century and of Otto Wagner and Price in the early twentieth century were not coincidences; rather they were based on a shared culture of progressive engineering that was rejected for the polemics of revolutionary European architecture after World War I. Lacking an interest or an awareness of the engineering culture, Price and his followers were ignored by American critics and scholars. Most crucially, Hitchcock might have discovered the direct sequence from Furness to Sullivan to Wright in the midwest, and of Furness to Price and Howe in the east, a genealogy that continues from Howe to Louis Kahn and Robert Venturi. The descendants of Furness have continued to equate form with function as the basis for modern work. Misinterpreting these values as "individualism," Hitchcock skewed the criticism of the 1930s toward "collective" values, insinuating geopolitical overtones that missed the point of American culture.

Will Price should have played a central role in this sequence. Drawing on sources that would have been obvious to veterans of the Furness office, Price in the twentieth century rejected the claims of the past to shape the present and future, achieving a conceptual amalgam that transformed Ruskin's English demand for honesty of construction and material (one that had priced the middle classes out of market) into an architecture of contemporary fact that could serve the mass markets in hotels, railroad stations, and shops.

---

13. For Hitchcock's initial view of Furness see *The Architecture of H. H. Richardson and His Times* (New York: The Museum of Modern Art, 1936), 293. Condit was appreciative of Price and McLanahan in both *American Building Art* (1960) and *Chicago 1910–1929* (1973).

Blending Carlyle's call for sincerity with Emerson's and Whitman's celebration of the present and democracy, Price represented his time and society, forming a bridge to our era while avoiding the trappings of imperial Rome which characterized most of the public architecture of the period. Spurred by his central thesis that each age had its own demands and values which ought to find expression in the material products of its society, Price shaped a contemporary architecture to serve the mass culture of democracy.

❧ *Toward an Inevitable Modernism*

Along with Sullivan and Wright, Price found a realistic and flexible design approach that contested the pompous classicism targeted by Lewis Mumford.[14] For Mumford this imperial classicism was an apt representation of the destructive forces of the American culture exemplified by trusts, monopolies, and big business, forces that had defeated Henry George and threatened to overthrow democracy itself. Emphasizing style over content, the new classicists broke the representational compact between form and function that characterized progressive design. Mumford understood the cultural dilemma implied in an architecture of "fancy dress" which he predicted would make "'mere building' become illiterate and vulgar below the standards of the most debased vernacular." The new formalism and its consequences were decried by Mumford.

> Correct in proportion, elegant in detail, courteous in relation to each other, the buildings of
> the [Chicago] World's Fair were nevertheless only the sumulcra of a living architecture;
> they were the concentrated expression of an age which sought to produce "values" rather
> than goods. In comparison with this new style, the romanticism of the Victorian Age, with
> its avid respect for the mediaeval building traditions, was honesty and dignity itself.[15]

In 1929 Mumford addressed American modernism in his preface to *American Architecture of the Twentieth Century*.[16] Written after Le Corbusier's *Vers une architecture*, and aware of the rise of European modern architecture which had already established its independent course but had yet to be christened by Hitchcock and Johnson, Mumford argued that Americans had already achieved an "inevitable modernism" which was best represented when constrained by utilitarian needs in "office buildings, the lofts, the factories and the hotels." In these circumstances "our architects have achieved a modern style, in contrast to the Europeans, without any definite program of modernism." Instead of being driven in the European style by top-down manifestos, American designers "were modern almost in spite of themselves," thereby avoiding the "stylistic posturing" that characterizes much

―

14. Lewis Mumford, "The Imperial Age," *Journal of the American Institute of Architects* (1925), 366–371.

15. Mumford, 367.

16. Oliver Reagan, ed., *American Architecture of the Twentieth Century* (New York: Architectural Book Publishing Company, 1927); republished as *American Architectural Masterpieces* (New York: Princeton Architectural Press, 1992).

of modern architecture. For Mumford the method of American modernism was the "straightforward facing of the problems of function" which in turn forced American architects to face reality. Moreover, Mumford argued, because so many of the issues of design were controlled by financiers and engineers, architects were forced toward ornament as the basis for expression.

The very aspect that the new theoreticians of the International Style eschewed, Americans celebrated. There could be no clearer statement of the fundamental contrast between American and European architecture, the former serving the many, the later the few. As the 1920s ended Mumford understood what Hitchcock and Johnson did not. Great architecture could not be imposed by an elite few. Disconnected from the wider public, architecture would be irrelevant no matter how politically or intellectually rigorous its program. Instead, Mumford concluded, Americans had goals other than manifestos: "We demand an architecture that is friendly to human beings, that meets their necessities and desires half way, that has its moments of exhilaration as well as its days of efficiency."[17] These values were in accord with the architecture of William Price and his turn-of-the-century contemporaries who had remained outside of the gates of the new Rome, and these are the values that interesting architecture is again taking as the twentieth century ends.

———

17. Reagan, 367.

1. Pillar House, Wayne, Pennsylvania (George E. Thomas, 1999)

2. Alan Wood residence, West Conshohocken, Pennsylvania (George E. Thomas, 1999)

3. Alan Wood residence, great hall (Lewis Tanner, 1999)

4. Louis Clarke residence, Bryn Mawr, Pennsylvania (Lewis Tanner, 1999)

5. Louis Clarke residence, dining room (Lewis Tanner, 1999)

6. Beulah H. J. Woolston residence, entrance hall, Chestnut Hill, Philadelphia (Lewis Tanner, 1999)

7. Beulah H. J. Woolston residence, reception room (Lewis Tanner, 1999)

8. Frank Stephens residence, Arden, Delaware (George E. Thomas, 1999)

9. Rose Valley Improvement Company house and gate (George E. Thomas, 1999)

10. Rose Valley Improvement Company house, fireplace (Lewis Tanner, 1999)

11. William L. Price residence living room fireplace, Rose Valley, Pennsylvania (Lewis Tanner, 1999)

12. Marlborough Hotel, from Park Place, Atlantic City, New Jersey (George E. Thomas, 1978)

13. Marlborough Hotel, window (Jack Boucher, 1978; Library of Congress Prints and Photographs Division, HABS NJ I-ATCI, 8-84)

14. Traymore Hotel, perspective, Atlantic City, New Jersey (drawn by Grant Simon; Price and McLanahan Archives, George E. Thomas Collection)

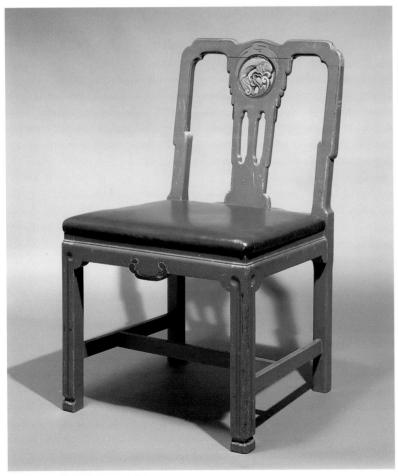

15. Traymore Hotel, dining room chair
(Julie Marquart, 1999, collection Robert Venturi and Denise Scott Brown)

16. Blenheim Hotel, from boardwalk, Atlantic City, New Jersey (George E. Thomas, 1978)

17. Blenheim Hotel, detail (George E. Thomas, 1975)

18. Blenheim Hotel, rear wing (George E. Thomas, 1978)

19. Beulhah H. J. Woolston residence, living room fireplace; watercolor and pencil on paper
(collection George E. Thomas)

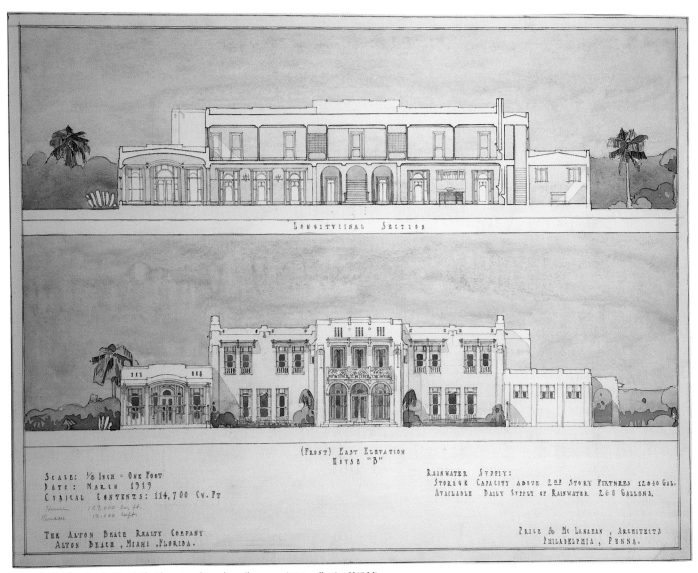

20. House B, Alton Beach, Miami, Florida; watercolor and pencil on paper (1919; collection H/S M)

21. N. C. Wyeth, *The Prince of Peace* (1915, collection Philip N. Price)

Catalogue

Swimming at Rose Valley pond, c. 1906 (Price and McLanahan Archives, George E. Thomas Collection)

◁ ROSE VALLEY ASSOCIATION
Rose Valley, Pennsylvania, 1901–16
William L. Price

see color plates 9–11

On 29 April 1901 Will Price and fellow incorporators John Gilmore, M. Hawley McLanahan, and Howard Stratton purchased 75 acres along Ridley Creek, just south of Media, Pennsylvania. On the property were two pre-Civil War water-powered mills and a workers' village as well as other houses. In July of the same year the Rose Valley Association was incorporated for "the manufacture of structures, articles, materials and products involving artistic handicrafts." That fall the furniture shops were opened in one of the smaller mill buildings with artisans housed in some of the existing residences of the mill village. Though the shops closed three years later and the village did not become the hoped-for center of craft production, artists and architects were attracted to its rural pleasures. They formed their own government and fostered a rich community life centered around theatrical and musical productions in the Guild Hall. Price designed new houses in an architectural style incorporating local stones and creek sands that made yellow-tan stucco walls. Ornamented with Mercer tile, the yellow walls and red roofs unify the buildings of Rose Valley. The association ceased existence in 1910 but a village path system still makes the community accessible

to its members, ensuring Price's democratic goals. In the 1920s, under Jasper Deeter's direction, the Guild Hall became the Hedgerow Theater, and continues to flourish.

Peter Ham and others, eds., *A History of Rose Valley* (Rose Valley, Pa.: by the Borough, 1973); William Ayers and others, *Rose Valley: A Poor Sort of Heaven, A Good Sort of Earth* (Chadds Ford, Pa.: Brandywine Museum of Art, 1983); George E. Thomas, "Rose Valley Community," in *Philadelphia: Three Centuries of American Art*, ed. Darrell Sewell (Philadelphia: Philadelphia Museum of Art, 1976), 465–467; George E. Thomas, "William Price's Arts and Crafts Community at Rose Valley, Pennsylvania," *The Ideal Home 1900–1920: The History of Twentieth Century American Craft*, ed. Janet Kardon (New York, Harry N. Abrams, 1993), 125–135.

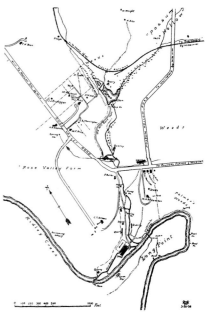

Harry Hetzel, "The Plot Plan of Rose Valley," *The Artsman*, 4, no. 2 (January 1907)

Rose Valley from McLanahan residence, looking northeast, c. 1908 (Price and McLanahan Archives, George E. Thomas Collection)

Guest House, looking northwest, c. 1902 (Price and McLanahan Archives, George E. Thomas Collection)

Bobbin Mill later converted to Guild Hall, looking northwest, c. 1902
(Price and McLanahan Archives, George E. Thomas Collection)

Interior of Guild Hall as Francis Day's studio, with portrait of Will Price, c. 1904
(Price and McLanahan Archives, George E. Thomas Collection)

"Small Plaster Cottage" (Warrington residence), 1903 (Price and McLanahan Archives, George E. Thomas Collection)

Warrington residence, interior, 1903 (Price and McLanahan Archives, George E. Thomas Collection)

above Fiske Warren (left), Will Price (right center), with Eleanor and Inky Stephens, and unknown woman, c. 1915 (Courtesy of Arden Archives)

right Plan of Arden, Ardentown, and Ardencroft, c. 1930 (Courtesy of Arden Archives)

ARDEN, DELAWARE
1901–9
William L. Price and G. Frank Stephens

see color plate 8

Arden was founded by Will Price and Philadelphia decorative artist G. Frank Stephens to test the Single Tax theory of Henry George. A 162-acre farm was purchased just across the Pennsylvania State line in Delaware and the following year a board of trustees was established that included Price. Price and Stephens designed a community based on the Garden City principles of Ebenezer Howard, with shared common spaces surrounded by houses and with the community border left as woodlands. Unlike Rose Valley residents whose access to capital resulted in a rich architectural style from the outset, the initial buildings of Arden were of flimsy materials unsuited to year-round residence. This gave the village the appearance of a workers'

camp meeting. The names (if not the craftsmanship) of the Red House, Gild Hall, and other buildings represented the allegiance of the founders to the ideals of William Morris and the English Arts and Crafts movement. A capital infusion from utopian industrialist Joseph Fels funded the construction of a group of more substantial group of buildings including Stephens' own house as well as the renovation of several of the community structures. Designed by Price, these depended on the vocabulary already developed in Rose Valley but in the smaller scale that reflected the economic differences between the two communities. Stephens described the community in 1907: *The little settlement of Arden . . . is an attempt . . . to develop a village community holding the land in common, in the spirit of medieval times, but under modern conditions, in accordance with the Single Tax philosophy of Henry George. The individual holders of plots of land pay the rental value of the land into a*

common fund, from which all the taxes levied by the state and county are paid, the remainder being spent upon the maintenance and improvement of the roads, woodlands and commons, with no profit to anyone as a private landlord. It is believed that even an experiment on these terms will give for all easier ways of earning a living, a simpler, more democratic and more peaceful manner of life than the characteristic of our time and country, and a freedom from mere wealth-slavery from which craftsmanship and art will develop. (From "Arden Boys Camp" brochure [1907], Arden Archives)

Mabel Tuke Priestman, "The Summer Camp at Arden Being an Experiment in Henry George Principles," *American House and Gardens,* 5 (May 1908), 180–183; Henry Weincek, "A Delaware Delight: The Oasis Called Arden," *Smithsonian,* 23, no. 2 (May 1992), 124–142; Eliza Harvey Edwards, "Arden: The Architecture and Planning of a Delaware Utopia" (master's essay, University of Pennsylvania, Program in Historic Preservation, 1993); Mark Taylor, "Arts and Crafts and the Single Tax: The Utopian Experiment at Arden, Delaware, *Style 1900,* 10, no. 3 (Summer/Fall 1997), 46–51.

Craft Shop, Red House, Village Green, and Millers Road, c. 1912 (Courtesy of Arden Archives)

Medieval pageant at Arden, Will Price on horseback on left, 1911 (Courtesy of Arden Archives)

Green Gate, c. 1910 (Courtesy of Arden Archives)

Rest Cottage, c. 1910 (Courtesy of Arden Archives)

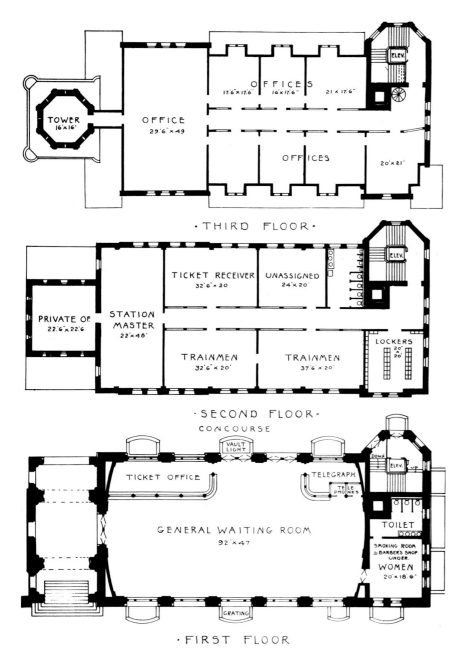

First-floor plan from *The Brickbuilder*, 16, no. 10 (1907)

◁ALLEGHENY STATION
Pennsylvania Railroad Station
Federal and Church streets,
Allegheny, Pennsylvania, 1905–6
Price and McLanahan
Hennebique Construction Company, engineers
Demolished

Passage of an ordinance to permit closing a portion of Church Street enabled the Pennsylvania Railroad to upgrade its station at an important suburb of Pittsburgh. Robert Trimble of the Pennsylvania Railroad engineering offices was responsible for overall site planning; the engineering for the reinforced concrete frame was undertaken by the Hennebique Construction Company of New York, one of the licensees of the nineteenth-century French engineer who pioneered reinforced concrete. The materials of the exterior were described as "paving brick, stone trimmed, with a reinforced concrete concourse and separate express building in the rear." The 50-foot clear span of the concourse was constructed of an armature of massive concrete beams sitting on the brick piers of the station, and on concrete piers at trackside. The ceiling of the concourse was infilled with glass block and the walls were filled with operable steel sash on the perimeter. The main waiting room was more refined, with Grueby faience tile cladding the reinforced concrete structure. The building was demolished in 1955.

Pittsburgh Dispatch (24 March 1905), 2; *The Brickbuilder*, 16, no. 10 (1907), 145–148; *Railway and Engineering Review*, 47, no. 38 (21 September 1907), 820–823; James D. Van Trump, *Life and Architecture in Pittsburgh* (Pittsburgh: Pittsburgh History and Landmarks Foundation, 1983), 226–228.

Photograph of lost watercolor perspective, 1905 (Price and McLanahan Archives, George E. Thomas Collection)

View from track elevation (Price and McLanahan Archives, George E. Thomas Collection)

Concourse, c. 1906 (Price and McLanahan Archives, George E. Thomas Collection)

Waiting room, c. 1906 (Price and McLanahan Archives, George E. Thomas Collection)

Street facade, 1912 (Price and McLanahan Archives, George E. Thomas Collection)

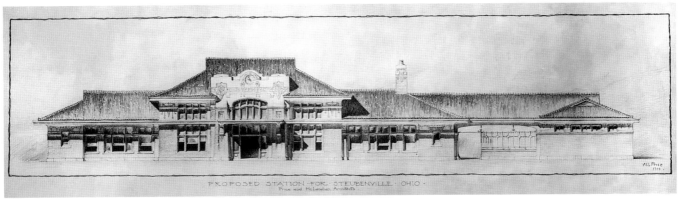

Photographic reproduction of lost pencil elevation drawing, 1910 (Price and McLanahan Archives, George E. Thomas Collection)

STEUBENVILLE STATION

Pennsylvania Railroad Passenger and Freight Stations
Steubenville, Ohio, 1910–11
Price and McLanahan
Cuthbert Brothers & Company, contractors
Demolished

Planning began in 1909 and the drawings for the new buildings were completed in 1910. They were to replace the Victorian board-and-batten structures that had served the city since the Civil War years. Price's scheme joined the passenger station and the express building under a continuous roofline which forms the dominant compositional element of both the trackside and the Sixth Street elevations. The building was constructed of a reinforced concrete armature clad in a sand-colored brick to weatherproof the structure Tile ornament embellished the parapet above the main entrance and the sculptural chimney, gave color to the upper walls of the express house, accented the ends of the concrete brackets that broke through the brick cladding to carry the canopies over the entrances, and added panels of color on the tapering concrete shafts that carried the electric lights at the Sixth Street front. Water infiltration into the concrete caused rust streaks on the main parapets which were reclad in brick during the summer of 1912. The building was demolished in the 1980s.

Philadelphia Real Estate Record and Builders' Guide, 25, no. 34 (24 August 1910).

Trackside, 1912 (Price and McLanahan Archives, George E. Thomas Collection)

Street facade, 1914 (Price and McLanahan Archives, George E. Thomas Collection)

View toward street facade, 1914 (Price and McLanahan Archives, George E. Thomas Collection)

Waiting room, detail of wall, 1914 (Price and McLanahan Archives, George E. Thomas Collection)

FORT WAYNE STATION

Pennsylvania Railroad Station

Fort Wayne, Indiana, 1910–15

Price and McLanahan

George B. Swift Company, general contractor

Altered

The first plans for the Pennsylvania Railroad station at Fort Wayne, Indiana, were announced in the summer of 1910 and drawings were revised in 1913. A four-year delay placed the construction of the building contemporary with the Traymore Hotel but the forms relate to the design mode of the previous decade centered around the Chicago Terminal project. Passengers exited the station under a reinforced concrete waffle slab with glass set into the slab to provide illumination, and entered a subway under the tracks from which stairs rose to the platforms. Unlike the light-steel framing of the main station, the subway, track elevation, and other elements at the rear were of reinforced concrete. Water penetration through unmaintained terra-cotta copings resulted in their removal in the 1950s. Efforts to restore the exterior were unsuccessful in the 1980s and the building is now badly altered in appearance.

Philadelphia Real Estate Record and Builders' Guide, 25, no. 34 (24 August 1910).

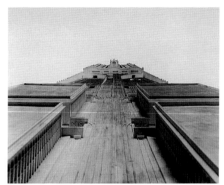

Plaster model of preliminary scheme, 1914 (Price and McLanahan Archives, George E. Thomas Collection)

⫷CHICAGO TERMINAL

Pennsylvania Railroad Freight Terminal

Chicago, Illinois, 1914–18

Price and McLanahan

Thomas Rodd, chief engineer, Pennsylvania Lines

West of Pittsburgh

Demolished

Carl Condit regarded the Pennsylvania Railroad Freight Terminal as "an overlooked masterpiece of Chicago architecture." Linked to the Burnham Plan's call for a new Union Station, its final location was only arrived at after much controversy. The station served two Pennsylvania Railroad subsidiaries, the Pittsburgh, Fort Wayne and Chicago Railroad, and the Pittsburgh, Cincinnati, Chicago and St. Louis Railroad. Because the new Union Station was to be built on the site of the existing freight terminal, this required the construction of a new freight depot. Planning began in 1911 but delays associated with politics pushed the construction of the building into the war years resulting in rising material and labor costs and a cessation of construction for eight months. The engineering and planning were largely the work of the railroad engineers while the architects handled the massing and treatment of the exterior. These features had been established by 1915 when construction began. Each floor encompassed an area of greater than seven acres and was lighted by internal light wells. The building was demolished in the 1970s.

Philadelphia Real Estate Record and Builders' Guide, 30, no. 24 (16 June 1915); "New Freight House of the Pennsylvania Lines in Chicago," *Railway Review* (16 March 1918), 365–380; *Construction News*, 38, no. 12 (19 September 1914); *Construction News*, 38, no. 14 (3 October 1914); *Western Architect* (July 1919), plates 1 & 2.; Carl Condit, *Chicago 1910–1929: Building, Planning and Urban Technology* (Chicago: University of Chicago Press, 1973), 265–268.

View of length of terminal, 1918 (Price and McLanahan Archives, George E. Thomas Collection)

Polk Street facade, 1918 (Price and McLanahan Archives, George E. Thomas Collection)

Plaster model of Polk Street facade, 1914 (Price and McLanahan Archives, George E. Thomas Collection)

Lighting study, 1916 (Price and McLanahan Archives, George E. Thomas Collection)

Reinforced concrete track elevation, 1919 (Price and McLanahan Archives, George E. Thomas Collection)

INDIANAPOLIS STATION
Pennsylvania Railroad Station
Indianapolis, Indiana, additions, 1915–20
Price and McLanahan
C. A. Paquette, chief engineer
Latham and Walters, concrete contractors

Designs for the Indianapolis track elevation and train station began in 1915 and construction was completed in two phases so that the main station, a vast Victorian hall by Thomas Rudd, could remain in service. Price and McLanahan's scheme called for a double-deck steel frame and reinforced concrete structure that elevated the train lines to avoid conflict with the newly important automobile. Station facilities were placed on the first floor below the tracks. The first phase, comprising four elevated tracks, was completed and put in service in the summer of 1918. The remainder was completed in 1920 when a new trainshed of steel arches (instead of columns) covering nearly five acres was competed from Price and McLanahan's designs. The station interior was converted into a shopping mall in the 1980s; competition from an adjacent mall caused the building to close in the 1990s. Its future is uncertain.

"Track Elevation in Full Blast," *Indianapolis Star* (23 July 1916), magazine section, 3; "Indianapolis Modern Union Station," *Indianapolis Star* (8 October 1922), 13, 22; "Union Station Is Rebuilt Without Interrupting Traffic," *Engineering News Record*, 83, no. 2 (10 July 1919), 84–87; "Trainshed Roof of Steel Arches Instead of Columns," *Engineering News Record*, 85, no. 8 (19 August 1920), 350–351; Wesley I. Shank, "Union Station, Indianapolis," Historic American Building Survey (1971).

Connection between track elevation and original building, 1919
(Price and McLanahan Archives, George E. Thomas Collection)

Concourse between old station and new, 1919 (Price and McLanahan Archives, George E. Thomas Collection)

Radiator cover, 1919 (Price and McLanahan Archives, George E. Thomas Collection)

View toward concourse, 1919 (Price and McLanahan Archives, George E. Thomas Collection)

Photogravure from *American Architect and Building News*, 33, no. 817 (22 August 1891)

Principal facade, c. 1902 (Library of Congress Prints and Photographs Division, Detroit Publishing Company Photograph Collection, LC-D4–14317)

Main parlor, from *Kenilworth Inn* (Asheville, c. 1902; courtesy of Mark Taylor)

◄ **KENILWORTH INN**

near Asheville, North Carolina, 1890–91

Frank L. Price and William L. Price

Demolished

The Kenilworth Inn was constructed near George Vanderbilt's mansion, Biltmore. Vanderbilt was the lead financier but Philadelphians played a role, including Isaac Clothier of Strawbridge and Clothier who provided the furnishings, Pennsylvania state senator Joseph Gazzam, and Dr. W. C. Browning. Surrounded by 150 acres devoted to tennis and golf, the hotel was aimed at the rising interest in outdoor recreation at the end of the nineteenth century. During construction exterior detail was simplified and of three projected wings, only the

central wing was initially built. The building incorporated modern comforts including steam heat, electric lights, an elevator, and telephone and telegraph connections. The most remarkable feature was a clear span hall 33 feet by 55 feet. A servants' wing was added from designs by Robert S. Smith, the Vanderbilt staff architect, in 1896. The hotel was destroyed by fire in 1909.

The Philadelphia Inquirer (29 July 1890), 7; *American Architect and Building News*, 33, no. 817 (22 August 1891), 124; *The Philadelphia Inquirer* (15 April 1909), 1; *The Kenilworth Inn* (Asheville, N. C., 1907); "The Kenilworth Inn," William W. Matos, comp., *Philadelphia: Its Founding and Development 1683–1908* (Philadelphia: Joseph and Sefton, 1908), 483; Jennifer Brown, "The Kenilworth Inn" (Urban Studies 272, December 1998).

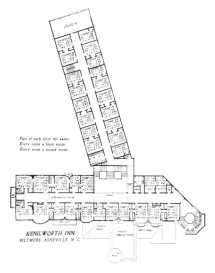

Plan, from *Kenilworth Inn* (Asheville, c. 1902; courtesy of Mark Taylor)

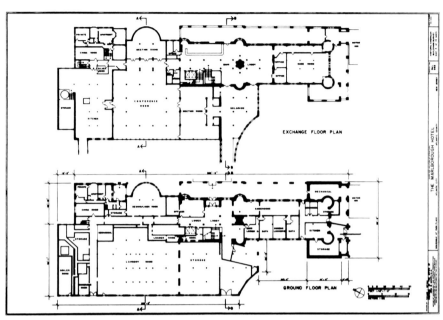

Exchange and ground floor plans (Richard I. Ortega, 1978; Library of Congress Prints and Photographs Division, HABS)

Dining room, 1902 (Price and McLanahan Archives, George E. Thomas Collection)

◁│MARLBOROUGH HOTEL
Atlantic City, New Jersey, 1902
William L. Price
Demolished

see color plates 12 and 13
Josiah White acquired the Luray Hotel in
1887 and was the first hotel operator in
Atlantic City to remain open year round.
Although he lost money the first year, by the
second he was successful. By 1895 the hotel
was so popular that it required a five-story
addition which was undertaken by Price's
firm, their first work in Atlantic City. Two
years later Price was at work designing a
200-room addition. In 1900 White acquired
the site of the Academy of the Sacred Heart
and commissioned the Marlborough Hotel
which, after a year of construction delay, was
opened in 1902. That delay spared it from
the great fire of 1901 which destroyed the
Luray Hotel among others and perhaps
resulted in the decision to use slate shingles
on the exterior of the building to provide
protection from fire. The hotel was demolished in 1978 in the midst of the casino boom.

The Philadelphia Inquirer (18 October 1895), 8; *The
Philadelphia Inquirer* (27 August 1897), 10; *Philadelphia
Real Estate Record and Builders' Guide*, 15, no. 35 (29
August 1900); William McMahon, *So Young...So Gay:
The Story of the Boardwalk 1870–1970* (Atlantic City, N. J.:
Atlantic City Press, 1970), 135; George E. Thomas,
"Marlborough Hotel, Atlantic City, New Jersey," Historic
American Building Survey (1978).

View from Park Place, 1902 (Library of Congress Prints and Photographs Division, Detroit Publishing Company Photograph Collection, LC-D4-14378)

Main lobby (Jack Boucher, 1978; Library of Congress Prints and Photographs Division, HABS NJ-863-41)

Detail of fish and seaweed bracket (Jack Boucher, 1978; Library of Congress Prints and Photographs Division, HABS NJ-864–95)

Boardwalk facade, 1906 (Library of Congress Prints and Photographs Division, Detroit Publishing Company Photograph Collection, LC-D4–71050)

BLENHEIM HOTEL

Atlantic City, New Jersey, 1905–6
Price and McLanahan
Trussed Concrete Steel Company, engineers
Demolished

see color plates 16–18
The Marlborough Annex, as the Blenheim Hotel was first called, was conceived in the summer of 1905 as an absolutely fireproof building. Linked to the Marlborough by a bridge across Ohio Avenue, its fifteen-story front block towered above the boardwalk and introduced a modern urban scale to the seaside resort. Described by Peter Collins as "the most strikingly rational attempt to

exploit both the structural and aesthetic values of concrete," it was the first important public building to utilize the new material without attempting to make it look like stone or some other material. Sunrooms at the boardwalk end framed an interior court, lighted with a shallow dome on the main axis to the hotel. A balconied polygonal music room surrounded by a ring of reinforced concrete columns and spanned by concrete beams and slabs represented the most public use of the material of its time. Despite a remarkable scheme by Venturi and Rauch that would have incorporated the central domed facade in a new casino hotel, the Blenheim was demolished in 1978.

The Philadelphia Inquirer (11 April 1905), 12; William L. Price, "The Possibilities of Concrete Construction from the Standpoint of Utility and Art," *American Architect and Building News,* 89, no. 1579 (31 March 1906), 119–120; J. Fletcher Street, "The Hotel Blenheim, A New Type of Construction," *The Brickbuilder,* 15, no. 4 (April 1906), 78–84; William L. Price, "Modern Architecture, Part 1," *The Artsman,* 4, no. 2 (January 1907), 227–238; William L. Price, "Modern Architecture, Part 2," *The Artsman,* 4, no. 3 (April 1907), 259–278; Jules Guerin rendering, *14th Annual Architectural Exhibition of the Philadelphia Chapter of the American Institute of Architects and the T-Square Club* (Philadelphia: T-Square Club, 1907); George E. Thomas, "Blenheim Hotel, Atlantic City, New Jersey," Historic American Building Survey (1978).

View of Blenheim Hotel from Marlborough Hotel, 1906 (Price and McLanahan Archives, George E. Thomas Collection)

View from beach, 1906 (Price and McLanahan Archives, George E. Thomas Collection)

View from boardwalk (George E. Thomas, 1978)

Main lobby, 1906 (Price and McLanahan Archives, George E. Thomas Collection)

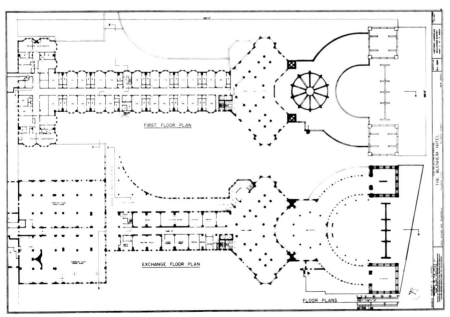

First and exchange floor plans (Robert E. Clarke, 1978; Library of Congress Prints and Photographs Division, HABS)

Photographic reproduction of lost pencil elevation, 1914 (Price and McLanahan Archives, George E. Thomas Collection)

TRAYMORE HOTEL

Atlantic City, New Jersey, 1906 and 1914–15

Price and McLanahan

Trussed Concrete Steel Company, engineers (first block); Otto Gentner and Dickinson Shaw, engineers (second block)

Demolished

see color plates 14 and 15

In 1906 Daniel White retained Price and McLanahan to construct a fireproof wing at the boardwalk end of the Traymore Hotel. Price had already worked on the hotel in 1899 when he added a dining room and parlor at the rear of the side lawn. Difficulties in waterproofing the concrete skin of the Blenheim Hotel, constructed only a year before, led to cladding the new tower in glazed terra-cotta tile. A cruciform plan tower maximized corner rooms with sea views, but its restrained detail was intended to accommodate later additions which would replace the existing wood-frame Victorian building. After White failed to raise funds to enlarge the hotel in 1912 Price and McLanahan were given the opportunity two years later to raise the capital and design a new extension. Constructed in little more than nine months between September 1914 and June 1915, the building was a triumph, setting standards for resort hotels for half a century. Its rooms were filled from the day it opened causing its owners to commission a 40-story addition but World War I made it difficult to raise capital. A decade later designs were made to build a twin building across Illinois Avenue. The Traymore Hotel was demolished in 1972.

H. Toler Booraem, "Architectural Expression in a New Material," *Architectural Record*, 8 (August 1909), 249–268; "Largest Fireproof Resort Hotel Completed in Atlantic City," *Engineering News Record*, 82, no. 1 (3 July 1915), 18–23; John J. Klaber, "America's Greatest Seaside Hotel: The Traymore, Atlantic City, New Jersey," *Architectural Forum*, 127 (November 1917), 119–128; Charles Whitaker, "The Traymore Hotel," *Masterpieces of Architecture in the United States*, ed. Edward W. Hoak and Willis Church (New York: Charles Scribner's Sons, 1930), 167–179; George E. Thomas, "A House Built on Sand," *Via 7: The Building of Architecture* (Philadelphia: University of Pennsylvania, Graduate School of Fine Arts, 1984), 9–21.

View from beach, c. 1915 (Price and McLanahan Archives, George E. Thomas Collection)

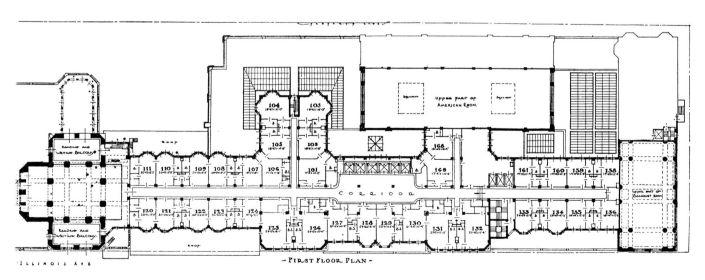

First floor plan, 1914 (Price and McLanahan Archives, George E. Thomas Collection)

1906 tower from boardwalk with pencil lines of proposed alterations, 1914 (Price and McLanahan Archives, George E. Thomas Collection)

Detail from boardwalk with Joseph Mott on balcony, 1915 (Price and McLanahan Archives, George E. Thomas Collection)

Music room with fountain, 1915 (Price and McLanahan Archives, George E. Thomas Collection)

Main lobby, 1915 (Price and McLanahan Archives, George E. Thomas Collection)

Stairs from ground floor to main lobby, 1915 (Price and McLanahan Archives, George E. Thomas Collection)

Exchange floor, 1915 (Price and McLanahan Archives, George E. Thomas Collection)

5 September 1914

21 September 1914

23 September 1914

29 September 1914

3 October 1914

The following photographs represent a selection from the 220 images taken as a construction log between 5 September 1914 and 10 June 1915 by Haworth's of Philadelphia (George E. Thomas Collection).

The construction log of the Traymore Hotel begins with Photograph 1 taken 5 September showing the site after the demolition of the old hotel. Many of the materials for the project had been assembled at the site beginning with timbers for pilings and machinery for mixing concrete. The site was surveyed to position the hundreds of foundations, each of which was numbered.

Photograph 18 (21 September) shows foundation 75 which was shored with planks caulked with straw to reduce the flow of water. Pumps removed water so that a reinforced concrete platform could be constructed atop the pilings.

By 23 September the forms were being placed for the slab of the exchange floor above which was a grillage of reinforcing bars held in place by wire spacers. The heavier bars of a column penetrate through the slab in the foreground. In the rear are the walls of the 1906 wing which was partially demolished to receive the new work.

A week later (29 September) steel girders were being laid from foundation to foundation and an iron column footing is visible in the foreground. In the rear is the construction shack and the portable steam engine that was used to mix and pump concrete.

Photograph 30 (3 October) shows foundation 93 still to be poured. Quicksand and underground streams made pouring difficult making it necessary to move some foundations.

Photograph 35 (8 October 1914) depicts the mushroom slab being formed for the deck above the Submarine Grill, with the formwork for the glass-bottomed pool in the center.

12 October 1914

Photograph 43 (12 October) is of the north concrete mixer and its conveyer belt. Concrete was provided by the Edison Company which was one of the large-scale manufacturers of the material in the early twentieth century. Surface water resulted from pumping foundation caissons.

Photograph 45 (12 October). Concrete was pumped to hoppers from which it was directed across the site by a complex system of chutes and booms. The earlier wing stands to the right, already prepared for the connection to the new construction.

Photograph 50 (21 October) shows the first steel columns being erected by riggers. These formed the core of the major reinforced concrete columns, carrying the weight of the upper stories during the lengthy curing of the cement and were an expedience to permit the rapid construction of the building.

Photograph 51 (28 October) shows the final form-work of the main exchange floor with the steel columns braced and a worker soaking the forms to ensure a tight seal just prior to the pouring of the concrete. The oversized coffers form the ceiling grid of the public spaces.

12 October 1914

21 October 1914

28 October 1914

Photograph 67 (20 November) taken from the 1906 wing of the hotel shows the massive girders joining the columns of the lobbies with a note that column 83 was out of line.

Photograph 74 (28 November) shows columns 145 and 147 out of plumb. These columns and girders framed the immense American plan dining room on the south side of the hotel.

Photograph 80 (11 December) shows the hotel rising rapidly out of the ground with the exchange floor poured and the mezzanine and the first bedroom floors being formed. Hollow tile units lighten these upper floors and form part of the slab. Forms were designed to be reused but the vast amount of debris suggests the extent of the carpentry work.

Photograph 82 (12 December) shows the framing of the American plan dining room. Thirteen men are visible including a group lining up with wheelbarrows to move concrete to places where the chutes could not reach.

20 November 1914

28 November 1914

11 December 1914

12 December 1914

1 January 1915

Photograph 93 (New Year's Day 1915) is of the pouring of the columns and beams of the mezzanine in the center of the building on the level of the roof of the American plan dining room while reinforcing is being finished for the slab.

Photograph 95 (also New Year's Day, dated in error as 1914) shows a dozen men at work on the new shops of the boardwalk facade. The sign is that of the Cramp Company, a Philadelphia ship building firm that had made the transition to construction. Here the new aesthetic of the building with its sand-colored brick and brilliant tile was first visible.

Photograph 97 (8 January) shows the construction advancing from the east toward the west with sheeting to hold in temporary heat.

The following day (9 January) a photograph shows the beams and columns of the second floor being formed, finally advancing beyond the level of the major steel columns and girders of the first floor public rooms.

Photograph 112 (29 January) is of the interior of the exchange floor. Columns are numbered for identification with windbracing brackets at their heads. The tracings of the planks of the formwork are clearly visible on the undersides of the slab above. Plumbing lines are being run through the building adjacent to columns.

Photograph 123 (18 February) shows floors one through seven poured and the south end of the eighth floor being poured. In five weeks six floors have been formed and poured. The exterior brickwork is beginning to rise at the left side in front of the American plan dining room.

Photograph 130 of the Illinois Avenue front (5 March) is of the tenth floor being formed and poured and the brick skin rising to the level of the fifth floor. Window frames are being set and the formwork has been removed on the first six stories so that interior finishes can get under way.

1 January 1915

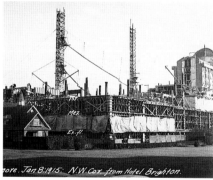

8 January 1915

9 January 1915

29 January 1915

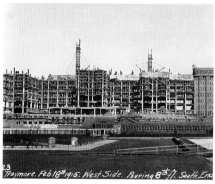

18 February 1915

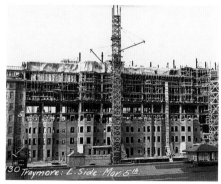

5 March 1915

Photograph 131 (9 March) shows the formwork of the eleventh floor. Rigging booms were raised to each new level to assist in moving heavy materials.

Photo 138 (12 March) shows thirteen masons constructing the exterior skin on the seventh story, without benefit of safety rails. Bay floors are cantilevered slabs.

Photograph 141 (18 March) depicts masons still on the seventh floor. The massive concrete brackets that support the balconies forming the crowning horizontal are above their heads. The rhythm of large and small windows indicates bedrooms and bathrooms.

Photograph 147 (23 March) shows the concreting chutes being used to pour the barrel vault roof in the center between the principal towers above the twelfth floor.

Photograph 148 (23 March) shows the testing of load capacity of the first sleeping floor which was poured in late December. Similar tests occurred during various stages of construction. The gypsum hollow blocks were plastered to form the finish of the corridors and bedrooms.

9 March 1915

12 March 1915

18 March 1915

23 March 1915

23 March 1915

23 March 1915

29 March 1915

2 April 1915

2 April 1915

3 April 1915

9 April 1915

Photograph 149 (23 March) returns to the pouring of the barrel vault between the towers. In the rear is the concrete tower showing the chutes descending from the hopper. A system of wood plank walkways elevated above the reinforcing bars permits moving wheelbarrows of concrete.

Photograph 151 (29 March) shows the forming of the thirteenth floor, the masonry skin reaching the top of the ninth floor, and sash being installed to the fourth floor. A new roof is being constructed to link the 1906 wing to the new work.

Photograph 153 (2 April) depicts the concreting of the fourteenth floor, windows being installed on the eighth floor, and the glazing and painting of the American plan dining room completed.

Photograph 154 (2 April) shows the storefronts on the boardwalk nearing completion with plate glass installed and transoms painted. A sign announces that the furnishing was being undertaken by Gimbel Brothers of Philadelphia. Pipe railings recall the industrial culture of the city.

Photograph 156 (3 April). The hotel is assaulted by a snowstorm that stopped work for a day.

Photograph 159 (9 April) shows the fifteenth floor being concreted and the framing for the upper roofs receiving tile. Masons are completing the perimeter wall on the eleventh floor and windows have been installed to the ninth floor.

Photograph 161 (10 April) shows the north tower concrete pump with some of the mixing crew.

Photograph 163 (10 April but apparently mislabeled) shows the decorative brickwork above windows, the voids left in the brick for the colored tile to be inserted, and the forming of the concrete copings of the balconies. The dome of the 1906 wing is in the distance.

Photograph 164 (10 April) is of the pouring of the fifteenth floor and carpenters at work finishing the outer planking of the forms over the roofs.

Photograph 165 (10 April) depicts the complex slab and beam system of the fifteenth floor roof which became the base for the domes of the facade. The Marlborough and Blenheim hotels are visible in the distance.

Photograph 166 (10 April) shows the poured slab of the fifteenth floor and the central barrel vault.

Photograph 169 (13 April) shows the formwork for the brick arches of the twelfth floor and the voids for ventilation of the bathroom windows.

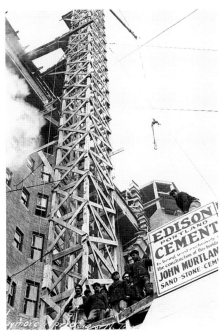

10 April 1915

10 April 1915

10 April 1915

10 April 1915

10 April 1915

13 April 1915

Photograph 173 (16 April) shows the forming of the ribs for the south dome with fifteen carpenters and the construction manager.

Photograph 174 (19 April) depicts the angled roof forms above the fourteenth floor. Deep beams mark recesses in the facade where decorative elements would be formed.

Photograph 177 (20 April). The crew is gathered on the north dome with circumferential reinforcing evident in the formwork and the outer surface of the forms being constructed.

16 April 1915

19 April 1915

20 April 1915

24 April 1915

24 April 1915

29 April 1915

31 May 1915

Photograph 179 (24 April) on the Illinois Avenue side shows both domes formed and concreting beginning on the south dome. Sculptural elements of the upper levels are taking place and the overall order of the facade is becoming evident.

Photograph 182 (24 April) shows the south dome being concreted with the masonry nearly finished on the middle wing.

Photograph 185 (29 April) depicts the gypsum block facing to the square columns of the exchange floor as well as the cast elements of the overhead lighting and decorative borders of the columns in place. The marble revetment of the base is also in place with the space ready for final plastering.

Photograph 202 (31 May) shows the essentially completed facade with the concreting towers still in place, sash still being installed on the upper levels, and the domes nearly finished.

The race to complete the hotel was on. N. C. Wyeth was completing his painting cycle in the Submarine Grill and the hotel would be opened less than a week later on 15 June. Despite some unfinished details the Traymore was ready for operation 40 weeks after construction began.

15 June 1915

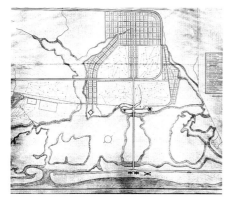

Detail of site plan, 1909 (Price and McLanahan Archives,
George E. Thomas Collection)

OVERHANOVER

Kirkland, North Carolina, 1909

Price and McLanahan

The effort to lure northerners to warm southern resorts accelerated in the 1890s when Henry Flagler established the Atlantic Coast Line railroad from Wilmington, North Carolina, into Florida and built the splendid Carrère and Hastings hotels at St. Augustine Florida to serve as the attraction for the route. Flagler continued pushing his railroads south, eventually building the overseas rail line that linked the Florida Keys as far as Key West. As the headquarter city of the railroad, Wilmington, with its proximity to the Atlantic Ocean, would have seemed a logical location for a resort, and attracted the Overhanover project. The scheme entailed an entire peninsula between Fitch and Page creeks with the hotels on Figure Eight Island. The present roads are perhaps a part of the scheme. It seems likely that most of the capital was to come out of New York, perhaps through contacts with Pembroke Jones.

18th Architectural Exhibition of the Philadelphia Chapter of the American Institute of Architects and the T-Square Club (Philadelphia, 1912).

William L. Price, View over boulevard toward Atlantic Ocean. Photographic reproduction of lost pencil perspective, 1909.
(Price and McLanahan Archives, George E. Thomas Collection)

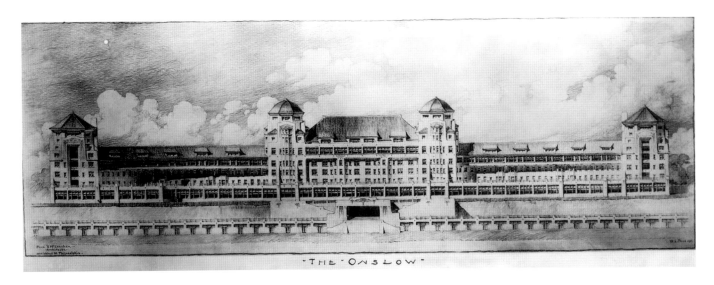

William L. Price, The Onslow and The Hanover, Overhanover. Photographic reproduction of lost pencil perspectives, 1909. (Price and McLanahan Archives, George E. Thomas Collection)

Photographic reproduction of lost pencil perspective, 1912 (Price and McLanahan Archives, George E. Thomas Collection)

EXPOSITION PIER

Atlantic City, New Jersey, 1912

Price and McLanahan

Hennebique Construction Company, engineers

The Exposition Pier was designed for a prominent position on the oceanfront on line with Tennessee Avenue essentially in the center of the developed stretch of the boardwalk and midway between the two existing ocean piers. First correspondence and reports began in the spring of 1912 and design was nearing completion in the fall with test borings for the observation tower paid for in October. In a desperate attempt to save the project, noted renderer Jules Guerin was commissioned to make an oversized watercolor for a promotional tour of the west in the summer of 1914. The outbreak of World War I effectively ended the project. The design of the reinforced concrete deck and pier structure was handled by the Hennebique Construction Company of New York. The pier was to be 2500 feet in length and of "oriental design." Perspectives show the pier as free standing and entered from the beach but it seems likely that it would have abutted the boardwalk. Later drawings show a shift away from the oriental motif toward a more sculptural free style. The paired domed towers flanking the entrance would have contained ticket booths and management offices with an array of facilities including a theater and a convention hall to the rear.

Philadelphia Real Estate Record and Builders' Guide, 27, no. 19 (8 May 1912).

Photographic reproduction of lost pencil elevation, 1912 (Price and McLanahan Archives, George E. Thomas Collection)

Photographic reproduction of lost pencil elevation, 1912 (Price and McLanahan Archives, George E. Thomas Collection)

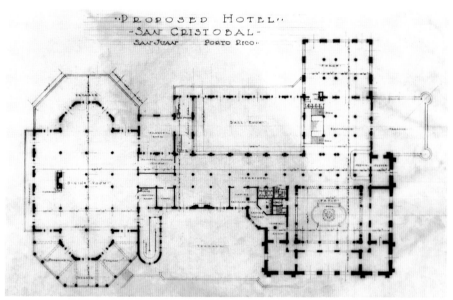

Photographic reproduction of lost plan, 1913 (Price and McLanahan Archives, George E. Thomas Collection)

Photographic reproduction of lost pencil elevation, 1910 (Price and McLanahan Archives, George E. Thomas Collection)

Photographic reproduction of lost pencil elevation, 1911 (Price and McLanahan Archives, George E. Thomas Collection).

SAN CRISTOBAL HOTEL

San Juan, Puerto Rico, 1910–12

Price and McLanahan

Conceived a decade after the Spanish-American War, the San Cristobal Hotel was part of an economic development scheme using tax incentives and offering a free site overlooking the harbor at San Juan subject to the condition that a hotel cost not less than $300,000 and be operated for ten years. A stock company was established in New York and Price and McLanahan were commissioned to make designs which could be used to raise the capital. The earlier scheme dated 30 August 1910 was based on the Overhanover project but with a more pronounced Spanish flair, incorporating motifs from San Juan churches and recalling the Spanish baroque which seemed analogous to reinforced concrete. Alternate two- and three-tower schemes were prepared, suggesting that the intention was to build the central block and then add the curving side wings if warranted by market conditions. A far more dramatic and original scheme followed two years later that pared away historicizing detail producing a clifflike mass that was in keeping with the harbor fortifications.

View looking southeast, 1904 (Photograph by William Rau; Price and McLanahan Archives, George E. Thomas Collection)

Detail of upper facade, 1904 (Photograph by William Rau; Price and McLanahan Archives, George E. Thomas Collection)

◁ JACOB REED'S SONS' STORE

Philadelphia, Pennsylvania, 1903–4

Price and McLanahan

Hennebique Construction Company, engineers

Jacob Reed established a custom men's clothing store in the old part of the city in 1824, but before the Civil War had shifted to ready-made clothing. With the removal of City Hall to Broad and Market streets, Jacob Reed's son, Alan, moved the family clothing business to the 1400 block of Chestnut Street in 1897 and in 1903 commissioned Price and McLanahan to design a retail building in the heart of the new downtown. The new building was to house various functions: men's clothing was manufactured on the upper levels; custom tailoring was provided on the second floor; and clothing was sold on the main floor. Completed in 1904, the building attracted widespread attention for its construction. The structural systems were largely concealed, appearing only in the reinforced concrete columns of the interior and suggested in the plaster vault of the ceiling. In 1983 Jacob Reed's Sons' Store closed and the building was adapted to other uses. It is now a certified historic building.

The Philadelphia Inquirer (1 December 1903), 9; *Philadelphia Real Estate Record and Builders' Guide*, 18, no. 48 (2 December 1903); *American Architect and Building News*, 97, no. 1532 (1905), 146; *Philadelphia Real Estate Record and Builders' Guide*, 28, no. 20 (14 May 1913); George E. Thomas, "Jacob Reed's Sons," *Philadelphia: Three Centuries of American Art*, ed. Darrell Sewell (Philadelphia: Philadelphia Museum of Art, 1976), 472–473.

Mercer tile figures of clothing making, 1904 (Photograph by William Rau; Price and McLanahan Archives, George E. Thomas Collection)

Interior looking southwest, 1904 (Price and McLanahan Archives, George E. Thomas Collection)

◄WAYNE TRACT DEVELOPMENT

Wayne, Pennsylvania, 1883–95
Frank L. Price and William L. Price
Wendell and Smith, builders

see color plate 1

In 1881 a consortium of Philadelphia investors headed by George W. Childs and backed by the Drexel Bank purchased 700 acres in the vicinity of Louella Station and laid out two suburbs, one north of the tracks in a simple grid for modest lots, and the other to the south with larger lots and curving streets that were typical of late nineteenth-century elite neighborhoods. Renamed Wayne, in honor of Revolutionary War General Anthony Wayne, by 1888 the growing town had its own steam plant that heated individual houses and produced electricity as a by-product, making it possible to light houses with electricity. It was possible to purchase a lot and commission an architect, but most buyers relied on Wendell and Smith's choice of the Price brothers whose drawings fill the promotional flyers published by the developers. Wayne attracted members of the rapidly growing professional and managerial classes as well as small business owners, all of whom could reach work using the Pennsylvania Railroad.

Samuel F. Hotchkin, *Rural Pennsylvania: In the Vicinity of Philadelphia* (Philadelphia: George W. Jacobs, 1897), 241–246; Wendell and Smith, *Overbrook, Pelham, St. Davids, and Wayne, Pennsylvania, Suburban Houses Built by Messr's Wendell and Smith* (Philadelphia, 1896); Wendell and Smith advertisement, "Wayne and St. Davids" (1890), reprinted by the Radnor Historical Society (1974).

View of North Wayne, from Wendell and Smith, *Overbrook, Pelham, St. Davids, and Wayne, Pennsylvania* (1896)

New Tower House, from *Builder and Decorator* (1888)

Flemish House, from *Builder and Decorator* (1888)

Pillar House, from Wendell and Smith, *Rural Homes*
(c. 1888; reprinted Radnor Historical Society, 1974)

Wendell and Smith offices, St. Davids, from *Builder and Decorator* (1888)

View of main facade, from *Woodmont Park, Residence of Hon. Alan Wood, Jr.* (Philadelphia, 1895, photograph by Frederick Gutekunst)

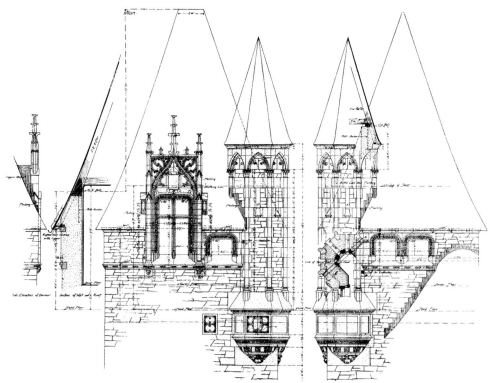

Construction details, from *Architectural Review* (1894)

Great hall, from *Woodmont Park* (photograph by Frederick Gutekunst)

Dining room, from *Woodmont Park* (photograph by Frederick Gutekunst)

ALAN WOOD HOUSE

Woodmont, West Conshohocken, Pennsylvania, 1892–94

Frank L. Price and William L. Price

see color plates 2 and 3

Alan Wood was the third generation of his family to operate iron works and rolling mills in Conshohocken. In 1892 Frank and William Price won the competition to design Wood's house on the west bank of the Schuylkill River, opposite his mill. Located at the highest point along the river, it has been a prominent landmark for a century. The house was constructed of the local stone trimmed with limestone and finished on the interior by many of Philadelphia's principal decorative artists. The estate included its own power plant as well as stables, barns, and extensive gardens. In 1952 the estate was acquired by Father and Mother Divine who have restored the house and grounds. It received National Historic Landmark status in 1998.

Theodore W. Bean, *History of Montgomery County, Pennsylvania*, Vol. 1 (Philadelphia: Everts and Peck, 1884), 593; *Philadelphia Real Estate Record and Builders' Guide*, 7, no. 8 (24 February 1892); [Frederick Gutekunst], *Woodmont Park, Residence of Hon. Alan Wood, Jr.* (Philadelphia, 1895).

◄ WILLIAM L. PRICE HOUSE
Overbrook Farms, Philadelphia, Pennsylvania, 1894
William L. Price

Drexel and Company through its operative builders, Wendell and Smith, repeated its success at Wayne with another development along the route of the Pennsylvania Railroad, this time at the westernmost suburb within the city limits of Philadelphia. In 1893 Will Price was retained as the principal architect for the suburb and in the following year made plans for his own house on Sherwood Road. Pencil sketches and an ink on linen show that the original plan called for a cluster of houses linked together as if they were one immense house; this in turn was developed as "Design for Houses 95, 96 and 97 on Sherwood Road, Overbrook Farms, Philadelphia." Only the central portion, # 96, was constructed as the home of the architect. Its elaborate carved verge boards, leaded glass windows, and special interior spaces denote its function as a show house and sales office for the development. The broad gable front supported on paired bays recalls the earlier Tuxedo Park house by Bruce Price and is contemporary with Frank Lloyd Wright's use of the same motif in his studio. In the case of the Sherwood Road house, the broad gable denoted a large third floor hall that functioned as both theater and studio for the architect.

Charles Edward Hooper, *The Country House: A Practical Manual of the Planning and Construction of the American Country Home and Its Surroundings* (New York: Doubleday, Page, 1903), 149; *The Philadelphia Inquirer* (9 June 1894), 5; Samuel F. Hotchkin, *Rural Pennsylvania: In the Vicinity of Philadelphia* (Philadelphia: George W. Jacobs, 1897), 22–37; Tello J. D'Apéry, *Overbrook Farms: Its Historical Background, Growth and Community Life* (Philadelphia: Overbrook Farms, Magee Press, 1936); George E. Thomas, "Sketch for a Street," and "Design for Houses Number 95, 96, and 97 on Sherwood Road, Overbrook Farms, Philadelphia," in James F. O'Gorman and others, *Drawing Toward Building: Philadelphia Architectural Graphics, 1732–1986* (Philadelphia: University of Pennsylvania Press, 1986), 169–172.

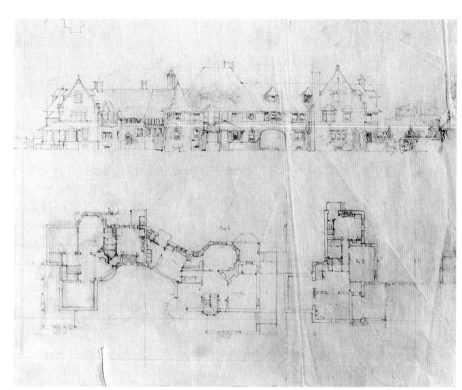

Sketch for a street. Pencil on paper, 1894. (Eleanor Price Mather Collection, Athenaeum of Philadelphia)

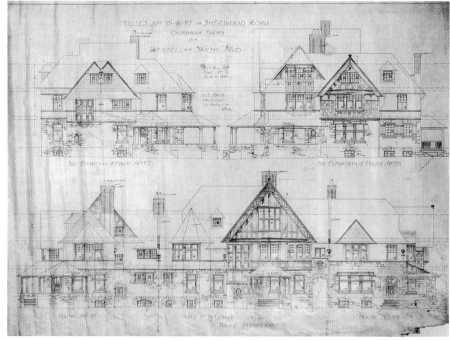

House no. 95, House for W. L. Price, no. 96, House no. 97. Ink and pencil on linen, 1894.
(Eleanor Price Mather Collection, Athenaeum of Philadelphia)

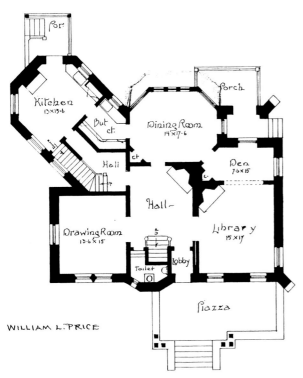

First-floor plan. Ink on paper, before 1903. (Eleanor Price Mather
Collection, Athenaeum of Philadelphia)

William L. Price residence, c. 1895 (Price and McLanahan Archives, George E. Thomas Collection)

Side and rear, c. 1895 (Price and McLanahan Archives, George E. Thomas Collection)

Front hall, c. 1895 (Price and McLanahan Archives, George E. Thomas Collection)

View of south facade, before 1903 (Price and McLanahan Archives, George E. Thomas Collection)

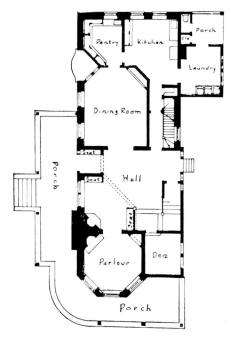

First-floor plan, from Charles Hooper, *The Country House* (New York: Doubleday, 1906)

HENRIETTA WALTER HOUSE
Wallingford, Pennsylvania, 1897
William L. Price

The Henrietta Walter house was among the most widely published of Price's early houses indicating a growing interest in nonhistorical design. Charles Hooper described it as "a most interesting stone house at Wallingford, Pa. Cost about $7,000." The plan placed living spaces on the south-facing front, with corridors and stairs along the rear, suggesting that Price was learning about siting from vernacular houses. A central living hall opens through an arch into a double parlor creating a large suite of rooms which can be closed off if needed, while the dining room on the west connects to the kitchen wing which gets the afternoon sun. The exterior is almost entirely lacking in the Gothic details of Price's houses of the period, with the exception of a truncated tower at the east end that becomes a favored motif in later houses. Masonry resisted the turn toward modern simplification, reflecting instead conventional stone-cutting patterns. Fenestration reflects the function of the rooms within, linking the building to the Wayne tract houses of the previous decade and ultimately to the Furness manner.

Philadelphia Real Estate Record and Builders' Guide, 12, no. 17 (28 April 1897); Charles Edward Hooper, *The Country House: A Practical Manual of the Planning and Construction of the American Country Home and Its Surroundings* (New York: Doubleday, Page, 1906), 36; *Catalogue of the Annual Architectural Exhibition of the T-Square Club, 1899–1900*, (Philadelphia: T-Square Club, 1899), 32, 175; William L. Price, "Choosing Simple Materials for the House," *Country Houses and Gardens of Moderate Cost*, ed. Charles F. Osbourne (Philadelphia: House and Gardens Publishing Company, 1909), 41.

ALAN H. REED HOUSE (CAR-ALAN)
Wayne, Pennsylvania, 1898
William L. Price

In the early 1890s Alan Reed hired Brown
and Day to design a row of houses on the
900 block of Pine Street where he
maintained his city residence, but in 1898 he
turned to Price for his suburban residence in
Wayne. By that time Price had established
himself as one of the principal designers of
Gothic mansions in the region, combining
historical detail with plans reflecting the
increasing openness of contemporary life.
Though black-and-white photographs give
the appearance of the dark red brick of
Victorian Philadelphia, in actuality the brick
was selected to mimic the soft orange-pink
tones of old English masonry. Entrance is
made into a multistory hall containing a
double stair to an encircling balcony. The
bay at the end of the house contains a parlor
that closes off the long axis through the
central hall; at the opposite end of the hall is
a pair of rooms forming a cross axis, the
dining room (adjacent to the kitchen wing)
and the library to which the gentlemen
could retire after dinner. The stable was
constructed from Price's design the
following year.

Philadelphia Real Estate Record and Builders' Guide, 13, no.
16 (20 April 1898); *Philadelphia Real Estate Record and
Builders' Guide*, 14, no.1 (4 January 1899); Thomas Nolan,
"Recent Suburban Architecture in Philadelphia and
Vicinity," *Architectural Record*, 19, no. 3 (March 1906),
167–193; *Inland Architect*, 42 (October 1903).

View from drive with carriage house, c. 1899 (Price and McLanahan Archives, George E. Thomas Collection)

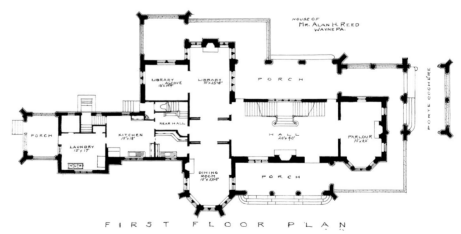

First-floor plan, c. 1899 (Price and McLanahan Archives, George E. Thomas Collection)

Great hall toward parlor, c. 1899 (Price and McLanahan Archives, George E. Thomas Collection)

View of main facade from lawn, c. 1900 (Price and McLanahan Archives, George E. Thomas Collection)

M. HAWLEY MCLANAHAN HOUSE
St. Davids, Pennsylvania, 1899
William L. Price

Born in western Pennsylvania and trained as an architect at Washington and Lee University, McLanahan became a partner in a real estate firm after his arrival in Philadelphia. Price was commissioned to design their suburban house in the fall of 1898 and construction began the following spring. Photographs of the interior at completion show important pieces of Rose Valley furni-ture, probably some of the earliest produced at the Rose Valley shops. McLanahan was an initial incorporator of Rose Valley and a partner with Price in the Rose Valley shops. In 1904 McLanahan moved to Rose Valley and sold the St. Davids house shortly afterward. The house was abandoned in the 1960s but was restored by real estate developer Michael Singer in the 1970s.

The Philadelphia Inquirer (5 October 1898) 12, (17 May 1899), 15, and (4 July 1900), 12; *Architectural Review*, 4, no. 8 (1903), 155.

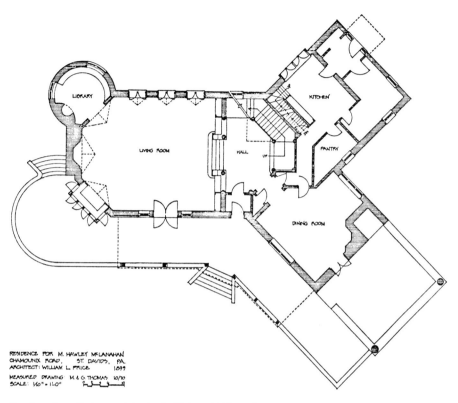

First-floor plan, 1971 (measured drawing by Marianna M. Thomas)

Second-floor stair hall, c. 1900 (Price and McLanahan
Archives, George E. Thomas Collection)

Living room fireplace, c. 1900 (Price and McLanahan Archives, George E. Thomas Collection)

Living room at end of construction, 1899 (Price and McLanahan Archives, George E. Thomas Collection)

Living room toward hall, c. 1900 (Price and McLanahan Archives, George E. Thomas Collection)

View of south facade, c. 1900 (Price and McLanahan Archives, George E. Thomas Collection)

⊰JOHN O. GILMORE HOUSE (YORKLYNNE)

Merion, Pennsylvania, 1899

William L. Price

Demolished

In 1891 John O. Gilmore, head of the nation's largest snuff producer, the W. E. Garrett Company, acquired a house in Wayne which he named Yorklynne. Seven years later, having become the president of the Colonial Trust Company, he purchased a 19-acre site on City Line Avenue across the northwest border of Philadelphia and held a competition to select an architect. Price was chosen in May 1899 and the house was completed two years later. By the spring of 1900 Gilmore had subdivided the western end of the property so that Will could build his own house (Kelty) facing Berwick Road. Gilmore was an early purchaser of many examples of Rose Valley furniture which appear in photographs of the interior of the house. He was also caught up in the political issues of the turn at the century, sponsoring meetings for Philippine independence held in the third-floor great hall of his house, and helping fund Price's purchase of Rose Valley by serving as an incorporator of the community. In 1921 the property was acquired as the new home of the Episcopal Academy, a church-related boy's school in Philadelphia. Among the students who passed through its doors was Robert Venturi. The building was demolished in the 1970s for a parking lot for the school. Price also designed a stable which survives as the power plant for the school, and in 1900 designed a smaller house on the same general design for Gilmore's son John, Jr.

Philadelphia Real Estate Record and Builders' Guide, 14, no. 7 (15 February 1899); Moses King, *King's Views of Philadelphia and Notable Philadelphians* (New York: Moses King, 1902), 75; *Catalogue of the Annual Exhibition of the T-Square Club, 1901–1902* (Philadelphia: T-Square Club, 1902), 37; *Inland Architect*, 41 (February 1903).

Carriage house, c. 1900 (Price and McLanahan Archives, George E. Thomas Collection)

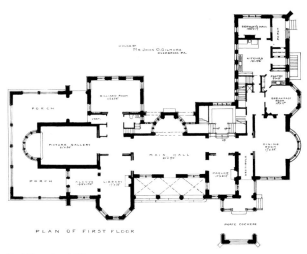

First-floor plan, 1901
(Price and McLanahan Archives, George E. Thomas Collection)

Stair, 1901 (Price and McLanahan Archives, George E. Thomas Collection)

Inglenook of main hall, 1901 (Price and McLanahan Archives, George E. Thomas Collection)

Main hall, 1901 (Price and McLanahan Archives, George E. Thomas Collection)

LOUIS CLARKE HOUSE
Bryn Mawr, Pennsylvania, 1901
William L. Price

see color plates 4 and 5

Louis Clarke, a pioneering manufacturer of automobiles, founded the Autocar Company in Pittsburgh in 1896. Over the next decade Clarke invented the spark plug, designed a car to be driven from the left side, developed a system of oil circulation for the engine, and made the shift from chain drive to drive shaft. Difficulties in raising capital caused him to move the business to the Philadelphia suburbs in 1900 where he began manufacturing commercial vehicles. He was joined by his brother John who had moved to Philadelphia in 1895. John Clarke had already retained Will Price in 1896 to alter a Frank Furness-designed house in Bryn Mawr toward more conventional taste of the period and is the probable link to Price for the Louis Clarke house. Described as "old French Style," mixing stone at the base with half-timber on the upper levels, the house is among the most successful of Price's historical designs. Like the McLanahan house of two years before, the entire front of the house is essentially one space, anticipating the free-flowing space of modern design. On the second floor, above the porte cochere, is the master bedroom suite with bathroom on axis with the main stair.

The Philadelphia Inquirer (9 September 1901), 16; *Philadelphia Real Estate Record and Builders' Guide*, 16, no. 37 (11 September 1901); Charles E. Hooper, *The Country House: A Practical Manual of the Planning and Construction of the American Country Home and Its Surroundings* (New York, Doubleday, Page, 1906), 25; Jean Toll, ed., *Montgomery County: The Second Hundred Years*, Vol. 2 (Norristown, Pa.: Montgomery County Federation of Historical Societies, 1983), 1331–1333.

View of Gulph Road facade, c. 1901 (Eleanor Price Mather Collection, Athenaeum of Philadelphia)

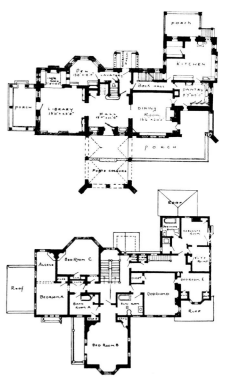

First and second floor plans, from Charles Hooper, *The Country House* (New York: Doubleday, 1906)

Detail of porch with Autocar, c. 1901 (Eleanor Price Mather Collection, Athenaeum of Philadelphia)

North facade with observatory added at top of stair tower, c. 1904 (Price and McLanahan Archives, George E. Thomas Collection)

CHARLES AND ALICE BARBER STEPHENS HOUSE (THUNDERBIRD LODGE)

Rose Valley, Pennsylvania, 1904
Price and McLanahan

Alice Barber Stephens trained at the Pennsylvania Academy of the Fine Arts under Thomas Eakins and became a well-known illustrator. Charles Stephens was a successful illustrator of Native-American subjects and served on the faculty of the School of Industrial Art. He was a cousin of Frank Stephens, founder of Arden. After

summering at the Guest House in 1904 the artists acquired the barn across Rose Valley Road from Will Price's house, adapting it to a two-level studio appended to a house. The house was designed so that all of the important rooms had a southern exposure, with circulation along the north side, while the north-facing double doors of the barn could be adapted to provide illumination for the studios. The interior forms a continuous sequence of modestly scaled spaces incorporating living room, entrance vestibule, and dining room which were unified by segmental headed arches spanning windows

and vestibule. Square sheets of gold Japan paper covered walls and ceilings above wainscoting, giving the interior an exotic flair that contrasted with Price's simply shaped and finished trim.

Catalogue of the Eleventh Annual Architectural Exhibit, 1904–5 (Philadelphia: T-Square Club, 1905), 41; Mabel Tuke Priestman, *Suburban Life*, 6, no. 1 (January 1908), 11–13; "The Home of Two Artists," *Town and Country* (20 November 1909), 17–19; Charles De Kay, "A Studio Home in Rose Valley," *Arts and Decoration* (March 1911), 198–201.

South elevation during construction, c. 1904 (Price and McLanahan Archives, George E. Thomas Collection)

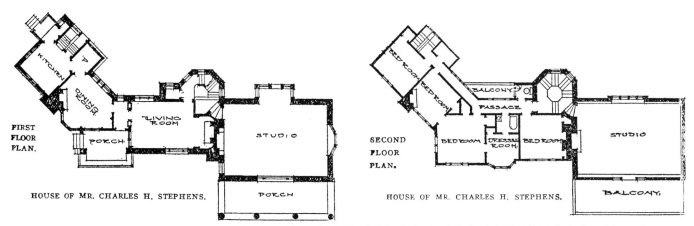

First- and second-floor plans, c. 1904, from "Some Buildings of Our Time: The Work of William L. Price, An Architect Who Stands by His Beliefs," *The Craftsman* (May 1910)

Stair, c. 1905 (Price and McLanahan Archives, George E. Thomas Collection)

Dining room, c. 1905 (Price and McLanahan Archives, George E. Thomas Collection)

Charles Stephens studio, c. 1905 (Price and McLanahan Archives, George E. Thomas Collection)

Alice Barber Stephens studio, c. 1905 (Price and McLanahan Archives, George E. Thomas Collection)

**M. HAWLEY MCLANAHAN HOUSE
(PEEWEE HILL)**

Rose Valley, Pennsylvania, 1905

Price and McLanahan

The McLanahan house had its beginnings as a modest frame tenant farmhouse on the ridge between Vernon Run and Ridley Creek. In 1904, when Hawley McLanahan decided to move to Rose Valley from his St. Davids house, he lived for a summer in the Guest House while the farmhouse was transformed into a family residence. Because it was intended largely to encase the building in an envelope of hollow tile and stucco, Price was free to rethink the entire composition. Large bays were constructed flanking the central entrance which were joined by a shallow segmental arch at the front plane of the bay that extended the second floor and added significant space to the small front rooms of the house. Overlaid in decorative patterns of Mercer tile, with a red tile roof, it was one of the first examples of Rose Valley architecture. Within, the house was focused on large stone fireplaces constructed of the local stone roughly stuccoed like the vernacular buildings and ornamented with Mercer tile.

South facade, c. 1907 (Price and McLanahan Archives, George E. Thomas Collection)

Living room, c. 1907 (Price and McLanahan Archives, George E. Thomas Collection)

Detail of entrance, c. 1907 (Price and McLanahan Archives, George E. Thomas Collection)

View of south facade, pergola, and water tower, c. 1906 (Price and McLanahan Archives, George E. Thomas Collection)

CHARLES SCHOEN HOUSE (SCHOEN HAUS)

Rose Valley, Pennsylvania, 1905
Price and McLanahan

The Schoen house had as its core a massive, hip-roofed stone structure, constructed in 1862 for Antrim Osborne, the owner of much of the Rose Valley property. It and additional adjacent properties were acquired by Charles and Lavinia Schoen, parents-in-law of M. Hawley McLanahan. Price transformed the house, combining interior spaces to create larger rooms, adding a service wing to meet the needs of the Schoen household, and wrapping much of the exterior in a stucco over hollow tile envelope which brought the house into the vocabulary of Rose Valley. A pergola whose columns recall those of local barns is terminated by a handsome multistory water tower that forms an important feature of the landscape. The interior was enriched with some of the best carving from the Rose Valley shops. Much of this carving has since been removed but the essential features of the house remain.

Francis Durando Nichols, "How a Pennsylvania Farm House Was Transformed into a Beautiful Dwelling, " *American Homes and Gardens,* 2, no. 6 (June 1906), 378–383; *Inland Architect,* 50, no. 5 (December 1907); *14th Annual Architectural Exhibition* (Philadelphia: T-Square Club, 1907); Rebecca Hunt, "The Schoen-Saul House and Its Role in William L. Price's Rose Valley Community" (Historic Preservation 525, May 1992).

Inglenook, c. 1906 (Photograph by Henry Troth; Price and McLanahan Archives, George E. Thomas Collection)

Osborne house before being converted into Schoen residence
(Price and McLanahan Archives, George E. Thomas Collection)

Stair, c. 1906 (Photograph by Henry Troth; Price and McLanahan Archives, George E. Thomas Collection)

Fireplace, c. 1906 (Price and McLanahan Archives, George E. Thomas Collection)

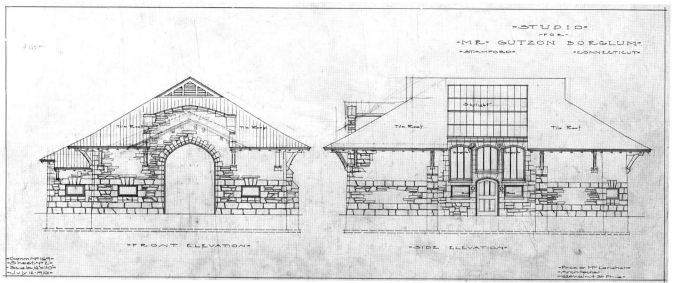

Front and side elevations, ink and pencil on linen, 1910 (Chrysler Collection, Athenaeum of Philadelphia)

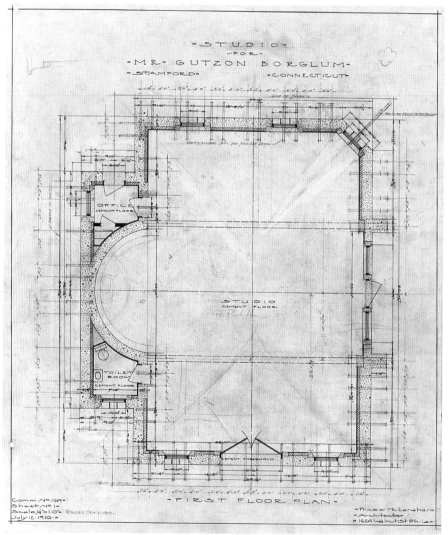

Studio, first-floor plan, ink on linen, 1910 (Chrysler Collection, Athenaeum of Philadelphia)

Exterior during construction, 1911 (Price and McLanahan Archives, George E. Thomas Collection)

GUTZON BORGLUM STUDIO
Stamford, Connecticut, 1910
Price and McLanahan

Price was already an "old friend" when
Idaho-born and Paris-trained sculptor
Gutzon Borglum acquired a scenic 400-acre
property outside of Stamford in 1910 and
commissioned Price and McLanahan to
design his studio. That relationship certainly
reached back to 1909 with the joint design
for the Newark Lincoln Monument, a work
which was eventually installed in 1913.
Rock-faced ashlar walls trimmed with
limestone convey the rustic sensibility of the
barnlike studio. Oversized doors permitted
the easy removal of monumental sculptures.
The studio is spanned by a massive hip roof
carried on simply shaped beams and lighted
by a north-facing skylight opposite which is
a gargantuan pink granite fireplace whose
details anticipate the monumental forms that
became Borglum's forte. Correspondence
from the office indicates that construction
began in the fall of 1910 and was nearing
completion the following summer.

Edward Bigelow, "Beauty in the Life of a Portrayer of
Beauty," *The Guide to Nature: Education and Recreation*, 4,
no. 5 (September 1911), 163–169; Robert J. Casey and
Mary Borglum, *Give the Man Room* (New York: Bobbs-
Merrill Company, 1952), 102, 108; Alan Burnham and
Virginia T. Davis, "Gutzon Borglum Studio," Connecticut
Historical Commission, Historic Resources Inventory
(May 1978); Jeremy Hildreth, "The Gutzon Borglum
Studio" (Historic Preservation 525, April 1992).

Interior toward fireplace during construction, c. 1910 (Price and McLanahan Archives, George E. Thomas Collection)

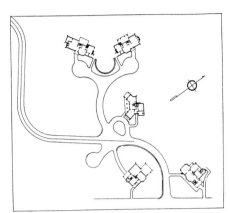

Site plan, from Price and McLanahan, "Group of Houses at Moylan, Rose Valley, Pa.," *The Brickbuilder*, 20, no. 9 (September 1911)

Hollow tile and concrete construction, from Possum Hollow Road, 1911 (Price and McLanahan Archives, George E. Thomas Collection)

Porter house and gates, 1912 (Price and McLanahan Archives, George E. Thomas Collection)

View from Possum Hollow Road, looking west, 1912 (Price and McLanahan Archives, George E. Thomas Collection)

HOUSES FOR THE ROSE VALLEY IMPROVEMENT COMPANY
Rose Valley, Pennsylvania, 1910
Price and McLanahan

When the original mortgage of Rose Valley came due in 1910, Hawley McLanahan and his father-in-law Charles Schoen took on the responsibility with the aim of recouping some of the value by developing a small group of houses that could be sold to reduce the community debt. As many as twenty houses were projected but only five were constructed. Price was commissioned to design the houses and Will Walton, also a Rose Valley resident, was the builder. In describing the planning and design goals Will wrote: "the unity of relation to the environment has been carefully preserved, and the types of dwellings, though largely a matter of personal taste with the architects, conform admirably to and appear to grow

easily out of the site." This was accomplished by using local stone at the foundations, and then shaping buildings of regional character in modern hollow tile and creek sand stucco ornamented in the Rose Valley fashion with Mercer tile. Interiors continued the materials of the exterior with rough plaster over tile and fireplaces ornamented with Mercer tile, producing a pleasing unity and resulting in some of the most progressive of Price interiors. The houses were constructed for $45,000 between the summer of 1910 and the spring of 1911 and were sold in the autumn of that year to Charles Schoen who held them as rental properties until his death in 1917. Designed as homes for artists, one of whom was stained glass master Nicola D'Ascenzo, they also attracted the lawyer of the Traymore Hotel project, L. Stauffer Oliver.

Price and McLanahan, "Group of Houses at Moylan, Rose Valley, Pa.," *The Brickbuilder*, 20, no. 9 (September 1911), 185–191; Charles Schoen Papers, Rose Valley Collection (Collection 41, Boxes 15 & 16), Winterthur Library, Greenville, Delaware; Elizabeth Tighe Sippel, "The Improvement Company Houses, Rose Valley, Pennsylvania: The Democratic Vision of William L. Price," (master's essay, University of Pennsylvania, Program in Historic Preservation, 1995).

View looking northwest at westernmost houses, 1912 (Price and McLanahan Archives, George E. Thomas Collection)

Details from "Group of Houses at Moylan, Rose Valley, Pa.," *The Brickbuilder*, 20, no. 9 (September 1911)

View of Woodland Avenue facade, 1912 (Price and McLanahan Archives, George E. Thomas Collection)

GEORGE G. GREENE, JR., HOUSE

43 North Woodland Avenue
Woodbury, New Jersey, 1911
Price and McLanahan

George G. Greene, Jr., was the son of Woodbury's most important industrialist, George G. Greene. Greene marketed almanacs with patent medicines and used his business profits for real estate purchases that spanned the country as far west as Pasadena, California, where he acquired and operated the Hotel Greene. Perhaps it was through the hotel business that Greene learned of Price and hired him for a modern house of the sort that he might have seen in California. The Greene house marked the maturation of Price's domestic style as he reached his fiftieth birthday. A brick base sets the building off from its sandy site, above which the walls are stuccoed and accented with Mercer tile below a red tile roof. The plan joins all of the public spaces to the central hall entered from the vestibule. To the left an open arcade partially screens the living room which opens in turn through French doors onto an enclosed porch. On the right of the hall is the dining room which is entered through a broad archway. The service wing continues from the back corner of the dining room.

Philadelphia Real Estate Record and Builders' Guide, 25, no. 34 (24 August 1910); Elise Vider, "The G. G. Greene House, Woodbury, New Jersey" (Historic Preservation 525, May 1992).

Living room, 1912 (Price and McLanahan Archives, George E. Thomas Collection)

View of entrance, c. 1914 (Photograph by H. H. Coburn Company; Drawings and Documents Archive, College of Architecture and Planning, Ball State University, Muncie, Indiana)

Entrance gate (Price and McLanahan Archives, George E. Thomas Collection)

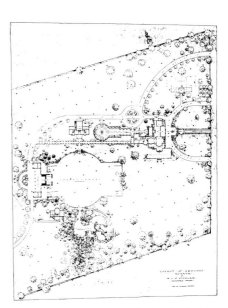

Layout of grounds, 1911 (Price and McLanahan Archives, George E. Thomas Collection)

FRANK WHEELER HOUSE

Indianapolis, Indiana, 1911

Price and McLanahan

The Sheibler-Wheeler Carburetor Company was the basis of the fortune of Frank Wheeler who in association with fellow automobile industry manufacturers and neighbors Joseph Allinson and Carl Fisher organized the Indianapolis Motor Speedway and later developed Miami Beach. Wheeler had lived nearer to the downtown of Indianapolis but with the increased reliability of the automobile acquired a large farm property on the outskirts of the city and retained Price and McLanahan as architects in 1911. Over the next three years Price and McLanahan designed the house and outbuildings, directed the interior design and furniture selection, and laid out the gardens and grounds. The water tower and lake were abandoned in the 1940s, and the house was painted white at a later date, resulting in damage to the glazes of the ornamental tile on the exterior. The house is now part of Marian College.

Philadelphia Real Estate Record and Builders' Guide, 26, no. 23 (7 June 1911); Henry Blackman Sell, "Good Taste and the Mansion," *International Studio*, 17 (November 1915), xi–xv.

Main hall, c. 1914 (Photograph by H. H. Coburn Company; Drawings and Documents Archive, College of Architecture and Planning, Ball State University, Muncie, Indiana)

Main stair from landing, c. 1914 (Photograph by H. H. Coburn Company; Drawings and Documents Archive, College of Architecture and Planning, Ball State University, Muncie, Indiana)

Sunporch, c. 1914 (Photograph by H. H. Coburn Company; Drawings and Documents Archive, College of Architecture and Planning, Ball State University, Muncie, Indiana)

Wheeler residence from Japanese garden, c. 1914 (Photograph by H. H. Coburn Company; Drawings and Documents Archive, College of Architecture and Planning, Ball State University, Muncie, Indiana)

Japanese garden and guest house from water tower, corn fields beyond, c. 1914 (Photograph by H. H. Coburn Company; Drawings and Documents Archive, College of Architecture and Planning, Ball State University, Muncie, Indiana)

Water tower and garage from landing, c. 1914 (Photograph by H. H. Coburn Company; Drawings and Documents Archive, College of Architecture and Planning, Ball State University, Muncie, Indiana)

Landing and water tower, c. 1914 (Photograph by H. H. Coburn Company; Drawings and Documents Archive, College of Architecture and Planning, Ball State University, Muncie, Indiana)

Entrance porch (Photograph by George E. Thomas, 1999)

BEULAH H. J. WOOLSTON HOUSE

Philadelphia, Pennsylvania, 1913

Price and McLanahan

see color plates 6, 7, and 19

Joseph Woolston, the husband of Beulah H. J., was a prominent wool merchant who resided in Germantown before building a house in Chestnut Hill across the street from his parents-in-law. Price adapted his Rose Valley architecture to the Woolston house, constructing the building of hollow tile, clad in stucco, covered with "pebble-dash," and ornamented with green-toned glazed tiles matching the roof. The house faces south but a glazed sunporch shields the house from heat in the summer and cold in the winter. The vestibule is paneled in Mercer tile while the interiors were more conventionally finished in dark stained wood. Many of the original fireplaces were removed during a renovation in the 1930s when Philip Price acquired the house. The exterior has been carefully restored by its present owners, Mr. and Mrs. John Levitties.

Philadelphia Real Estate Record and Builders' Guide, 28, no. 5 (29 January 1913).

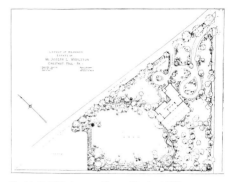

Beulah H. J. Woolston residence, Chestnut Hill, Philadelphia, layout of grounds, June 1912 (Price and McLanahan Archives, George E. Thomas Collection)

South facade (Photograph by George E. Thomas, 1999)

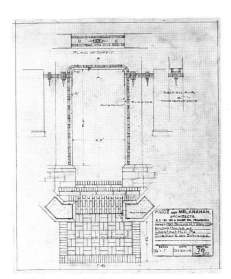

Detail of entrance. Pencil on tracing paper, 1913.
(Chrysler Collection, Athenaeum of Philadelphia)

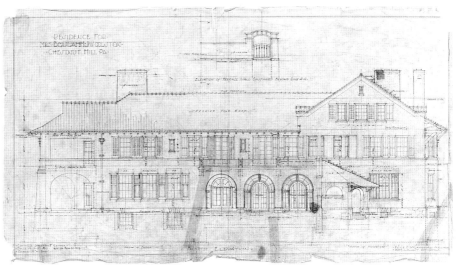

South elevation. Pencil on tracing paper, 1912. (Chrysler Collection, Athenaeum of Philadelphia)

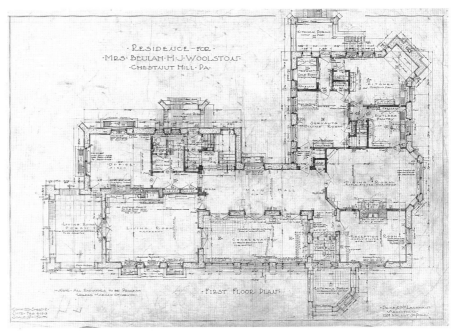

First-floor plan. Ink on linen. (Chrysler Collection, Athenaeum of Philadelphia)

Detail of living room fireplace. Watercolor wash and pencil on paper.
(Price and McLanahan Archives, George E. Thomas Collection)

Living room, c. 1935 (Courtesy of Mr. and Mrs. John Levitties)

ROSE VALLEY FURNITURE

Beginning in the late 1890s, William Price designed Gothic furniture that was incorporated into many of his large houses. In 1901 a shop for manufacturing furniture was constructed in the newly founded community of Rose Valley, Pennsylvania. The pieces of furniture on the following pages are products of that shop. By 1905 labor difficulties caused the shop to close, although Price's firm continued to take commissions and produce new work into the 1920s. For more on Rose Valley furniture, see Robert Edwards' *"When You Next Look at a Chair": The Arts and Crafts Furniture of William L. Price*, which follows these images.

Rose Valley table (Price and McLanahan Archives, George E. Thomas Collection)

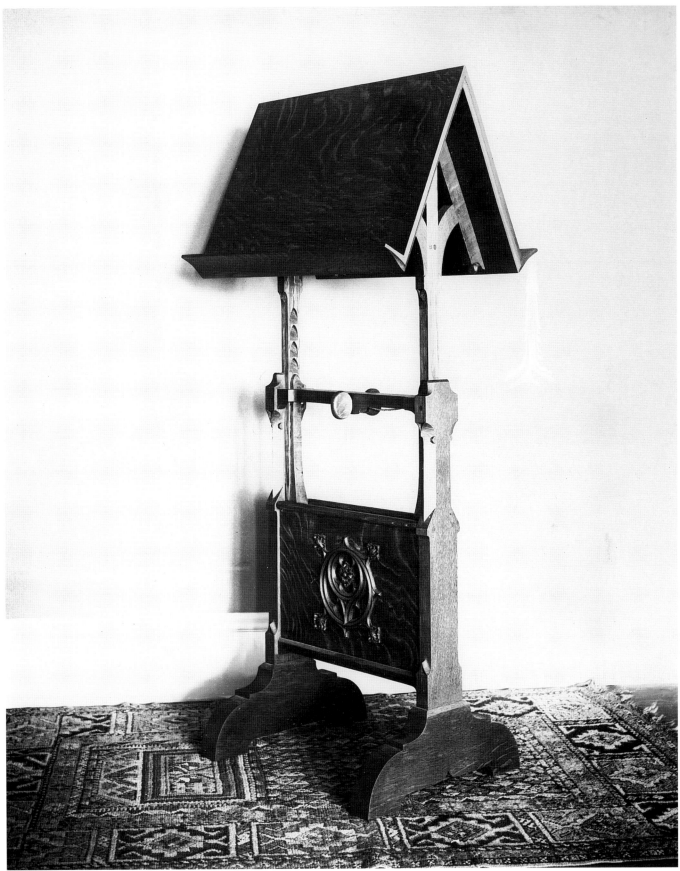

Rose Valley music stand (Price and McLanahan Archives, George E. Thomas Collection)

Shakespeare folio case with figures of Portia and Shylock, for William Harrison (Price and McLanahan Archives, George E. Thomas Collection)

Rose Valley reading table and chair (Price and McLanahan Archives, George E. Thomas Collection)

Mackay-Smith typewriter case, table, and chair (Price and McLanahan Archives, George E. Thomas Collection)

Rose Valley sideboard (Price and McLanahan Archives, George E. Thomas Collection)

Rose Valley mahogany five-legged table for W. F. Davidson
(Price and McLanahan Archives, George E. Thomas Collection)

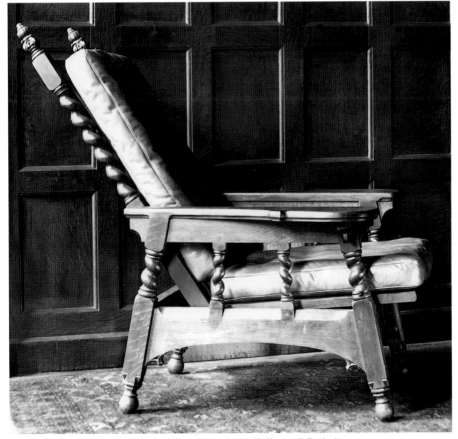

Rose Valley Morris chair (Price and McLanahan Archives, George E. Thomas Collection)

Figure of woman with shield, newel figure from James Clarke residence, 1896 (Courtesy of Robert Edwards)

"When You Next Look at a Chair": The Arts and Crafts Furniture of William L. Price

Robert Edwards

The furniture designs of William Price have been discussed in the context of the Arts and Crafts movement. This helps greatly to define the movement in general but adds little to an understanding of Price's furniture in particular. A progressive thinker, Price would have been drawn to the philosophy of the movement but the furniture and woodwork designs emanating from his Philadelphia office before he established Rose Valley were exactly the same as those made during the short time the Rose Valley shops were producing (1901–6). Most converts, like Gustav Stickley, found the Arts and Crafts movement and then made furniture to fit the philosophy. Price made the philosophy fit his furniture. He was already using the best grades of quartered white oak for the hand-carved woodwork in his domestic interiors.[1] Oak happened to be the wood of the medieval era, the greatest flowering of handcraft. Quartered oak of lesser quality had been, since the 1890s, the overwhelming choice of huge factories such as those in Grand Rapids, Michigan, that spewed out furniture of every style, including Arts and Crafts or "Mission." The anti-industrial Arts and Crafts movement would eventually be remembered by the pejorative Mission oak simply because other woods were so little used in the machine-made furniture industry until the oak supply was seriously depleted by 1915. Price also finished the oak without varnish so that the wood's texture would remain evident as Ruskin had recommended.[2] Gustav Stickley learned the business of furniture making from his uncles

---

The title of this piece is excerpted from a text by William L. Price: "When next you look at a chair, look below the varnish, and if you can't find the pins of honest construction, shun it as you would the evil one of which it is a product." William L. Price, "The Building of a Chair," *The Artsman*, 1, no. 8 (May 1904), 283.

1. A female figure holding a shield was carved for use on the newel post in the 1896 remodeling of the John S. Clark house. It is identical in every way except for a more developed facial expression to the figures decorating the tops of two pins on a marked Rose Valley table now in the Metropolitan Museum of Art.

2. The usual finish applied to Rose Valley furniture was described in a letter Price wrote to the superintendent of the Louisiana Purchase Exposition, St. Louis, 11 April 1904, and quoted in William Ayres, ed., *A Poor*

who produced just the kind of "golden oak" chairs he would rail against after he discovered the honest simplicity American intellectuals identified as the Arts and Crafts style.

Closer parallels to Price may be found in Ralph Radcliffe Whitehead who founded a utopian community, Byrdcliffe, in Woodstock, New York, and George Vanderbilt's Biltmore Industries in Asheville, North Carolina.[3] Whitehead studied cabinetmaking in Germany before emigrating from England to the United States. The furniture he made before his colony was established bears little resemblance to what the Byrdcliffe craftsmen produced in 1904 and after. While Byrdcliffe furniture used flat, bi-level relief carving and subtle colored transparent stains for decoration, Biltmore furniture was decorated with panels of fully modeled carving which, like the pieces made at Rose Valley, required highly skilled craftsmen.

Price's style, which in the years before 1910 relied primarily on Gothic forms and decoration, was at odds with the mainstream of American Arts and Crafts production. However, his writings explain how purely his furniture represented the movement's modern ideas. His critiques show how the products of the Stickleys, the Roycrofters, and most of the Grand Rapids factories used the cant of the movement as merely a marketing tool. Just as Price had *The Artsman* to disseminate his ideas, Gustav Stickley had *The Craftsman* (for which Price wrote) and Elbert Hubbard of the Roycrofters had several periodicals, among them *The Philistine* and *The Era*. Each of these journals put a distinctive spin on rhetoric that was essential to encouraging public acceptance of furniture which seemed to lack all the traditional standards of high quality such as exotic wood veneers, virtuoso inlay or carving techniques, and reference to court styles of the Renaissance and eighteenth-century France. By comparison to Hubbard's facetious tone or Stickley's pedantry, Price's erudition seems to explain the incontrovertible rather than preach a new religion. Hubbard's furniture proclaimed what it was meant to be in a very literal way: the parts were obviously heavy giving good measure for the price and the Roycroft insignia was usually written large so all could appreciate the medieval (i.e., Arts and Crafts) lineage. Stickley resorted to symbols: his exposed tenons were seldom functional and sometimes fake yet they suggested honest, handcrafted construction to consumers who knew little of furniture-making techniques.

Sort of Heaven, A Good Sort of Earth: The Rose Valley Arts and Crafts Experiment (Chadds Ford, Pa.: Brandywine Conservancy, 1983), 54. A creosote stain was "applied with a brush and rubbed down with cotton waste within an hour." After drying for 12 to 24 hours the wood was given a thin coat of boiled linseed oil, the oil "rubbed, as the stain was and left to stand for twenty-four hours," and "finished with wax … and rubbed with an ordinary shoe polishing brush."

3. For an account of the Byrdcliffe experiment see Robert Edwards, "Byrdcliffe: Life by Design," in *Life by Design: The Byrdcliffe Arts and Crafts Colony* (Wilmington, Del.: Delaware Art Museum, 1984).

Price never designed furniture to look like Arts and Crafts style; rather, his furniture looks the way it does because of the way it is built. He abhorred what he called "mixed construction" or the use of glued joints combined with loose-pinned joints. His joinery actually held a piece of furniture together and, when appropriate, allowed it to be taken apart. Such construction techniques were not standard in factories which relied heavily on dowels, glue, and varnish to hold their products together.[4] Factories had to use machinery extensively and efficiently to meet production demands requiring the introduction of several new "lines" each year.[5] The Charles P. Limbert Company developed lines in quick succession, first offering rustic "Old Hickory" furniture, then "Arts and Crafts," then "Holland Dutch Arts and Crafts," then "Holland Dutch Arts and Crafts Straight Line and Flanders Furniture," and then, perhaps bowing to the limited space on a normal-sized label, "Ebon-oak" and "Rainham."

Gustav Stickley also responded to market dictates although he did not generally tack catchy names on his lines of inlaid or spindle furniture. Modern historians like to call these changes of appearance "development" but there is little evidence of any conscious design evolution. Stickley's first designs derived from the attenuated Japonesque of European art nouveau. Next he began making ludicrously heavy if endearing pieces (like the "Eastwood" chair) which were, in 1901, *retardataire* interpretations of mid-nineteenth-century furniture made by British designers such as Ford Madox Brown. Harvey Ellis is credited with the next changes that again relied (sometimes literally) on the lighter proportions and inlay decorations of British and European art furniture. But heavier designs continued to be offered along with Ellis designs until 1915 when Stickley went bankrupt. At the end Stickley introduced the "Chromewald" line which, even though it allowed him to exercise his interest in painted finishes, must be seen as an attempt to survive the demise of popular taste for the Mission style. The market did not drive style in smaller shops such as Price's Rose Valley or Whitehead's Byrdcliffe. They were productive for a much shorter period of time than the factories and were never set up to churn out thousands of pieces. It has been estimated that fewer than one hundred pieces were made at Byrdcliffe and fewer than five hundred at Rose Valley. It was the style of living that mattered in these communities not the style of the furniture; the latter was the inevitable result of the former.

During the early years of his architectural practice, Price did not design furnishings to outfit an entire building as his mentor Frank Furness sometimes did and Frank

---

4. William L. Price, "The Building of a Chair," *The Artsman*, 1, no. 8 (May 1904), 277–284; "Some Humors of False Construction," *The Artsman*, 1, no. 9 (June 1904), 321–328; "From the Artsman Himself," *The*

Artsman, 1, no. 12 (September 1904), 481–483.
5. Jane Perkins Claney and Robert Edwards, "Progressive Design in Grand Rapids," *TILLER*, 1 (September/October 1983), 42.

Lloyd Wright, with whom Price was often compared, usually did. The grand houses he built before establishing Rose Valley were furnished in an eclectic manner typical of the late nineteenth century and undoubtedly determined by the owners. The Gilmore and McLanahan houses had Colonial revival chairs, bronze sculptures, Moorish lanterns, bamboo furniture, tiger skins, and oriental rugs but they also had a few pieces designed by Price. Close examination of the carving on the Price-designed pieces and on furniture bearing the Rose Valley mark suggests the same craftsmen made both although it is not yet known when or where the unmarked pieces were made. A desk commissioned by William Harrison to hold his Shakespeare folios seems to have been a very important job for Price's office.[6] It was photographed from every angle and during every state of production—from the modeled-clay sketches for the figures of Shylock and Portia, which were later carved in oak to decorate the base of the desk, to the finished desk with and without its brass fittings. The background in each of these photographs appears to be a shop other than the one in Rose Valley even though a date (22 August 1903) appears on a sign visible through a window. This establishes the time of manufacture of the piece at least two years after the shop opened in Rose Valley in 1901. The desk could have been photographed in the Philadelphia workshop of Edward Maene whom Price usually employed to execute carved woodwork. Maene's carving style is evident on the woodwork and built-in furniture found in Price's domestic interiors designed before 1901 but it is also apparent on furniture made at the Rose Valley location. Perhaps Price's story about his search for skilled cabinetmakers is apocryphal and the woodworkers employed at the furniture shops in Rose Valley were trained by Maene.[7]

The question of training is worth discussing. Henry Hetzel taught at the Drexel School of Industrial Art and Price attended the Pennsylvania Museum School of Industrial Arts, an institution of major importance in disseminating Arts and Crafts philosophy—where tile maker Henry Chapman Mercer, ironworker Samuel Yellin, and writer Howard Fremont Stratton all taught at the time Rose Valley was founded. Hetzel had a large workshop in Rose Valley where he made furniture for his home. Of these pieces a bench, a chair, and two footstools were illustrated in *The Artsman* where they are identified simply as a "Rose Valley Gothic Bench," a "Rose Valley Chair," and "Rose Valley

---

6. Harrison purchased his folios from noted Philadelphia book dealer Phillip Rosenbach for $17,500 in 1903. In May of the same year he asked Rosenbach for "the exact size in *every* way of the four volumes of Shakespeare and what kind of a book-case you would suggest putting them in? In some way or other, it should be both burglar and fire proof." Original letters are in the Rosenbach Museum and Library. There is no record of Rosenbach's response but the cabinet was near completion by August 1903.

7. According to his great-granddaughter, Paula W. Healy, John Maene came from his birthplace in Bruges, Belgium, around 1880 to work in the stone-carving shop of his uncle, Edward Maene. John Maene became the foreman of the Rose Valley furniture shops.

WHEN YOU NEXT LOOK AT A CHAIR"   323

Footstools."[8] The bench is not marked with the shop's stamp but is otherwise indistinguishable from any of the many plain pieces produced by the Rose Valley shops. Students of Hetzel and Yellin produced objects that imitated their teachers' styles and methods. Furniture has been found that seems to be very similar to Price designs. For example a Gothic-style library table was assumed to be Rose Valley-made until close inspection revealed chisel marks evenly distributed over the entire surface and an uncharacteristic drawer under the top. This table may, in fact, be a student's piece or simply one made independently by Maene, Hetzel, or any of their workmen. Of course students had access to the same design sources as their teachers and those sources were interpreted, sometimes quite literally, by artisans on both sides of the Atlantic, thus making attributions difficult.[9]

Documentation of student work rarely survives but in the case of Parke Edwards there is extensive information about how and what he learned before he graduated from the Pennsylvania Museum School in 1913. Examples exist of his exercises in ceramics, metalwork, and woodwork. The carving on an oak sewing stand Edwards designed and built shows a level of skill equal to what was required to produce most Rose Valley pieces. Surely Price would have been aware of such talent and would have wanted to encourage graduates of the area's manual arts schools.[10]

The modern observer must keep in mind that designers such as Price made a strong distinction between style and ornamentation. Because in the late twentieth century we equate simplicity with modernity, a comparison of a simple, monolithic Stickley Craftsman trestle table to a Rose Valley trestle table embellished with sculpted pins and Gothic tracery might lead one to the conclusion that Stickley's work was progressive. Indeed, Price's work is often seen as regressive because his ornamentation derived from antique sources. Another argument views the plainness of the Mission style as a manufacturing exigency while the hand carving on a Price-designed piece of furniture may be seen as the timeless expression of an essential Arts and Crafts tenet. Price wrote:

> There is still another serious defect to be admitted, especially in mission furniture, and
> that is the use of excessive wood. It is just as bad construction to use too much wood as

---

8. *The Artsman*, 2 (August 1905), 352; *The Artsman*, 2 (April 1905), 232; and *The Artsman*, 2 (April 1905), 224 respectively.

9. As Mark Taylor has pointed out, a copy of Jacob Von Falke, *Mittelalterliches Holzmobiliar* (Vienna: Verlag Von Anton Schroll, 1894) survives in the Rose Valley archives. A chair with monkey finials illustrated in this book was obviously the inspiration for the design of the Rose Valley chair now in the Philadelphia Museum of Art. There are at least two surviving Rose Valley examples of this form (for the other, see catalogue #95

in *A Poor Sort of Heaven, A Good Sort of Earth*). Details of the Rose Valley chairs differ and the proportions of their structural members vary significantly from the historic example cited above.

10. Parts of the Parke Edwards archive are at Winterthur, the Metropolitan Museum of Art, and in the possession of Robert Edwards. The sewing stand was illustrated in *19th & 20th Century Decorative Arts from the Collection of Robert Edwards* (New York: Phillips Auctions, 1987), lot #207.

Rose Valley furniture shop, c. 1902 (Price and McLanahan Archives, George E. Thomas Collection)

too little. Mere absence of shaping and ornament is not necessarily good taste. Where common sense dictates the shaping of the part, appropriate ornament is both reasonable and desirable. Take the simple chair in cut seven, without any attempt at shaping or ornament. It is necessarily heavy, and to my mind, clumsy as well, and this necessity grows out of a perfectly reasonable structural feature—the need of strength where the leg and brace meet and are properly framed together. And here the size of the leg cannot safely be reduced, because of the cutting away of the wood in making the mortise. Between these points there is no reason for the same weight of wood. Common sense suggests that it be reduced, and taste suggests that, being reduced, it be reduced along the lines of beauty, with the same strength as before, less weight and more grace. Besides, this offers a chance for indefinite variety in treatment, and opportunity for much pleasure and growth in the making of it, without lessening a whit its essential simplicity, for simplicity is not a matter of form or lack of it. Simplicity is directness, and absence of meaningless parts, and not absence of ornament.[11]

The barley twist turnings Price sometimes used, when viewed abstractly, need not refer to the antique but only a decorative way to reduce wood weight. We can never accurately determine the perceptions of those who lived in a time other than ours—we now find the mid-nineteenth-century interpretations of mid-eighteenth-century French furnishing to be fanciful and often amusing in their inaccuracies. As well, at the turn of the century, there was a now-difficult-to-perceive vocabulary of decoration that distinguished "Flemish," "French Gothic," "Tudor," "Elizabethan," "Florentine," and "Lombard" among many other subtle modes. Even under the rubric Arts and Crafts, finishes were described as Flemish and reference to antique Spanish or Moorish styles was more or less played up. Price understood how the use of motifs found in the antique might not be mere imitation if we "put off the cloak of pretense, cease judging our work by dead standards, and work in the material at hand to meet the daily needs of contemporary life."[12] He further noted that there can never be such a thing as style until after it is dead. He could not have known the death of the Mission style was near when he criticized its avoidance of shaping or ornamentation as "bordering on self consciousness and fad."[13]

Price was not the only one who thought the ponderous proportions of Mission furniture could be improved by reducing its weight with appropriate ornamentation. Charles Edward Hopper, writing in *The Art World* (which subsumed Stickley's *Craftsman* in 1916), characterized Mission style as a throwback to the brutal and primitive efforts of our prehistoric forebears: "The fact that most of it is heavy and ungainly in form makes it

11. William L. Price, "Some Humors of False Construction," *The Artsman*, 1, no. 9 (June 1904), 326–327.

12. Price, "Some Humors of False Construction," 327.

13. William L. Price, "Man's Expression of Himself in His Work," *The Artsman*, 1, no. 6 (March 1904), 209–220.

the better for our purpose, as in the reduction of its necessary bulk we are arriving at two good ends: that of effecting a pleasing transformation and a corresponding reduction of weight." Hopper made an important point that is often overlooked by modern scholars of the Arts and Crafts movement: examples of the Mission style "surely do *not* fit into any surrounds that may lay claim to architectural excellence, hence, their use, at least wisely, is very limited."[14] If photographs published in shelter magazines such as *House Beautiful* or *House and Garden* during the years between 1890 and 1920 provide an accurate indication, few American homes were decorated in Mission or Arts and Crafts style. The interiors of Price-designed houses were no exception. Even in Rose Valley, where furnishing selection was often guided by Arts and Crafts principles, there were few examples of Rose Valley furniture.

Price ran into the same problem that had confounded William Morris. Arts and Crafts philosophers made much of the democratic and socialist nature of their utopian visions but, in practice, the production of objects meeting their standard of handcraftsmanship was an expensive and, therefore, elitist proposition. Stickley's mass-produced dining table (#631) cost $66 in 1904, putting it well beyond the reach of most Americans. A grand, hand-carved Rose Valley table cost $150, which only a rich patron could afford. Louis Comfort Tiffany won the job to furnish a Chicago clubhouse because his bid was lower than Price's.[15] Still, the Rose Valley order book and the photographs of furniture in the process of being built or just finished suggest that the furniture shop was very busy during the few years it operated.

The closing of the shops in Rose Valley has been characterized as failure. While it is true that the shops were not a financial success, the furniture made there represents a major achievement in realizing the Arts and Crafts ideal as defined by the movement's founders. After the shops closed in 1906, Price's office continued to design and supply furniture for various patrons. Most notable of this later production are the furnishings designed for the Traymore Hotel (1914–15). These pieces, having none of the dour burden of Arts and Crafts philosophy, were playful and somewhat fantastic as is fitting for a seaside resort. A suite of red-painted Chinoiserie furniture was produced for the hotel dining room. From a late twentieth-century perspective this furniture appears to presage art deco styles of the 1920s and so seems much more modern than the Gothic-referenced Rose Valley production of the previous decade. However, what we know belies what we see. The socialist bent of the Arts and Crafts movement was radical and progressive while art deco was not and was not intended to be much more than a change in fashion.

———

14. Charles Hopper, "Suggested Change of Lines for Mission Furniture," *The Art World*, 2, no. 5 (August 1917).

15. From a letter at the Athenaeum of Philadelphia.

There are several different styles of drawing evident in renderings of furniture made for Price. They range from the confident, knowing pencil sketches initialed "WLP" to barely competent ink tracings which may be the work of newly apprenticed draftsmen. Few, if any, appear to be actual designs. Some marked "approved" were presentation drawings. Others are graphite drawings that have been drawn over in ink probably for reproduction in *The Artsman*. Of these many are based on photographs of completed furniture or actually traced from photographs. In addition to Price's initials, drawings bear the monograms of John J. Bissegger, a draftsman in Price's city office; Henry Hetzel and William Walton, both Rose Valley residents; draftsman W. T. Karcher; and Alice Barber Stephens, a nationally recognized illustrator whose home and studio were in Rose Valley. *The Artsman* drawings are identical in style, which may have been the result of the way they had to be adapted for transfer to the metal plates used for printing illustrations in the magazine. Certainly Stephens' style was not at all like that of Price. It would be difficult, therefore, to use these drawings as a reliable guide in determining which furniture Price may have designed and which may have been designed by others.

A survey of drawings may not help determine who was responsible for particular designs but it does provide an overview of the influences other than Gothic used by Price and his designers. "Colonial" is well represented usually more in spirit than in faithful reproduction of eighteenth-century details. In Price's day the term Colonial included objects from the 1830s and 1840s, and Price designed Stephens' dining room around a secretary in that style. What we now sometimes call "Empire" was often of bizarre design and ersatz construction, difficult to align with Price's constructional theory, so he relied on simplified Hepplewhite or Sheraton designs for his Colonial pieces. Symbols allow these to be "read" as easily as his Gothic pieces. There are no exaggerated loose-pinned tenons, but the flush-cut pins are obvious and refer to the honest simplicity of America's founders who were cast in the noble role of workers using their hands. It mattered little that many of those cabinetmakers chose to cover humble construction details with gorgeous veneers. Just as oak was usually used for Gothic pieces, mahogany and, less often, walnut were specified for Colonial. The designers seemed to be aware of their limitations. Among the drawings is a note to a client stating that they did not like to do sofas but they would prepare some sketches for the client to see. Sure enough, their drawings of sofas show awkward affairs that would be better not built. In 1906 they even attempted a Louis XV-style armchair for C. E. Morris. The chair may never have been made, however, because, as Bissegger wrote to Morris, the shop manager had left and no more orders were being taken until Price returned from Europe.[16]

---

16. Letter to C. E. Morris, dated 9 March 1906, now #139–63 in the collection of drawings at the   Philadelphia Museum of Art.

While certain details in *The Artsman* are more rhetorical than reliable, John Maene's "Modeling and Carving" sheds light on the designing process as Price conceived it.

> Drawing is of vast preliminary importance in modeling and carving. But drawing may be only suggestion. In executing designs variations spontaneously occur, some of them wonderfully advantageous—variations that it would have been impossible even to imitate on paper. This is no doubt where the creative mind of the carver or modeler will ascertain itself.... It is fortunate if the executant is also the designer of his work.[17]

John Maene speaks of his work "in the Rose Valley shop." Much of the furniture completed during the five years the Rose Valley shops existed was photographed in a shop interior with windows giving on to an urban street, not the pastoral Ridley Creek which ran beside the converted mill in Moylen. A great deal of furniture was hand-carved from 1904 to 1905 and it seems unlikely that the little group in Price's utopian experiment could have made it all. As noted, the Harrison Shakespeare folio cabinet commissioned in 1903, while the Rose Valley furniture shop was operational, was probably made in Edward Maene's shop. Since John Maene complained that schools did not teach a carver to design or model, either he or Edward would have done the expert carving on this cabinet. He further worried about how American craftsmen were to attain any individuality or national style if they were not taught fundamental design skills. To him carvers were merely being taught a way to earn wages because carving was looked upon as "a commercial commodity at so much a yard." In practice the style of carving found on Price-specified woodwork and furniture is seamless and without expressions of individuality. As well, carving of the quality Maene was capable of has always been a very expensive commodity and, in a large part, was the undoing of the Rose Valley furniture shops. Such artistry is achieved by only a few craftsmen and affordable by only a few patrons.

A small number of pieces were made to be sold through the Price and McLanahan office on Walnut Street in Philadelphia, the Society of Arts and Crafts in Boston, the Guild of Arts and Crafts in New York City, and a few commercial outlets such as Taft and Belknap also in New York. However, the order books show that rich people who had no intention of participating in "the Art that is Life" commissioned the majority of these pieces. These patrons expected to buy their carving by the yard. In a 1904 letter addressed to "Messers. Price & McLanahan" (not to the Rose Valley shops), Alfred Percival Smith groused, "in regard to the larger of the two chairs, I wished one with a little more work on it than the one which was sent on approval." Having dealt with aesthetics he continues: "In regard to the cost of the box, you will remember that as originally contemplated there was to have been more lettering on the front which has never been put on, yet the total cost seems to have exceeded that at first mentioned by nearly 50%."[18] The Maene and Price

---

17. John Maene, "Modeling and Carving," *The Artsman*, 1, no. 6 (March 1904), 201–208.

equations did not match those of the consumer: for the former, carving (as long as it was "honest") ought to equal beauty; for the latter, carving equaled luxury. Hitching concepts of honesty or nature to skills like carving is an intellectual exercise of interest primarily to philosophers. The rest of us would need a good deal more time to discover what Maene means when he says, "the best carving of all ages has been nearest nature, nearest simplicity," than we would need to pick out a chair with which to furnish a home.

For Price carving was honest when it expressed the craftsman himself. But how was this to be accomplished? Archly, Price disdained the efforts of a lady "who with great pride showed [him] some tiles on which she had herself painted lovely sprays of orchids. That is just about as senseless as most of our notions about art, and we have got the idea that we cannot afford to do differently."[19] The balance of the text implies that this hapless Arts and Crafts acolyte decorated her tiles as an economy measure which was surely not the case especially at a time when ceramics decoration was a hugely popular means of self-expression. Maene's carved figures in medieval costume holding shields are no less senseless or more natural or honest. Popular taste won out and much Rose Valley furniture ended up in "heterogeneously furnished homes." This was discussed in an article, "Ugly Homes and Bad Morals," by Mrs. Herbert Nelson Curtis and reprinted in *The Artsman*. The Harrison Shakespeare desk went into a home, "Grey Towers," which was an exemplar of the worst fears of Curtis. This stone mountain harbored cavernous rooms encased in enough gilded-gesso frills and carved cupids and garlands to corrupt an army's morals. Such American interpretations of seventeenth- and eighteenth-century French styles unjustly bore the brunt of criticism. "Generally speaking, elaborate pieces of furniture are most dangerous because they are most aggressive to the eye and, most distracting to the mind" lectured Curtis, but she probably had not seen the elaborate Shakespeare cabinet or, if she had, she would have seen it differently than we do today.[20] Price wondered how this insubstantial furniture was going to wear, choosing to ignore the fact that the delicate marquetry, porcelain plaques, or gold leaf embellishing these pieces hardly needed to wear in the court of Louis XV or in the baronial halls of America's merchant princes. In an article in the issue of *The Artsman* just preceding the one in which Price's ruminations appeared, artist Everett Shinn's effort to tart up an ordinary piano for a French room in composer Clyde Fitch's home was praised: "The piano as finished is in its proper environment. The room is a perfect Louis XIV apartment."[21]

Price recognized some of the contradictions and inconsistencies in his theorizing; some he tried to rationalize and some he never addressed. Those cited above are included

---

18. Letter from Alfred Percival Smith, dated 28 December 1904, at the Athenaeum of Philadelphia.
19. Price, "Man's Expression of Himself in His Work," 216.
20. Mrs. Herbert Nelson Curtis, "Ugly Homes and Bad Morals," *The Artsman*, 3, no. 3 (December 1905), 73–78.
21. Reprinted from the *New York Sun*: "Plea for Beautifying Things of Daily Use," *The Artsman*, 3, no.4 (November 1905), 46.

not to discredit him or his foray into Arts and Crafts philosophy. They illustrate why he insisted over and over again on calling the Rose Valley community, which included the furniture shops wherever they physically stood, an experiment. The old mill provided a laboratory where Price could try out ideas about how furniture should be constructed and carved. Meanwhile the architectural office downtown had to continue to function regardless of the results of the Rose Valley experiment. Furniture was still being ordered on Rose Valley shops stationery as late as 1913 although by then the process was fragmented. Price designed a table for a Mrs. Scott, the design was sent to Bissegger to be rendered, Bissegger's drawing was sent to Mrs. Scott for approval, and then Mrs. Scott sent drawings and wood to John Maene who, at this point, had his shop back in the city.[22] Drawings from the architectural office dated 1921 (five years after Price's death) show a Colonial revival dressing table, a step back from the modern furniture designs for the Traymore Hotel. Had Price lived longer he would have continued to be interested in modernism. As it happened the style he left behind in Rose Valley survived for several decades as "executive Tudor." Architects like Mellor, Meigs and Howe designed furnishings in the antique styles of the Arts and Crafts movement's revered medieval. Handmade for use in country houses built across America, this furniture often met and sometimes exceeded Price's philosophical requirements but, if it was intended to express anything, it was only how much such craftsmanship cost.

———

22. A letter to Mrs. H. L. Scott written on stationery from the Rose Valley shops, dated October 1915, and at the Athenaeum of Philadelphia, lists Maene's address as 181 South 4th Street, Philadelphia.

Is American Art Captive to the Dead Past?

William L. Price

Originally published in The Craftsman *(Gustav Stickley, editor and publisher), 15, no. 5 (February 1909), 515–519.*

How long, I wonder, will the Renascence hold us in its grasp? How long will the fetters of the past bind us to the arts of other days? How long will Art be led captive to education and be shackled to precedent? For that period following the glorious, if barbaric, Gothic age, which we call the Renascence, was for Architecture no re-birth of art, but a grave-digging resurrection. The people of that day, realizing the crudeness and barbaric splendor of the Gothic, and having rediscovered the classic art and literature of Greece and Rome, made a fatal mistake. Instead of refining the barbaric out of their own art and keeping its glory and its frank expression of materials and the wants and customs of their own day, the educated and refined said, "We can never hope to equal the classic beauty of the past; let us spend our lives in imitating it."

And now the general public, especially the educated public, and the vast majority of the artists and architects, still in the Renascence, are "laying the flattering unction to their souls" that we have achieved a great advance in architecture and the arts in the past twenty years. We have awakened, it is true, but our eyes are still heavy with the sleep of the Renascence. Lulled by the slumber song of a gorgeous past, we think to dream art back into the hungry world. We think to let the mantle of our education cover the bareness of popular apathy and creative thought. We think to lift the masses to an understanding of the excellency of revived styles and resurrected cultures, while we should be studying those very masses for an inspiration, while we should be raised to a pitch of enthusiastic interpretation of their great qualities—those very qualities of which as patriots we boast and at which as artists we sneer. If there is no inspiration for the architects and artists in the life of our own people, then there will be no art of our own people, and this is the fault of the artists, not of the people.

When the naked savage, pushed by the wants of his body, fashioned clay to his uses, or with rude flint tool shaped his weapons for their fell purpose, something happened to him. He was no longer merely a weak and naked animal in a cold and strenuous world. He had slipped into the god class. He had become a creator, a man who wills, not the blind follower of instinct or racial habit, and the tale of his birth is told in the work of his hands. Having created, he looks with new eyes on creation. Having fashioned for man's service he sees his fellow man, still "but as trees walking," "as in a glass darkly." Yet he sees. And the tale of that emotion is written large on pot and bow, or on the painted bauble for a love's sake that has become more than mere physical sex attraction.

And this is art, fine art, all there is to art, and it is enough. I like to quote to my friends, the artists, the cloistered painters and sculptors, the words of Blount, "The scratched line around the porringer and the carved motto over the cottage door,—these are the beginning and almost the end of the fine arts."

We have hedged about the artists and their work as if they were something apart, their works we have enshrined as gods, and themselves we look upon as the inspired priests of a holy of holies that common men must approach with bowed reverence. But I say to you artists, come out from your dead cloisters. Come out into the free air where men really live, and take the shoes from off your feet, for this is holy ground. You are not the end and aim of life, but interpreters of life as it is, and prophets of life as it shall be. Come out as the savage did and tell the tale of life, and if that life be savage and vulgar, tell the tale so that it will shame the vulgarity and lift the vulgar; but tell the tale, for your job is the same as that of the savage: to show to your fellow men the new point of view, the new beauty in common things, to trace dimly the paths of promise, to break a few steps in the steep path of the hill difficult; and this must be done in the sight of the people. You must also sit at the door of your tents to chip the stone and mold the pregnant clay.

Oscar Wilde says, "The educated man's idea of art is always the art that has been; the artist's idea of art is the art that is to be." And he knew. So if you would be hailed by men as great artists and great architects, build according to your knowledge and their knowledge. Sit satisfied in your Renascence, but if you would lead men on to greater heights and new achievements, build from your secret souls. Let your knowledge guide and conserve, but let your intuition rule.

Oh, you artists who think yourselves above the pots and trappings of a common life—you who think fine art above the chipping of useful stones and the fashioning of the commonplace—you are not fit to shape the instruments of man's daily needs. You who think that art is to paint silly pictures for silly gilded frames, whose greatest ambition it is to have them hung in some silly gilded Luxembourg, come out into life and help the people to build a new art for a new day. Better, a thousand times better, the rock-ribbed Gothic of a Whitman than all the curled darlings and simpering niceties of a borrowed culture. And you painters and sculptors who think to get closer to architecture by decorating the stolen and effeminate glories of our modern Renascence, who in the end only emphasize the emptiness of the temple by accenting or ignoring its banalities, come out from among the tombs, join you fellow craftsmen, the quarryman and the woodman, and realize that the cornerstone comes before the capstone. Realize that until the work of our hands in fashioning the necessities of life has been glorified, there can be no art that shall move men's souls.

And you architects who think that architecture can be made in offices, that paper and pencil can express the hopes and aspirations of a people, learn that you cannot save your souls alone, that you cannot drop architecture down on a waiting earth like manna. Architecture comes up from the soil, not down from the skies. And it is the mother of arts because not man but men must create it. Only as you can influence your fellows, the stone-mason and the joiner, can you hope for architecture.

And your great organizations of builders and of workmen, they hold out no hope. And your machines! Only as they free men, not *from* work, but *to* work, shall they help.

The artists of the past about whose graves you linger, who were they? Not the pattern-makers, but the doers. Most of the great buildings of the past are bad architecturally, but they are great as craftsmanship. They shadow forth the hopes and the failures of their makers. They are alive today because men's lives were built into them. Your classmen in architecture can imitate them but they cannot make them. They can point out their failures and their inconsistencies, but with all their machines and knowledge and organization they can of themselves no more create architecture than the architects of that day could. The difference is that those men did not try. They designed with their fellows, the craftsmen, not for them. They accepted the limitations of materials of use and of the workman, and no sculptor was too great or painter too exalted to interpret the common life around them, and if their madonnas were not Jewish, at least they were maternal. If the Gothic sculptures were not natural, at least they were architectural. They tell no tale of anatomy, but they tell the tale of a people's aspirations. "But," says Shaw, "your modern academicians think to paint Giotto's pictures without Giotto's inspiration and correct his perspective into the bargain."

Until we get craftsmen who are architects and architects who are craftsmen, we shall have no architecture. And until we get architecture, or set ourselves in the way of getting it, we shall have no fine art. For fine art is only the fine way of doing things that are worth the doing. And as long as our educated men, whether they be laymen or architects, think that the Madison Square tower which has no meaning, is greater than its prototype, the Giralda, we shall build Madison Square towers, we shall build marble temples for banks, Italian palaces (nearly Italian) for dwellings for the vulgar rich, and English villas in miniature for the vulgar poor. We shall build Colonial houses such as the Colonials never built, for cultured do-nothings, and hotels that are not even French, for snobs and commercial travelers. If our American life is half-way worth the boast we make for it, why is it not good enough to be our inspiration? If our rich men are worth catering to in paint and marble, why are they not worth interpreting in brick and stone? If our Republic is worth defending and upholding, is not its seat in Washington or elsewhere worth housing in something better or at least more representative than the cast-off vestures of monarchy? And that our capitols speak more of feeble-minded monarchy than of strong young Democracy I challenge anyone to deny.

There is only one thing worse than ignoring precedent, and that is following it. Carlyle says, "Originality does not consist in being different, but in being sincere." And there is not only the very soul of individuality in art, but also of style in art. For if we were sincere, our work would vary from type as we individually vary, but also as we are much alike in the same environment, so our sincere work would have much in common, and that is the thing we call Style. Not a fixed form, but an expanding expression of a common impulse. So if we were sincere as we are like our fathers, so would our works follow theirs, not as imitation but as like expression, and as we are different and beyond our fathers, so would our work be different and beyond their work.

Not the feeble, book-learned Colonial of our day, for we are no longer colonists, but the full-blooded expression of a giant Democracy; the strong, rude conqueror of a continent, not the feeble dependent of an outworn social creed. And some there are, groping for this real Renascence, not a resurrection, mind you, but a re-birth of Art. Here and there a free man lifts his head. Here and there a potter lifts his clay out of the common plane of style. Here and there a carver or a sculptor dares say his new day's say. And architecture is creeping to our doors almost unnoticed, close to the soil, still finding its birth, as always, in the simple dwellings of the countryside. And architects whose great and costly buildings are mere banal European architecture, and not true even to that, are hiding away in the countryside cottages and country houses that are real,—that are neither French nor English, that are just houses, for here they are not afraid. Here they dare be themselves and dare frankly express their fellows.

But our big buildings! It is to laugh. Five-story bronze and steel buildings masquerading as marble temples, orders piled on orders, detail thrown bodily to the top of high buildings for the birds to see. Marble palaces at Newport, chateaux on Fifth Avenue, alleged Pantheons on Broad Street, marble detail cast in clay or painfully wrought in granite. Wood fashioned like stone and stone like wood. As an architect from Ghent, recently here, said, "Oh, that your forests were fire-proof and your buildings were not. I came full of hope to find a great, new, modern architecture, and I find but bad European architecture." And he had been to Boston, too, and to New York and Albany and Philadelphia. But he had not seen our nestlings, our suburbs, our little real houses in the country.

Our hope of art, like our hope of health, lies in the pregnant call of "Back to Nature." Back to the fields and forests for our nerve-broken health. Back to man and his needs, his common daily needs, for our art.

And, my friends, don't fool yourselves that there is any other way. Look at your own achievements. Look at the architectural triumphs of even ten years ago, and ask yourselves if they will live, if they have anything to say, any new thought to thunder down the hollow vault of time. We are a people in the forming, and so have all peoples been when they really lived, and we must build for the moment and go on , and if you don't care to build for the scrap heap, don't build, for it will all go there. But if you build truly, some stones shall stand, some detail will cling to the robes of art and become part of the great whole. Better to lay two bricks together in the new way that tells a tale, than to build a temple for the money changers with no thought in it less than two thousand years dead.

Modern Architecture
William L. Price

Delivered before the Ontario Association of Architects in January 1907 and originally published in two parts in The Artsman, *4, no. 2 (January 1907), 227–238 and 4, no.3 (April 1907), 259–278.*

What I want to say will be, I hope, rather anarchistic—rather in the direction of taking a shot at certain ideals and ideas that seem to me to be false in our architectural work. In talking about modern architecture perhaps I ought to define a little what I mean. It is very differently looked at. The Beaux Arts man says that modern architecture consists in following out certain continuous historical precedents, as expressed in the Schools of Paris, and that the Beaux Arts people are in line with that succession architecturally; that though the work may be bad in every other way, still that is the path we should pursue. However, that is not the kind of modern architecture I want to talk about. I was told today that Mr. Cram in his lecture before you took the very opposite view from that suggested by Prof. Nobbs yesterday. He thinks that the Gothic architecture was nipped in the bud by an obtrusive and immoral Renascence, and that what we ought to do is to go back and take up the Gothic where our predecessors left off, and arrive at something really splendid. I think he is partially right in his premise but entirely wrong in his conclusion. He is right when he says the Gothic was interrupted before it reached its full flower. What I mean by modern architecture is not the Art Nouveau with its pulled candy motive. That does not seem to be essential modern art, though it has in it a good substantial kick against existing lines of thought, and I do not forget that as one of my friends paraphrases the old saying, "he also serves who stands and kicks." Sometimes it is necessary to have these refractory and unpleasant people around to do the kicking for us. My own ancestors were kicked out of England as Quakers because they were so obnoxious and upsetting to things as they were.

What I mean by modern architecture is architecture that accepts its own age and its own wants and its own feelings as its standard, rather than any mere standard of excellence or beauty in design. That seems to me what constitutes the modern way of looking at things. Now, we have in the records of the civilized world very little except its architecture, and only a very small fragment of that. We know comparatively little about what people have thought. We know that in Greece they reached a very high perfection along certain lines architecturally; that in expression of beauty pure and simple, they have probably never been equaled, and may never be equaled again. We know that the Romans appropriated and made great use of much that the Greeks have worked out; they did blend Greek architecture with their own as an expression of their life—of their tremendous force and virility. Their architecture is the expression in stone of imperialism, of the majesty of the state. Now, we do not look at the state in quite the same way that the Roman did, any more than we look at life and art as the Greek did, and for us to adopt either one of their architectures would be very stupid—just as stupid as it would have been for the Roman to try to make the Greek express his life. Carlyle says that originality does not consist in being different but in being sincere. If you are sincere you will be different enough but not very different. None of us look alike: very few of us act exactly in the same way under the same circumstances. Very few of us dress alike; we come as near to it as we well can; but we all have a certain distinction and distinctiveness about our manners of thought; consequently if we really express ourselves frankly in what we are trying to do we would not express ourselves as other men do. That is where the originality would come in if we were sincere: that is where modernity would come in if we were modern. That does not mean that one man would work in Gothic or Renascence or Greek because he happened to like these things. In the average we are very much the same. That is where style comes from—the fact that men in the same conditions do actually think and act very nearly alike: so that while their individual character would be reflected, if they were sincere in their work, their style would be much alike. Style is the general average of thought of any period.

Now, it has always seemed to me that the Gothic period was the only truly modern period that we have any historical knowledge of. Possibly the Greek period was just as modern: we know less about it. But the Gothic was absolutely modern. The Gothic builder threw aside practically all precedent, so far as we can see—or nearly all of it: he still had to have windows, he still had to have doors, he still had to build a building of stone, but he built on a different basis from any of the known architectures that preceded. I am not an archaeologist, so that I may get tripped up on these facts: as Mr. Shaw says, all of our facts get disproved in time, so that it does not make much difference—but there is every evidence that the Greek column and lintel architecture is primarily wood construction. We go back and reverse the thing, and do what the Greek or Renascence man did properly in stone, in wood, and it becomes absolutely foolish. You have, for instance, the example of your Renascence door trim. You would not think of framing that door with the stiles cut off and the top bottom rails run through: never in the world. It would not appeal to you as being good wood construction: in point of fact, it would be bad wood construction. But, when you get to the frame that surrounds the door you do precisely that thing. You have a stupid wood construction: you have a wood construction which is not essentially wood or essentially plaster, essentially anything but stone—a series of blocks laid one upon the other, built up by the Greeks and Egyptians before them, from their wood column and their lintel. Shortening the lintel, they made it so that the block of stone will rest across, and get a legitimate construction in that way. The Gothic seems to me to have realized, as no other period has realized, a fitting use of material. Prof. Nobbs spoke of that yesterday. It understood the material with which it worked and the end which it was trying to accomplish, and it worked its design to the material in which it was working. You never find a piece of Gothic woodwork that is not properly framed: never, examining any of the good work, will you find it: neither will you find in the stone work of the Gothic period any attempt to make stone look like wood, or to use it in any way, except as block built upon block, carrying the strains to the ground. Of course, in later periods of Gothic, as in all periods, its votaries do run to excess. They came to a point where they tried to see how little stone they could put in, where it was not a questions of how much stone should go in to do this work, but of how little could be made to do it; of how delicate it could be made. All that was very stupid. It stands just as our modern architecture stands. It has no relation to the real acceptance of material. But they still clung to the fundamental structural ideas in these materials. When you see the iron work on the architecture of that period, you find the iron changes the design. It is never treated like cast iron if it is wrought iron: it is treated as hammered out twisted bent pieces of metal. That runs all the way through the Gothic period.

If we were to take up the Gothic work where its masters left off, and go on, as has been suggested, with that—that is, taking up their designs—we would absolutely lose sight of the underlying principles which compelled them to build in that way. We would be simply taking patterns from their work and trying to improve on those patterns. That is not architecture. I do not care whether it be Greek or Roman, or whether it be Renascence or Gothic, looking at design in that way puts it on a wrong basis towards architecture. What we have a right to do, and what we should do, in examination of all these efforts of the past, is to examine their work, the purpose in their work, and try to find out why they did so and so, and say: "That is the thing for us to know; not what they did, but why they did it." Where the same principle that underlies their work will carry us, it is safe to follow. The result would not be Gothic architecture. Gothic architecture was barbaric in many ways. We think those cathedrals and those great works over there are perfectly magnificent: so they are: they are perfectly beautiful; but you would not want to create them now. You would not want specially to live with them. If they were painted in the three primary colors, as they largely were at that time, it would be harsh and grating on us to live with them. In point of fact, Gothic architecture expressed a new flamboyant boisterous age in art—a newly-found craft spirit. That alone would prevent us from going on, from where they left off. As Prof. Nobbs said yesterday, we have not the craftsmen to put in the wonderful imagery and the fun and frolic of it all, because our craftsmen are not humorous, frolicsome or very artistic. We might just as well try to paint the pictures of some of the old masters, and say: "We have not colors such as they had and will therefore paint them in monotone," and then expect them to have the same glory, as to expect to have Gothic architecture without craftsmanship, because Gothic architecture is primarily craftsmanship and not design. Of course we can reproduce, or make some attempt to reproduce, the majesty of their buildings and all that, but it is not Gothic architecture unless it is produced in the same way that Gothic architecture was produced.

Now, we come to Mr. Cram's position that the Renascence was an immoral interruption of a very important art. I absolutely agree with him. I believe that the great mistake which underlay the Renascence movement—and we are still in that movement absolutely, as much as they were at the time it started, as far as I can see—was, just as ours is today, that its disciples never were modern, that they did not try to fit themselves and their life with architecture that expressed that life in the materials in which they worked, but that they set up standards, and said: "We can never do anything as fine as the Greek or Roman did: we can never do it in literature, we can never do it in architecture; therefore, the thing for us to do is to try to do as nearly like they did as possible, merely fitting it to our needs." The moment any man sets up that standard, that man dies. The moment any man sets up as his standard of excellence the standard of another man's growth, that man ceases to grow. It is all right to worship the work of these great masters. But if you really believe that they were greater than you can ever become, you will never do any worthy work in God's world. The work that has been worthwhile, the work that has lived in the world's history, has been the work of men who have believed that their work was to be better than any other man's ever was. That is what makes art, that is what makes the artist successful in his career. He does not do it primarily for fun. He does it because he believes he has something to say. It may be only be a fraction of what other men have said, but that he has something to say that no other man ever could have said: that is the spirit that accepts today as the best day, that accepts the heritage of the past as the stairway to today, that realizes that the past is dead and today is dying, that we only have tomorrow, that tomorrow always comes, and that I if we today express ourselves to our fullest and best then tomorrow we will be bigger men than we are today. Now, the Gothic architects did just that. They did not set up the standard of the Greek column and say: "Here is our pattern: we will modify it, but we will do something like it, because these men were better than we are." Possibly they knew nothing of the character of the Greek. Whether they did or did not, they said: "Glory be to God, we are going to have a church; we will build it as magnificently as we know how, and we will build better tomorrow than we did today." The proof of that is that they changed all the time. They started to build one thing, and the man who started that died, and the church went on and built itself up from day to day, growing into a bigger and better thing than the first man's church would have been or could have been. The Renascence period did that only in one of the arts, as far as I know, and that is in the art of painting. They were great masters, great original thinkers. But in architecture they undoubtedly accepted the standards of the past as they did in literature.

Now, Gothic architecture has had all that to say, it seems to me, and that is enough. All we have to get from the Gothic workman is his point of view, not what he did. If Gothic architecture has any message today, it must, it seems to me, be under those circumstances which are primarily the same as the life the Gothic man was living. In the Church, which has been of continuous growth, and a continuous body, and practically a continuous form, there may be an absolute excuse for Gothic architecture. It may be that the Church is—and I believe it is in many ways—still medieval in its line of thought; the Catholic church undoubtedly is in its forms, in its ceremonies, very much the same as it was then. The surrounding that fitted it then would fit it today, if we were ready to build it. So it is with the college. The college, as we have it, is only beginning to cease to be medieval: we are only just beginning to realize that the college is for today and not for yesterday. We have hardly yet thrown aside the mass of fetish worship in our colleges. We still believe that we have to go through certain courses of study. But if the college is to be the same today as at that time, the architecture of that time undoubtedly fits this period in that direction. The question is whether it is right to go on with the college today as it was then. The question is whether we have not, as architects, a message that they require to learn; if we are leaders of thought, we cannot get away from responsibility for that fact. If we preached in architecture that the college should be modernized, we would tend to modernize the college; if we preached in our work that the Church should be modernized we would undoubtedly tend to modernize the Church; and it is just that point that I am desiring to make here.

We have a general condition that is not Medieval, that is not Classic, that is not like the period of the Renascence. I do not mean to say that the Renascence architecture did not express the people of that time, but what I mean to say is that the people of that time had not the modern point of view, were not moderns even then, because they did set up these standards of dead ages; but insofar as their architecture expressed their life, insofar as it indicated their peculiar genius, it is good. The great minds which lived and produced splendidly proportioned monuments in the Renascence period, would have produced splendidly proportioned monuments in the Greek period, or Roman period, or now, or any time. That is not a question of the soil in which they worked. That is a question of their own ability and power to see proportion.

Here we are in a condition which is certainly not Classic, not Renascence, not Gothic in its habit of thought. It is a business age; yet also much more than that. We talk a great deal about the sordidness of our life and the hurry and rush of our life. That is only a momentary matter: it is incident to all new countries it is incident especially to people who have gone out from their own country into other countries. The very contact with nature, and the very thought that they must put up with the hard knocks that they have to endure, has produced the kind of character that gets in a hurry and lives strenuously, and it takes generations to overcome that and strike a reasonable balance in our lives, and I see at the present time a very distinct tendency in that direction. There are very many of us who are not so much in a hurry as we were a few years ago; maybe because we are older, but I think it is because we are getting a little more sense. I know young men who are turning aside from careers, or what we would call careers, that promised all kinds of monetary success. Young men have ideals: they are beginning to take time to think about these things. Fifty years ago people were too busy to bother about architecture: they did not care, so long as it kept you warm, what the house looked like. We are getting to a different point of view in these matters, and we must meet that point of view.

I say we are preachers as well as mere interpreters of the public mind. But we must primarily be interpreters of the public mind and public feeling and public habits. If we have a factory to build, and that factory is to be a place where little children are ground to death, as they are in the silk mills in Pennsylvania, we ought to make the gates of that factory look like the gates of Hell, and we should paint over the door, "Abandon hope, all ye who enter here," and be honest about it. If we did that, the man that owned that building would be one of the people that would rise in the end with their bloody finger nails to tear it down brick by brick. If we really expressed the sordidness that exists in our time in the architecture that surrounds that life, it would not stand a minute, or at least but for a very short time. If we built our big financial institutions to look like the robbers' dens they are, how long would they last? We adorn them with bronze and gold and purple and fine linen, and sumptuousness, so that we have got to go in there and drop in our nickels. That is what it is for: no other reason under heaven but to induce the people to go in there and lose their money, because the men that run those institutions do not run them for fun. They do not produce wealth, except in a very incidental way, and they get enormously rich. Why, even Mr. Carnegie, himself a producer and organizer of production, says he made the discovery of his life when he discovered that the men who make the wealth never get rich. And if we could express, and if we did express, exactly these things, I am not joking about it when I say I believe it would be perfectly possible for the architecture of the country, if the architects were really sincere, to be a large factor in the reform of the country. We do form public opinion now. I will build a marble bank or anything else, just as quickly as any of you. But I will try to build that bank or that hotel or that house in some way or another, as nearly as lies in my power, to express the use and purposes, the ambitions, of those people, and I will try to make it hurt just a little. I built a hotel last year, and I know it hurts a little. I know there are architects that it hurts, and yet they cannot help but admit many of them at least, that it is an expression of the purpose for which it was built and of the place where it was built: that it is an expression of the gay and sumptuous life, as it was meant to be, of the people that go to Atlantic City. That seems to me to be possible in a great measure, but remember this: that if you do not want to erect buildings for the scrap heap of futurity, do not build, because that is where they all go.

A few centuries ago the Parthenon was practically perfect. You know that the columns of Carnack are falling now; and the lovely Campanile of Venice—where is it? All these shall pass away. This little bit of history we know about is but a fragment, but humanity goes on. It makes all the difference in the world how we build—very little what we build. It makes all the difference in the world, not only to the people who see our buildings and who live in our buildings, but still more to the people that build our buildings, the people that ought to be our best friends, and are, next to our clients, our hardest problems—the builders, the craftsmen, that work in the shops. If we stand out for good work, for work that pretends to be what it is, we will very soon see that we will build up craftsmanship—that carpenters and joiners and real brick masons and real stone layers and stone cutters, will come back to us, if we insist on having the materials treated for what they are. If, on the other hand, we always treat our terra cotta as stone—and usually our stone as terra cotta—we are corrupting and debauching, not only the popular taste, but infinitely more the men we rely on to help us create good buildings.

Every sham we build into a building means sham ideas built into the workman. We complain a great deal about the trades unions, and their attitude towards labor, and their effect on labor, and we complain justly. I believe in trade unions, but much of the effort of trade unions is put in a direction that tends to destroy the unionists ideals as a builder altogether—that tends to reduce him to a mere automaton that lays so many bricks a day. You cannot get architecture that way. You cannot get architecture out of that kind of labor, and this to me is the most important point of all that I have to say, the question of the attitude of labor towards architecture, because it is labor that must produce architecture.

When our plans are made, architecture is not born: it is possibly engendered, but architecture does not depend upon the excellence of our drawings, except in a certain degree. It is important enough, but only in a degree does it affect the final result of architecture. You have all had this experience: you have all made details that you thought were pretty fine, and gone to look at the work and found it pretty bad, and yet you could hardly have told wherein it departed from that drawing you have made. In point of fact, your drawing was a suggestion to an artist or artisan to go to work, and only suggested something that you could not draw until after it is carved or built, because you cannot draw carving until after it is carved. Unless you can find people who will accept your suggestion, modern people who are thinking of the problems of today, people that can put something into the building that was not possible to be put in the drawings, the result cannot be architecture. Architecture is the building of these concrete materials, this mud and clay and stone, up into enduring forms, to a fitted purpose, and to beautifully express that purpose, and unless it does that, I do not see that its majestic proportion, that its exquisite detail (nearly all copied, and mostly copied stupidly, without regard to the material), is going to produce architecture; it certainly is not going to produce modern architecture.

Now, I was asked to come here and talk about house design, because they think I know a little about house design and nothing about architecture, and in the perversity of human nature I do not want to talk about house design, but I will just a little. We have a great many more houses to design, the average of us, than we have monumental buildings. In point of fact, our every day problem is a problem of the cheap and simple, rather than the magnificent. It seems to me we have gone too much to Europe and the past in this regard. In the *Architectural Record* I see an article about brick houses—one a Jacobean house and the other a Georgian house, and the article starts out by stating that when a man wants to build a brick house in the country, that there are only two styles to build it in: that he has either to build a Jacobean house or a Georgian house. Who said so? Who said bricks had to be laid up in this form or that?

We go to England and we see styles instead of seeing architecture. We go through a shire there and we see a wonderful unity, and we are able to say "this house belongs to Warwickshire: this house is a Devonshire house," and we know them at once. Why is that? What gives them their character over there? Largely the fact that these men who built these houses looked about and picked up the first material they found. In one place they have stone roofs, and this gives one character to a countryside. In another place they had no friable stone but good clay, and there you find brick houses with tile roofs. You will find where local material was used, there is the architecture that is significant, that has some real character.

We only need to be modern in thought when we are doing work for this or that locality. If each one would do that as he works from place to place, there would soon be local style. If we would say: "Here is such and such a material to our hand. Here is a country that is flat, or that is high rolling, that suggests a certain type of house." We do these things to a certain degree now. We all do pretty much the same kind of thing for the same sort of places. But they have no local significance nor modern significance. If we would go to work and build in these places with the materials at hand, all materials suggested by the locality, we would soon commence to build up typical country architecture. There would not be any hard and fast style of house there any more than there is in those shires in England. But there would be countryside houses of stone, brick, or whatever was local and suggestive, that would tend towards style. That is the reason we do not get any style or any real significance into our architecture while we are looking for styles from the outside—while we are trying to think of styles as fixed things, instead of a natural growth brought into being by the intelligent use of materials in meeting the needs of the people.

Colonial work or Georgian work does in a large measure fit many of our houses. Our life is in very many ways like their life. That is the reason it fits. English architecture goes better, as a rule, in this country than French does, and why? Not because there are not any Frenchmen here, or that their houses are not beautiful, but because our life is more nearly like that of the people of England than France. But we have to remember that the houses, after all, are only a background for the life: that when the Colonial or the

Georgian was in vogue, with its simple white paint and its severe classic lines, and all that, the life for which it was the background was very flowery. I can scarcely conceive of a great big sweeping drive up to the entrance of a Colonial or Georgian house without a coach and four in front, with people in flowered waistcoats and flowered gowns, and all the pomp and color incident to their life. When your artist paints it he always paints it that way, and with propriety. When he paints pictures of the Gothic period, he does not picture men in dress suits. Even we would properly say it does not fit.

The architecture of the past does not make the proper background for our life, as I see it: and we architects have not consciously tried to make a fitting background for our life. That is what is the matter with modern architecture. You cannot imagine anybody living in dress suits and our horrible funeral clothes and all that kind of thing in the Gothic period. Why, then, should we try to bring down the form without the life? Now you are talking about your new Government buildings here, and the buildings are to be the houses of your politicians and your public servants.

[Mr. Darling: Do not ask us to make it suit the politician. Mr. Price proceeds.] That is what I do ask you to do. We do it with the gaols, and that is what I would have you do with your government buildings, except that they should also express the aspirations of your best citizens, as your gaol not only fits the prisoner but expresses the sordidness of the community as well; and if the next generation pulled them down, so much the better for the next generation and so much the better for you, because you would have helped make the next generation worthy to pull them down. It is the people that we have to think about. We architects get very indignant about Cromwell and his crowd that went around and smashed off the heads of the angels on the churches, and broke in the windows; in fact we are a great deal more worried about that than we are about that other revolution in France where they cut peoples heads off. Those people would have died anyhow, we say, and we might still have had the angels' heads in the churches. Just the same, there was a reason in what Cromwell and his people did. It was better that the architecture and the angels' heads should suffer than that the people should go on suffering. It was better even that the heads of the gilded darlings of the French court should fall into the basket, savage as it was, criminal as it was, than that they should go on breeding innocent little children to live in such an atmosphere as to make them capable of such savagery.

The next generation, the future, tomorrow, is our business. Build your halls for your legislatures, even to fit your legislators. Even that. That would seem to me to be modern. It might be too modern. It might be revolutionary, but tomorrow is always revolutionary. We are always disbelieving what we believed yesterday. I will go a step further and say that if the church as an organization stands back of the corruption of our civic life, of our political life, of our business life, as in some measure it does, that then we ought to reverse the old order, and put the statues of the angels on the outside and the statues of the fiends on the inside.

There is nothing in religion or in politics or in legislatures or in governments that we the people have a right to respect or to honor that interferes with our right and our duty to respect and honor men. These institutions are made for men and women and little children, not they for the institutions, and if we would frankly express in our houses, in our factories, in our churches, even, as I say, in the halls of our legislatures, the kind of work that goes on there, we would very soon have a different kind of work going on. People would not stand for it if they could see it. You and I do not believe that thousands of little children, seven or eight years old, work all night, whipped at times to keep them awake, in factories in Pennsylvania. If we did believe that, then we would get up and tear those places down piece by piece. And yet it is a fact. We do not see these facts. We go on from day to day joking and laughing about our corrupt politicians. We go on accepting that corruption in politics, because we want jobs; of all the low-down motives in the world, because we want money. That is the reason. That is the reason I do not go down there in Pennsylvania and raise a ruction about those children in those terrible hells. And that is only a sample of what happens everywhere, all over our country. I do not do it because I am afraid to do it, because I am afraid to let my life represent my beliefs. But great architecture does not come that way.

Great architecture comes and always has come, whether it was the wonderful worship of beauty by the Greek, the worship of the state, and of the power and dignity of the state, by the Roman, the worship of pomp and glory and magnificence by the Renascence, or worship of high ideals, as in the Gothic period, because these men said what they thought. They did the thing that was in their mind to do. They were modern to that extent, even in the Renascence period. They frankly accepted the magnificence of the palace as an offset to the squalor and misery of the poor. They frankly accepted it and they were modern to that extent. The Greek frankly accepted his slavery. He did not lie about it. He was modern in that way. If we are to be modern we have to approach this thing in that way also. Whether it is a question of mere construction, whether it is a question of allowing our beams and columns to be what they are, whether it is a question of working in concrete or working in wood or stone, or this, that or the other thing, if we do not accept our problem as a problem of the proper use of material for a certain purpose, and frankly and honestly try to express that purpose in that period, we will never be modern, and we never will have architecture.

[Mr. Price in the discussion following.] I do not know that I have very much to admit or take back. I entirely agree with Mr. Langton as to the greater immorality of honest half timber over dishonest half timber. I have done honest half timber dishonestly, as he suggests, and also have quit doing it either honestly or dishonestly. I think he received a wrong impression of what I meant to say, when he suggested that each one of us should try to go round and create a style. That is the last thing I should suggest. We do not create by trying. We put these problems to ourselves, and in some mysterious way we get the answer, correct or otherwise, which we jot down on paper, and shove out on an unsuspecting world as representative architecture, and it is representative architecture just as was the Renascence. The question is, is it representative of anything worth while? Or can we make it better by questioning whether we shall accept standards of beauty ready-made, or try to make the standards those of our own time and place? This is the point of the modernity I am trying to urge. It is not that we should be very different from those older people; if we are sincere we shall eventually and certainly produce great types of architecture, not as individuals, but in the mass; and if I have acted as Cromwell did, and knocked off a few angels' heads, you will have to forgive me on the same ground that we forgive Cromwell, because he meant well. He had no grudge against the angels' heads, but he had against the system. My own ancestors were Quakers, and they shut down on music, which is one of the most ennobling arts—shut it out of their lives for many generations, and it was not such a stupid thing that they were trying to do after all. They did it in a mistaken idea as to the use of music. Music was one of two things at that time. It was either a form in a church, which they had a protest against, or it was an adjunct to balls and revels, for which they had no use whatever. So that these very radical stands people take (even being called a Socialist does not hurt me greatly, because I am not a Socialist and do not believe in Socialism) result in some good, if the motives of people are honest. I came here and said what I did because you stood so well for what I said before, and I thought I would try this thought on somebody.

When the Blenheim Hotel was about half finished, some man met the owner and said: "Look here how in the world did you ever have the nerve to start a building like that?" and he replied: "My architect said he had to have some damned fool to try his experiment on, and I guess I am it." He asked me what style it was and said: "I do not know, unless it is Atlantic City, period of 1906." That is what it was trying to be. I think Mr. Langton is mistaken in one important point, and that is that it is ever really good architecture to change the construction and not change the design. In the Blenheim Hotel I tried to be honest to a certain extent in that very direction We had in the Exchange, concrete construction, which is absolutely expressed in the resultant forms in the ceilings, and where we had big beams there are still big beams, and where the spans were smaller they were smaller beams. The construction is honestly accepted, and it does not seem to be very shocking, either to the public, or to many of the architects who have seen it. They do not like to admit it, but they do like certain things about it: at least they tell me so. You can say what you please about it after I go. But it is a fact that in that building I really was trying to accept the problem as I found it, against the judgment of my entire office, and I had to do the work in the face of considerable opposition. I fortunately, or unfortunately, as remains to be seen, had a client that I had built for before, and as he had made a good paying concern of the other hotel, he was amenable to reason, or amenable to unreason, as the case may be, and he let me do pretty nearly what I pleased. In point of fact it is not an absolute concrete structure. The walls of the building are hollow tile curtain walls, and I think it is perfectly proper so to build. But the forms that those walls take and the projections and mouldings are all of such a type as can be cast in wooden moulds, and were actually so cast in wooden moulds, as concrete is usually built. It is it perfectly possible to develop forms in concrete that shall be pleasing, forms of openings, forms of roofs and balconies, and what not, any shape that is desired, without the use of sham cornices or any sham parts. It is possible also to develop types of moulding that do express the material. Now, concrete is cast or it is built with a shovel and a trowel, and I believe it is perfectly possible by proper designing to express the shovel and trowel work in its finished state, and to get good effects that way. I think it is also proper to encase the weatherings and exposed surfaces with materials like glazed or unglazed terra cotta in a frank and legitimate way, which does not interfere with its looking like concrete, and which adds color and variety in the building.

Mr. Langton is correct when he says we have to have something more than mere bare bones to look at. We are not satisfied with that. Our esthetic side is much more important than our physical side. We would not be architects if that was not true, because physically we live poor, but esthetically we live high. We get more satisfaction out of trying to design, and really doing some designing, than we can in pulling in the shekels in some other way; otherwise we would be getting our wealth in a less difficult way. My only point is that we should endeavor to use these materials frankly for what they are, to fit the purpose for which the building shall be erected.

As to the question of local materials, which Mr. Langton has raised, his point is entirely well taken. The difference is that our shire is not simply a little local shire; it is whatever we are in touch with, whether it is by the railroad, or steamboat, or the immediate surrounding. Our shire is extending all the way to Africa, it is extending all the way to China and Japan. We are getting the materials we can build with from any of these places, and proper material; that is all true. But there is something that is worth while in the use of rough local materials, in the cheaper form of work, like country houses, that will produce local types to meet local conditions. We would not build the same house on the top of the hill as down in the hollow. We do already tend towards these styles, whether we consciously think about it or not, and it seems to me we might go a step further, and we are going a step forward, and we do not load up our cottages now, as we did in the Queen Anne period, with "round and square stuck here and there and everywhere." We do not believe all the balustrades on our stairways in our cottages have to be copies of balustrades in an opera house in Paris, as we did a few years ago. We are beginning to see that the natural structural forms of wood work and stone work are quite adaptable to our houses at the present time.

Chronology of the Works
and Projects of William L. Price

In 1886 the city of Philadelphia began requiring building permits. This soon resulted in the publication of a daily column on building activities in *The Philadelphia Inquirer* (*PI*) and the establishment of a new publication, the *Philadelphia Real Estate Record and Builders' Guide* (*PRER&BG*). Together these sources make it possible to produce a relatively complete list of projects in the various Price offices beginning in that year. Fortunately an account book of the office of F. L. and W. L. Price and later of W. L. Price provides additional information on the years between 1893 and 1902. In the account book commissions are noted in the shorthand of names and fees, with later entries indicating the progression of the job. These entries lack the details of address and project description which were recorded elsewhere. These documents together with drawings and materials from the office acquired by the author at auction in 1969, family papers, and the working checklist of the drawings of the firm acquired from the Chrysler Museum by the Athenaeum of Philadelphia are the source for the following chronology. It is intended to provide a sense of the scope of the firm's work. Where it is known that a building was unexecuted or has been demolished, it is noted. All commissions are in Pennsylvania unless otherwise noted.

◑⊺ Frank L. Price

1878–79

Frank L. Price in office of Frank Furness; Will Price in Addison Hutton's office and then in Furness' office

1880

Frank L. Price opens own office at 731 Walnut Street, Philadelphia

1881

William L. Price listed in *Gopsill's Philadelphia City Directory for 1880* as an architect, with his brother Frank L. Price

◑⊺ Frank L. and William L. Price

1883

Frank L. Price, treasurer of T-Square Club; William L. Price, member

1) Residence for Herman Wendell (attribution), Powder Mill Lane, Frankford, Philadelphia
James Martin Price to Walter Price, 11 November 1883 (Walter F. Price Papers, Rose Valley)
2) Twenty houses for Drexel and Childs, Wayne
James Martin Price to Walter Price, 11 November 1883 (WFP Papers)
3) Courthouse project at Tacony, Philadelphia
James Martin Price to Walter Price, 11 November 1883 (WFP Papers)
54th Exhibition of the Pennsylvania Academy of the Fine Arts showed the following:
#491, "Sketch for Porte-Cochere" (whereabouts unknown)

1884

55th Exhibition of the Pennsylvania Academy of the Fine Arts showed the following:
#313, "Hard Luck" (whereabouts unknown)

1885

56th Exhibition of the Pennsylvania Academy of the Fine Arts showed the following:
#469, "Lower Falls, S.A.K. Glen" (whereabouts unknown)

1885

1) Twelve houses for Drexel and Childs, Wayne
Frank L. Price to Walter Price, 28 November 1885 (WFP Papers)

1887

1) Two pairs of residences at Lansdale (one "all brick, and the other brick to the second story, and frame")
Philadelphia Real Estate Record and Builders' Guide, 2, no. 9 (7 March 1887)
2) Pair of residences at Mount Airy, Philadelphia
PRER&BG, 2, no. 9 (7 March 1887)

3) Residence at Newtown
PRER&BG, 2, no. 9 (7 March 1887)
4) Residence for E. W. David, Chestnut Hill, Philadelphia
PRER&BG, 2, no. 15 (25 April 1887)

1888

1) Three-story house in colonial style, Wayne
PRER&BG, 3, no. 5 (6 February 1888)
2) Store for Dives, Pomeroy and Stewart, Reading
Builder and Decorator, 6, no. 1 (March, 1888)
Demolished
3) Plans for "Pillar House" for Wendell and Smith, Wayne
B&D, 7, no. 2 (October 1888)
4) Plans for "Bruin Lodge" for Wendell and Smith, Wayne
B&D, 7, no. 2 (October 1888)

1889

1) Additions to Friends' School, 4th and West streets, Wilmington, Delaware
PRER&BG, 4, no. 19 (15 May 1889)
2) Three house types "Round End," "Tower," and "Flemish" for Wendell and Smith, Wayne
B&D, 13, no. 1 (September 1889)

1890

61st Exhibition of the Pennsylvania Academy of the Fine Arts showed the following:
456, "Kenilworth Inn" (whereabouts unknown)
457, "Country House" (whereabouts unknown)
458, "Country House, Wayne, Pa." (whereabouts unknown)
459, "Frame Cottage" (whereabouts unknown)
1) Wayne Title and Trust Company, Wayne
The Philadelphia Inquirer (4 February 1890), 7
Demolished
2) Five houses for Mrs. Thomas Parker, Cranberry, North Carolina (with Edward Paxon)
Drawing in collection of author
3) Seven different house types for Wendell and Smith, Wayne
PI (17 March 1890), 8
4) Kenilworth Inn, near Asheville, North Carolina
PI (29 July 1890), 7
Destroyed by fire 1909
5) Office of Wendell and Smith, St. Davids
BD&W, 14, no. 6 (August 1890)
Demolished

1891

1) Addition to Utopian Club, 1417 Locust Street, Philadelphia
PI (17 February 1891), 7
Demolished
2) Many houses at St. Davids and Wayne ("diversified in detail in the approved style")

PRER&BG, 6, no. 17 (29 April 1891)
3) Residence for E. M. David, Germantown, Philadelphia
PI (22 May 1891), 7
4) Stone residence for John Miller at Overbrook, Philadelphia
PRER&BG, 6, no. 23 (10 June 1891)
5) Residence for Monroe Smith, 3911 Chestnut Street, Philadelphia
PI (27 June 1891), 7
Demolished

1892

62nd Exhibition of the Pennsylvania Academy of the Fine Arts showed the following:
#515, "Sketch for Railroad Station" (whereabouts unknown)
#516, "City Front" (whereabouts unknown)
#517, "House at Wayne" (whereabouts unknown)
#518, "Afternoon Paradise" (whereabouts unknown)
#519, "Greenway Lane"(whereabouts unknown)
#520, "Spring Mill" (whereabouts unknown)
#521, "Scranton Row" (whereabouts unknown)
#522, "Manheim" (whereabouts unknown)
1) Alteration to residence for Monroe Smith, 3911 Chestnut Street, Philadelphia
PRER&BG, 7, no. 3 (20 January 1892)
2) Residence for Alan Wood (Woodmont), Conshohocken
PRER&BG, 7, no. 8 (24 February 1892)
Architectural Review, 3, no. 8 (1894), plates 50–57
3) Competition for refacing Academy of Natural Sciences, Philadelphia. Other competitors Wilson Eyre, Jr., James H. Windrim, and the winners, the Wilson Brothers
PI (6 July 1892), 7
4) Residence for J. L. Twadell, Devon
PRER&BG, 7, no. 38 (21 September 1892)
5) Plans for "House F," for Wendell and Smith, Wayne
Drawings at Athenaeum of Philadelphia

1893

1) C. H. Skirmer commission
Account Book of F. L. Price and W. L. Price (7 January 1893), 1 (Collection of author)
2) Regina Jungerich commission
Account Book (21 January 1893), 19
3) Roland Park Company, Baltimore, Maryland
Account Book (3 March 1893), 20
4) J. W. Leatt commission
Account Book (7 March 1893), 21
5) W. C. Stoever commission
Account Book (13 March 1893), 21
6) W. F. Monroe commission, 330 Gowan Avenue, Mt. Airy, Philadelphia
Account Book (10 April 1893), 22

Frank L. and William L. Price (contd.)
1893
7) New Jersey church, final payment
Account Book (25 April 1893), 22
8) Mrs. J. S. Baldwin commission
Account Book (27 April 1893), 22
9) M. L. Phillips commission
Account Book (29 April 1893), 22
10) Ida Garber commission, house at Bryn Mawr
Account Book (3 June 1893), 23
11) T. L. Noble commission
Account Book (11 August 1893), 26
12) Twelve or more houses including "House
no. 10, 1893," "House no. 11, 1893," "House no.
14, 1893," "House no. 16, 1893," and a stable, for
Wendell and Smith, Overbrook, Philadelphia
Account Book
Drawings at Athenaeum of Philadelphia

William L. Price
William L. Price successor to Frank L. Price
and William L. Price, 12 August 1893
13) Residence for Alfred Wayne, Oak Lane,
Philadelphia
Account Book (5 September 1893), 28
14) Miss Jordan commission
Account Book (25 September 1893), 29
15) Ida Alpaugh
Account Book (26 November 1893), 30
16) M. B. Sayre commission, Baltimore, Maryland
Account Book (22 November 1893), 30

1894
64th Exhibition of the Pennsylvania Academy of
the Fine Arts showed the following:
#57, "Summer Sketch" (whereabouts unknown)
1) J. W. Patterson commission, Gladwynne
Account Book (17 January 1894), 33
2) Residence for Charles Scott, for Wendell and
Smith, Overbrook, Philadelphia
PRER& BG, 9, no. 17 (25 April 1894)
3) Two "handsome dwellings," for Wendell and
Smith, Overbrook, Philadelphia
PI (18 April 1894), 6
4) Sherwood Road Row and residence for W. L.
Price at 6334 Sherwood Road, for Wendell and
Smith, Overbrook, Philadelphia
Account Book (17 April 1894), 36
Charles Edward Hooper, *The Country House*
(New York: Doubleday, Page, 1903), 149
Drawings for "Houses 95, 96, 97, Sherwood
Road," Athenaeum of Philadelphia
5) Five houses for Wendell and Smith,
Overbrook, Philadelphia.
PI (9 June 1894), 5
6) Residence for Charles Hires, Devon
American Architect and Building News, 55, no. 970
(July 1894)
Unexecuted

7) Plans for four-story rear addition to 925
Walnut Street, Philadelphia
PI (26 July 1894), 6
8) E. H. Bouton commission, Baltimore,
Maryland
Account Book (13 August 1894), 41
9) Charles Scott Spring Company
Account Book (13 September 1894), 42
10) House for Wendell and Smith,
Germantown, Philadelphia (with Chester Kirk)
AABN, 55, no. 970 (28 July 1894), 36
11) Four houses for Wendell and Smith,
Overbrook Avenue south of Lancaster Avenue,
Overbrook, Philadelphia
PI (18 September 1894), 6
12) Residence for Mrs. F. D. Sweeney, 6346
Sherwood Road, Overbrook, Philadelphia
Wendell and Smith Papers, Radnor Historical
Society
Account Book (21 June 1894), 39
Drawings at Athenaeum of Philadelphia
13) "House for Wendell and Smith, 1894,"
"Houses no. 1 & no. 2, 1894," "Houses no. 6 &
no. 7, 1894," "Houses no. 11 & no. 12, 1894,"
"House no. 30, 1894," "Houses no. 81 & no. 82,
1894," "Houses no. 84 & no. 85, 1894," "House
no. 86, 1894," "House no. 88, 1894," "Houses no.
89 & no. 90, 1894," "Houses no. 91 & no. 92,
1894," "House no. 94, 1894," "Houses no. 95, 96,
97, Sherwood Road, 1894," and "House no. 98,
Sherwood Road, 1894"
Drawings in Eleanor Price Mather Collection,
Athenaeum of Philadelphia
14) Residence for Captain R. D. Pike (Pillar
House), Bayfield, Wisconsin
(brownstone house, enlarged Wayne Tract
design)
Susan McCue, part 1 certification form on file
with Wisconsin State Historic Preservation
Office, 1985

1895
1) W. L. Emley commission, 1529 Girard
Avenue, Philadelphia (?)
Account Book (17 January 1895), 46
2) Dr. B. Okie commission
Account Book (2 February 1895), 47
3) Three-story stone residence for Henry Petit
and George W. Bacon (The Beeches),
Overbrook, Philadelphia
PI (6 March 1895), 5
Drawings at Athenaeum of Philadelphia
4) Alterations to residence of Andrew G. Wood,
1425 Poplar Street, Philadelphia
PI (17 May 1895), 9
The Ladies' Home Journal designs begin June
1895 and continue through April 1898
Account Book (1 June 1895), 54
Drawings for several, including Houses 1, 5,

and 6, are in the Chrysler Collection,
Athenaeum of Philadelphia
5) Dreher commission
Account Book (23 July 1895), 55
6) Wayne Library Company
Account Book (9 August 1895), 56
Demolished
7) Alfred Sidney commission
Account Book (11 September 1895), 57
8) Five-story frame addition to Hotel Luray for
Josiah White, Atlantic City, New Jersey
PI (18 October 1895), 8
Destroyed by fire 1901
9) Miss Baldwin commission
Account Book (31 October 1895), 58
10) Marshall of West Chester commission
Account Book (30 November 1895), 59
11) Graham commission
Account Book (11 December 1895), 59
12) Drawings for Pennlyn Improvement
Company, Wynnewood
PRER&BG, 10, no. 50 (11 December 1895)
13) Residence at Brighton and Pacific avenues,
Atlantic City, New Jersey
PRER&BG, 10, no. 50 (11 December 1895)
14) Charles H. Dickey commission
Account Book (17 December 1895), 59
15) Mrs. Howard Wood commission, Woodlane
Station, Conshohocken (?)
Account Book (24 December 1895), 59
16) Lutheran Parsonage at Ardmore
Wendell and Smith Papers, Radnor Historical
Society
17) "House no. 95," "House no. 95C," and "Store
Buildings on Germantown Avenue," for Wen-
dell and Smith, Pelham, Mt. Airy, Philadelphia
Drawings at Athenaeum of Philadelphia

1896
1) Dining hall for Haverford College, Haverford
PI (10 January 1896), 8
2) Alterations to residence of John S. Clarke
house, Yarrow Street, Bryn Mawr
Account Book (11 March 1896), 62
3) Captain P. A. Nicholson commission,
4 Cresheim Road, for Wendell and Smith,
Pelham, Mt. Airy, Philadelphia
Account Book (17 March 1896), 63
Co-organizer of the annual exhibition of the
T-Square Club. *PRER&BG*, 11, no.13
(25 March 1896)
4) Lodge building at Stafford [sic]
PRER&BG, 11, no. 17 (22 April 1896)
5) Henry D. Cooper commission
Account Book (26 June 1896), 66
6) Residence for W. S. Schellinger, Wyncote
Account Book (1 July 1896), 67
7) William H. Cope commission
Account Book (24 July 1896), 67

William L. Price (contd.)

1896

8) "A large amusement park is to be erected in this city by a stock company which has engaged Mr. Price, and he is presently obtaining a few pointers from European architects."
PRER&BG, 11, no. 31 (27 July 1896)

9) Swarthmore United Presbyterian Church
Account Book (7 August 1896), 67
Demolished

10) Three-story residence, Roland Park, Maryland
PRER&BG, 11, no. 39 (23 September 1896)

11) Three houses of three stories each for E. Bouton, Roland Park, Maryland
PRER&BG, 11, no. 40 (30 September 1896)

12) Wharton Square Presbyterian Church, Wharton Street, Philadelphia (one-story, brick with stone)
PI (21 November 1896), 15

13) Addition to residence of Mrs. C. D. English, Bryn Mawr (three-story, stone and frame)
PRER&BG, 11, no. 48 (23 November 1896)

14) Colonel A. L. Wetherill commission
Account Book (24 December 1896), 72

15) Three houses for Joseph Stein, Eden Terrace, Maryland ("to cost $6000 each")
PRER&BGI, 11, no. 53 (30 December 1896)

1897

1) House for Joseph Stein, Baltimore, Maryland
PI (1 January 1897), 9

2) Charles Reed commission
Account Book (8 January 1897), 73

3) Victor G. Bloede, Eden Terrace, Baltimore, Maryland
Account Book (11 January 1897), 73

4) Eighty-room brick-and-frame hotel for Mrs. M. S. Lightfoot, Asbury Park, New Jersey
PRER&BG, 12, no. 13 (31 March 1897)
Demolished

5) Bryant house for developer Milton Young
Account Book (8 February 1897), 74

6) Stone-and-frame residence for E. L. Farr, Wenonah, New Jersey
PRER&BG, 12, no. 14 (7 April 1897)
Architectural Review, 5, no. 7 (1898), plates 50–54

7) Office building in Baltimore or Washington (six stories, with basement and sub-basement)
PRER&BG, 12, no. 14 (7 April 1897)
Unexecuted?

8) Stone-and-frame residence for Mrs. William Walter, Wallingford
PRER&BG, 12, no. 17 (28 April 1897)

9) Additions to school house for Society of Friends, 5418 Germantown Avenue (two stories, stone and pebble dash)
PRER&BG, 12, no. 25 (23 June 1897)

10) Residence for W. O. Freytagg, 334 North 3rd Street, Philadelphia (brick and terra-cotta)
PRER&BG, 12, no. 27 (2 July 1897)

11) Four-story addition to Charles Scott Spring Company, Germantown Avenue and Newmarket Street, Philadelphia
PI (5 August 1897), 10

12) Residence for John C. Winston, 5208 Wayne Avenue, Germantown, Philadelphia
PI (13 August 1897), 10
Drawings at Athenaeum of Philadelphia

13) Pair of houses in suburbs (brick and stone)
PRER&BG, 12, no. 34 (25 August 1897)

14) Two-hundred room enlargement to Hotel Luray, Atlantic City, New Jersey (four stories with slate roof) (with Frank Price)
PI (27 August 1897), 10
Demolished by fire 1902

15) Residence and stable for William B. Gest, Merion
PI (27 August 1897), 10

16) Residence for Hermann Hessenbruch, Merion
PRER&BG, 12, no. 38 (22 September 1897)
"Sketch of Hall Mantel," drawings at Athenaeum of Philadelphia

17) Dr. A. R. Cooke commission
Account Book (24 September 1897), 81

18) Estimates for several houses in Overbrook, Philadelphia
PI (5 November 1897), 11

19) Alterations and additions for Church of St. Paul, Chester
T-Square Club Annual, Philadelphia, 1897–98
Drawings at Athenaeum of Philadelphia

20) Residence for John M. Gest, Overbrook, Philadelphia
Account Book (2 December 1897), 84
Inland Architect, 41, no. 5 (February 1903)

21) Residence for E. W. Bok, Lower Merion
Account Book (31 December 1897), 86
Inland Architect, 42, no. 2 (November 1903)

1898

1) David Scull, Cherry Cottage, Overbrook, Philadelphia
Account Book (18 January 1897), 87
Expert Testimony for State of Pennsylvania
Account Book (17 February 1898), 89

2) Charles Crosman on account
Account Book (17 February 1898), 88

3) J. E. Carter commission
Account Book (30 March 1898), 90

4) Gardener's cottage for Hermann Hessenbruch, Merion
PRER&BG, 13, no. 16 (20 April 1898)

5) Residence for Allan Reed, Devon
PRER&BG, 13, no. 20 (18 May 1898)
Inland Architect, 41, no. 1 (February 1903)

6) Residence for Samuel Croft, Merion
Account Book (3 August, 1898), 96
T-Square Club Exhibition 1899–1900 (Philadelphia, 1900), 165
Drawings at Athenaeum of Philadelphia
Demolished

7) Young Friends' Association building at 15th and Cherry streets, Philadelphia
PI (10 August 1898), 12
Demolished

8) Residence for Jesse Nalle, Bryn Mawr
PI (12 August 1898), 10
Architectural Review, 4 (1903), 178
Demolished

9) Mary Buzby commission
Account Book (3 October 1898), 98

10) Sketches for Fernwood Hotel for F. L. Riggs
Account Book (2 November 1898), 99
Unexecuted?

11) Competition for First Baptist Church, 17th and Sansom streets, Philadelphia
Other competitors Addison Hutton, D. K. Boyd, David S. Gendell, Rankin and Kellogg, and the winner, Edgar V. Seeler
PI (13 December 1898), 12

12) Alterations for Daniel S. White to Traymore Hotel, Atlantic City, New Jersey
Account Book (5 December 1898), 100
Demolished

13) Residence for Walter B. Smith, Ardmore
Drawings at Athenaeum of Philadelphia

14) House for Milton W. Young, Overbrook, Philadelphia
Drawings at Athenaeum of Philadelphia

1899

1) Stable for Allan Reed, Devon
PRER&BG, 14, no. 1 (4 January 1899)

2) Mrs. J. H. Wright commission
Account Book (10 February 1899), 104

3) Winner of competition for residence for John Gilmore, City Line Avenue, Merion
PRER&BG, 14, no. 7 (15 February 1899)
Inland Architect, 41, no. 1 (February 1903)
Demolished
Lecture at Cornell University
Account Book (17 March 1899), 106

4) Two-story stone stable for W. B. Saunders, Overbrook, Philadelphia
PI (10 April 1899), 13
Architectural Review, 4 (1903), 178

5) House for Wendell and Smith, south side of Drexel Road west of 60th Street, Overbrook, Philadelphia
PI (18 April 1899), 11

6) N. J. Clark, for Boys' Club, Chatauqua
Account Book (8 May 1899), 109

7) Residence for William Cox, Hillside
PRER&BG, 14, no. 20 (17 May 1899)

William L. Price (contd.)
1899

8) Residence for Martin Hawley McLanahan, St. Davids
PI (17 May 1899), 15
9) Joseph E. Rhoads commission
Account Book (20 May 1899), 110
10) M. C. Fenton commission
Account Book (14 June 1899), 111
11) Residence for Wendell and Smith, Drexel Road south of Lancaster Avenue, Overbrook, Philadelphia
PI (14 September 1899), 9
12) Henry M. Tracy commission
Account Book (26 September 1899), 116
13) Additions and alterations for Daniel S. White to Traymore Hotel, Atlantic City, New Jersey
PI (28 September 1899), 9
Demolished
14) F. H. Mahan commission
Account Book (2 October 1899), 116
15) Charles E. Hires commission
Account Book (7 October 1899), 117
16) Addition to residence of W. B. Saunders, 925 Walnut Street, Philadelphia
PI (28 December 1899), 9
17) Residence for C. W. Borton, Moorestown, New Jersey
T-Square Club Exhibition 1899–1900 (Philadelphia, 1900), 209
18) Residence for Frank Cooper, address unknown
Inland Architect, 42, no. 5 (November 1903)
19) House for Milton W. Young, Overbrook, Philadelphia
Drawings at Athenaeum of Philadelphia

1900

1) Alterations and additions to residence for Ferdinand Keller, 1517 Girard Avenue, Philadelphia
PI (30 January 1900), 13
2) House for Wendell and Smith, Pelham, Mt. Airy, Philadelphia
PI (17 February 1900), 14
3) Additions and alterations to residence of George Higley, Conshohocken
PRER&BG, 15, no. 10 (7 March 1900)
4) Residence for George Evans, north side of Cresheim Road southeast of Carpenter Street, Pelham, Mt. Airy, Philadelphia
PI (20 March 1900), 9
5) Improvements to residence of David Scull, City Line Avenue, Overbrook, Philadelphia
PI (20 March 1900), 9
6) Residence for William Bradley, Camden, New Jersey
PRER&BG, 15, no. 26 (27 June 1900)

7) Residence and automobile stable for Helen Pierson, Bryn Mawr
PI (4 July 1900), 12
8) Stable for Martin Hawley McLanahan, St. Davids
PI (4 July 1900), 12
9) Tower Methodist Church, Margaretta and Tackawanna streets, Philadelphia
PRER&BG, 15, no. 29 (18 July 1900)
10) Additions and alterations to residence of W. B. Saunders, Overbrook, Philadelphia
PI (25 July 1900), 5
11) Alterations and additions to shop of Lewis King, 929 Pine Street, Philadelphia
PI (28 July 1900), 7
12) "Immense stone and brick hotel for the Messrs. White," Atlantic City, New Jersey
PRER&BG, 15, no. 35 (29 August 1900)
Demolished
13) Residence for John Gill, Haddonfield, New Jersey
PRER&BG, 15, no. 40 (3 October 1900)
14) Residence for Charles Scott, City Line Avenue, Overbrook, Philadelphia
PI (12 November 1900), 6

1901

1) Additions to residence of Ferdinand Keller, 1517 Girard Avenue, Philadelphia
Account Book (20 February 1901), 144
2) J. B. English commission
Account book (2 February 1901), 143
3) Residence in colonial style for Henry P. Glendenning, near Media
PI (3 February 1901), 7
4) Houses for C. E. Frick, Tioga Street, Philadelphia
Account Book (20 February 1901), 144
Drawings at Athenaeum of Philadelphia
5) Additions to residence of John S. Clarke, Yarrow Street, Bryn Mawr
Account book (19 April 1901), 147
6) Interior alterations to residence of William Elliott, 317 South 17th Street, Philadelphia
PI (27 May 1901), 9
7) Interior alterations to showroom of Haines, Jones and Cadbury, 1136–40 Ridge Avenue, Philadelphia
PI (27 May 1901), 9
8) Addition of billiard room and laundry to residence of Robert Hoyle, Overbrook, Philadelphia
PRER&BG, 16, no. 22 (29 May 1901)
9 Residence for Louis J. Clarke, Palm Beach, Florida
Account Book (1 June 1901), 150
10) Residence for J. W. Patterson, Devon
PRER&BG, 16, no. 28 (10 July 1901)
11) Residence in "old French style" for Louis J. Clarke, Old Gulph Road, Merion

PI (9 September 1901), 16
12) Winner of competition for Overbrook Presbyterian Church, Overbrook, Philadelphia
PI (16 October 1901), 11
13) Residence for C. C. Price, Tyrol (three story, stone and plaster)
PI (16 October 1901), 12
14) Project for Charles Schoen
Account Book (30 October 1901), 158
15) House for Milton W. Young, Overbrook, Philadelphia
Drawings at Athenaeum of Philadelphia

1902

1) Plans for ten-story apartment house at Broad and Jefferson streets, Philadelphia
PI (4 January 1902), 6
Unexecuted
2) Residence and carriage house for C. M. Dahlstrom, Ardmore
Account Book (10 February 1902), 163
Drawings at Athenaeum of Philadelphia
3) Plans for Josiah White for new Luray Hotel, Atlantic City, New Jersey (to replace building destroyed by fire)
PI (5 April 1902), 7
Unexecuted
4) George Graham residence, Bryn Mawr
PI (5 April 1902), 7
Scientific Building Monthly, 38, no. 3 (September 1904)
5) Two-story stone stable for John C. Winston, Germantown, Philadelphia
PI (11 April 1902), 7
6) Providence Baptist Church, 37th and Filbert streets, Philadelphia
PI (7 May 1902), 7
7) Residence for C. S. Warfield, 52nd Street and Wynnefield Avenue, Philadelphia
PRER&BG, 17, no. 26 (25 June 1902)
8) Residence for John G. Winston, Hansberry Street and Germantown Avenue, Germantown, Philadelphia
PI (26 June 1902), 15
9) Additions and alterations to residence of W. S. Schellinger, Wyncote
PI (1 July 1902), 9
10) Residence for F. M. Bordon, Carpenter and Cresheim streets, Germantown, Philadelphia
PI (3 July 1902), 14
11) Addition to residence of Richard Tilghman, St. Davids
PI (31 July 1902), 14
12) Alteration to residence of Mrs. S. L. Parrish, 313 South 10th Street, Philadelphia
PI (9 August 1902), 14
13) Alterations to store at southeast corner, Thirteenth and Pine streets, Philadelphia
PI (3 September 1902), 11

William L. Price (contd.)

1902

14) Residence for Mrs. C. W. Borton, Haddonfield, New Jersey

PRER&BG, 17, no. 40 (1 October 1902)

Drawings at Athenaeum of Philadelphia.

15) Alterations to residence of Miss A. E. Wilcox, Simsbury, Connecticut

Drawings at Athenaeum of Philadelphia

Price and McLanahan

1903

"The architectural business heretofore conducted by William L. Price at 731 Walnut Street is now conducted by Mr. Price and M. Hawley McLanahan under the firm name of Price and McLanahan."

PI (9 January 1903), 12

1) Stable for J. H. Ristine, Ardmore (large size with quadrangle in center)

PI (6 February 1903), 10

2) Hollidaysburg National Bank, Hollidaysburg

PI (5 March 1903), 6

3) Old English style residence for Mrs. Lawrence Bodine, Berwyn

PI (19 March 1903), 5

4) Competition for Bucks County Historical Society building, Doylestown

Competition won by Horace Trumbauer

PI (21 April 1903), 4

5) Additions and alterations to property of Colonel William G. Price, 808–810 Sansom Street, Philadelphia

PI (4 May 1903), 5

Demolished

6) Alterations to residence of Mrs. Edward Martin, 1506 Locust Street, Philadelphia

PI (11 May 1903), 16

Demolished

7) Alterations to residence of Dr. Thomas Morton, School House Lane, Germantown, Philadelphia

PI (15 May 1903), 9

8) Interior alterations to Penn National Bank, 7th and Market streets, Philadelphia (including balcony)

PI (25 July 1903), 5

Demolished

9) Residence for William C. Scott, Ardmore

PI (25 November 1903), 7

10) Jacob Reed's Sons' Store, 1426 Chestnut Street, Philadelphia

PI (1 December 1903), 9

AABN, 97, no. 1,532 (1905), 146

Drawings in Chrysler Collection, Athenaeum of Philadelphia

1904

1) Clubhouse for Spring Haven Country Club, Wallingford

PI (26 January 1904), 14

Catalogue of the Eleventh Annual Exhibition, 1904–5 (Philadelphia: T-Square Club, 1905), #266

Demolished

2) Sunday school addition and pastor's study, Overbrook Presbyterian Church, Overbrook, Philadelphia

PI (3 February 1904), 9

3) Residence for Frank Gould, Roland Park, Maryland

Price and McLanahan Archives

4) Residence for Walter Dewey, Glenside

Working drawings in Price and McLanahan Archives

PRER&BG, 19, no. 28 (13 July 1904)

Unexecuted

5) Unidentified residence, Chestnut Hill, Philadelphia

PI (29 August 1904), 12

6) Residence for Fred Gruger, Avon-by-the-Sea, New Jersey

PRER&BG, 19, no. 44 (2 November 1904)

7) Alterations and additions to residence of S. K. Mulford, Wyncote

PI (28 November 1904), 6

8) Unsuccessful competition for National Mechanics Bank, Baltimore, Maryland (with Owens and Sisco)

Price and McLanahan Archives

9) Bench for University of Pennsylvania campus (H. D. Wood, designer)

Ink on linen drawing in Philadelphia Museum of Art

1905

1) Residence for Frank Van Camp, Indianapolis, Indiana

PRER&BG, 20, no. 6 (8 February 1905)

Demolished

2) Passenger and freight station for Pennsylvania Railroad, Allegheny

The Brickbuilder, 16, no. 10 (1907), 145–148

Demolished

3) Residence for Thomas Jackson, Indianapolis, Indiana

Price and McLanahan Archives

4) Residence for James Turner, 5220 Ellsworth Avenue, Pittsburgh

PI (10 April 1905), 6

5) Residence for James Crosley Brown, 63rd and Jefferson streets, Philadelphia

PI (11 April 1905), 6

6) Blenheim Hotel, addition to Marlborough Hotel, Atlantic City, New Jersey

PI (11 April 1905), 12

Demolished

7) Residence for O. W. Hewitt, Hollidaysburg

Price and McLanahan Archives

8) Extensive alterations to Colonial Trust Company, 13th and Market streets, Philadelphia

PI (8 June 1905), 11

Demolished

9) Competition for extension of Union League clubhouse, 140 South Broad Street, Philadelphia

Competition won by Horace Trumbauer

PRER&BG, 20, no. 30 (26 July 1905)

10) Store for Jules Junker, 1630 Chestnut Street, Philadelphia

PI (10 August 1905), 12

Demolished

11) Passenger station for Waynesboro and Washington Railroad, Washington

PI (16 November 1905), 12

Drawings in Chrysler Collection, Athenaeum of Philadelphia

12) Passenger station, Brownsville, Ohio

Price and McLanahan Archives

1906

1) Alterations to residence of Colonel William G. Price, 806–808 Sansom Street, Philadelphia

PI (5 January 1906), 6

Demolished

2) Two-story addition to residence of Louis Clarke, Haverford

PI (9 April 1906), 4

3) Residence for Colonel John Legg, Roland Park, Maryland

Price and McLanahan Archives

4) Concourse and shelter for subsidiary of Pennsylvania Railroad, Federal and Stockton streets, Chicago, Illinois

PI (9 May 1906), 9

5) Additions for Daniel S. White to Traymore Hotel, Atlantic City, New Jersey

PI (16 August 1906), 6

Engineering News Record, 54, no. 19 (10 November 1906)

Demolished

6) Alterations to Warwick Apartments, 19th and Sansom streets, Philadelphia

Drawings in Chrysler Collection, Athenaeum of Philadelphia

1907

1) Three-story stone residence for H. L. Keiper, Lancaster

PRER&BG, 22, no. 3 (16 January 1907)

2) Residence for Chalkley Palmer, near Media

PI (16 January 1907), 9

3) National Guard Armory, Chester

PI (21 May 1907), 4

4) Plans for Chicago Terminal for Pennsylvania Railroad, Chicago, Illinois

Price and McLanahan Archives

Price and McLanahan (contd.)

1907

5) Residence for J. Howard Pugh [sic, Pew],
Ardmore
PI (16 April 1907), 6
6) Residence for William Halkett, Ridley Park
"Entry #433," *Yearbook and Catalogue of the T-
Square Club* (Philadelphia: T-Square Club, 1909)
Drawings in Chrysler Collection, Athenaeum of
Philadelphia
7) Competition for railroad station, Scranton
Competition won by Kenneth Murcheson
Carroll L. V. Meeks, *The Railroad Station* (New
Haven, Conn.: Yale University Press, 1956)

1908

1) National Guard Armory, Media
PRER&BG 23, no. 3 (15 January 1908)
2) Stone-and-frame residence for J. C. Stillwill,
Stroudsburg
PRER&BG, 23, no. 13 (25 March 1908)
Drawings in Chrysler Collection, Athenaeum of
Philadelphia
3) Competition for master plan for Western
University of Pennsylvania
Competition won by Palmer and Hornbostel
PRER&BG, 23, no. 18 (29 April 1908)
4) Alterations to Colonial Trust Company
Building, 13th and Market streets, Philadelphia
PRER&BG, 23, no. 27 (1 July 1908)
Demolished
5) Additions and alterations to residence of
Charles Marlatt, Washington, D. C.
Price and McLanahan Archives
Drawings in Chrysler Collection, Athenaeum of
Philadelphia
6) Christian Union Congregational Church,
Upper Montclair, New Jersey
Price and McLanahan Archives
7) Residence for Caroline Parke, Wynnefield and
Lancaster avenues, Philadelphia.
PRER&BG, 23, no. 44 (28 October 1908)
8) Residence for Mr. Pilling, Windermere
Avenue, Lansdowne
American House and Garden, 6 (1908), 113
9) Garage and conservatory for William
Halkett, Ridley Park
Drawings in Chrysler Collection, Athenaeum of
Philadelphia

1909

1) Alterations to National Guard Armory, Media
PI (26 February 1909), 9
2) Overhanover project, Kirkland, North
Carolina
Yearbook of the T-Square Club for 1912
(Philadelphia: T-Square Club, 1912)
Price and McLanahan Archives
Unexecuted

3) One-and-one-half-story stone bungalow for
Henry Young, Kirklyn
PI (18 August 1909), 9
4) Alterations to residence of William Sproul
(Lapidea Manor), Chester
Price and McLanahan Archives
5) Design for base of Gutzon Borglum's statue
for Lincoln Memorial, Newark, New Jersey
Drawings in Chrysler Collection, Athenaeum of
Philadelphia

1910

William L. Price dropped from T-Square Club
for nonpayment of dues, 5 January 1910
1) Five-story concrete-and-stone hotel for
Dr. E. L. Potter, Hotel Clarendon, Sea Breeze,
Daytona, Florida
PRER&BG, 25, no. 2 (12 January 1910)
Demolished
2) Palmetto House Hotel, Daytona, Florida
Price and McLanahan Archives
Unexecuted
3) Stone bungalow for Harry Young, Kirklyn
PRER&BG, 25, no. 4 (26 January 1910)
4) Designs for hotel, Newport, Rhode Island
Price and McLanahan Archives
5) House, near Wallingford
AABN, 97, no. 1791 (20 April 1910)
6) Alterations to residence of Charles Pilling,
Lansdowne
PRER&BG, 25, no. 17 (27 April 1910)
7) Cow barn for William C. Sproul, Chester
PRER&BG, 25, no. 23 (8 June 1910)
8) Office for *The Morning Republican*, Chester
PRER&BG, 25, no. 23 (8 June 1910)
9) Studio for Gutzon Borglum, Stamford,
Connecticut
Price and McLanahan Archives
Drawings in Chrysler Collection, Athenaeum of
Philadelphia
10) Stable at studio of Gutzon Borglum,
Stamford, Connecticut
Drawings in Chrysler Collection, Athenaeum of
Philadelphia
11) Passenger station for Pennsylvania
Railroad, Converse, Indiana
PRER&BG, 25, no. 34 (24 August 1910)
12) Passenger station for Pennsylvania
Railroad, Fort Wayne, Indiana
PRER&BG, 25, no. 34 (24 August 1910)
13) Passenger station for Pennsylvania
Railroad, Steubenville, Ohio
PRER&BG 25, no. 34 (24 August 1910)
Drawings in Chrysler Collection, Athenaeum of
Philadelphia
Demolished
14) Residence for G. G. Greene, Jr., Woodbury,
New Jersey
PRER&BG, 25, no. 34 (24 August 1910)

15) Design of residence for Reverend E. M.
Ferguson, Swarthmore (prepared by J. F. Street
of Price and McLanahan)
PRER&BG, 25, no. 39 (28 September 1910)
16) Meeting House for Society of Friends,
Swarthmore College, Swarthmore
PRER&BG, 25, no. 42 (19 October 1910)
17) Residence for Frank Van Camp, Jr.,
Indianapolis, Indiana
PRER&BG, 25, no. 44 (2 November 1910)
Unexecuted
18) Residence for C. W. Fairbanks, Indianapolis,
Indiana
PRER&BG, 25, no. 46 (16 November 1910)
19) Hospital addition, Chester
PRER&BG, 25, no. 49 (7 December 1910)
Demolished
20) Alterations to Potter residence, Swarthmore
Price and McLanahan Archives
21) Competition for passenger station for
Pennsylvania Railroad, Wilkinsburg
Records of Consulting Practice of Warren P.
Laird; unpublished materials in Fine Arts
Library, University of Pennsylvania (vol. 66)

1911

1) Passenger station for Pennsylvania Railroad,
Hartford City, Indiana
PRER&BG 26, no. 6 (8 February 1911)
2) Passenger station for Pennsylvania Railroad,
Ridgeville, Indiana
American Architect, 100, no. 1867 (4 October
1911)
3) Passenger station for Pennsylvania Railroad,
Dunkirk, Indiana
American Architect, 100, no. 1867 (4 October
1911)
4) Passenger station for Pennsylvania Railroad,
Trimmer, Indiana
Drawings in Chrysler Collection, Athenaeum of
Philadelphia
5) Passenger station for Pennsylvania Railroad,
Ava, Ohio
Drawings in Chrysler Collection, Athenaeum of
Philadelphia
6) Shelter for Pennsylvania Railroad,
Logansport
Drawings in Chrysler Collection, Athenaeum of
Philadelphia
7) Milepost for Pennsylvania Railroad,
Indianapolis, Indiana
Drawings in Chrysler Collection, Athenaeum of
Philadelphia
8) Manse of Third Presbyterian Church,
Chester
PRER&BG, 26, no. 14 (5 April 1911)
9) Alterations and additions to residence of
Josiah White, Cardington
PRER&BG, 26, no. 19 (10 May 1911)

Price and McLanahan (contd.)

1911

10) Residence, stables, lagoon, gondolas, and landscaping for Frank Wheeler estate, Indianapolis, Indiana
PRER&BG, 26, no. 23 (7 June 1911)

11) Tenant house for William C. Sproul estate, Chester
PRER&BG, 26, no. 23 (7 June 1911)

12) One-and-one-half-story building for Hollidaysburg Academy, Hollidaysburg
PRER&BG, 26, no. 25 (21 June 1911)

13) Wheeler Heights Apartments, Indianapolis, Indiana
PRER&BG, 26, no.25 (21 June 1911)
Unexecuted

14) Red Man Hotel for Frank Wheeler, Indianapolis, Indiana
Price and McLanahan Archives
Unexecuted

15) Residence for Horace Forman, Haverford
PRER&BG, 26, no. 29 (19 July 1911)

16) Details of residence for H. L. Bass, Indianapolis, Indiana
Price and McLanahan Archives

17) Residence for H. Edgar Barnes, Swarthmore
PRER&BG, 26, no. 29 (19 July 1911)

18) Bungalow for E. A. Harvey, Brandywine, Summit
PRER&BG, 26, no. 30 (26 July 1911)

19) Office and residence for Fiske Warren, Harvard, Massachusetts
PRER&BG, 26, no. 35 (30 August 1911)
American Architect, 105, no. 2000 (22 April 1914)

20) Passenger station, South Chicago, Illinois
PRER&BG, 26, no. 36 (6 September 1911)

21) Residence for F. Wallis Armstrong, Moorestown, New Jersey
PRER&BG, 26, no. 37 (13 September 1911)

22) Addition to Dunes Hotel, Spring Lake, New Jersey
PRER&BG 26, no. 40 (4 October 1911)

23) Residence and grounds for J. L. Woolston, 164 West Chelten Avenue, Philadelphia
PRER&BG, 26, no. 43 (25 October 1911)

24) Residence for James Clarke, Media
Price and McLanahan Archives

25) Residence for E. A. Howell, address unknown
Price and McLanahan Archives

26) Residence for J. Street Fletcher, Indianapolis, Indiana
Price and McLanahan Archives
Unexecuted

27) Alterations and additions to Mott–Parrish residence and fountain for grounds, Radnor
Price and McLanahan Archives

28) Rochester Yacht Club, Rochester, New York
Price and McLanahan Archives

29) Essex and Sussex Hotel, Spring Lake, New Jersey
Price and McLanahan Archives
Unexecuted

30) Alterations to residence of Edward L. Farr, Wenonah, New Jersey
Price and McLanahan Archives

1912

1) Addition to Traymore Hotel, Atlantic City, New Jersey (construction delayed until 1914)
PRER&BG, 27, no. 6 (7 February 1912)
Demolished

2) Clubhouse for Riverton Yacht Club, Riverton, New Jersey
PRER&BG, 27, no.10 (6 March 1912)

3) Absecon Pier Company for 2500-foot-long pier of "oriental design," Atlantic City, New Jersey
PRER&BG, 27, no. 19 (8 May 1912)
Unexecuted

4) Residence for W. H. Hall, Atlantic City, New Jersey
PRER&BG, 27, no. 20 (15 May 1912)

5) Alterations and additions to Sixth Regiment Armory, Media
PRER&BG, 27, no. 26 (26 June 1912)

6) Additions to Overbrook Presbyterian Church, Overbrook, Philadelphia
Price and McLanahan Archives

7) Solarium and alterations to residence of Joseph Allinson, Indianapolis, Indiana
Price and McLanahan Archives

8) Market Street Ferry Terminal, Philadelphia
Price and McLanahan Archives
Unexecuted

9) Ridley Park Church, Ridley Park
Price and McLanahan Archives
Unexecuted

10) Alterations to residence of Thomas Baldridge, Hollidaysburg
Price and McLanahan Archives

11) Passenger station for Pennsylvania Railroad, Canton, Ohio
Price and McLanahan Archives
Unexecuted

12) Track elevation tower, Park Manor, Chicago, Illinois
Price and McLanahan Archives

13) Bridge for P. C. C. & St. L. Railway, Chicago, Illinois
Price and McLanahan Archives

14) Proposed hotel for E. W. Grove Park, Asheville, North Carolina
Yearbook of the T-Square Club for 1912 (Philadelphia: T-Square Club, 1912)
Unexecuted

15) Hotel project, Aumond, Georgia
Price and McLanahan Archives
Unexecuted

16) Presbyterian Cemetery Gate, Hollidaysburg
A. Margaretta Archambault, *A Guide Book of Art, Architecture and Historic Interests in Pennsylvania* (Philadelphia, 1924), 475

17) Designs for grandstand for Philadelphia Historical Pageant (October 7–10)
Ellis Paxon Oberholtzer, *Philadelphia Historical Pageant, Official Program* (Philadelphia, 1912), 22

1913

1) Clubhouse for Delphic Literary Society, Swarthmore
PRER&BG, 28, no. 2 (8 January 1913)

2) Residence for Beulah H. J. Woolston, Chestnut Hill, Philadelphia
PRER&BG, 28, no. 5 (29 January 1913)

3) House for the Reverend William Prall, Princeton, New Jersey
PRER&BG, 28, no. 18 (30 April 1913)

4) Residence for Philip Price, Johnstown
Price and McLanahan Archives

5) Alterations and additions to Jacob Reed's Sons' Store, 1424 Chestnut Street, Philadelphia
PRER&BG, 28, no. 20 (14 May 1913)

6) Designs for San Cristobal Hotel, Puerto Rico
Price and McLanahan Archives
Unexecuted

7) Stable for the Reverend William Prall, Princeton, New Jersey
PRER&BG, 28, no. 47 (19 November 1913)

8) Designs for stable for J. Horace McFarland, Harrisburg
Price and McLanahan Archives
Unexecuted?

1914

1) Residence for Dr. E. O. Janney, Media (of hollow tile construction)
PRER&BG, 29, no. 5 (4 February 1914)
Drawings in Chrysler Collection, Athenaeum of Philadelphia

2) Dairy buildings for William Gable, Altoona
PRER&BG, 29, no. 17 (29 April 1914)

3) Residence for Mr. Barney, Media
Interview with Eleanor Price Mather (1972)

4) Alterations and additions to residence of James Crosley Brown, Ardmore (former residence of William Scott)
PRER&BG, 29, no. 17 (29 April 1914)

5) Sixteen-story addition to Traymore Hotel, Atlantic City, New Jersey
PRER&BG, 29, no. 20 (20 May 1914)
Engineering News Record (1 July 1915), 18–23
"Hotel Traymore, Atlantic City," *The North American* (15 June 1915), sec. 2, pp. 1–20
Demolished

6) Residence for William Gable, Altoona
Price and McLanahan Archives

Price and McLanahan (contd.)

1914

7) Residence for L. Stauffer Oliver, Moylan
PRER&BG, 29, no. 32 (12 August 1914)
Drawings in Chrysler Collection, Athenaeum of Philadelphia
8) Residence for Morris Saul, Moylan
PRER&BG, 29, no. 32 (12 August 1914)

1915

1) Residence for Mr. McDonald, Sherbrooke, Quebec (served as design for Howard residence, Sherbrooke, 1918)
Price and McLanahan Archives
Unexecuted
2) Competition for station for Pennsylvania Railroad, Johnstown
Warren P. Laird Records (vol. 66)
3) Unsuccessful competition for Deshong Memorial, Chester
Price and McLanahan Archives
4) Residence for Joshua Holmes, Germantown, Philadelphia
Price and McLanahan Archives
Drawings in Chrysler Collection, Athenaeum of Philadelphia
5) Alterations and additions to residence of W. W. Turner, Swarthmore
Price and McLanahan Archives
Drawings in Chrysler Collection, Athenaeum of Philadelphia
6) Barn for Lowell Gable, Chester County
Price and McLanahan Archives
7) Freight Terminal for Pennsylvania Railroad, Chicago, Illinois
PRER&BG, 30, no. 24 (16 June 1915)
Demolished
8) Residence for Carolyn King, address unknown
Price and McLanahan Archives
Unexecuted
9) Designs for passenger cars for Pennsylvania Railroad, Lines West of Pittsburgh
Drawings in Chrysler Collection, Athenaeum of Philadelphia

1916

1) Newark Founders Monument, Newark, New Jersey (with Gutzon Borglum)
The National Architect (May 1916), plate 49
2) Offices for C. A. Wagner and Company, Philadelphia
Price and McLanahan Archives
3) Alterations to residence of Mrs. Montgomery, 2019 Cypress Street, Philadelphia
PRER&BG, 31, no. 9 (1 March 1916)
4) First Christian Church, 10th Street and North East (now Roosevelt) Boulevard, Philadelphia
PRER&BG, 31, no. 16 (19 April 1916)

5) Alterations and additions to offices of Haines, Jones and Cadbury, 11th Street and Ridge Avenue, Philadelphia
PRER&BG, 31, no. 25 (21 June 1916)
6) Track elevation, bridge, and station for Pennsylvania Railroad, Indianapolis, Indiana
Engineering News Record, 83 (2 July 1919), 84
7) Thirty-story reinforced concrete addition to Traymore Hotel, Atlantic City, New Jersey
The New York Times (8 September 1916), 8
Unexecuted
8) Design for Musical Arts Club
Drawings in Chrysler Collection, Athenaeum of Philadelphia

A variety of other projects are known only from names and photographs in the architect's papers. Dates are unknown in most cases.
Tomb for Wertz family, Geesytown
Alterations and new structures for Miss Cowle's School, Hollidaysburg
Alterations to residence of Miss Kimball, near Chester
Alterations, including fireplace, to residence of Mrs. Jungerich, Germantown, Philadelphia
Alterations to residence of John King McLanahan, Hollidaysburg

William L. Price: Buildings at Rose Valley

1901

1) Alterations to eight row houses, creating the Guest House
Price and McLanahan Archives
2) Alterations to existing suburban house for residence of William L. Price
Price and McLanahan Archives

1902

1) Alterations to preexisting house for Harrison family
Price and McLanahan Archives
2) Alterations to Bishop White house
Price and McLanahan Archives
3) Water tower house, an accretionary structure built around a water tower on William Price property
Price and McLanahan Archives
4) Renovations and alterations to preexisting mill buildings creating meeting facilities, studios, and theater
The Artsman, 1, no. 4 (January 1904)

1904

1) Residence and related structures for Charles and Alice Barber Stephens
Ralph de Morten, "An Artist's House in Rose Valley," *American Homes and Gardens*, 6, no. 3 (March 1909), 93–98

2) Residence for Charles Schoen (additions and alterations to preexisting farmhouse)
F. Durando Nichols, "How a Pennsylvania Farm House Was Transformed into a Beautiful Dwelling," *American Homes and Gardens*, 2, no. 6 (June 1906), 378–383

1905

1) Residence for M. Hawley McLanahan (alterations and addition)
Price and McLanahan Archives
Drawings in Chrysler Collection, Athenaeum of Philadelphia

1906

1) Van Santenhoff Cottage
Aymar Embury, *The Livable House* (New York: Moffett and Yard, n. d.), 167
2) Cottage for Mrs. Warrington
F. Durando Nichols, "The Model House, Costing $1200 to $2400," *American Homes and Gardens*, 2, no. 3 (March 1906), 161–165
3) Henry Hetzel Cottage
F. Durando Nichols, "The Model House, Costing $1200 to $2400," *American Homes and Gardens*, 2, no. 3 (March 1906), 161–165
4) Office for Charles Schoen
AABN, 93, no. 1687 (22 April 1908)
5) Alterations, renovations, and additions to Tod Morden Farms for Charles Schoen
Price and McLanahan Archives

1909

1) Residence for Martin R. Jackson
AABN, 99, no. 1842 (12 April 1911)
2) Schoen Mill (alterations and additions to preexisting mill buildings)
Price and McLanahan Archives
Drawings in Chrysler Collection, Athenaeum of Philadelphia

1910

1) Twenty houses for Rose Valley Improvement Company (five constructed)
PRER&BG, 25, no. 36 (7 September 1910)
2) John Maene Cottage
Price and McLanahan Archives

1916

Garage for Charles Schoen
Drawings in Chrysler Collection, Athenaeum of Philadelphia
Small cottage for Charles Schoen
Drawings in Chrysler Collection, Athenaeum of Philadelphia

1901–16

Ice houses, water towers, bridges, pergolas, and other secondary structures

Bibliography of William L. Price

William L. Price

"Designs for Houses," *The Ladies' Home Journal* (1 June 1895 through April 1898); published as *Model Homes for Little Money*. New York: Doubleday, Page and Company, 1904.

"Is Rose Valley Worth While?" *The Artsman* 1, no. 1 (October 1903): 5–11.

"A Philadelphia Architect's Views on Architecture." *American Architect and Building News* 82, no. 1452 (23 October 1903): 27–28.

"Let Us Be Practical." *The Artsman* 1, no. 2 (November 1903): 45–48.

"Do We Attack the Machine?" *The Artsman* 1, no. 5 (February 1904): 169–174.

"Man's Expression of Himself in his Work: A Speech." *The Artsman* 1, no. 6 (March 1904): 209–220.

"The Building of a Chair." *The Artsman* 1, no. 8 (May 1904): 277–284.

"Some Humors of False Construction." *The Artsman* 1, no. 9 (June 1904): 321–328.

"What is the Arts and Crafts All About?" *The Artsman* 1, no. 10 (July 1904): 363–374.

"The Relation of Arts and Crafts to Architecture." *The Artsman* 1, no. 11 (August 1904): 407–414.

"The Educational Rebels." *The Conservator* 15, no. 7 (September 1904): 101–103.

"What do We Mean by Artsmanship?" *The Artsman* 2, no. 1 (October 1904): 11–16.

"Architecture and Rathskellers." *Architectural Review* 11, no. 11 (November 1904): 233–237.

"The Attitudes of Manual Training to the Arts and Crafts." *Proceedings of the Eastern Manual Training Association, 1904*. Philadelphia: Eastern Manual Training Association, 1904: 15–18.

"Simplicity in Arts and Crafts." *The Artsman* 2, no. 3 (December 1904): 93–98.

"The Rose Valley, Fact and Spirit." *The Artsman* 2, no. 4 (January 1905): 129–134.

"Architecture and the Chair." *The Artsman* 2, no. 5 (February 1905): 161–164.

"Use and Value of Common Materials in the Home." *The Artsman* 2, no. 1 (September 1905): 385–398.

"Several More Answers for Charles Cantor." *The Artsman* 2, no. 8 (May 1905): 265–272.

"The Joy of Love." *The Conservator* 16, no. 10 (December 1905): 151–152.

"Man Must Work to be Man." *The Artsman* 3, no. 4 (January 1906): 101–108.

"The Possibilities of Concrete Construction from the Standpoint of Utility and Art." *American Architect and Building News* 89, no. 1579 (31 March 1906): 119–20.

"The Art of a Free People." *The Artsman* 4, no. 1 (October 1906): 195–200.

"Modern Architecture." *The Artsman* 4, no. 2 (January 1907): 227–238.

"Modern Architecture, II." *The Artsman* 4, no. 3 (April 1907): 259–278.

"All Architecture." *The Conservator* 18, no. 4 (June 1907): 58–59.

"Is American Art Captive to a Dead Past?" *The Artsman* 15 (February 1909): 515–519.

"Mural Painting in Relation to Architecture." *The Craftsman* 16 (April 1909): 3–12.

"Democracy in the Domestic Architecture of America." *The Craftsman* 16 (June 1909): 251–256.

"Beautiful City." *The Craftsman* 17 (October 1909): 53–57.

"Choosing Simple Materials for the House." In Charles F. Osbourne, ed. *Country Houses and Gardens of Moderate Cost.* Philadelphia: House and Gardens and John C. Winston Co., 1907, 33–44.

"Clouds and Swallows." *The Conservator* 21, no. 8. (October 1910): 117–119.

"The Decorative Treatment of Plaster Walls." *The Brickbuilder* 20, no. 9 (September 1911): 181–184.

"The House of the Democrat." In Gustav Stickley, *More Craftsman Homes.* New York: Craftsman Publishing Co., 1912, 7–9.

"Peace Man or War Man." Philadelphia: c. 1915. Quaker Collection, Magill Library, Haverford College, Haverford, Pennsylvania.

Price and McLanahan

"The Designing of Small Railway Stations." *American Architect* 100, no. 1867 (4 October 1911): 130–132.

"Group of Houses at Moylan, Rose Valley, Pa." *The Brickbuilder* 20, no. 9 (September 1911): 185–191.